INTERPRETATION IN

Piers Plowman

For Patrick, with thanks.
     Bill Rogers

WILLIAM ELFORD ROGERS

INTERPRETATION IN
Piers Plowman

THE CATHOLIC UNIVERSITY
OF AMERICA PRESS
WASHINGTON, D.C.

LIBRARY OF CONGRESS CATALOGING-IN-PUBLICATION DATA

Rogers, William Elford.
    Interpretation in *Piers Plowman* / William Elford Rogers.
        p. cm.
    Includes bibliographical references (p.) and index.
    ISBN 0-8132-1092-5 (alk. paper)
        1. Langland, William, 1330?–1400? Piers the Plowman.
2. Hermeneutics—Religious aspects—Christianity—History
of doctrines—Middle Ages, 600–1500.   3. Christian poetry,
English (Middle)—History and criticism.   I. Title.
    PR2015 .R64 2002
    821′.1—dc21

                                        2001028534

To the fellows and the faculty of the 1995 Chaucer/Langland Institute

CONTENTS

Acknowledgments / ix

Introduction / 1

1. The Beginning and the End / 31

2. Three Authoritative Figures / 79

3. The Dreamer and Piers / 169

Works Cited / 283

INDICES

Authors / 289   Passages / 291
Subjects / 295

ACKNOWLEDGMENTS

This book was inspired by the Chaucer/Langland Institute sponsored by the National Endowment for the Humanities at the University of Colorado at Boulder in the summer of 1995. This institute will always stand for me as my model of collegial inquiry. It is impossible for me to acknowledge the many debts, intellectual and personal, that I owe to the fellows and to the faculty of the institute. This book is dedicated to them. Where the book is strong, it is so often because of what I have learned from them. Where it is weak, it is so often because I have not listened to them carefully enough. I name them here:

Fellows: Joan Baker, Louise Bishop, John Bowers, Jim Flynn, Cata Folks, James Goldstein, Tom Goodman, Eloise Grathwohl, Michael Hanly, Matt Hearn, Kathy Hewett-Smith, Linda Holley, Patrick Horner, Eileen Jankowski, Judith Kellogg, Sandra McEntire, Kate McKinley, Susan Morrison, Karen Mura, Teresa Nugent, Daniel Pigg, Katy Rehyansky, Jay Ruud, Stephen Shepherd, Jo Koster Tarvers, Deborah Uman.

Faculty: David Benson, Beth Robertson, James Simpson.

David Benson, to whom I owe a double debt, also read the manuscript for The Catholic University of America Press. His thoughtful and generous comments, along with those of Denise Baker, the other reader, have made this a better book than it otherwise would have been.

Much of this book was written during a sabbatical leave from Furman University. I thank Furman University for making the sabbatical possible. I thank the library staffs at Furman, at Emory University, and at the University of Colorado at Boulder for their help with my research.

Earlier versions of portions of Chapters 1 and 2 appeared originally in *Sewanee Mediaeval Studies,* as follows.

"Spiritual Love and the Hard Counsel of Need: *Piers Plowman* C.XXII.1–50." In *Earthly Love, Spiritual Love, Love of the Saints: Sewanee Mediaeval Studies 8,* ed. Susan J. Ridyard (Sewanee, Tenn.: University of the South Press, 1999), 269–81.

"Knighthood as Trope: Holy Church's Interpretation of Knighthood in *Piers Plowman* B.I." In *Chivalry, Knighthood, and War in the the Middle Ages: Sewanee Mediaeval Studies 9,* ed. Susan J. Ridyard (Sewanee, Tenn.: University of the South Press, 1999), 205–18.

I thank the editor of *Sewanee Mediaeval Studies,* Susan J. Ridyard, for permission to incorporate the revised material into this book. I thank the Sewanee Mediaeval Colloquium for providing me with opportunities to try out some of my ideas by presenting them as papers.

INTRODUCTION
A Little Treatise of Methodology

Spiritus Prudencie *the firste seed highte;*
That whoso ete that, ymagynen he sholde,
Er he dide any dede, devyse wel the ende . . .

(XIX.278–80)

Going about Interpretation

The approach to William Langland's *Piers Plowman* represented by this book is, I hope, not particularly eccentric. Nor is it intended to be exemplary. There is not much reason to talk about my approach, except to prevent confusion about the extent of my claims. They are modest.

My modesty is motivated partly by my minimal credentials. Like Dante, Langland deserves the tribute of many critical lifetimes; indeed, half a person's lifetime would be needed just to brush some of the bloom of strangeness from his poem. My approach is naturally determined by my own sense of Langland studies. I stand on a humble hill that offers only a restricted view of a complex landscape, with continents of terra incognita. Anne Middleton maps that landscape about as well as anyone could in a small space, in her introduction to the excellent collection edited by John Alford (*A Companion to "Piers Plowman"*). But it does not take much reading about Langland to be reminded irresistibly of the parable of the blind men and the elephant. Much has been said that is locally indispensable; there are recurring attempts to put everything together; but the poem seems too big, loose-limbed, and sprawling for any single description to work thoroughly and for long. Most critics of Langland, in fact, seem not foolishly blind but Socratically ignorant. Not everywhere, but for the most part, a refreshing breeze of humility blows through this currently peaceful province—maybe because scholars of Langland, even more than other beleaguered medievalists, need each other to talk with. Few even pretend to have come to terms with this most difficult poem. We all try to describe as accurately as possible the part of the elephant we most proximally rub. But in general, the texture of local effects successfully resists the structure of the overall argument. George Kane mentions "the fact (at least in my observation) that no two people genuinely familiar with the text of the poem will agree about its larger meaning" ("Reading" 17–18).

For critics of Langland, precisely the friction between texture and structure makes *Piers Plowman* crackle with energy. There is pressure to perform the magical explanation that will bleed off what seems peculiar or merely obsessive into political, philosophical, or theological channels. We want to build the circuit that turns all that voltage into useful work.

3

So getting a handle on the poem seems to mean first looking for a world picture or theme or motif or genre or technique (or anything) that might lend a sense of relationship at least, if not strong coherence, to its disparate parts. It helps to understand how much of the poem can be subsumed under the search for the three lives, or how much of it counts as a quest for *kynde knowynge* of Christ or as an example of the genre of the apocalypse, or how much of it arises from a kind of riffing on the Latin quotations. My notion of structure is, for the moment, simple: *structure* refers to the parts of the poem and the relationships of those parts to each other and to some postulated whole. In this sense of the term, critics of Langland virtually always find themselves talking about structure, essentially. It might be possible to write the history of criticism of *Piers Plowman* as a narrative of the quest for structure.

Setting *texture* and *structure* in opposition as a way of talking about poems generates the theoretical apparatus of John Crowe Ransom (see, for example, 91). It sometimes seems that nostalgia for Coleridgean unity in multeity still mediates the critical thought of my own generation, in spite of the theoretical and practical problems that seem to doom that quest from the outset. There are, for example, the lessons of the various historical methods that have been applied to *Piers Plowman*. These methods seem necessary; even Britton Harwood, who describes his book as "another New Critical book," ultimately aims to produce an alloy that he calls "formalist historicism" (ix). Historical critics at least have provisional explanations for the conspicuous lack of closure in the poem. Maybe Langland or any other fourteenth-century author thought of "unity," if at all, in terms radically different from Coleridge's. Ample evidence in Langland's work, and in Chaucer's as well, points to the dominance of "inorganic" structuring, as opposed to "organic" Coleridgean structuring. Besides, the controversies over authorship and editing show how hard it is to draw any firm conclusions about how Langland's poem might have looked or felt in its author's mind when he tried to see it whole. Thus we have no firm control on interpretation, no standard of correctness, and anachronistic excesses are loosed in the name of the search for the "theme of *Piers Plowman*." These are historical problems.

There are also philosophical problems. Today we are much worried about whether the human self is the kind of thing that is able to have a coherent vision, not being necessarily coherent itself. This is the central question in the postmodern critique of the Cartesian ego subject. The philosophical assumptions implicit in the critical quest for Coleridgean unity are indicted by that same critique. I will argue later that the critique was not invented by postmodernism, but that Langland himself was much worried by his own version of this same question. To my mind, the philosophical problems go deeper than the historical problems. When the concept of "intention" itself has become problematic both for the fourteenth-century author and for us, there seems to be little point in worrying about an author's intention as a control on interpretation.

The philosophical problem I have just been talking about is exactly the problem that David Lawton finds implicit in the critical vocabulary that is "derived from the New Criticism and so looks for such things as unity and integrity" (2). When applied to *Piers Plowman,* such a vocabulary "tends to confine us to a teleological and sequential reading of the poem and virtually imposes metaphors of 'growth' and 'development,' the dreamer's 'progress' towards a 'goal'" (2–3). Though "*Piers Plowman* critics have not yet given up the attempt to package Langland's sprawling monstrosity of a poem into a well-wrought urn" (the reference, of course, is to the title of Cleanth Brooks's most famous book), for Lawton M. M. Bakhtin's terms seem more useful for talking about Langland's work: "For *Piers Plowman* is a dialogic, not a monologic, poem" (3). Though he admits that in fact "there are many monologic passages in *Piers Plowman,*" ultimately Lawton argues that the poem "conforms more . . . to the dialogic structure of plural and autonomous discourses freed from an author's control" (4). Thus, "we need a different model of 'consciousness' and 'personality' to understand the dialogism of Langland's poem. Such a model is to hand, in the theory of the subject that has been produced since the 1960s mainly in France" (4).

The reflections in the last few paragraphs might seem to demonstrate decisively that we need terms for thinking about *Piers Plowman* that are less naïve than those Lawton scorns. Nevertheless, most criticism of *Piers Plowman* that I know of still in one way or another quests for the Grail, the unifying theme that will rationalize the hermeneutic frustrations of Langland's structure. Why? Is there anything more interesting here than reflex?

Obviously, I am going to say yes. I say yes because I think the poem is about interpretation. This is by no means an original idea. Burt Kimmelman, for example, puts it quite explicitly: "[T]o view the poem as a demonstration of its own poetics is to be able to loosen many of . . . the poem's critical knots" (204). In fact, of all the unoriginal ideas in this book, the idea that *Piers Plowman* is about interpretation is maybe the most unoriginal. But it is also the most important idea: the value of this book, if it has any, is its thoroughgoing insistence on this idea. It is important to note that I am not proposing "interpretation" as the name of a theme that will subsume all the parts of *Piers Plowman* into a Coleridgean unity. I do not mean that every part of the poem makes some explicit or implicit statement about interpretation (although many parts of the poem do make such statements), or that all of these statements can be put together into some complex but coherent intellectual structure—for example, into some consistent theory of or some paradoxical attitude toward textual hermeneutics. When I say that the poem "is about" interpretation, I mean "is about" more in the sense of "goes about": what the poem *does* is to cause its reader to reflect on the activity of interpretation itself. To borrow a distinction from Wittgenstein, interpretation is not what the poem "says," but what it "shows."

The poem shows Langland (and the speaker and the dreamer as his surrogates) searching for a viable hermeneutic, a principle of interpretation that will make sense of all Langland knows or thinks he knows about human experience. To say "Langland" here is maybe a little misleading, since after all I know very little of importance about William Langland beyond what I infer from *Piers Plowman*. If anyone has done so, Lawrence M. Clopper has illustrated in detail the processes of inference by means of which a reader might work back from *Piers Plowman* to its author. Clopper concludes that Langland himself had a "Franciscan mentality, ideology, and spirituality" (*Songes of Rechelesnesse* 3). But as Clopper says,

> I had felt that there was something distinctive in this voice and in the interests expressed in the poem that ought to enable us to place the poet within clearly defined intellectual, theological, social, even historical contexts. It would have helped . . . if we had had a document that told us William Langland was a monk, a friar, a chantry priest, or whatever. In the absence of such documents, we are thrown back on the poem—not on the details of the persona's life par-

ticularly but on the disposition of the mind of the person who created the poem. By "disposition," I mean quite literally the mentality that selects and arranges elements within a system or line of reasoning in a distinctive and identifiable way. (*Songes of Rechelesnesse* 3)

In other words, when we say "Langland," generally we mean just the individual human consciousness postulated at the limit of the text as a condition for the possibility of *Piers Plowman.*

Neither I nor (I would judge) Clopper means to imply that trying to reconstruct the historical Langland is a futile or uninteresting activity, or to suggest that there is no evidence besides the poem on which to base such a reconstruction. The recent collection edited by Steven Justice and Kathryn Kerby-Fulton (*Written Work: Langland, Labor, and Authorship*), for example, demonstrates how New Historicist methods yield biographical conclusions that bear directly on the interpretation of the poem. *Written Work* focuses mostly on the C-text and will receive only this mention here. But its agenda—to think of Langland as an author with all that implies—has affinities with my own agenda. The human consciousness at the limit of *Piers Plowman* is a medieval intellectual (see Wittig, *Revisited* 8), and therefore paradigmatically a *litteratus*. His intellectual movements replicate the movements of a reader in the hermeneutic circle, the movements between the parts of a text as experienced temporally (and over and over again) and the evolving sense-of-the-whole. These movements in the poem call for a particular kind of oscillation between texture and structure.

The concept of the "hermeneutic circle"—maybe the most important theoretical concept in this book—is obviously correlative with the concepts of "texture" and "structure." But since we tend to think of structures as objectively verifiable, the term *structure* already seems to connote some sort of formalist orientation, as if parts and wholes of poems were somehow objectively knowable like rocks and starfishes. The term *hermeneutic circle,* on the other hand, suggests the provisional interpretive movements of readers as they encounter interesting texts (that is, texts that they can "be in") again and again. The term *hermeneutic circle* also suggests a long history of hermeneutic theory, going back to such texts as Augustine's *De doctrina christiana* that were paradigmatic for medieval thinking about interpretation. But I will not discuss here the history of hermeneutics, for two reasons. First, in this book I want to abstract from—without, however, devaluing—historical criticism. Second, and more important, I want to keep the concept of "hermeneutic circle" as open-ended as possible, because this book is arguing that that very concept is the one most at issue in *Piers Plowman*. If, as I think, Langland's poem is about how readers fail to master texts, then to adopt some fixed idea—even Augustine's idea—of how correct interpretations are generated would preempt Langland's agenda and short-circuit the critical enterprise. The easy assumption (nowadays, almost the cliché) is that methodology and ideology are of a piece. If we cannot separate methodology from ideology, then the best we can do is to be reflective about our methodology.

We need a provisional, open-ended notion of the hermeneutic circle that will force us to attend to the interpretive process itself, instead of foreclosing interpretive possibilities. *Hermeneutic circle,* then, refers to the process by which readers come to texts with expectations—highly complex, implicit, and often unconscious—and construe the parts of these texts, as those parts are experienced in temporal sequence, in accordance with those expectations. The expectations are determined by history, economics, politics, religion, genre, individual circumstances—but nobody comes to a text "clean," or comes to it in exactly the same way as anybody else does. The parts of the text, however a reader might decide to divide the text into "parts" (another interpretive decision), appear as they do because of the reader's expectations that govern their apprehension. The proof of this is the "ironic" text, where, because of the expectations a reader brings to it, the text appears to mean exactly what it does not say. Deconstruction has demonstrated that even texts that are not "intended" ironically, and that have no obvious "internal cues" to suggest irony, can be read as meaning what they do not say—because of the various contexts (expectations) within which it is possible to construe them.

But, on the other hand, the reader's temporal experience of the parts of a text can alter the expectations with which the reader initially approaches the text. We know this because it is possible, for example, to distinguish one sonnet from another, or to identify "developments" in a genre, or, ultimately, to talk about "originality." Where the parts of a text in fact do not substantially alter a reader's expectations, there is a "dead" text; or there is, what is equally uninteresting, doctrinaire criticism.

This process, the movement between mutually determining expectations and experiences, is repeated every time a reader encounters a living text. The metaphor of the circle here suggests not closure but endlessness. The turning in the hermeneutic circle in a kind of Derridean free play is delightful to some readers. To others (to Langland, I am arguing), it is at worst a torture and at best a necessary discipline. But the point is to pay attention to the movement itself, and not to close the circle by settling on some unimaginable interpretive "truth" that everyone agrees about. We need critical concepts to speak about texts at all, but the crucial thing is somehow to keep those concepts from deciding what the text is and is not allowed to say to us.

It is a matter of using concepts that might in themselves seem naïve, but using them nonnaïvely. Oddly, I think Thomas Kuhn's reflections on the history of science help here. Certain schools of literary criticism in the United States, in France, and elsewhere have at various times aspired to the condition of science. That is, literary criticism has at times taken on the project of producing objective judgments about poems, by which literary criticism would attain the same degree of intellectual respectability as, say, chemistry. At such times, literary criticism aspires to become what Kuhn calls "normal" science: "research firmly based upon one or more past scientific achievements . . . that some particular scientific community acknowledges for a time as supplying the foundation for its further practice" (10). These exemplary achievements are Kuhn's "paradigms." Once we have the paradigm—that is, once we agree that poems work the way the critics say they do—we and our students can go to work cranking poem after poem through the machine, much as a chemist cranks compound after compound through a magnetic-resonance imager. Criticism becomes normal science, what Kuhn calls "puzzle-solving" (36) or "mopping-up operations" (24). The reigning paradigm, whatever it may be, is supposed to become "an object for further articulation and specification under new or more stringent conditions" (23).

In fact, though, humanistic study is never really like Kuhn's normal science. It is obvious that literary critics never really achieve agreement with each other, as scientists often do. In fact, we remain (and there is much reason to resist the odds and insist on remaining) in a situation resembling what Kuhn calls the "preparadigm" period of a science. This period is characterized by "frequent and deep debates over legitimate methods, problems, and standards of solution, though these seem rather to define schools than to produce agreement" (47–48). We literary critics have come to expect perpetually what Kuhn says happens in science only in periods of crisis: "proliferation of competing articulations, the willingness to try anything, the expression of explicit discontent, the recourse to philosophy and to debate over fundamentals" (91). What is a description of science in crisis is for the humanities a description of business as usual.

Operating constantly in the mode of crisis, as we do, means that all assumptions are always up for grabs, that the self-evident propositions and the undefined terms and the specifications of methodology appear in the discourse not as ends to argument, but as the beginning of argument. That means operating nonnaïvely.

The Sense-of-the-Whole

The false trail that it is necessary to avoid at once is a set of tacit assumptions about the sense-of-the-whole, and the relationship of that sense-of-the-whole to the parts of the poem. One fallout from that set of assumptions is the idea that writing criticism is continuous with understanding poems, that criticism flowers naturally from reading the way laboratory reports flower from experiments. But one never comes to a poem *critically* with an open mind. In writing criticism, we are always in the middle of a project of some kind. As I have said, we cannot come upon the poem newly, as if it were a self-subsistent rock or starfish, the way some people think science tries to come upon its objects as objective, without preconceptions. If Kuhn is right, this is even a misunderstanding of normal science, which always approaches its puzzles like the characters in *Ghostbusters,* with the heavy equipment of its paradigm on its back.

Be that as it may, one never writes criticism without preconceptions and ongoing projects. To say otherwise is a rhetorical pose. One could argue that all rhetoric is poses, and as poses go, this one is not bad. But what gets elided in the pose, and what is for my purposes in this book essential to keep, is the explicit awareness of the hermeneutic circle. In fact, what happens is that one reads a poem, and more or less laboriously develops a sense-of-the-whole, as a condition for being able to write criticism at all. By the time the criticism gets written, however, what gets presented is the perfect circle of the mandala, and the agony of turning in the wheel is forgotten. The cool objectivity of science presumably demands this pose.

We can even tighten the screw another turn, and push this whole problem of elided awareness back to an earlier stage in the process of interpretation. We could say that we never *read poems* without preconceptions and ongoing projects. Thus we have to admit that any sense-of-the-whole is perhaps an illusion (that is, is nonobjective), an illusion that might be countered or corrected in various ways, though not necessarily replaced with something else that is not an illusion. Roland Barthes's division of the work into "lexemes," Stanley Fish's concept of the "self-consuming artifact," and the various methods of "deconstruction" considered as the quest for incoherence, for example, are all ways of undermining our confidence in any sense-of-the-whole we might happen to come up with. Such postmodern critiques strike directly at the root concept of Coleridgean "unity."

One might predict that the concept of "unity" would force attention to the hermeneutic circle, since, after all, one must usually invent the sense-of-the-whole. The sense-of-the-whole is usually not given explicitly, as the moral of one of Aesop's fables might be given to a child. In practice, however, the concept of "unity" usually functions rather to displace attention onto the finished structure. The rhetorical pose is that the sense-of-the-whole works like a quasi-scientific hypothesis to be tested against the details of the poem. Look, we say, these parts fit together this way, under the hypothesis that the poem is getting at such-and-such.

But scientific hypotheses explain things, and (at least until quantum theory) they explain on a causal model. Even formalist critics who abstract from causal explanation of "why the author wrote what he wrote" do not necessarily abstract from causal explanation of "why the poem as linguistic artifact behaves as it does." But this is not a well-formed question unless we can agree on "how the poem behaves." If the "text" were an objective thing, then we could talk about how the "materials" of the poem woven together into the text interact with each other according to certain linguistic norms that function like natural laws, and so we could explain objectively the causes of the greatness (or sentimentality) of the poem. We could explain why its parts behave together as they do. In this picture, the poem is like the solar system. Given the stuff of the planets and Newtonian mechanics, we can explain the orbits of the wandering stars.

In the picture just articulated, it might look as though there is clear movement between parts and whole, and therefore explicit awareness of the hermeneutic circle, at every stage of the interpretive process from first picking up an unfamiliar text to publishing an article about it in a learned journal. But something crucial is missing from this picture. The sense-of-the-whole is (is presented as) provisional and revisable as a result of encounters with the parts. But the quasi-scientific nature of the enterprise demands that the parts not be provisional or revisable. When hypotheses are tested in the laboratory, everybody has to agree on what happens in the laboratory. The "same thing" that happens in your laboratory has to happen in mine as well. If the sense-of-the-whole is going to be tested as hypothesis, everybody has to agree about how the parts of the poem behave under standard conditions of temperature and pressure. What is missing—elided or repressed—is the explicit awareness of how the parts can change as well in the light of the altering sense-of-the-whole. As Blake puts it, "For the Eye altering alters all" ("The Mental Traveller," line 62). To grasp the hermeneutic circle in full awareness means to recognize that the "text itself" is exactly as protean as the sense-of-the-whole.

What does all of this have to do with *Piers Plowman?* If I am right, the poem shows Langland's questing for a viable hermeneutic. On the one hand, then, we will expect the speaker and the dreamer, functioning as Langland's surrogates and in complex relationships with each other, again and again to make the Coleridgean movement, the reaching for logical and aesthetic unity in multeity. Whether the movement succeeds or fails—mostly it fails—it is nevertheless the same movement. We want a methodology designed specifically to talk about how that movement happens in texts, without, on the other hand, repressing awareness of the hermeneutic circle. Explicit awareness of the hermeneutic circle is, I am arguing, the name of the game in *Piers Plowman* (compare Raabe 78ff.). Everything will depend upon how we handle the problematic concept of "unity." We must use the concept to open questions about the interpretive process and not to repress the crucial moments in that process when we (with Langland, and sometimes with the speaker, and even more rarely with the dreamer) realize that everything is up for grabs.

What we need, in short, is a sense-of-the-whole that does not act like a scientific hypothesis. Our sense-of-the-whole must not demand for its functioning in our discourse an objective text, already set over against us like a rock or a starfish, that is what it is no matter what we happen to think about it, and that is always capable of decisively falsifying incorrect hypotheses. Instead of a hypothesis, we need what I would prefer to call a "methodeutic principle." The term *methodeutic* comes from the philosophy of Charles Sanders Peirce. Another of Peirce's terms for this branch of study is *speculative rhetoric*. The terms refer to the study of the ways people connect signs. So instead of asking, "What is the unifying principle of *Piers Plowman?*," I am asking, "How does Langland connect signs?" I am trying to articulate the rule, as it were, according to which one verbal sign (word, sentence, or larger unit) gets connected with another in *Piers Plowman*.

Briefly put, the rule I am proposing is that Langland connects signs as if he were interpreting a text. He reads his world as if it were a book. This was not an uncommon thing to do in the Middle Ages, as Jesse M. Gellrich has shown in *The Idea of the Book in the Middle Ages: Language Theory, Mythology, and Fiction*.

But anybody who has reflected deeply on the matter, including Langland, knows that reading a text is a complex and perhaps ultimately mysterious activity. What it means to interpret a text is itself an open-ended question. Gellrich also shows how Dante and Chaucer deconstructed the "mythological," monolithic "idea of the book." Therefore, we cannot say that *Piers Plowman* embodies a clearly worked-out hermeneutic theory that Langland applies to the understanding of fourteenth-century society. All the while Langland is trying to read his world like a book, he is interrogating the nature of textual interpretation itself. Textual hermeneutics is at the center of concern in *Piers Plowman,* but it is not the unifying Coleridgean theme. The poem is not "about" textual hermeneutics; it "goes about" textual hermeneutics.

At first glance, it might look as though the distinction between Coleridgean hypothesis and methoduetic principle is without a difference. Certainly, paying attention to textual hermeneutics in *Piers Plowman* will foreground certain things and push other things to the background. A book written on the premise that *Piers Plowman* is concerned with textual hermeneutics will look very different from a book written on the premise that the poem is concerned with political theory, or with doctrinal issues, or with religious psychology. The methoduetic principle, just like a Coleridgean hypothesis, seems to direct me where to look and what to look for in the poem.

But things get unclear when I try to talk about how things in the poem "confirm" or "disconfirm" any particular methoduetic principle. Most of the time, I will be forced to acknowledge that particular parts of the poem look one way if I assume that they are connected by one rule, and another way if I assume they are connected by another. That is, I am forced to recognize the protean nature of the text. If I were doing science, I would slice through the threatening chaos with Occam's razor. But in literary interpretation the critic is under no compulsion to select the simplest rule. Indeed, the more complex the methoduetic principle, the more meanings I will actually find, and the "richer" the work will seem. Reading being the complex and mysterious activity it is, I venture to propose that the methoduetic principle "Read the world like a book" is about as complex a principle as anybody could hope to deal with. I am certainly conscious of not having dealt with it adequately in this book.

It is especially important to note that a methoduetic principle is not a causal explanation. It does not in any interesting sense explain what caused the author to write what is written. If I say that the author wrote what is written because the author was following such and such a rule for connecting signs, then that only opens the historical question of why the author selected that particular rule. Nor does the methoduetic principle explain how the material (or other) conditions of the author's culture produced such a work. The interesting question in that case is why some particular rule for connecting signs came to prevail in the author's culture. Nor does the methodeutic principle explain causally why I had all the ideas I had while I was interpreting. That explanation would be business for psychology. The methodeutic principle is a rule for connecting ideas, and it makes no statement about the genesis of these ideas or the genesis of these connections. We *can* make causal statements about some or all of these things. I do that when I say, for example, that Langland reads his world like a book because he is a medieval intellectual who is obsessed with texts. But the methodeutic principle by itself does not constitute a causal explanation.

In articulating methodeutic principles, we are making not historical statements about the causal past of the work, but instead predictions about its evolutionary future. We are participating in the evolution of the work as a living sign. We are trying to articulate not "where the poem or its interpretations came from," but instead "what the poem will come to mean (in some indefinitely future state of complete information), in all of its possible complexity." In asserting my sense-of-the-whole, I am predicting that whatever *Piers Plowman* is finally thought to mean altogether, textual hermeneutics will have something important to do with that. My sense-of-the-whole is not a hypothesis to be tested on the model of causal explanation. Instead, it is a methodeutic principle that allows me to articulate meanings that are fallible and partial, but (I am betting) probably in many cases (though I do not know which) fated to endure.

I have now lapsed completely, and for the last time in this book, into the language of Peircean semiotics, which forms the philosophical foundation, to the extent that there is any, of my enterprise. Those who want a fuller explanation of this philosophical foundation may read my book about that (Rogers). I want a Peircean analogue to the Coleridgean hypothesis, an analogue that will activate some powerful methodologies without at the same time resurrecting timely buried philosophical machineries that have rationalized those methodologies.

Langland and Critical Methodology

The task now is to articulate my sense-of-the-whole more fully so as to point to the methodologies I think I need. I perform this articulation by making some statements about Langland. These are not statements purely about the speaker (or the dreamer), as they would be with doctrinaire formalist criticism, which abhors any trespass into the province of biography. By *Langland,* I mean here the consciousness who creates the speaker and the dreamer, who off and on seems to become identified with the speaker or the dreamer, but who always is *inferred* as the other pole of a relation with the speaker and/or the dreamer.

On the other side, as I have mentioned before, the statements I make about Langland are not necessarily statements about some real, historical person named William Langland. About him I know nothing except what the poem and its scholars, working from mighty thin evidence, might tell me. The thin evidence is presented succinctly in Ralph Hanna's thin monograph *William Langland. Langland* in my book is the name of a function, the name of a sign among other signs—shorthand for the individual human consciousness, at least sometimes distinguishable from both the speaker and the dreamer, who is postulated whenever we say that *Piers Plowman* is written and read. Nor should the term *individual* be read too strongly here. I am not talking about, and I infer that Langland would not have talked about, the individual in the sense of a self-subsistent Cartesian ego. The problematic of textual hermeneutics, at least whenever we want to say that "private reading" is possible, is inseparably fused with the problematic of the self.

I will make three statements articulating my sense-of-the-whole. All three, as methodeutic principles, are statements of "how things get done in the poem," as opposed to statements of "what the poem is about." All three are implicitly statements about how Langland reads, since I am proposing that whatever gets done in the poem gets done on the model of textual hermeneutics. Each of the three statements implies a particular interpretive method. And finally, all three statements are debatable. Some critics of Langland will think the statements are trivially obvious, and some others will think they are perversely wrong. I am not interested in "demonstrating," in some unimaginable way, that these statements are "correct." I am interested only in showing that there exists a standpoint that will produce a particular description of the poem among other possible descriptions, and that the text of *Piers Plowman* is rich enough to pay out these meanings too.

First, then, Langland is a highly *original* poet. As John Alford has remarked, to address the question of Langland's learning is to develop "a deeper appreciation of the man's originality and complexity of thought. He belongs to no tradition, popular or courtly. He stands by himself" ("Learning" 7). That does not mean that Langland creates everything he says out of whole cloth or imagines his poem ex nihilo. Nobody does that, not even Coleridge. It does mean that we do not understand Langland just because we know and thoroughly understand whatever texts are quoted, or are "alluded to," or are "in the background." Placing the poem in the context of other medieval texts almost never fails to seem highly illuminating. Most of the best work ever done on Langland is precisely of this sort. If that were not so, I might not need this initial essay to rationalize another methodology. But Langland's relationship with texts other than his own is never simple. He interprets those texts, and I am arguing that the process of his interpretation itself is at issue. Almost always, what he "makes of" other texts is the center of interest.

Second, Langland is a highly *textual* poet. By this I mean that the reality in which he habitually moves is the reality of texts. Other people's texts are the spaces where he circulates, the mountains on his horizon, the obstacles in his path, the personalities he lives among, the objects of his world that oppose and obstruct him and provide him with the raw materials for his own making and doing. This will perhaps seem the most controversial of my statements about Langland. He seems so much of the time to be talking not about books, but about his society with its real, gritty people and places and things. On the other hand, of course, Alford ("Quotations") has argued that the Latin quotations in Langland serve as the nuclei around which his whole composition condenses. Much of this book will be trying to show that the gritty reality in Langland appears in the service of hermeneutic activity: that he construes "extratextual" reality as if it were a text, and that he talks about this extratextual reality in the first place as the terminus of some particular interpretive system, as the "stuff" that provides material for the definitive human activity of interpretation. Extratextual reality, for Langland, exists only as the limit of some particular interpretive act.

Finally, Langland is a highly *recursive* poet. By that I mean, roughly, that his poem interprets interpretation. For example, Holy Church in-

terprets money, but Lady Meed may be said implicitly to interpret Holy
Church's interpretive activity, and Piers's attempt to set up a just economy on the half-acre implicitly critiques Lady Meed's way of interpreting
the world, and the dreamer is always interpreting everybody's interpretive activity, and so on. This at first may not seem so controversial a
statement as the preceding one. Every reader of *Piers Plowman* notices
that the "same themes" come up again and again, like complex objects
seen from radically different perspectives and under lights of different
spectral distributions. Morton Bloomfield says that *Piers Plowman* "is perhaps the first poem in English . . . that concentrates on the problem of
the self. . . . It is a literary work which itself deals with the problem of
interpretation rather than offering a text for interpretation" ("Allegories" 37). And everywhere interpretive activity proceeds on the model
of textual hermeneutics. Several books about Langland focus on his concern for language, in particular, as the paradigmatic way of interpreting
the world: for example, Mary Carruthers's *The Search for St. Truth: A Study
of Meaning in "Piers Plowman,"* Pamela Raabe's *Imitating God: The Allegory of
Faith in "Piers Plowman B,"* and Gillian Rudd's *Managing Language in "Piers
Plowman."* And Burt Kimmelman's *The Poetics of Authorship in the Later Middle
Ages* reads Langland by placing Langland's reflections on language in the
literary, theological, and philosophical contexts of his time.

This third statement, as noncontroversial as it may seem, is nevertheless for me the most important and far-reaching statement of the
three. It is obvious that the dreamer constantly reflects on the inadequa-
cies of his own interpretations of the world, and that he evaluates the
interpretations of the authoritative figures he meets. It is obvious that
the various authoritative figures explicitly and implicitly critique each
other's interpretive activity. In Steven Justice's words,

> This is Langland's technique throughout the *vita*: to juxtapose theological vo-
> cabularies and presuppositions that are discontinuous with each other because
> of the conflicting institutional functions they serve; the fluidity and digressive-
> ness of the poem signal not exactly a "decentering," but a proliferation of com-
> peting discourses, each of which tries to promote itself as the authoritative cen-
> ter to which all others must appeal. (*Writing and Rebellion* 113)

Anne Middleton in fact uses the word *recursive* to describe *Piers Plowman*:
citing her own earlier article "Narration and the Invention of Experi-

ence: Episodic Form in *Piers Plowman*," she says that the poem "in all its versions is essentially recursive, an episodic re-enactment in various scenes of a fundamental struggle over the power to determine what counts as edification and in particular to authorise memorial reconstructions of the past" ("Making" 250). I will argue that the recursiveness of the poem goes this deep and deeper—that in fact the preachments of the authoritative figures have as primary agenda to illustrate how the interpretive process itself works, that the intrusions of the gospel narrative are meant primarily to show how the gospel should be read, and that Piers Plowman himself is ultimately a hermeneutic principle that must seem multifarious because, as the central hermeneutic principle of the poem, Piers must do all the hermeneutic work the poem wants done. The poem is a hermeneutic quest for a viable hermeneutic.

In summary, then, my sense-of-the-whole is as follows: at every level in his poem, Langland connects signs as if he were interpreting a text; and when he interprets, he reads originally, intertextually, and recursively. He is always trying to make up his own understanding (*kynde knowynge?*) of the world. But he is a medieval intellectual, and so the world he wants to understand is the world as it appears or might appear in texts. And since texts are arbitrarily mysterious objects, he is always questioning his own interpretive processes.

Corresponding to the three articulated parts of this sense of the whole are three methodological principles.

Langland's Originality: Nonparaphrasability

First, if Langland is highly *original,* then the poem itself would be the unique statement of its meaning. We might illuminate, but could not exhaust, Langland's meaning by repeating something Augustine or Aquinas said. Like every great poem, *Piers Plowman* is, strictly speaking, nonparaphrasable. Britton Harwood identifies as one of the characteristic and enduring techniques of the New Criticism "the construction of redundancy by . . . taking some portions of a text as figurative or ironic restatements of other portions" (ix). The methodological slogan is something like, "Look at the *text itself!*" or "Back to the *text!*" But the postmodern critique, if it has accomplished nothing else, has harried us into a state of terminal skepticism about the concept of the "text itself": *"il n'y a pas de hors-texte"* (Derrida 158).

We need to restate the methodological principle less naïvely. A first approximation might be something like this: "The text, whatever it may be ultimately, glosses itself; each part counts as an explanation, at least at first resort, of all the other parts." In medieval theories of scriptural interpretation, this is how the Bible itself was supposed to work. If Langland mentions Augustine or Aquinas, that is, the *first* place to look to decide what Langland means is in the (perhaps ever-widening) vicinity in Langland, and not in the works of Augustine or Aquinas. *Eventually* we get to the works of Augustine or Aquinas, because we constantly widen the vicinity as we "deepen" our understanding.

But even this principle does not do all the work we want it to do, especially with a text like Langland's. In querying the text for explanations of its difficult parts, we experience irresistible centrifugal force. We naturally find ourselves spiraling ever outward into the contexts. We find "quotations" of Augustine or Aquinas, or "mentions" of Augustine or Aquinas, or "allusions" to Augustine or Aquinas, or vague "influences" of Augustine or Aquinas; and these quotations or mentions or allusions or influences justify our substituting Augustine's or Aquinas's words as paraphrases of Langland's. Once we are pretty sure that Langland quotes or mentions or alludes, how can we argue that Augustine and Aquinas are not, in some sense at least, "in" Langland's text?

That last question addresses one of the repressed contradictions of doctrinaire formalist criticism. Is *The City of God* "in" *Piers Plowman?* No, because Langland's text is different from Augustine's text. Is *The City of God* "in" *Piers Plowman?* Yes, because Langland mentions Augustine's text. The problem here is the usual one: namely, the assumption that texts are discrete objects like rocks or starfishes. The apparent contradiction would go away if we were prepared tacitly to agree that a mention of a text works pretty much the same way as a mention of a rock or a starfish. We see no problem in saying that a rock or a starfish can be mentioned in a poem without saying that the poem is made of granite or protoplasm. Similarly, we can say that the text called *The City of God* is not in Langland's poem, but a "mention" of the text called *The City of God* is certainly in Langland's poem.

There is a difference, though, between texts, on the one hand, and rocks and starfishes, on the other. No one offers a rock or a starfish as a paraphrase of a poem that mentions them, whereas critics often do offer passages from other texts as paraphrases of Langland. This observation points to what seems to me the more precise statement of the methodological principle. To talk about what is "in" the text or what is "outside" the text is confusing. Rather, the crucial notion is the notion of nonparaphrasability. No other text, including (or perhaps especially) the critic's interpretive text, adequately paraphrases the poem.

It is, of course, a deep and troubled philosophical question whether there is any such thing as a nonparaphrasable utterance in general. Nevertheless, it does seem possible to conceive of a literary criticism that does not present itself as paraphrasing poems, as "saying what poems mean." What is original (nonparaphrasable) about Langland—*especially* Langland—occurs precisely at the fuzzy contested border between what is taken as being "in" the text and what is taken as being "outside" the text. That is because for Langland the notions of "quoting" or "mentioning" or "alluding to" are themselves open-ended concepts, concepts under investigation, so that we do not immediately know how a mention works just because we can identify what is mentioned. Langland, as he goes about textual hermeneutics, is always also questioning what a mention is. So we do not immediately know *how* Augustine is in the text just by knowing that Langland mentions him. Lawrence M. Clopper points out this problem:

> Literary scholars who are medievalists often have recourse to the writings of Thomas Aquinas to illuminate a particular point in a poem or tract. But what are the implications of this appeal? Does it mean that the critic is saying the medieval writer was a Thomist? In many studies, the existence of a causal relation is finessed: Aquinas is a great systematizer; he is a kind of "medieval" mind; therefore, he is an authority on all medieval subjects and can be a source of illumination. (*Songes of Rechelesnesse* 12–13)

I resist the usual caricature of patristic criticism: I do not believe that because of Augustine's immense authority, Langland would have had to believe what Augustine believed, if only Langland could have managed to figure it out. And unlike Clopper, I do not want to apply refined methods of historicism to reconstruct Langland's "disposition" (*Songes of*

Rechelesnesse 3). What we do know is that substituting Augustine's words for Langland's does not provide an adequate paraphrase for Langland's text, since Augustine's text does not question its own presence or demand its own warrant. It is more useful to talk about "how Langland works" than to try to paraphrase "what Langland believes."

The methodological principle, then, is this: If we want to deal appropriately with Langland's originality, to meet him on his own ground, then we should not think of ourselves as paraphrasing, as substituting other texts for Langland's, as saying in other words what Langland says. We should, instead, think of ourselves as articulating the modes through which other texts appear in *Piers Plowman*. On the level of explication, that means paying closer attention than usual to the features of the poem that seem most resistant to paraphrase: tone, style, flavor, quality, nuance, attitude (notice how vague our vocabulary can be for this sort of thing). On another level, that means always keeping in the foreground the hermeneutic question, and keeping the question open: How should one interpret texts? What counts as a quotation or an allusion or a mention or an influence, and what are the possible ways that quotations or allusions or mentions or influences work? How do other people's texts figure in our own?

Langland's Intertextuality: Dramatic Reading

The preceding line of reflection leads me to my second point about Langland, which has to do with *intertextuality*. The intertextuality of *Piers Plowman* suggests to me that there would be much value in approaching Langland as a highly *dramatic* poet. I am interested not so much in what *Piers Plowman* says, but in what it shows. Drama is the genre that *shows*.

If Langland is as much a medieval intellectual as I suspect, obsessed with books, living his life in a world of texts, then texts are for him dramatis personae. They contend with each other. They constitute mutually incommensurable interpretive systems that struggle to devour each other. Anne Middleton says something very much like this about Langland's fundamental unit of composition, which she calls the "episode": "[T]he episode in *Piers* presents a combat. . . . [A]t some point the interaction becomes charged with opposition. The injection of a countervening force, rather than the logical or rhetorical limits of the discursive topic, shapes the further course of the episode and determines its often abrupt end" ("Narration" 96–97). Indeed, in her determination to answer "what happens" as opposed to "what does it mean," Middleton seems to me very close to the methodology I am trying to formulate here.

Thus Langland's authoritative figures are not mouthpieces for Langland himself, but dramatic characters whose relationships with Langland and each other always remain implicit and complex. At the level of the dreamer's interaction with the authoritative speakers, it is therefore necessary to pay closer attention than usual to the dreamer's own agenda as he questions them. The dreamer's interactions with the authoritative speakers are not just the Socratic disciple's interaction with the master, not just occasions to elicit authoritative commentary. Sometimes the point is obvious, as when the dreamer argues feelingly with Scripture (X.343ff.) or rebukes Reason (XI.372–74). Elsewhere, the point is perhaps less obvious—thus, as I shall argue, there is considerable impertinence in some of the dreamer's questions to Holy Church in Passus I.

The methodological principle, therefore, is to read *Piers Plowman* dramatically, so that the function of any part of the text ("What happens?") becomes as much an issue as its content ("What does it mean?"). Different pieces of Langland's text behave with respect to each other just as other people's texts behave with respect to Langland's; they contend. Texts become the real force in Langland's world, interruptions, "others" that must be reckoned with as obstacles in the otherwise foolishly tranquil stream of human consciousness.

Doctrinaire formalist criticism requires fixed linguistic norms that explain the objective behaviors of bits of text. If we have something called the "text itself" that can be fixed as an object of quasi-scientific inquiry, then at the level of the "text itself" interpretation must be controlled by cultural norms that function analogously with natural laws. What can a poet do with such norms in a text? There seem to be no choices except to reiterate them—moon–June–spoon–croon, the Hallmark greeting—or to set them against each other. The first alternative produces sentimentality. The second supposedly produces interesting poetry precisely because every good poem turns into a site of dramatic conflict between culturally sanctioned ideas.

But it is not necessary to believe that there is a fixed entity called the "text itself" in order to read dramatically. Instead of seeing the text as the site of conflict between implicitly defined cultural norms, we can see it as the white-hot furnace in which those norms are being forged, in which the norms do not preexist the text, but are themselves at issue in it. Human beings can contend with each other without being certain what the argument is about, and we can understand the drama of a conflict without knowing what is at stake. That sort of uncertainty is part of the characteristic experience of reading *Piers Plowman*. Again and again, we find that we can tell that some sort of argument is going on, but we cannot quite get straight what is at issue. The drama produces not a standoff or the momentary crystallized paradox, but a sense of constant meltdown, the fluidity of evolutionary change. In short, the concept of drama does not necessarily entail the concept of well-defined entities in opposition. There can exist a drama of identity, where the natures of the dramatis personae themselves are at issue. That, I am arguing, is what we have in *Piers Plowman*.

Langland's Recursiveness: Pattern

And now I must talk about Langland's *recursiveness*. The drama in *Piers Plowman* does not come from conflicts among well-defined entities. Instead, the drama is a drama of relations that place the entities involved in those relations in flux. So we expect the "same ideas" to return again and again. The same figures return in different relationships. How would we have apprehended that Langland's notion of Conscience, for example, is in flux, is an issue, if Conscience did not keep returning under changed aspects? The same problems too return in different guises—for example, the apparently insoluble problem of money, which begins with *Reddite Cesari* (I.52) and ends with *Redde quod debes* (XIX.394). These returns give the poem its spiraling pattern, the most blatant rhetorical symptom of Langland's recursive thought. Michael L. Klein, for example, bases his reading of *Piers Plowman* on the hypothesis of "spiral" structure.

But *recursion* does not mean just "returning." I employ the term in something closer to its mathematical sense, in which any particular value of a function is defined in terms of previous values of that same function. So, for example, the Fibonacci series of integers can be defined recursively: 1, 1, 2, 3, 5, 8, 13, and so on. I always get the next term in the series by adding the two preceding terms. Just as the rule or function here is "Add the two preceding terms," the rule or function for *Piers Plowman* is "Treat the earlier discourses as texts to be interpreted." That is, Langland is not providing successive approximations to some final oracular statement about Conscience or about money. Instead, he is exploring the process of textual interpretation by causing interpretation to operate again and again on its own results. That is why reading *Piers Plowman* often produces a dizzying sensation similar to that of exploring a self-similar fractal surface—the same pattern seems to repeat itself again and again, but each time on a different scale or with a different orientation.

Obviously, the crucial notion is "pattern." I think Roman Jakobson's reflections can be helpful here. Jakobson, a structural linguist, tries to make rigorous the distinction between "poetic" language and "ordinary" language. I think Jakobson's project is misguided, but his approach to the problem is nevertheless instructive

In Jakobson's formulation, the distinctive feature of the poetic text is the primacy of the *"poetic function,"* which *"projects the principle of equivalence from the axis of selection into the axis of combination"* (358). To put it crudely, the message calls attention to itself as linguistic object. I say "I like Ike," instead of saying, for example, "Bill admires Dwight," or "Rogers votes Republican," or any other of the utterances that might, depending upon the context, count as semantic equivalents. I select *I* from one list of semantic equivalents (*Bill, William, Rogers, professor,* and so on), *like* from another such list (*admire, vote for, prefer,* and so on), and *Ike* from still another (*Dwight, DDE, Eisenhower, Republican candidate,* and so on). But this particular utterance "I like Ike" calls attention to itself because the three words that have been combined are in another sense "equivalents." They exhibit assonance, and two of them rhyme. "Equivalence is promoted to the constitutive device of the sequence" (Jakobson 358). I have created a pattern by *combining* words according to the principle of equivalence, and in the process have added some sort of meaning to the utterance—perhaps nonparaphrasable meaning, certainly meaning that is difficult or tedious to paraphrase, the way it is difficult or tedious to explain a joke.

So, for Jakobson, the message calls attention to itself when we recognize linguistic patterning. Thus we are enabled to divide a pile of randomly selected texts into "poetic" texts and "nonpoetic" texts. Much formalist practice amounts to the recognition of pattern in just this sense. Jakobson's disciples tend to confine themselves to descriptions of grammatical patterning (How many present participles and second-person pronouns do we find in this poem, and where do they occur? and so on) and to concentrate on poetry where this grammatical patterning is especially apparent (Marvell, e. e. cummings, and others). The more interesting practice tends to concentrate on imagery patterns and large structural patterns of various other sorts. But there is no theoretical reason why patterns of relatively large linguistic units cannot function like patterns of morphemes in compelling us to recognize a "poetic" text. It is just that in Jakobson's project morphemes and other relatively small linguistic units seem more like scientific objects—that is, likelier to attract universal agreement about their presence or absence.

The rub, however, comes precisely at the point where we cannot agree about patterns. It seems that if we cannot treat patterns as objective, we will never get over the fence of dictionary definitions and into the wide open spaces of nonparaphrasable meaning that is created precisely by patterns. The notion of recursion will, I hope, keep us from getting snagged on this particular barb.

The notion of recursion implies that there is patterning in *Piers Plowman,* just as there is a pattern in the Fibonacci series. So far, I have described this patterning loosely as "spiraling." What I want to retain is the idea that nonparaphrasable meaning comes from patterning. What I want to reject is the idea that pattern is somehow objective, that the patterns we "discover" function in the argument as features that confirm our hypothetical sense-of-the-whole. Can the notion of recursion perform this work?

Let us look at it this way. Many times in the poem Langland talks about money. As I have just mentioned, one of the first explicit statements is *Reddite Cesari* and one of the last is *Redde quod debes.* That looks like a pattern in the strongest Jakobsonian sense, depending among other things upon the repetition of the same Latin verb. Thinking about these two statements in relation with each other and in the context of other parts of the poem that talk about money occasions much reflection. Now Meed comes early in the poem, and she has one notion about money; Need comes late in the poem, and he has another. Their names rhyme. Is that a pattern? Perhaps not so obviously as the other one, but let us say that this is a pattern too. Thinking about Meed in relation with Need occasions much reflection. But now what about setting Meed in correspondence with *Reddite Cesari* and Need in correspondence with *Redde quod debes?* Does that work? Is that a pattern?

This question, I judge, would be very difficult to settle. In practice, I venture to predict, the answer would depend upon what meanings are said to "follow" from erecting these correspondences, and whether those meanings can be made to support whatever critical agenda is being proffered. The formalist move here is to see the pattern as "objective" if it confirms the hypothetical sense-of-the-whole. There is a linguistic norm that explains (and thereby closes) the pattern once and for all, just as the Newtonian law of gravity explains the eternal motions of the planets.

But if we were not sure how to interpret texts, the question would remain open. We would say something like, "Whether this counts as a pattern depends upon who is doing the interpreting." The question Langland broaches by presenting characters with rhyming names at either end of his poem is not the question of what the correspondence means, but precisely the question of *whether there is* a correspondence— that is, what rule we should use for making connections in texts. We see *that* meaning comes from patterning, without ever being ready to conclude *what* meaning finally emerges. We see the *possibility* of patterns without ever being sure that a pattern is *meant.* That experience, I submit, is the experience most characteristic of reading Langland.

Reading Langland as a recursive poet, in my sense of the term, means that the rules for connecting signs never get fixed. The function of Langland's recursiveness is to reopen again and again the question of how one should interpret. The poem ends with the beginning of what I, at least, hear as another never-ending hermeneutic quest:

> "By Crist!" quod Conscience tho, "I wole bicome a pilgrym,
> And walken as wide as the world lasteth,
> To seken Piers the Plowman, that Pryde myghte destruye . . ."
> (XX.381–83)

Pride here, besides being the name of a personage in the allegory, means a misinterpretation of the self. Just as the Fibonacci sequence is infinite and nonconvergent, all hermeneutic patterns are open-ended and provisional, even after the poem is over.

Now I offer a couple of final words about my own rhetoric. I would not object if someone wanted to describe what I am doing here as "close reading." But a close reading of the whole of *Piers Plowman* would run to thousands of pages and bore even its author. In what I take to be Langland's own spirit, I reject the whole idea of a definitive work. So there is no sense in which I am presenting a "reading" of the whole poem. I am trying only to illustrate one way of reading, and meanwhile doing the best I can to argue from a limited set of samples that textual hermeneutics is a central concern for Langland. In that sense, I am already a failure as a formalist critic because there is nothing like Coleridgean unity either at the center of my project or on its horizon.

I proceed in three movements. Chapter 1 reads the beginning and the end of *Piers Plowman* in the light of the exegetical tradition surrounding the story of the Tower of Babel in Genesis 11. It develops that for Langland, the intelligibility of both the social organism (the "estates") and the individual self depends upon construing both as texts. The subtext of the chapter is to demonstrate Langland's originality in his use of traditional material. Langland does not invoke the tradition to suggest solutions to the problems he poses. The exegetical tradition aims to enforce orthodoxy, but Langland uses the tradition to suggest that the normal state of life on earth is a Babylonian cacophony of conflicting texts, with a corresponding interior Babel of the fragmented self.

Chapter 2 analyzes the dreamer's dialogues with Holy Church (Passus I), Anima (Passus XV), and Need (Passus XX) to show how *Piers Plowman* construes the interpretive activity of these authoritative figures on the model of textual hermeneutics. But contrary to the normal procedure of historicist criticism (which has nevertheless proved very fruitful in analyzing these passages), the chapter argues that Langland does not provide anything resembling an unqualified endorsement of any authoritative figure's conclusions or interpretive methodology. Although Holy Church, Anima, and Need essentially represent a sampling from

the many authoritative speakers in the poem, these three have been chosen also because they represent distinctive movements in the narrative
of the dreamer discussed in Chapter 3. The subtext of Chapter 2 is to
demonstrate what it means to say that Langland is a "textual" poet, by
demonstrating how texts become for him entities with whom it is possible to experience dramatic interactions.

Chapter 3 argues that there is a narrative of the dreamer—albeit inconclusive—a spiritual development in which the dreamer learns that
the intellectual's lust for self-justification on the model of textual argument is futile and self-destructive. And yet the intellectual as *litteratus*
must approach God, if at all, through texts. The dreamer and Piers, as
the only private symbols in the poem, are reciprocally determining. Piers
represents the space that is always opening in the poem between God
himself and all the embarrassingly inadequate human interpretations of
him. Literacy turns out for the intellectual to be itself instrumental like
sin: an understanding of the wrongness of wanting to master texts in order to justify oneself provides the stimulus for a necessary refocusing of
one's life. The subtext of the chapter is to demonstrate Langland's recursiveness by showing how the dreamer's narrative consists in revisit-
ings and refigurings of his previous interpretive activities in constantly
renewed interpretive activities.

I am talking about the B-text, with only brief glances at the C-text,
because the B-text is what most critics talk about. I quote from the edition of A. V. C. Schmidt because that edition is inexpensive, accessible,
and good.

In the main body of my text I will not in general carry out arguments with other critics of *Piers Plowman*. Nor will I generally acknowledge intellectual indebtedness in any detail, except when I actually
quote something or take over wholesale someone else's line of thought.
Otherwise, this book would quickly snap under the weight of critical
quibbling. Those with a professional interest in Langland and the scholarship about *Piers Plowman* will easily be able to infer my intellectual indebtedness (and the blank spots in my reading about Langland) from
the list of works cited at the end of the book. That intellectual indebtedness is in general considerable. In fact, as I have suggested already,
there is scarcely one *completely* original thought in anything I have writ-

ten. Those who are interested in a more comprehensive bibliography for Langland or for scholarship on *Piers Plowman* cannot do better than to avail themselves of the excellent book by Derek Pearsall (*An Annotated Critical Bibliography of Langland,* 1990) and the annual bibliographies in the *Yearbook of Langland Studies.* Periodic "Bibliographical Essays" in my book will (nonsystematically) take up some of the critical issues that impinge on my reading. But apart from these digressions, I will not pay much attention to anything anybody except Langland says.

CHAPTER I

THE BEGINNING
AND THE END

Sestow this peple—
How bisie they ben aboute the maze?
(I.5–6)

The Tower of Babel

The Tower of Babel casts a long shadow over Langland's Prologue. But having argued that we cannot understand *Piers Plowman* just by knowing the exegetical tradition, I need to demonstrate Langland's originality in extending that tradition.

In the moment of "historical" or patristic criticism, we would note that the tradition interprets *Babylon* as meaning "confusion." This exegesis occurs paradigmatically in Augustine's *The City of God* (2.112), and also, for example, in *Glossa Ordinaria* (PL 114.431), and in Rabanus Maurus's *Allegoriae in Sacram Scripturam* (PL 112.872) and *Commentarium in Genesim* (PL 107.528). There are obvious superficial resemblances between the Babel story and Langland's vision. Langland's Castle of Wrong is a "dongeon" in a "dale" (Prologue 15) that strikes the dreamer as both "derke" (Prologue 16) and "merke" (I.1). The Tower of Babel in the Latin of the Vulgate is a *turris in campo;* as Gregory the Great explains, the Tower was constructed not on the height of virtue but in the plain of vices, *planitie vitiorum (In Septem Psalmos Poenitentiales Expositio, PL 79.598)*. Nimrod, a type of the devil, built it (Augustine, *The City of God* 2.112; *Glossa Ordinaria, PL* 113.114; Rabanus, *In Genesim, PL* 107.528; Isidore, *Allegoriae Quaedam Scripturae Sacrae, PL* 83.103). Certainly the babble of competing and often mutually unintelligible voices is an image central to Langland's Prologue. Having gone so far, we might reasonably conclude—as Robertson and Huppé in fact do conclude—that the scene on the "fair feeld ful of folk" (Prologue 17) represents a "kind of Babylonian confusion" (21–22). At some level, then, Langland is talking about Augustine's Babylon, the type of the earthly city.

And by extension, Langland is talking also about the Fall. As Edwin D. Craun points out, pastoral treatises about sins of the tongue treat "deviant utterance" as "a fall, not a slip of the tongue. Particular types are often traced not to the Babel of Genesis, that story of linguistic multiplicity which fascinates fabulists like Dante and Gower, but to the Fall of Genesis, where the first sins involve the conscious abuse of words" (37). Craun's whole discussion of *Piers Plowman* (157–86), in fact, places the poem in the context of pastoral discourse concerning sins of the tongue.

This sort of analysis is indispensable, and I do not want to suggest otherwise. Again and again, patient scholars of Langland uncover some new bit of context that thenceforth seems indisputably part of the meaning of *Piers Plowman*. Again and again, this book and subsequent books will say silly things about *Piers Plowman* because the writers of the books do not know enough about the texts Langland knew. My point, however, is that it is a mistake to stop short after performing this archaeology, as if we had exhausted the meaning of Langland's "allusion" to the commentaries on Genesis 11 once we have remarked that Langland must have been thinking about Augustine. That would be to relegate *Piers Plowman,* and *The City of God* as well, to the museum case of archaic—that is, dead—ideas.

To ask about Langland's originality does not mean to ask, "What can the exegetical tradition tell us about the meaning of *Piers Plowman?*" That is an always respectable and often indispensable question, but in its form it abstracts from the whole issue of originality as I am trying to understand it in this book. The question that I want to ask is rather, "What can *Piers Plowman* tell us about the meaning of the exegetical tradition?" How does Langland extend the meaning of *The City of God,* so as to make both Augustine's text and *Piers Plowman* living texts? How does Langland "do hermeneutics" on the story of the Tower of Babel?

The rest of this chapter is a long answer to that short question. But let me begin by quoting a passage from Mary Carruthers that could almost serve as an abstract of the chapter.

> [I]n the Prologue Langland utilizes many possible types of sign, many possible kinds of language. . . . [H]is procedure focuses attention on the signs of intellection themselves; the world of the Prologue demands to be understood, by the very fact of its confusion. The signs used to give it order and understanding are inadequate, in conflict with one another rather than in harmony. The leaves of Langland's universe are not only scattered; they seem to have come from unrelated volumes. (33)

I want to especially develop two notions: first, that the Babylonian confusion of the Prologue provides the context within which the problems posed in the rest of the poem make sense as problems ("the world of the Prologue demands to be understood, by the very fact of its confusion"); second, that the cacophony by its constant returns calls attention to the inability of the speaker to make sense of his world in spite of his constantly reiterated attempts to do so ("[H]is procedure focuses attention on the signs of intellection themselves"). We are left asking, "What can the speaker, or I, or anyone, do to sort out this messy convocation?"

The Prologue presents two separate catalogs of folk. One comes before the entrance of the King and his court at line 112. The other, shorter catalog comes after the fable of the rats and the mice, and begins with the deluge of lawyers at line 211. It is already an interesting question why Langland separates the catalogs this way, and I shall address that question later. For now, I want to look at the first catalog (20–111), with the shadow of the Tower of Babel in mind.

There is no suggestion that these folk are speaking mutually unintelligible languages. The issue of Latin literacy does keep coming up by implication—as, for example, with the friars who "Glosed the gospel" (60), or with the cardinals whose power to elect a pope pertains partly to their "lettrure" (110). But, for the most part, the scene seems Anglicized. The dreamer is apparently able to construe everything he hears. If there is "Babylonian confusion," then, it arises from something other than (or more than) linguistic diversity. This is not a simple replication of Babel. So what is the source of the confusion, if Babylon is itself the very archetype and meaning of confusion?

Clearly, part of the problem is that people tell lies. The exegetical tradition treats the Babylonian confusion as a type of heresy, which causes disunity in the Church. We find this exegesis, for example, in the *Glossa Ordinaria* (PL 113.114) and in Rabanus's *In Genesim* (PL 107.530). In *Piers Plowman,* the "japeres and jangeleres, Judas children, / Feynen hem fantasies" (35–36). The "Bidderes and beggeres" beg falsely: they "Faiteden for hire foode" (40–42). The pilgrims are famous for lying: having gone on a pilgrimage, they "hadden leve to lyen al hire lif after" (49). The uniforms of the false hermits (one of which the speaker himself seems to be wearing in line 3) are an implicit lie by means of which they "shopen hem heremytes" (57). The friars "Glosed" (60); the pardoner "blered hire eighen" (74); the bishop's seal, with or without the bishop's connivance, was "sent to deceyve the peple" (79). The emphasis on lying prepares the way for the allegory of Passus I, where Holy Church, who naturally construes herself as the custodian of truth and the enemy of heresy, interprets the "tour up the toft" (I.12) as the castle of Truth and the "dongeon in the dale" as the castle of "Wrong" who is the "Fader of falshede" (I.59–64).

I believe that Langland's emphasis on lying also constitutes an interesting reflection on the exegetical tradition. The exegetes insist that God in confusing the languages at Babel did not create anything new. Instead, he merely mixed up the letters and syllables of the original language (presumably Hebrew). Versions of this exegesis occur, for example, in Augustine's *The City of God* (2.121–22), in the *Glossa Ordinaria* (PL 114.430), in Rabanus's *In Genesim* (PL 107.530), and in Isidore's *Allegoriae* (PL 83.103). Also, God dispersed reference, so that the same word (that is, the same sequence of sounds) might refer to different things in different languages. Examples of this exegesis occur, for example, in the *Glossa Ordinaria* (PL 113.115) and in Rabanus's *In Genesim* (PL 107.530). As Robert Myles puts it in his discussion of Chaucerian "realism," the story of the Tower of Babel assumes an "intentionalist realist view of language," in that "while the words may change, the things they are directed towards and attempt to name and reveal remain the same" (9).

Langland's reflection on the exegetical tradition suggests an interesting inference: the biblical account of linguistic diversity also provides an account of the nature and possibility of falsehood. Lying consists in intentionally misapplying a word—in applying the word *minstrel,* for example, to a jangler; or in using the word *hermit* to refer to a con man; or in misappropriating the word *hunger* to stand in for gluttony. "To lie" means to intentionally construct another language, in which words that sound familiar are in fact being used to refer to something entirely different. This account of lying differs, for example, from that of Jonathan Swift's Houyhnhnms, who, having no word for falsehood, describe lying as saying "the thing which was not." Misnaming for Langland is not the same as creating fictions ex nihilo. The possibility of misnaming implies that there is something there already, God's good reality, and the only human question is what we are going to call it. If we believe that Langland "alludes to" the story of the Tower of Babel and the exegetical tradition surrounding that story, then it seems that he is extending the concept of Babylonian confusion to include also category mistakes and the confusion that results from lying. Babylon is not just an "image" of the Church divided by heresy. Instead, it is a *type* in the deep sense. The diversity of languages at the Tower is an *instance* of the same phenomenon that causes disunity in the Church. Langland suggests how that can be so. That phenomenon is, at base, a failure of interpretation brought about by uncertain reference.

It is not surprising that Langland extends the concept of Babylonian confusion to include lying. Lying and its devastations are obviously prominent features of the earthly city, both then and now. But the more striking implication is that the only possible response to Babylonian confusion is, strictly speaking, hermeneutic activity. We cannot redeem the earthly city just by becoming polylingual. The descent of the Paraclete at Pentecost does not constitute the end of sacred history, but instead the beginning of Christian action in the world. We must find out how to be sure that the words of any particular language are applied truly. Arguments directed against Babylonian confusion are, at base, hermeneutic arguments.

We have to say, in short, what things *mean*. That is, after all, the first thing the dreamer wants to know from Holy Church, and the first question he asks in the poem: "Mercy, madame, what [may] this [be] to meene?" (1.11). I am arguing that Langland invokes the exegetical tradition as the background against which the hermeneutic combats of the rest of the poem will be played out. I am also arguing that Langland's originality consists in part in extending the tradition to apply to hermeneutic activity *within* the single language that most concerns him: namely, the English vernacular of the late fourteenth century. Langland seems not especially interested in the orthodoxy for which heresy is always clearly heresy. At the Tower of Babel it was presumably easy enough to tell when someone else was speaking some other language. Langland goes deeper. He is interested in the phenomenon of interpretation itself (and by implication, misinterpretation) that makes different languages, and heresy, possible. Confronted with Babylonian confusion in the heart of his own language, he wants to explore where that confusion comes from.

Besides all the lies, another part of the problem in the Prologue seems to be the confusion of the estates. The catalogs look like catalogs of occupations, and that fact lends the Prologue the shape of a sort of inchoate estates satire. But clearly, part of the confusion of the estates is linguistic. "Hermit" is a legitimate social category (as in line 28), but the "Grete lobies and longe" who head for Walsingham with "hire wenches after" (54–55) do not belong in the category—they only call themselves hermits. The "preaching" of the friars and the pardoner falls well short of preaching in the highest sense, and the "absolution" the pardoner offers (70) is not legitimate absolution. There is a hint that some "pilgrims" are not really pilgrims: they "*seiden* thei hadde ysought seintes" (50; emphasis mine). And the cardinals, if they were really to live up to the deepest meaning of their name, would cultivate the cardinal virtues (100ff.), but they do not. At the root, their name does not correspond with their reality.

But a deeper problem with the confusion of the estates is the system of categories itself. That is, it seems no longer clear in the world Langland describes that the traditional terminology is adequate to the observable society. The problem unfolds almost immediately, with the first three categories listed: "Somme putten hem to the plough" (20), "somme putten hem to pride" (23), and "In preieres and penaunce putten hem manye" (25). Except for the second category, this passage sounds as though it should be the listing of the traditional three estates, a matrix for the further specification that follows. Laboring with the hands and laboring at prayer are clear enough, but we are left wondering whether laboring at sartorial splendor (23–24) is meant to characterize the knightly class. The principle of division blurs. Is the dreamer availing himself of the traditional division of labor, or is he contrasting those who do useful work with those who waste and preen? If he does insinuate that the knightly class is corrupt, is that an indictment of that class only? Or does Langland's critique extend also to the old system of categories itself, appropriate to the feudal economy but inadequate to analyze the complexities of the new money economy?

In fact, the dreamer immediately moves on to the merchants and the minstrels: "somme chosen chaffare" (31) and "somme murthes to make" (33). Both of these are especially problematic categories in that it is not easy to see how they fit the schema of the traditional three estates. Merchants and minstrels do not defend the realm, and they neither labor nor pray. This nagging problem does not go away. Later, for example, the merchants have a place only in the margin of Piers's pardon (VII.18), and Haukyn's minstrelsy as *Activa Vita* is at best ambiguous (XIII.222–25).

The dreamer's fumbling with the traditional categories of social analysis alerts us to something else original in Langland's understanding of the Babel story. The suggestion here is that social corruption flourishes at least in part because of our inability to erect an adequate set of categories to talk about it. We cannot think well without good terminology. Dividing the social body into the traditional three estates, for example, might provide a story that justifies class distinctions, but it seems to elide the more pressing problem of economic injustice. On the other hand, to undermine the traditional classification seems to invite chaos, where nothing is understood and no one is able to construe his or her proper relation to the social organism. Certainly it is possible to read Langland as nostalgic for the feudal economy and deeply skeptical of the new money economy. But my point is that both this nostalgia and this skepticism, if Langland felt them, would have arisen from the acute discomfort he, or any fourteenth-century intellectual, would have felt when trying to think through social problems in terms of the familiar categories of social analysis. Langland is extending the Babylonian confusion of Genesis 11 and the exegetical tradition to include not only linguistic diversity and lies, but also the confusion that results from erecting systems of analytical categories in terms of which to interpret, and therefore to some degree control, human experience. The dreamer's confusion about categories is not a sign of philosophical clumsiness or half-baked thought on Langland's part, but instead a dramatic device to show what happens when we try to construe the world on the hermeneutic model.

As I have said before, I am concerned mainly with textual hermeneutics. That is because I believe that a fourteenth-century intellectual, a *litteratus,* would understand interpretation on the model of textual hermeneutics and would in general try to read the world like a book. In one sense, I have already been trying to show how Langland's poetic activity in the Prologue reads fourteenth-century society as a text of Babylonian confusion. It is not just that fourteenth-century society provides a contemporary token of the Babylonian type. Fourteenth-century society can be turned into a text by a hermeneutic consciousness—in fact, the text of *Piers Plowman* and the consciousness that is the condition for its possibility. Langland's Prologue understands his society as a text that both illuminates and is illuminated by the Babel story and its exegetical tradition, in a relationship that is perhaps best described as "intertextual." But more remains to be said about texts in the Prologue. So far, I have concentrated on lying, heresy, and category mistakes, all of which presumably can exist in the absence of literacy. What evidence is there, other than his own literacy, that Langland thinks of *textual* hermeneutics as paradigmatic for interpretation in general?

I want to approach this question in a somewhat roundabout way, by considering the overall structure of the catalog in lines 20–111 of the Prologue. I think there is something to be gained from comparing Langland's Prologue with the General Prologue of Chaucer's *Canterbury Tales*. To navigate all the shoals and reefs of such a comparison would be difficult and dangerous. Many different points might be made from this comparison; see, for example, Helen Cooper's "Langland's and Chaucer's Prologues" and James Simpson's interesting reading (21–23). But I want to limit my discussion to one fairly superficial observation. Both Langland's catalog of occupations and Chaucer's catalog of pilgrims—who are also identified by occupation—have an overall structure that might be described as "loose."

That is, Chaucer begins with the Knight, the highest ranking pilgrim, and ends with the churls (and himself). *In general,* he moves from highest to lowest. But I would be hard-pressed to demonstrate that this principle is rigorously applied throughout the General Prologue. Other principles of arrangement and various opportunistic juxtapositions cut across the overall plan, much as seems to happen with the overall plan of *The Canterbury Tales* themselves.

I want to argue that Langland does something similar in his catalog: there is an overall pattern, but it is loosely applied, cut across by other patterns and opportunistic groupings. Joseph Wittig's reading of Langland's catalog (*Revisited* 34–45, 47–48) is an instructive illustration of how a thoughtful reader might move through the catalog, applying various principles of association—what Wittig calls "associative logic" (48)—to account for Langland's juxtapositions. But I want to start from the notion that once we are past the confusion about the three estates, and the problematic categories of merchant and minstrel that serve to intensify that confusion, Langland's catalog moves *in general* in reverse order from Chaucer's: that is, from lowest to highest, from beggars to cardinals.

The "Bidderes and beggeres" (40) can even be read as a transitional category. On the one hand, beggars present a category as problematic in its own way for the theory of the three estates as are the categories of merchant and minstrel. The theory of the three estates is based on a division of labor. Legitimate beggars are precisely those who cannot labor. How can the theory of the three estates account, then, for these marginal members of the social organism? As for Piers's pardon, "Beggeres" and "bidderes" are not there at all unless "the suggestion be sooth that shapeth hem to begge" (VII.64–65). Like merchants and minstrels, beggars pose a nagging problem that surfaces again and again in different contexts. One such occasion, for example, is Piers's discussion with Hunger about how beggars should be treated: "Of beggeris and of bidderes what best be to doone?" (VI.203). On the other hand, of the categories that follow the merchants and the minstrels, beggars have the least social sanction, in the sense that they by definition make no economic claim to deserve what they receive. The pilgrims (46–52) presumably pay their own way, or, if they receive donations, they can make the argument that they are doing useful spiritual work. The hermits (53–57) presumably can make the same argument. The friars (58–67) preach and shrive; the pardoner (68–82) preaches and (he says) absolves. Parsons and parish priests (83–86) abandon their congregations, but they are paid for singing masses in London. Masters and doctors (87–99) take administrative posts, and cardinals (100–110) do what cardinals do to cultivate the cardinal virtues.

In fact, it is possible to read these categories as fitting loosely on a scale of increasing social sanction, if not of actual social rank—with a typically Langlandian bite in relegating the friars to a position below even the villainous pardoner. But the more interesting point is that as soon as we get to the clergy in the catalog—that is, beginning with the friars—the nature and degree of social sanction depend precisely upon the nature of the relationship with some text.

The friars, as literate, "Glosed" and "construwed" (60–61), but their relationship with the gospel text that ultimately sanctions their activity is, in a way, distant. Langland presents the friars' activity as opening up a space between reading and preaching. The friars use (or, in this case, abuse) the gospel for purposes not necessarily connected with the purposes of the gospel itself: "Prechynge the peple for profit of [the] womb[e]" (59). The activity of the pardoner, on the other hand, is specifically warranted by the text of his "brevet" (74) or his "rageman" (75). Whereas the gospel may well be absent in every sense from the friars' preaching, even the physical parchment containing the pardoner's warrant is an important prop for him. His relationship with his relevant text is more intimate. The text itself creates the space within which the pardoner operates.

One of the reasons Langland's structure seems "loose" is that it is hard to tell whether the "Persons and parisshe preestes" (83) form a separate category from that of the "Bisshopes and bachelers, bothe maistres and doctours" (87). Schmidt's edition, by its paragraphing, suggests that all these clergy constitute a single category, perhaps with subdivisions. Pearsall's edition of the C-text, on the other hand, breaks the passage into two paragraphs. The argument for separate categories, as I have hinted, is that different clergy end up in different jobs, some as chantry priests and some as bureaucrats. All of these clergy, however, have at least two things in common. One is that they are failing to perform their pastoral functions (84, 88–90). This is the point that C reinforces, introducing a rebuke by Conscience that includes the story of Ophni and Phinees, types of slack priests. One failing of slack priests in C is that they allow "vntrewe sacrefice" (98). That criticism suggests the other thing that all these imperfect clergy have in common: all of them are contributing to the corruption of spiritual labor. Because of their avarice, the liturgy is not performed properly. Some of them "syngen . . . for symonie" (B.86); others are so busy with worldly affairs that "Hire messe and hire matyns and many of hire houres / Arn doone undevout-liche" (B.97–98). What should provide these clergy with their social sanction is precisely their spiritual labor, their devout and wholehearted absorption in the texts of the divine liturgy. As opposed to merely providing a warrant for their activities, the texts of the liturgy constitute those activities. Realizing the texts is their proper labor, and there should be no space in the moment of that realization between the liturgical texts and the purposes of the clergy.

Finally, the definitive activity of the cardinals is to elect a pope, and thereby to extend the power of Peter as Vicar of Christ "To bynden and to unbynden, as the Book telleth" (101). Langland expresses that power of election in an interesting way: "in love and lettrure the eleccion bilongeth" (110). In the first place, the line rhetorically elevates literacy to the level of love itself, the chief Christian virtue and perhaps the defini tive name of God in *Piers Plowman*. In the second place, the line suggests that, like love, literacy is not just an attainment among other attainments, but instead a way of life. Their literacy should permeate the cardinals' lives at every moment, and not only when they are singing masses or saying matins. They should, in the deepest sense, live by the Book. That perfectly and continuously intimate relationship with Scripture is what sanctions their high social position as well.

It is possible to argue, then, that the structure of Langland's first catalog of occupations implies, within the limits of its looseness, a potential ordering of society based on the notion of literacy itself. The looseness is important, in that it suggests the perpetual incompletion of the hermeneutic circle, the open-endedness of any living text. On the one hand, that reading fits with many other passages in *Piers Plowman* that demonstrate Langland's awareness of the actual importance of texts of various kinds in conferring social sanction on various human activities. On the other hand, that reading also constitutes an argument that Langland means to show in his poem what the world looks like when we take reading itself as the definitive human activity.

The First Foundation and the Social Drama

After the cardinals have had their chance to impose order on the Babylonian confusion, and after the dreamer pointedly refuses to say outright that they have failed (107–11), the King enters the field. This looks like the attempt of secular authority to succeed where ecclesiastical authority has bungled. And in fact, the King, with the help of Knighthood and the clergy and the commons and Kynde Wit, immediately begins to sort things out in terms of the traditional three estates.

The episode is the first of many "founding moments" in the poem, in which some sort of social or spiritual order is established that is doomed to break down because of its own internal contradictions. *Piers Plowman* ends with a cracking of the monolithic establishment of Unity, the Church, as Conscience departs to search for Piers.

The episode of the King in the Prologue is also the first example of how Langland structures parts of the poem around dramatic interactions. The dramatic interactions in this case consist of hermeneutic arguments: specifically, they consist of arguments about which texts should actually found the social order, and about how those texts should be interpreted. As such, the whole scene is deeply ironic, because it is by no means clear at first that the secular authority consciously cares about texts at all. As Langland puts it in the B-text, "*Might* of the communes made hym to regne" (113; my emphasis); and C revises the line in the direction of political conservatism, to make it seem as though it is the might of the knights ("Myght of tho men"—140) that makes the King reign. In either case, might, as opposed to a text, makes right. And in the debates about texts that follow in the Prologue, everybody is talking to the King, but the King himself is pointedly silent. Silence can have as much dramatic impact as speech. One has to wonder whether the King is much interested in textual guidance for his rule or in textual justification of his power.

The issue is sharpened by the fact that the first to presume to give the King advice is a "lunatik" (123). I identify this figure with Langland himself, who elsewhere in the poem portrays himself as mentally unstable and as failing to show proper deference to the great and the good (XV.3–10). The line introducing the lunatic, like most of this scene in my reading of it, is richly and comically ambiguous. The King, with the commons and Kynde Wit, has just in the line immediately preceding established "lawe and leaute—ech lif to knowe his owene" (122), and certainly it does not seem to be the proper place of a lunatic to advise a king. This lunatic, moreover, speaks "clergially" (124), trespassing on the function of the counselor (114–15), which is the last function one would want performed by a lunatic. On the other hand, since the lunatic's advice in fact sounds theologically unexceptionable and appropriately clergial, the whole point might be that only a lunatic, no matter how good his advice, would presume to give that advice unsolicited to a king. And finally, there is an irony like Chaucer's: that Langland-author, constructing himself as Langland-lunatic and a character in his own poem, pretends to worry about advising a fictional king whom he himself has constructed.

The lunatic tries to subsume secular authority under divine authority. The King is responsible for "rightful rulyng" because he is subject to Christ and wants to be "rewarded in hevene" (127). The angel apparently supports the lunatic, coming to his aid with a Latin quotation, because "lewed men ne koude / Jangle ne jugge that justifie hem sholde" (129–30). But this is also potentially a comic moment. The sudden appearance of the angel suggests, on the one hand, that the bumbling attempts of the "lewed" lunatic have to be corrected at once by somebody who can speak Latin, and suggests, on the other hand, that kings are likely to be snobbish about whom they listen to. The angel, by rushing in to repair the damage where fools have not feared to tread, seems to imply both that the lunatic is a fool for offering advice in the vernacular and that the King is a fool for being unwilling to listen to it. The angel literally lowers himself ("Lowed"—129) to give his advice. Langland-author ostensibly rebukes Langland-lunatic for arrogating to himself the role of the clergy without the literacy of the clergy. But the rebuke is rendered ironic by the fact that the angel's advice, though Latin, is doggerel, whereas the lunatic's advice is perfectly good English. A small and funny skirmish is going on here in the immense and continuing struggle over the capacity of the vernacular as a medium for authoritative discourse.

In a way, the angel's advice is not a faithful translation of the lunatic's and represents a step backward. The lunatic's advice is completely and self-consciously open-ended: "Please Christ." The angel's advice pretends to be a further specification of that principle. The King will please Christ by tempering justice (*jus*) with mercy (*pietas*). But how does one do that? Far from explaining lucidly how to please Christ, the angel's advice opens one of the most tangled cans of worms in the poem—precisely by erecting this rhetorical opposition between justice and mercy. This opposition maps onto the opposition between works and faith, and presages the later, seemingly interminable, debates about the virtuous pagan. Maybe only Jesus, in fact, can reconcile justice with mercy, and even he has to work like a lawyer in Passus XVIII to finish the job.

The goliard horns in next. His point is that the essence of being a king *(rex)* is to rule *(regere)*, which the goliard identifies with enforcing the laws *(jura tenere)*. Of course, the angel never said that the King should not enforce the laws. What the angel wants to treat as a complementary pair *(jus, pietas)* the goliard, misunderstanding the angel's rhetorical technique, treats as mutually exclusive terms. But the goliard's objection functions to highlight the problem with the angel's advice. Is there ever any occasion when being merciful entails failing to enforce the law? Or, put the other way around, is there ever any occasion when it is possible to enforce the law and at the same time to be merciful? Can *jus* and *pietas,* as the angel presents them, ever be reconciled?

The goliard himself, however, as a "gloton of wordes" (139), gets hold of the wrong end of the stick. No doubt he expects the King to overhear the debate, but he focuses more on refuting the angel than on advising the King: "to the aungel an heigh answeres after" (140). The goliard would be dismissed by postmodernism as an "essentialist," and he seems to believe furthermore that the essence of anything is entailed in the etymology of the Latin term *(nomen)* that names it. By contrast with the speaker who earlier in the catalog jokes about the cardinals' name ("the Cardinals at court that kaughte of that name"—107), the goliard seems quite serious about the principle. Certainly, the maxim the goliard quotes could be taken to imply that a king should be subject to the law, but that is not the point the goliard uses the maxim to make. The goliard's point is rather that a king should be subject to the Latin language, to which the goliard himself, by the way, implicitly asserts proprietary rights. Surely, no one could object if a king managed on some occasion to enforce the law and at the same time to be merciful. The goliard "greved hym" (139) not because the angel preaches mercy, but because in the goliard's opinion the angel deviates from etymology.

In particular, with the goliard's interjection, it emerges that what has been going on here is an argument about interpretation. The angel implies, among other things, that only Latin texts can be truly authoritative; and that the way to understand human experience is to construe it under some pattern of opposition, just as texts must be understood in terms of patterns of opposition. Justice and mercy in the social organism must be understood in relation to each other, just as the terms *jus* and *pietas* in the Latin text must be understood in relation to each other. The goliard chooses as his authority a different text from the angel's, but his argument with the angel is primarily about how to understand texts. The goliard rejects the angel's text because of the way the goliard interprets. The goliard construes rhetorical opposition as implying logical contradiction. The goliard's principle is that we understand texts by understanding the words that constitute them, and we understand those words by uncovering their etymologies. Words mean what they mean (and kings either rule or they are not kings), no matter what patterns of opposition the words happen into in particular texts. Then, once we know what the words mean, we can understand (and control) social reality by living up to the language by means of which we describe it.

At this point, the commons stick in their oar. They have apparently been impressed by the display of Latin literacy, and so they themselves "crye in vers of Latyn" (143). The moment is perhaps somewhat reminiscent of the entrance of the goose into the courtly love debate in Chaucer's *Parliament of Fowls*. The commons' maxim makes sense, but there is some reason to doubt that the commons themselves really understand all its resonances and implications. Langland's ironic aside, "construe whoso wolde" (144), suggests among other things that the meaning of the commons' maxim is up for grabs, since there is no clear intention behind it to be uncovered. "Make of it what you will," and what we should make of it is, again, thoroughly ambiguous.

One possible interpretation is that the commons, though they might not be subtle political philosophers, are nevertheless clever political animals. They have a keen eye for their own self-interest, and they can always rummage up some political cliché to justify their position. Then, the maxim *Precepta Regis sunt nobis vincula legis* serves as a rhetorical countermove to the goliard. The goliard misses the point, maybe, but he thereby introduces into the discourse a maxim that could be dangerous for the commons. To subject the King to the law shifts power, in general, from the King himself to his council—that is, to the ones who will interpret the law to the King, and the only ones who are in any position, practically speaking, to insist that the King observe the law. If members of the King's council are greedy and bad (as there are both historical and textual reasons to believe they were, at the period of the B-text), then the commons will suffer from this shifting of power. It might be better for the commons to depend on the mercy of a more absolute monarch. Their remarks, then, are directed "To the Kynges counseil" (144), and the "construe whoso wolde" appears as another instance of Langland's ironic distancing of himself from a position that might offend powerful people.

Another possible interpretation is that the commons are so much at sea that they do not understand either the implications of what they are saying or its relation to what has gone before. Then, the "construe whoso wolde" means exactly what it says: "This maxim could be taken to mean whatever anybody wanted it to mean." The commons just repeat some Latin tag that they have heard somewhere and that they judge will be inoffensive to everybody, because who could possibly deny that the King rules the commons?

A third possible interpretation is that the commons might understand the implicit debate over political philosophy, but that they have no faith that the issue can be settled and no interest in having everything completely clarified anyway. They want to nip the developing debate in the bud. They are just being practical: "However this debate about the King and the law might turn out, for all practical purposes we commons have to do what the King says. Let's not provoke a constitutional crisis; let's just get on with business." Then, the "construe whoso wolde" might be taken to mean something like, "The commons were willing to let anybody who wished do the interpreting; interpreting was not their concern." The irony here is that the commons' own intervention is premised on a belief in the power of texts to control behavior. They are wrong to think that they need not be concerned with interpreting.

These are not the only possibilities. But my point is that by opening this Pandora's box of ambiguity, Langland forces us to pay attention to the dramatic context of the commons' maxim. If we want to work out what the commons mean, we have to ask ourselves what they are trying to do. The meaning of a text depends at least in part on how it functions as a speech act. Thus Langland constructs his political world as the site of contending texts. But the texts, like persons or political action committees, are not simple unchanging essences. If we thought of texts that way—the goliard's way, maybe—we could not construe the complexities of the world as if the world were a text. But Langland's drama demonstrates, among other things, that the behavior of texts can be adequately complex to model political behavior.

That brings me to the fable of the rats and the mice. In the drama of the Prologue, the fable is apparently motivated by the hermeneutic debate that precedes it. The commons contribute their maxim, and "*With that* ran ther a route of ratons" (146; emphasis mine). In what sense, exactly, does the fable follow dramatically from the commons' maxim?

One way to look at the fable is to regard it as a parable of the political situation implied in the commons' speech. Depending upon how one reads the lines preceding the fable, the fable illustrates either the cluelessness of the commons or their pain of being politically savvy without having any real political power. Whichever way we go, however, the political situation implied in the commons' maxim sets the limits to the possibility of action in the world of the fable. It is as though the commons (the rats and the mice) have to go through a stage of codifying their situation, of rendering it in a maxim, before they know what to do next. We have to know what verbal rule we are following before we know how to behave.

The main point I want to make about the fable, however, is that it is about the failure of interpretation. In the story the "raton of renoun" (158) tells at first, what one knows from bells on collars is whether the wearers are present: "Were ther a belle on hire beighe, by Jesu, as me thynketh, / Men myghte witen wher thei wente and awey renne" (165–66). But in his actual proposal, somehow the rodents are supposed to be able to tell from the bell what mood the cat is in:

> . . . here we mowen
> Wher he ryt or rest or rometh to pleye;
> And if hym list for to laike, thanne loke we mowen
> And peeren in his presence the while hym pleye liketh,
> And if hym wratheth, be war and his wey shonye.
>
> (170–74)

The strategy is not to avoid the cat entirely, but to play with him when he is happy and to avoid him when he is angry. It is not clear how the sound of a bell is supposed to convey this information. This is information about intention. Whatever the bell might represent in the political allegory, the fact that the rat apparently does not notice that he has confused an indication of simple presence with an indication of intention bodes ill for his hermeneutic, not to mention his survival. His argument is like saying that because an author is present in a text, we can immediately and nonproblematically divine the author's intentions from the text.

The mouse who has the last word implicitly questions that naïve hermeneutic. But I also read considerable irony in the speech of that mouse. In the first place, the line that introduces him is metrically interesting: "A mous that muche good kouthe, as me tho thoughte" (182). The second half-line requires primary stress on *me,* as containing the alliterative stave; and then either *tho* (missing in some manuscripts) or *thoughte* must receive the other primary stress. Thus, the half-line goes either "As it *seemed* to *me,* then," or "As it seemed to *me, then.*" Either reading stresses the relativity of the judgment. Perhaps things seem different at some other time, to the speaker who is presumably learning as he goes along.

Also, we might notice that the mouse's speech is, in one sense, jejune. Nobody is going to do anything more about the bell, whether this mouse speaks or not. The only real function of his speech is rationalization ex post facto. He is providing an interpretation of the situation that will let the rats and mice be more comfortable with their cowardice.

Because I am reading *Piers Plowman* as going about textual hermeneutics, I see the mouse's argument as being more dependent on textual authority than modern editions might suggest. All the manuscripts put lines 189–92 after line 197 (see Schmidt's note on theses lines), but Schmidt and Kane-Donaldson emend on the grounds of apparent incoherence in the argument. I think the manuscripts need not be read as all that incoherent, if we suppose that the mouse is in fact basing his whole argument on the scriptural text he quotes from Ecclesiastes 10:16: *"Ve terre ubi puer est rex!"* (196). The argument goes like this: "We should not try to bell the cat (188). For my father always told me that, as the Bible says, the court is bad off when the cat is a kitten (193–96). For in such a situation, nobody can rest at night for the rats (197). While the king catches rabbits, he doesn't want our sorry bodies (189). He feeds himself with venison, and so let us never curse him (190; compare Ecclesiastes 10:20). For a little loss is better than a long-lasting sorrow—a confusion for us all, even though we get rid of one villain (191–92)! For we mice would destroy many men's malt (198)," and so on.

The difference between this argument and the emended ordering is that here the mouse is clearly basing his whole case on a particular interpretation of an authoritative text. He interprets the passage from Ecclesiastes as meaning that the land with a child king is unfortunate because the child is not strong enough to restrain the greed of his subjects. The mouse's use of the text—by no means a logically necessary conclusion from it—is to enjoin political quietism. Since the Bible describes the land with a child king this way, then this is the way things must be in England while Richard is a child, and there is nothing to be done about it except to keep one's head down: "ech a wis wight I warne—wite wel his owene!" (208). This advice also perhaps counts as further exegesis of Ecclesiastes 10, which has a great deal to say about the behavior of the wise and the foolish.

So the fable of the rats and the mice after all appears to continue the debate about which texts properly define the relationship between king and subjects and the proper interpretation of those texts. The debate seems to end by saying that things are bad and that there is nothing to be done. It shows that hermeneutic activity ultimately deconstructs itself, and terminates in the conclusion that no founding texts can be found. Intentions cannot be determined, debate turns out to be impotent, and everyone is left selfishly scrambling for what he or she can get. Langland again ironically disclaims responsibility, simultaneously suggesting that the point of the exercise is to determine meaning (to do hermeneutics), and yet abdicating the author's authority: "What this metels bymeneth, ye men that ben murye, / Devyne ye, for I ne dar, by deere God in hevene" (209–10).

This, then, is the day of the lawyers: "Yet hoved ther an hundred in howves of selke" (211). The *Yet* is interesting. Is the primary meaning "still," that no matter what evil occurs, there will always be plenty of lawyers to try to profit from it? Or is the *Yet* adversative, referring back to Langland's disclaimer of responsibility: *he* does not dare to say what his dream means, but lawyers are always happy to say what anything means—for a fee? Or does the *Yet* refer further back, to the mouse's advice that everybody should mind his or her own business—for money, lawyers mind everybody's business?

Be that as it may, the lawyers are the logically predictable and dramatically appropriate result of the failure of the hermeneutic enterprise. When everybody is out for whatever is to be had, the name of the game is to make hermeneutics work for private and therefore selfish ends. In the structure of the Prologue, this second catalog of occupations seems to be Langland's glance at nihilism, and the lawyers are its champions. Langland's image of the mist on the Malvern Hills works on more than one level: "Thow myghtest bettre meete myst on Malverne Hilles / Than get a 'mom' of hire mouth er moneie be shewed!" (215–16). The immeasurable mist is also an image of the nihilistic fog, the obscuring of all values resulting from the absence of a viable hermeneutic. In the second catalog, unlike the first, the occupations quickly jumble together into a mere disorderly list, and the whole social order degenerates into the cacophony of the street-criers' invitations to gluttony: "Goode gees and grys! Go we dyne, go we!" (227). But the possibility of this cacophony is to be understood in terms of what has intervened between the first and the second catalogs: that is, the failure of the hermeneutic enterprise to establish the social organism. The dramatic structure of the Prologue explains why cacophony reigns. In the first catalog, there are traces of purpose, allusions to possible orders. Here, finally, there is truly Babel.

The Interior Babel

When human pride at the Tower of Babel incurred the punishment of dispersed reference, it incurred also the possibility of what the philosopher Paul Ricoeur calls the "illusions of the subject" (144). Linguistic uncertainty about intention penetrates even into the first-person pronoun. We cannot know ourselves fully. Because we know through language, each of us knows himself or herself primarily as an *I*. Each of us is that to which the first-person pronoun refers. But that word too is as elusive as all the rest. The inability to share knowledge of our intentions accurately with other human beings entails our inability to know those intentions accurately ourselves. A necessary moment of the quest of *Piers Plowman* is therefore the dreamer's quest to know himself—to know his own *Will*. The Prologue also establishes the context for that quest, which, I will argue, is precisely the hermeneutic quest. As many readers of *Piers Plowman* have said, implicit in the allegory of the dream-er's name *Will* is the notion that the search for Truth as a name of God is at bottom also the search for the self. The self is the subject of the poem in both senses of *subject*.

Another quick comparison with Chaucer might be useful here. Crit-ics of Chaucer argue about whether there really are two Chaucers ("Chaucer-author" and "Chaucer-pilgrim") or whether there really is only one Chaucer, who speaks in a highly sophisticated voice capable of rapid and subtle shifts of tone. This debate, at base, seems to be about whether we should construe *The Canterbury Tales* as a "dramatic" work or as a "narrative" work. Be that as it may, in neither interpretation is it im-plied that Chaucer ever "loses control." Either he is the cool dramatic ironist, constructing his bumbling alter ego with consummate skill so as to infallibly convey his own attitudes; or else he is the devilishly clever and insinuating interlocutor, infallibly carrying us along with him by the literary equivalents of significant winks and nods.

The point is that the kinds of things that are always said about Chaucer are precisely the kinds of things that do *not* get said about Langland. An exception might be Pamela Raabe's discussion of the "two distinct voices, one willful and fallible and one divinely authoritative," in Langland's poem (82ff.). But *Piers Plowman* seems difficult, among other reasons, precisely because we never seem to know "where Langland is," because we often have the feeling that he "gets carried away," because he often seems to lack the polish or savoir faire that assumes or creates that comfortable sense of consensus that is the closest literary equivalent to the atmosphere of a gentlemen's club. With Chaucer, critics have always felt in reading him that he is "one of us." (Incidentally, I believe that it is a mistake to read Chaucer this way.) With Langland, on the other hand, we always want to ask, "Who is this fellow?" One way or the other, we feel that we know Chaucer. But as Malcolm Godden puts it, we feel that the *I* in *Piers Plowman* is "really a complex of different identities and voic-es rather than a single personality" (23).

What is the source of this feeling? I think that one of the most intel-ligent statements is James Simpson's, so I will begin by recapitulating briefly some of Simpson's ideas. Throughout his book on *Piers Plowman*, Simpson is concerned with the question of genre. Langland's task as author is to match literary genres with his obsessions, to coopt whatever literary forms will enable him to talk about what he wants to talk about. Simpson's main project is not to trace Langland's concern with hermeneutics, but instead to articulate Langland's Christian thought. Nevertheless, Simpson is one of the critics who in some sense, and with a different emphasis, has already said what I want to say. His book in many passages counts as an extended argument that Langland is "doing hermeneutics" in the course of his poem—that is, Langland is showing what happens when one interprets experience in terms of given literary modes.

Specifically, in the Prologue and the first two lines of Passus I Simpson (17–38) dissects out three distinct discourses, where *discourse* means, roughly, text with ideology ("the authoritative claims made by a given way of writing or speaking"—15): dream vision, estates satire, and sermon. All these forms, as genres, are literate forms—even the medieval sermon, to a large degree, was already in the fourteenth century, and certainly is now as *we* can know it, a literate form. The three *I*'s of these discourses differ from each other. Admittedly, human beings are complex, and most of us can, on occasion, adopt different tones and voices. But Simpson seems to think (as do I) that here we do not get the sense, as we might with Chaucer, that some authorial *I* is deliberately shifting voices and carrying us along with him in a medley of literary forms. Instead, the *I* exists in the Prologue as a reflex of the discourse and its associated ideology. The dreamer becomes the conduit for the genre he speaks, for the duration of the speaking. Thus, as Simpson puts it, in spite of the appearance in the Prologue and Passus I of commitment to "closed" literary forms, Langland ultimately succeeds in creating "a profoundly original and open-ended text" (38). The text is original in calling attention to its own provisional alliances with traditional genres; it is open-ended in relativizing the pretensions of any genre to become definitive for analyzing the experiences Langland talks about—or, I might add, for articulating the human personality who temporarily inhabits the genre.

Now I would like to look more closely at the shiftings of voice in the Prologue, to see exactly what happens along the fault lines. As the poem modulates from dream vision into estates satire, there is a corresponding modulation from what might be called a "receptive I" to a "judgmental I." At the beginning, the speaker *defines* himself as the type of person who is appropriate to the genre of dream vision. This speaker wants to see and hear things, without making any demands that he understand them: he "Wente wide in this world wondres to here" (4). First-person pronouns cluster thickly at the beginning: "I shoop *me* into shroudes as I a sheep were" (2); "*Me* bifel a ferly, of Fairye *me* thoghte" (6); "I was wery [of]wandred and wente *me* to reste" (7); "I lay" (9); "I slombred" (10); "gan [*me*] to meten" (11); "I was in a wildernesse, wiste I nevere where" (12); "I biheeld" (13); "I seigh" (14); "A fair feeld ful of folk fond I ther bitwene" (17). The verbs at the beginning of the poem suggest intellectual passivity. The most the speaker does is to see or to dream or to find. The dreamer evinces a self-absorbed determination literally to *enjoy himself*, to contemplate phenomena without participation or responsibility.

And then, with the introduction of the first occupational catalog, the first-person-singular pronoun disappears conspicuously for fourteen lines. The estates satire, initially in third person, is sharply judgmental, as the genre demands: "thise wastours with glotonye destruyeth" (22); "somme putten hem to pride" (23); "*Qui loquitur turpiloquium* is Luciferes hyne" (39); "Sleep and sory sleuthe seweth hem evere" (45); "hire tonge was tempred to lye" (51); and so on. The difference between the implicit consciousness of the dream vision and that of the estates satire is focused sharply by Langland's repetition of the word *ferly*. In the world of the dream vision, the *ferly* has positive connotations. "Me bifel a ferly, of Fairye me thoghte" (6): this is exactly the sort of thing the dreamer was looking for when he went out into the world. In the world of antifraternal satire, however, "sith charite hath ben chapman and chief to shryve lordes / Manye ferlies han fallen in a fewe yeres" (64–65). Whatever the *ferlies* are specifically here, they are bad signs; and furthermore, the word itself is used ironically in a way that implicitly denigrates the genres that value a *ferly*. Only the naïve or the trivial-minded—maybe the people who appreciate dream visions—could seriously think of these events as "marvels," as opposed to signs of human corruption. Far from enjoying himself, the dreamer is satirizing not only the friars, but also those who are wide-eyed enough to derive pleasure from thinking of the world as primarily a scene of *ferlies*.

But the modulation from one genre to another is not smooth. Nor do we seem to have a Coleridgean unity, a successful balancing of op-posed attitudes in tension. The poem rather makes it *more* difficult for us to imagine both of these genres cohering in the same consciousness. The poem is full of sudden strangeness and interpretive puzzles. At first in the modulation, the dreamer hides behind the plural pronoun, ab-sorbed within what the philosopher Heidegger calls the "they-self." Of the merchants, the poem says: "it semeth to *oure* sight that swiche men thryveth" (32; emphasis mine). Who is this *we*? With whom, exactly, is the dreamer claiming solidarity? We began, after all, by hearing the re-port of some individual's private dream. Are these merchants in the dream or out of it? Are *we* in the dream or out of it? There is a moment of otherworldliness worthy of Lewis Carroll, where we begin to wonder which world will disappear when the White King wakes up.

The modulation into the estates satire is made stranger by the treat-ment of the first-person pronoun, which as it returns continues to ap-pear often with verbs of intellectual passivity: "I leeve" (34); "I seigh" (50); "I fond" (58). By the time the dreamer gets to the cardinals, at the end of the first catalog of occupations, he is perhaps willing to admit to having exercised some mental energy: "I *parceyved* of the power that Pe-ter hadde to kepe" (100; emphasis mine), as if this theological point is something that has required at least a little reflection on his part. But usually in the catalog verbs of judgment with the first-person pronoun are explicitly negated: "I wol nat preve it here" (38); "impugnen I nelle" (109). At most, "I kan and kan naught of court speke moore" (111). The effect is an interesting blurring and even inversion of the genres, as if we have a speaker who goes to sleep in the land of fairy and dreams the mundane world. The satirical speaker of the estates satire, moreover, in his self-understanding seems to come trailing clouds of fairy, the intel-lectual habit of wide-eyed receptivity. He is forced by the genre to take implicit responsibility for satirical judgments that he is not quite ready to grasp.

We have here, then, not the smooth and sophisticated Chaucerian shifting of narrative voice, but a clashing of gears, a sense that some rad-ical discontinuity of thought underlies the conflict of genres. When Chaucer tumbles from the rhetorical sublimity of "Of which vertu en-gendred is the flowr" to the mundane observation that "Bifel that in

that seson on a day," we conclude that the same self-identical consciousness is either making fun of Chaucer-pilgrim's inability to sustain
rhetorical sublimity or making fun of Frenchified rhetoric itself. With
Langland, it is not so easy. In part because there is a modulation from
genre to genre, as opposed to an obvious and abrupt juxtaposition, we
feel that the speaker has somehow been drawn from one genre to another insensibly—as if not the speaker, but the drift of the discourse, is determining his consciousness.

   The blurring of genres in the Prologue, then, demonstrates that in a
profound sense the *I* who is speaking does not know who he is. At times
he seems to be a wide-eyed denizen of the world of dreams, and at times
he seems to be a hardheaded satirist of the mundane. It is interesting
that he tends to name himself with the first-person pronoun—explicitly
to call attention to himself as a private individual—at those points
where he broaches the subjects that will prove most problematic
throughout the poem. "And somme murthes to make as mynstralles
konne, / And geten gold with hire glee—synnelees, I leeve" (33–34). The
dreamer is himself at this moment making poetry (whether it counts as
"mirth" is maybe another issue); and, as already mentioned, Haukyn (*Activa Vita*) later, a figure resembling the dreamer in several ways, is also
a "mynstrall" (XIII.225). In Passus XI Lewte apparently grants the
dreamer license to write satirical verse (XI.101–2), whereas in Passus
XII Imaginatyf rebukes the dreamer because "thow medlest thee with
makynge" (XII.16). The question of the dreamer's "making" also figures
in the long "autobiographical" passage of the C-text (V.5). The issues
here are the dreamer's (and Langland's) identity as a poet and his self-
justification. The *I* in the Prologue is most concerned to distinguish true
minstrels from those *Qui loquitur turpiloquium,* and his concern is precisely
to construct a space that he himself has sanction to inhabit.

   Of the pilgrims, the dreamer says, "I seigh somme that seiden thei
hadde ysought seintes" (50). The issue here is the nature of true pilgrimage, a theme pervasively reiterated throughout *Piers Plowman.* "I fond
there freres" (58), the social class whose corruption Langland seems to
have found particularly nauseous, and the villains who, by corrupting the
sacrament of confession through the avarice of "Sire *Penetrans-domos*"
(XX.341) and his cronies, threaten to succeed where even Antichrist has

so far failed, and to destroy Unity at the end of the poem. The *I* of the Prologue explicitly struggles to understand the power of the cardinals ("I parceyved of the power that Peter hadde to kepe"—100; "To han the power that Peter hadde, impugnen I nelle"—109), thus anticipating the debates in the long middle of the poem about the necessity and function of clergy (VIII–XII). And finally, the ambiguous half-line already mentioned, in which the *I* of the Prologue seems simultaneously to assent to and to dissent from the mouse's opinion ("as me tho thoughte"—182), implicitly prepares the reader for all of the political debate that follows. It is worth noting that the ambiguity of the half-line and the later refusal to interpret the parable (209–10) sort ill with the genre of the sermon, to which the fable apparently belongs. Sermons do not normally evince uncertainty about their meaning or coyness about their conclusions. In this deviation from the conventions of the genre there is a further blurring of the *I* who speaks.

The *I* of the Prologue is foregrounded, then, at those very moments when the knottiest problems of the poem surface for the first time. These are the questions that will obsess the *I* of the poem, the problems whose solution is most intimately bound up with his identity. How he answers those questions will determine who he is. Conversely, those questions being unsettled, so is his identity.

Settling the questions, solving the problems, seems at first to mean choosing a discourse and committing oneself to it wholeheartedly. But the Prologue is full of refusals—through modesty or timidity, as it is implied—to choose a discourse. I have already mentioned most of these examples: "of Fairye me thoghte" (6); "I wol nat preve it here" (38); "impugnen I nelle" (109); "I kan and kan naught of court speke moore" (111); "construe whoso wolde" (144); "as me tho thoughte" (182); "Devyne ye, for I ne dar" (210). This abdication is part of Langland's recursiveness. The *I* who is speaking replicates in himself the hermeneutic impotence he describes in the social organism. The *I* blurs, becomes itself a site of conflicting discourses, precisely where it should be most individual and wholehearted, precisely at the points of its own inmost obsessions.

The clear implication is that the self is normally determined by its discourses. As David Lawton puts it,

> [I]n practice human beings are surrounded by monologic discourses that clam-
> or for our attention, yet differ and conflict in the demands they make. Such dis-
> courses are therefore lived and experienced as being dramatically plural. Will's
> search is indeed for "a single Truth," but his consciousness is itself plural and
> split: necessarily so, for it is constituted by the discourses that divide it. If truth
> cannot be seen as single or stable, the seeker cannot be either. (4)

The phenomenon of dispersed reference, the condition of human beings after Babel, is a necessary condition for the shifting voices in the
Prologue. That is, the same word, the *I,* apparently can refer to many
different subjects, depending upon the discourse that has taken it over
at any particular point. The Babel story provides, among other things, a
theological explanation of what Langland as author has observed: namely, the possibility that the code itself can undermine intentionality. Confusion comes when we do not know what people are saying. But it also
comes sometimes when we think we *do* know what they are saying. We
are confused because they seem to be using words we know. Various discourses entail various speakers as reflexes of the discourses themselves.
The various discourses that thus determine their different subjects
thereby confuse or even disperse the true subject, alienating it from it
self, because we always think we know what *I* means. We do not know
what we want (our *Will*); we know only what the discourse wants that
for the moment has taken us over as its speaker. And so we do not know
who we are.

This is another part of Langland's recursiveness. He cannot *tell* us
outright in so many words how the subject exists as the reflex of its discourse. What unimaginable metadiscourse could he use to do that, without making himself and us victims of the illusion that we finally know
who we are because we know what we think? He must instead *show* us
various discourses struggling for control of the fuzzy subject. We read
this experience as part of the difficulty of *Piers Plowman,* the impossibility
of telling for sure at any particular moment exactly who is talking to us.

Normally, of course, we do not think of our discourses as controlling
us, but instead think of ourselves as controlling our discourses. That is
why we tend to be so worried about what genre *Piers Plowman* is, and to
suspect that if we cannot assign it to a genre, then Langland has "lost
control of his material" and is at least with respect to his literary skill a

lesser poet than, say, Chaucer, who is always so perfectly "in control of his material."

But the exegetical tradition surrounding the story of the Tower of Babel has something fairly straightforward to say about that line of reflection as well. It is clear in Genesis 11 that the builders of the Tower are exhibiting hubris, but it is perhaps not immediately obvious why God should decide to mix up human language as a punishment for human pride. Augustine says, in the definitive explanation widely repeated in the exegetical tradition, "As the tongue is the instrument of domination, in it pride was punished" (The City of God 2.112; repeated, for example, in Glossa Ordinaria, PL 113.115). Human beings use language to dominate each other. The desire to dominate is in itself prideful, and so pride is punished in the tongue.

I think that Langland, as he does also with the notion of dispersed reference, is alluding to and extending Augustine's notion. Language is not only the human tool for dominating other human beings, but also the chief human strategy for getting control of our environment and our experience in general. Certainly, it is the strategy of intellectuals like the dreamer in Piers Plowman, who, as it develops in the autobiographical passage in the C-text (C.V.1–104), is too weak, too lean, too well bred, too well educated, or too lazy to work with his hands. Anne Middleton puts the matter succinctly:

> What is pursued in every encounter [in Piers Plowman] is not knowledge but power: the power to wield the text that "makes" the world as a world. As a mode of knowing, but perhaps even more fundamentally as the organizing center of a philosophically serious long poem in English, the status of worldly experience, and the cultural authority of what the subject "makes" of it, is on trial. ("Narration" 104)

In the Prologue, Langland is establishing the context that will make sense of what comes next. He wants to show us—must show us, since he cannot tell us—what happens to human beings who attempt to dominate by means of discourse.

He is also showing us at once what is wrong with the attitude that demands an author who "takes control of his material." The desires to judge, to classify, to sermonize, even to describe—the desires behind the discourses of the Prologue—are all at bottom the desire to dominate.

But the more one feels successful at dominating, the more one has become a function of the discourse itself, and the more there is no there
there. In his own terms, to be sure, Langland understands, as postmodernism might say, the mistake that Descartes had not yet made: understands, that is, the impossibility of founding knowledge on an indu-
bitable *cogito,* since in the very moment of trying to take control of its
experience by means of its discourse, the self inevitably becomes a function of that discourse.

The hermeneutic paradox, then, is that the more one believes oneself to own one's discourse, the more one loses oneself. The hermeneutic
analogue of Babylonian pride is to grasp at control over one's experience
by describing, judging, classifying, explaining. I will have a great deal to
say in later chapters about this trap. What hope is there for self-knowledge, if to make discourse "mine," using it to extend my own power, immediately results in the dispersion of the subject, if the self is always
merely a reflex of one or another of the competing discourses of the culture? To avoid the trap is enormously hard, especially for the intellectual—but not, I think Langland thinks, impossible. But for now, I want to
argue only that in the Prologue Langland tries to show us what the trap
is, to show us what Babylon really means for a *litteratus.*

The speaker of the Prologue starts with the wide-eyed receptivity appropriate to the dream vision and the world of fairy. But ultimately he
becomes obsessed with the question of meaning, because to know what
something means is the intellectual's way of gaining control of it. What
intellectuals do with the world first, if they do anything at all beyond
looking at it, is to construe it. With the first catalog of occupations, the
speaker immediately begins not only classifying, but also valuing and dis ·
tinguishing truth from falsehood; he notes that the friars' characteristic
activity is that they "construwed" the gospel (61); he declines to construe
("construe whoso wolde"—144) the maxim of the commons; and he invites others to say of the fable of the rats and the mice "What this metels
bymeneth" (209). For him, the definitive human activity is to construe.

Perhaps most significant, there is another startling blurring of the *I*
in the first lines of Passus I: "What this mountaigne bymeneth and the
merke dale / And the feld ful of folk, I shal yow faire shewe." Who is
this *I* who is so concerned with meaning, and who believes that he can
control the discourse so as to lay out the meaning of all the experience

he has witnessed? Is this the unmediated voice of Langland himself, the author of the poem, and is he saying that he will now create an allegorical character (or maybe a whole poem) to explain everything? If so, the authorial ambition produces more problems than it solves. The discourse of Holy Church in itself is far from nonproblematic, and the whole poem resembles a freeway pileup of incommensurable interpretive systems. Or is this *I* once again the dreamer, who after being exposed to the implicit lessons of the Prologue, and when he should know better, explicitly tries to take control of the discourse, like the preacher whose role he momentarily assumes? If so, the dreamer does not succeed in his authorial ambitions, but immediately becomes instead a reluctant and slightly obtuse disciple of an authority figure.

The point, then, is that in the Prologue Langland shows us an interior Babel corresponding with the earthly Babylon, and institutes the search for the self as an essential part of the quest for a viable hermeneutic. The Prologue establishes the context for everything that follows, but it gets us nowhere in terms of the quest. In fact, whoever the speaker may be at the beginning of Passus I, his assertion that he knows everything and can explain it clearly shows as convincingly as possible that he is at the zero point of self-understanding. The fact that we readers for a moment think we are going to get a clear explanation, and the fact that we are prepared to welcome it, show us that we as readers are at the zero point alongside the speaker. If we have truly paid attention to the Prologue, and taken the depiction of Babylonian confusion quite seriously, then we should be deeply suspicious of anybody's claim to explain everything. But for a moment, inevitably, we expect it to happen. Like the speaker, we have for a moment been absorbed into the sermon genre, with its assumption that all human experience can be explained. This is still another feature of Langland's recursiveness. Again and again in *Piers Plowman* he catches us out as readers in our weak interpretive movements and our misdirected interpretive desires.

The Healing of the Babylonian Wound

I will need to return later to the events of Passus XIX, and not everything that needs to be said about that Passus can be broached now.

But in the exegetical tradition the story of the Tower of Babel is presented as the antitype of the story of the descent of the Holy Spirit on the day of Pentecost—which happens in *Piers Plowman* in Passus XIX. The Pentecostal gift of tongues heals the Babylonian wound.

A passage from one of Augustine's sermons "On the Day of Pentecost" is worth quoting at length here, if only because the sermon ties together several strands of allegorical imagery that are also important throughout *Piers Plowman*. After quoting Acts 2:2–4, Augustine says,

> That gust was purging their hearts of worldly chaff; that fire was consuming the straw of ancient lusts; those tongues they were speaking in, filled by the Holy Spirit, were prefiguring the Church of the future through the languages of all nations.
>
> I mean, just as after the flood the ungodly pride of men built a high tower against the Lord, and the human race was deservedly divided by languages, so that each nation would speak its own language and thus not be understood by the others; so in a similar way the devout humility of the faithful has brought to the unity of the Church the variety of their different languages; so that what discord had dissipated charity might gather together, and the scattered members of the human race, as of one body, might be attached to their one head, Christ, and so reunited, and fused together into the unity of the holy body by the fire of love.
>
> ... You ... my brothers and sisters, members of the body of Christ, seedlings of unity, sons and daughters of peace, keep this day joyfully, celebrate it without anxiety. Among you, after all, is being fulfilled what was being prefigured in those days, when the Holy Spirit came. Because just as then, whoever received the Holy Spirit, even as one person, started speaking all languages; so too now the unity itself is speaking all languages throughout all nations; and it is by being established in this unity that you have the Holy Spirit; you that do not break away in any schism from the Church of Christ which speaks all languages. (*Works* 298–99; also *PL* 38.1245–46)

The editor of the sermon notes at the end of the second paragraph quoted above, "An elaborately extended metaphor, taking us all the way from the threshing floor to the baker's oven!" As such, the metaphor is reminiscent of Langland's multifoliate development of the parable of the sower that grounds the figure of Piers himself. We find here also the image of the Church as the Body of Christ. This image is developed paradigmatically in 1 Corinthians 12, a scriptural passage on which Lang-

land draws—compare, for example, XIX.251 with 1 Corinthians 12.25—
and from which he quotes: *"Divisiones graciarum sunt"* (1 Corinthians 12.4,
quoted after line 229).

Corresponding exegeses of Pentecost as the cure for Babylon are repeated, for example, in the *Glossa Ordinaria* (PL 114.430–31) and in Bede's
Super Acta Apostolorum Expositio (PL 92.947).

Personification allegory dominates the discourse of Passus XIX;
when I return to this passus, I shall have something to say about personification allegory. Like every other form of discourse in the poem,
personification allegory proves satisfactory for some purposes and unsatisfactory for others. I am emphatically *not* arguing that the establishment of Unity in Passus XIX counts as some sort of final solution to all
of Langland's hermeneutic problems. If for no other reason, that conclusion seems counterintuitive because another whole passus still remains in the poem, and at the end of Passus XX Conscience, the dreamer's chief instructor in Passus XIX, departs from Unity to seek Piers,
who also has somehow disappeared. But one thing that personification
allegory does sometimes prove satisfactory for is laying out doctrine in a
theoretical (that is, overly schematic) sort of way. So while the allegory
of Passus XIX might ultimately seem to lack the muscle and blood that
would make its doctrine live for real human beings, I am arguing that it
does provide at least a barebones anatomy for understanding the hermeneutic quest in abstract terms. In short, because Passus XIX seems in
many ways to be a reversal of the Prologue, I am using Passus XIX here
as a gloss on my reading of the Prologue.

Passus XIX begins, significantly, with a discourse about terminology.
The dreamer, having encountered Jesus in the body—that is, dressed in
the arms of Piers—asks why Conscience applies the name of *Christ* to Jesus, since there "is no name to the name of Jesus" (XIX.19). Conscience
answers by demonstrating that the same person, depending upon his
deeds, may be called either knight, king, or conqueror: "knyght, kyng,
conquerour may be o persone" (27); and that Jesus is all of these, as he
also instantiates Dowel, Dobet, and Dobest. In the process of instruct-
ing the dreamer in the uses of words, Conscience actually reiterates the
gospel account of Jesus' life, which has already been articulated in different ways in Passus XVI and in Passus XVIII. The point seems to be
that the "same thing," the same person Jesus or the same gospel story,

can be intended by many different words or many different interpretive systems. Like the different sets of terminology earlier, Conscience's set of terms also provides a complete articulation of the truth about Jesus. Crucially, linguistic truth is not contradicted by bodily truth, as the episode of Thomas (170–83) shows. Jesus demonstrates empirically that his post-Resurrection body is his identical body, before he can actually become Dobest and invest Piers with his earthly authority. He appears to Thomas, "And whan this dede was doon, Dobest he [thou]ghte, / And yaf Piers power, and pardon he grauntede" (183–84).

In one way of looking at this passage, Conscience is addressing the problem of dispersed reference that underlies the Babylonian confusion of the Prologue. We need not become confused by the application of different words to the same thing, as long as we keep in mind that identity is not a simple matter. We cannot think, like the dreamer in Passus XIX, that there must be exactly one name per thing. Nor can we think, like the goliard in the Prologue, that the name determines a simple essence that constitutes identity. Identity, like words themselves, is relational. Words do not stand alone, but take their meanings from the discourses in which they appear. What we are, similarly, consists in our relations to others: the identities of the members of the Body of Christ consist in their functions in that body.

Thus, what appears as a division of labor in the Prologue appears in Passus XIX as a *divisio gratiarum*, a dealing-out of gifts. James M. Dean makes this point in his discussion of the various transformations in *Piers Plowman* of the *felde* with which the poem opens:

> Grace's depiction here [Passus XIX] of man's diverse occupations represents for the dreamer a quick glance back to the *felde* of the prologue, which was also a display of mankind's vocations. . . . The original *felde*, however, appears very different now. . . . Grace structures his portrait of the *felde* around humans' God-given capabilities, setting it . . . in the specific context of the Christian community and in the era *sub gratia*. (219)

In the Prologue, the King when he appears is already a king. There is no discussion of how one gets to be a king or how to tell whether one deserves to be a king. In the Prologue the King is just precipitated, as it were, into the middle of the dream as a given. And the same is true of the knights and the commons: "Thanne kam ther a Kyng: Knyghthod hym ladde; / Might of the communes made hym to regne" (112–13). Only with the clergy in the Prologue is there a suggestion that anything besides social class has anything to do with one's function in the social organism: "thanne cam Kynde Wit and clerkes he made" (114). Langland suggests, perhaps too kindly, that one needs at least a modicum of native intelligence to fulfill the clerical function. But then the clerks cooperate with the King and the knights to enforce the theory that class is destiny: "The Kyng and Knyghthod and Clergie bothe / Casten that the Commune sholde hem [communes] fynde" (116–17). The commons have to labor because they are the commons—perhaps because their name hints that they are consumable like the food they provide—and not necessarily because they have any particular vocation or talent for physical labor. In other words, there is an arbitrary division of labor among social classes that are already an unquestioned given.

Things work exactly the other way in Passus XIX. As Grace deals out the gifts, social positions are determined by the functions that people are best able to perform. Langland puns: Grace, Latin *gratia,* deals out to each person a gift, Latin *gratia.* God's image in the human being here is the human being's *craft,* the knowing-how-to that establishes the human being in the world. The dealing-out of gifts begins with the establishment of literacy, as if the founding of the social organism in this articulation depends crucially upon reading and writing:

> Some [wyes] he yaf wit, with wordes to shewe—
> Wit to wynne hir liflode with, as the world asketh,
> As prechours and preestes, and prentices of lawe—
> They lelly to lyve by labour of tonge,
> And by wit to wissen othere as grace hem wolde teche.
>
> (230–34)

Line 231b, "as the world asketh," echoes Prologue 19b, where the phrase is deeply ambiguous. The phrase in the Prologue seems to hint that the world inevitably corrupts the work. Here the suggestion seems to be that one can pay Caesar his penny incidentally, while always rendering God his due. The apprentices of law who live "lelly" are the answer to the lawyers in the Prologue who batten on nihilism.

The whole passage about the gifts of the Holy Spirit implies a theological justification for social class, including, of course, the standard disclaimer that we are all nevertheless siblings and members of the same body:

> ". . . he that useth the faireste craft, to the fouleste I kouthe have put hym.
> Thynketh [that alle craftes," quod Grace], "cometh of my yifte;
> Loke that noon lakke oother, but loveth alle as bretheren."
>
> (254–56)

One point that Passus XIX makes about the Prologue, therefore, is the obvious point, made in many ways and in many places in the poem, that the standard forms of political discourse need to be questioned in terms of theological discourse. But more important for my immediate argument is the notion that Babylonian confusion results in part from false notions of identity: namely, the notion that any self-identical thing has a mode of being such that it can be fully and finally named by a single word, and the correlative notion that words have a mode of being such that they always signify whatever they signify apart from any discourses in which they might appear. The catalogs of occupations in the Prologue, in particular, function as lists, where a *list* means a collection of words with separate identities, unrelated to each other except in terms of some purpose that cannot itself appear as an item on the list and perhaps gets repressed. Passus XIX argues that neither the person of Jesus, nor the words that describe him, nor his followers, nor the words that describe them have identities in that sense. Passus XIX shows, without explicitly saying, that the Prologue is about hermeneutics—about understanding things and persons on the model of the understanding of words, and about understanding confusion in the social organism on the model of textual unintelligibility.

Another obvious point made in Passus XIX is that the new establishment of the social organism, the rewriting of the field of folk in intelligible terms, is a matter of explicitly making the social organism over into the image of a text. Piers has as his function to "tilie truthe" (263), where *truth* is, among other things, an attribute of propositions. Langland, as also in VII.2, is punning here: "for to tilie truthe a teeme shal he have" is both "to till truth he shall have a team," where *till* and *team* are to be read allegorically; and "to tell truth he shall have a theme." The oxen in Piers's team are the Evangelists (264–68), and the "stottes" that pull his harrow are the Fathers of the Church (269–74). That is, the definitive activity of God's representative on earth—Grace's "procuratour," "reve," "registrer," "prowor," and "plowman" (260–62)—is to deal with scriptural texts and the commentaries on those texts.

But the allegory now grows interesting and a little tricky. Scripture is what gets harrowed, but the blades of the harrows themselves are the two Testaments of Scripture (as also later in lines 312–13): here the Fathers

> . . . harewede in an handwhile al Holy Scripture
> With two [aithes] that they hadde, an oold and a newe,
> *Id est, Vetus Testamentum et Novum.*
>
> (274–75a)

Schmidt goes some way toward solving the interpretive problem when he says in his note to the passage that "the Bible is to be used to interpret itself" (487). At the most obvious level, one blade harrows the other: the Old Testament prepares for the understanding of the New Testament, and the New Testament completes the meaning of the Old. But what soil have the Evangelists been plowing, exactly, since what they themselves write is apparently included in the New Testament that is being harrowed and that is itself a harrow? The soil in lines 277 and following is clearly the human soul (as in the parable of the sower), where the cardinal virtues are being sown (and, incidentally, *named*) in hopes of producing love (as in line 313): "And Grace gaf Piers greynes—cardynales vertues, / And sew it in mannes soule, and sithen he tolde hir names" (276–77). And it makes sense to say that the Evangelists, by telling the gospel, prepare the human soul to know and to foster the cardinal virtues so as to produce the fruits of love.

But in translating the allegory we cannot avoid saying that the soil is both (perhaps, at once) the Scripture and the human soul. The clear implication is that the soul itself must become assimilated to the text of Scripture. Not only must the soul become prepared ("harrowed," with the connotation of purging and pain) by the Scriptures, but the soul must actually be construed and construe itself as a text—must be understood, that is, as the Fathers of the Church understand the Scriptures and as the Scriptures understand themselves.

The healing of the Babylonian wound by the Holy Spirit, then, involves essentially the explicit attempt to understand the human soul on the model of textual hermeneutics. How satisfying that attempt turns out to be is a matter for another chapter. Already in Passus XIX the perverse ingenuity of human sinfulness quickly finds ways to distort Conscience's interpretation of the cardinal virtues and to resurrect Babylonian confusion in various shapes. The commons, as greedy and self-centered as the rats and the mice in the Prologue, reject the counsel of Conscience to pay their debts (395ff.). The "lewed vicory" is at least acute enough to perceive the dissonance between the behavior of the cardinals and their ostensible position as keepers of the cardinal virtues, in a passage (413ff.) reminiscent of the discussion of the cardinals in the Prologue. The king in Passus XIX, who enters in a line that echoes the entrance of the King in the Prologue ("thanne cam ther a kyng"—469), makes bolder claims than the King of the Prologue made for himself, and raises the specter of tyranny as the dark side of the cardinal virtue of justice.

The events of Passus XIX, however, as Langland's redaction of a portion of sacred history, in one way represent a rewriting of the Prologue in terms of orthodox scriptural hermeneutics. The conflict of discourses does not go away—it never goes away in the poem—but Passus XIX seems a long way from the Babylonian confusion of the Prologue. In spite of the almost mechanical stasis of the allegorical discourse, there now seems a potential for a different understanding of identity and the self, a definition of the I in terms of Unity. The interior Babel comes from failure to recognize that the self can in fact be defined only in relation to other selves, as a member of the Body of Christ.

I will argue later that the dreamer's intellectual progress results from a hard-won understanding of how textual interpretation for him has served and can continue to serve as the model for understanding human experience. The word *progress* here perhaps implies something I do not want to imply. I mean the word in somewhat the same way as I take Langland to mean *passus*. Steps are taken; some sort of understanding is achieved; but I believe that it is not right to say that Langland proposes some goal to himself, works steadily toward that goal, and finally grasps it. David Lawton's points about the failings of New Critical premises as applied to *Piers Plowman* are well taken here: we should not fall victim to a desire to impose a "teleological or sequential" reading on the poem or to "defend the orthodoxy of Langland's work" (3). The point of the poem is to consider how the steps are taken, how the signs that constitute human consciousness get connected.

I know that this all sounds like a very postmodern reading of a medieval poet, and I am as worried as the next person about any critic's tendency to "impose" his or her modern obsessions on an old text. But I think it is not impossible that intellectuals of Langland's time shared a concern for some of the problems surrounding the phenomenon of literacy that obsess us today. As Gillian Rudd says, "[A]ttitudes toward texts which twentieth-century readers tend to regard as modern, are not only well suited to reading medieval literature but also are not as far removed from some medieval conceptions as may be supposed" (xi–xii). In a comment more specifically relevant to the concerns of this book, Robert Myles points out that "[a] shared medieval and modern presupposition . . . is the linguistic model of intentionality: all structures that operate intentionally may be understood to operate as language operates" (37). And, as Helen Barr argues, even Langland's literary disciples of the early fifteenth century seem to have regarded *Piers Plowman* as being in some sense "about" reading and the struggle of conflicting authoritative discourses:

> In *Piers*, . . . interrogation of established discourses is a very characteristic poetic technique. Its perpetuation in the poems in the tradition [*Pierce the Ploughman's Crede, Richard the Redeless, Mum and the Sothsegger, The Crowned King*] suggests it was one of the chief stylistic lessons learnt from reading *Piers Plowman*. Often, institutional discourses provide the narrative schemes of the poetry but with the result that the inadequacies or contradictions of these discourses are exposed. The poems can be seen to supplement institutionalised discourse in the Derridean sense of "supplement": that which is simultaneously both an enrichment of something already full, and a replacement of something which is deficient. (42–43)

Barr's study suggests that the "tradition" stemming from Langland's work often reads that work much as I am trying to read it here. At the same time, it interesting that Barr, as I often do, finds the vocabulary of postmodernism helpful in describing what is going on in *Piers Plowman*.

Admittedly, there is no meaningful sense in which Langland's problems could be said to be "exactly the same as" our problems. But I think it might make sense to talk about Langland's problems as counterparts of ours. And anyway, the choice is very simple. Either Langland is an enormously subtle and interesting poet who is concerned with all the things I suspect he is concerned with (and more), or he is a poet who cannot sustain a consistent allegory or a coherent voice or an intelligible structure, and who is therefore clumsy and to that degree uninteresting. The article of faith that underwrites this book is that Langland is subtle and interesting.

Bibliographical Essay 1

These short Bibliographical Essays distributed throughout this book have several purposes. First, I use them to acknowledge my major intellectual debts, insofar as I am aware of them and insofar as they are not adequately acknowledged in the sparse documentation of the chapters. Second, I employ them to some degree to map the critical territory in which I am working, so as to establish the context for my arguments, and occasionally to explain where and why I disagree with the critics whose ideas I summarize. Finally, I will utilize them sometimes to pursue ideas that are relevant to my argument but somewhat peripheral, and that might have been distracting had I dealt with them fully in the chapter itself.

In this chapter on Langland's Prologue, I am operating in general in the territory defined by the critical debate about Langland's attitude toward language. Pamela Raabe neatly summarizes this debate (1–3). Raabe and Mary Carruthers might be seen as defining its poles. Raabe and Carruthers themselves are operating within the larger territory most clearly mapped by Jesse M. Gellrich in *The Idea of the Book in the Middle Ages*. Gellrich summarizes Jacques Derrida's "idea of the book" as presented in *De la grammatologie:* "The idea of the book is the idea of a totality, finite or infinite, of the signifier; this totality of the signifier cannot be a totality, unless a totality constituted by the signified preexists it, supervises its inscriptions and its signs, and is independent of it in its ideality" (Gellrich, *Book* 34). Gellrich argues that this idea of the book was bound to arise, and did arise, in the Middle Ages "as soon as a signifying system—words in Scripture, things in nature—became a metaphor for divinity: the entire preexistent 'totality' of God's plan was potential in the signifying means" (35). On the other hand, much of Gellrich's book consists of detailed demonstration of how the great medieval writers of "fiction," Dante and Chaucer, deconstruct the medieval "idea of the book":

> Both poets look away from the medieval past in that their allegories of reading are so different from those that they read in explication of the Bible and that organized the *aedificium Scripturae* and the Book of culture. However firmly such models stabilized the institution of interpretation in the middle ages, the allegories of reading in Dante and Chaucer open the way for rereading. (247)

The tension reflected in the debate between Raabe and Carruthers, in other words, is a tension already immanent in the intellectual and literary history of the later Middle Ages.

For Carruthers, "Langland's desire to achieve a new understanding expresses itself in his discomfiture with a corrupted rhetoric and his desire to forge a new one" (11); the "partialness and inadequacy" of religious language is "the anguished premise of his poetry" (173). For Raabe, on the other hand, the paradoxical truth of the Word of God "has been embodied in every allegory in the poem, each requiring readers to read the whole ambivalent Truth of all God's texts: the text of the poem, of humankind, of society, and of the cosmos"; Langland understands that "faithless readers will not read his allegory correctly and that he cannot teach them faith. But Langland also understands that in making his poem he is imitating God" (167). For Carruthers, in short, Langland's theme is that the corruption of language prevents humans from knowing the truth. For Raabe, Langland is saying that the ambivalence of language kindles faith. Both Carruthers and Raabe seem to be working to some degree under the presupposition that it is the business of criticism to find a Coleridgean "theme" that unifies the poem. One way of articulating their disagreement is simply to say that they disagree about the hierarchy of attitudes constructed in the text.

As I have already hinted, Carruthers seems very close to describing what I have called "Babylonian confusion" and the "quest for a viable hermeneutic." On the other hand, Raabe seems very close to describing what I have called "reading the world like a text." My project depends upon believing that for Langland, as medieval intellectual or *litteratus,* textual hermeneutics provides the paradigm for human knowing in general (Raabe), but that for Langland textual hermeneutics is always more or less an exercise in frustration (Carruthers). Textual hermeneutics fails to give us what we want, especially when interpretation is conceived as a means of getting power over one's experience and oneself. In other words, I want to read Carruthers's and Raabe's theses not as contradictory, but as complementary. Reading Langland does not permit us to choose between these theses, but instead forces us to explore the antinomy as such.

At this point, I am very nearly repeating Gillian Rudd, whose study of Langland's attitude toward language will appear pervasively influential in this book. Rudd distinguishes between *scientia* and *sapientia* as modes of knowing. *Scientia* attempts to "define things in precise terms" and relies on the discourse of definition and deduction, whereas *sapientia* tries to reach beyond language and uses discourse more "emotive and figurative" (x). *Piers Plowman* is concerned with the "ambiguous nature of language" (xi), and is

> an exposition of the play between the discourses of learning *(scientia)* and wisdom *(sapientia)*, of the interaction between knowledge and understanding and an exploration of how power and authority can be gained, bestowed and undermined; and because it is all this, it is also a demonstration of the creative power of language. Above all it is a vivid example of how the impossibility of finding a form of language which expresses any form of comprehension fully and unambiguously can provide the basis for a rich and demanding text. For Langland's poem illustrates that there is only the attempt, which fails. (xiv)

As I do, Rudd reads *Piers Plowman* as going about hermeneutics. Here is Rudd's description of what I have called Langland's "recursiveness":

> [T]here are dialogues between the various characters and discourses within the poem as well as between the text and its audience. For, just as we readers bring to bear on the poem "a grid of interpretation" . . . we are brought to act as witnesses to a similar process enacted in Wil's journey through the text. For Wil is an interpreter of the events in the poem as well as an enactor of them. He can thus be regarded as a figure of a reader who brings to the events he witnesses his own "grid of interpretation." . . . [T]he literary perspectives and the dialogues between the discourses of knowledge, language and authority and how they are used . . . form the centre of interest. (42–43)

Finally, then, for Rudd as for me, "the major pre-occupation of the poem is . . . a presentation of, and movement within, the difficulties and play of language or discourses which arise when one is confronted with desire for authoritative renderings and interpretation" (201); "The question of the articulation and interpretation of a text lies at the heart of Langland's poem" (204). Rudd's approach seems to me a kind of Hegelian *Aufhebung* of the apparent antithesis articulated by Carruthers and Raabe.

My arguments about Babylonian confusion and the interior Babel in general take up the program outlined by David Lawton's influential article "The Subject of *Piers Plowman*," from which I have already quoted more than once. Lawton wants *Piers Plowman* to be read as a "dialogic" text, and that move would imply giving up the nostalgia for a single unified subject—in either sense—of the discourse. My arguments often assume that the human person is to be identified with intentionality, or will. *The Crisis of Will in "Piers Plowman,"* by John Bowers, is the fullest treatment of Will in the poem as an allegory of the human will—though Lawton takes Bowers to task for Bowers's deeply ingrained New Critical presuppositions (Lawton 2). Robert Myles summarizes Augustine's doctrine of intentionality in *De Trinitate*:

> The *intentio* is the active principle in the mind which governs both meaningful external perception and thought, choosing that to which the organ of sight will be bound, and binding together "objects" from the memory to the understanding, the result of which is thought *(cogitatio)*. . . . The principle upon which *intentio* operates is love, desire, or passion. Will is the motor which leads to subsequent action and knowledge. (42)

The important issue here for me, however, is the relationship between literacy and intentionality. For discussions of medieval notions about the relationship between language and human personality, see John Alford, "Grammatical" 739; Judson Boyce Allen 280–81; and Myles 66–73. I have already mentioned Anne Middleton's interesting comments on how the human subject gains power through narrative. For Middleton, Will presents himself as "a writer for whom the business of writing is *finding things out*" ("Narration" 120). He thus "presents to the mythic order of explanation and authority the prospect of a rival which offers to supplant it," namely, "a record of personal labors" (120). Middleton goes on: "Although this way of conceiving literature as subjective testimony was perhaps the major literary invention of the fourteenth century, for its first major practitioners it was . . . fraught with tonal insecurity and moral risks" (121). I am deeply indebted to Middleton's way of reading the poem as built from clashes of incommensurable interpretive systems. Ultimately, I shall diverge from her conclusion that the narrative subject gains power in the combative "episodes" of the poem precisely by means of the narrative. I shall argue that some of the crucial encounters with authoritative texts in the poem do not look like "episodes" in Middleton's sense ("Narration" 106). And Middleton herself is well aware of the perils for the narrator of first-person narration:

> [F]irst-person narration, even if nominally confessional, also carries within it a . . . hazard. In the psychology of sin implicit in the medieval handbooks, in which the subject's capacity to see and tell the truth about himself is circumscribed by the empty recursiveness formed by his own *habitus,* such utterance is in practice equally capable of deflecting and deferring penitential contrition, enacting a fruitless and endless auto-exegesis which keeps the narrative subject *in medias res.* . . .
>
> . . . From the first to the last version of Langland's poem the confessional imperative that underwrites both allegorical self-representation and penance— and hence the impulse to narrate—never loses this deep subjective danger and duplicity. Indeed, it would be hard to find an "idea" in the poem more basic to the workings of Langland's moral and literary imagination, and more fundamental to the form of its realisation, than this notion that "makyng" is a kind of endless lecture upon the shadow that nevertheless is powerless to deliver us from the "body of this death" that it can so compellingly envision. ("Making" 248–49)

Britton Harwood also emphasizes the moral dangers of literacy, which had "already been a theme for centuries by the time Langland wrote": "[L]iteracy creates not only the possibility of an integration of abstractions but also suspicion of the motive behind such a goal and uncertainty about its relevance" (20). For Harwood, the abstractness implied in literacy itself stands opposed to the *kynde knowynge* that is the proper object of the dreamer's quest. I am arguing that for Langland, turning away from literacy as the paradigmatic mode of knowing was not really an option. Texts were for Langland *there,* the significant objects of his world. It was necessary for him not to avoid them or in some way to turn aside from literacy, but to work through the problems posed by his own literacy and the texts he encountered. My main point here, howev-

er, is that the context I am working in is the context in which it is as-
sumed that literacy itself poses moral problems, and that the search for
a viable hermeneutic also entails the search for the human self of the
interpreter.

In a related discussion, Judson Boyce Allen argues that in the Prologue of the B-text, Langland is running a concordance on the themes
of speech and bonds or chains—*sermo* and *vinculum*. The root text is
Colossians 3:11ff. Verse 14 refers to charity as the *vinculum perfectionis*. The
goliard in the Prologue

> is explicitly concerned for the relation between words and things, the angel for
> the spirit in which legal formulae should be applied, and the commons for the
> relation between legal authority and what the king says. All three, in comple-
> mentary ways, are concerned to define language, and to define it for that cru-
> cially operative and powerful case, the law. . . . The law and legal process are
> verbal procedures which render the world true by describing it. . . . Thus law is
> a language which seeks to be absolutely descriptive, and absolutely performa-
> tive, at the same time. (279)

The poem asks, at the same time, how a person may become a true person: "The answer, crucially, has to do with language, with *sermo* which
binds, which is a *vinculum,* supremely in the activity of right law under
pietas, but also in one's own name, and in all the metaphors and relations
of *nomen* and *res* in between proper naming and legal judgment"
(280–81). Thus, Allen concludes, "The self is the *vinculum* in which reference takes place" (281). Although my reading of the dramatic interactions among the angel, the goliard, and the commons is different from
Allen's, nevertheless I heartily endorse his general points that the political debate in the Prologue is about language, and that the debate about
language impinges crucially on one's understanding of the human self.

Part of the debate about language concerns the ideology of genre,
the social and moral implications of adopting a certain way of writing.
Simpson comes back to the question of genre again and again in his
book, and his remarks are in general the most illuminating I know.
Morton W. Bloomfield's book *Piers Plowman as a Fourteenth-Century Apocalypse* (1962) has, of course, been enormously influential in focusing critical attention on the question of literary genre and in helping us to understand why that question is important. While reading the poem as an
"apocalypse," Bloomfield finds there "three literary genres: the allegori-

cal dream narrative; the dialogue, *consolatio* or debate; and the encyclope-dic (or Menippean) satire," and "three religious genres (or forms): the complaint, the commentary, and the sermon" (10). Steven Justice ar-gues that Langland successively chooses different genres that "progres-sively abandon claims to poetic authority" ("Genres" 305), thus antici-pating specifically in terms of genre theory an issue that I will discuss more fully later: namely, the crisis in the dreamer's own narrative that involves a change in his attitude toward authoritative texts.

Most of the themes I have discussed so far in this Bibliographical Essay are taken up also by Burt Kimmelman in *The Poetics of Authorship in the Later Middle Ages*. Citing a number of the scholars and critics I have also cited, Kimmelman compares *Piers Plowman* with Dante's *Commedia* and Chaucer's *Canterbury Tales*. Kimmelman's study, valuable for his treatment of the philosophical and theological traditions informing late-fourteenth-century speculations on language, is especially con-cerned with the relationships among literacy, literary genre, and ideas of the self. Like my study, Kimmelman's at times sounds postmodern; but he provides the historical underpinnings from which I have mostly ab-stracted. Kimmelman argues that *Piers Plowman* is Langland's "critique of, and attempt to undo, the poetic and otherwise epistemological form of inquiry known as allegory" (161); Kimmelman concludes that "what finally holds the poem together is its trenchant meditation on language, indirectly and directly . . . which is ultimately accomplished through Langland's poetics" (165). *Piers Plowman* is "an allegory about the failure of allegory to express the truth" (226).

As for Langland's politics, finally, I think my reading of the Prologue does little to add to or light up what others have said before. In *The Theme of Government in "Piers Plowman,"* Anna Baldwin argues that Lang-land himself, by the time of the C-text, had decided in favor of an ideal of government involving "absolutism" in the monarchy: that is, the king should be limited only by reason and conscience, and not by common law or Parliament—both of which had proved to be easily corruptible in practice (5–23). As Baldwin recognizes, *absolutism* was not the medieval term; but the point of the theory was that in some cases only by being above the common law and Parliament could the king preserve "equity," or the right ("reasonable") relation among his subjects according to "conscience"—where *equity, reason,* and *conscience* were the current terms in legal discourse in Langland's time. Certainly one can see my reading of the B Prologue as describing one stage in the evolution of political thought that Baldwin details. Baldwin also provides an excellent short discussion of "The Historical Context" in general, in her essay in John Alford's collection (*Companion* 67–86).

In his commentary on the episode of Lady Meed, James Simpson discusses the tension reflected in *Piers Plowman* between the old feudal economy and the new cash-based economy (32–36). Interestingly, Daniel Pigg specifically connects the new economy with failures of language: "Imaged in the B text, Langland's . . . attempt at addressing the problem of significative corruption brought on by social unrest imagines a feudal ideal but sees the ideal's own undermining by the forces of greed and false signification" (33). Part of the cause of Babylonian confusion is what Langland portrays as (and what we disparagingly refer to today as) "political rhetoric"—spin doctoring, demagoguery, and outright lies characteristic of politicians who regard language precisely and solely as a tool of power. As I have suggested in my brief excursus above into Passus XIX, Langland concludes—in a perfectly orthodox manner—that political discourse needs to be taken up into theological discourse. And even when that happens, though a certain clarity of thought might result, no real practical problems are likely to be solved in the social organism. Langland is less interested in reforming the body politic than in deciding what to think about it. It seems strange to say so, but Langland is not, finally, a political poet.

CHAPTER 2

THREE
AUTHORITATIVE
FIGURES

Thanne Scripture scorned me and a skile tolde,
And lakked me in Latyn and light by me she sette,
And seide, "Multi multa sciunt et seipsos nesciunt."

(XI.1–3)

Dramatizing Authority

In the Babylonian cacophony, everybody speaks an idiolect. Things become even more confusing when all the languages sound like plain English. Then we have to overcome first the illusion of understanding what is being said. Langland exposes his dreamer to instruction from many authoritative figures. These figures all "speak their own languages," "impose their different perspectives," "articulate their different world-views," or, as I prefer to put it, represent mutually incommensurable interpretive systems. That the instructors are not in tandem laying out a system of dogma is obvious from the fact that individual instructors appear transmogrified in the speeches of other instructors. Anima, or Soul, for example, is female in Passus IX (7) and male in Passus XV (14ff.). Holy Church, herself an instructor dressed in linen in Passus I, reappears in Passus XIX as a barn named Unity (XIX.331). And so on. The point is that, having decided which speakers can reasonably be considered authoritative, we critics of *Piers Plowman* cannot stop with paraphrases of the contents of their speeches. We must always ask besides, "Why do things appear this way *to this particular speaker?*"

It is also possible to get confused about that question. If we ask why things appear a certain way to, say, Conscience, with the idea in mind of determining what Langland finally means by *conscience,* then we are still looking for a Coleridgean unity to subsume all the parts of the poem that happen to mention Conscience. We have not surrendered our nostalgia for the shining surface structure that, as I am arguing, gets in the way of our seeing the deep currents of hermeneutic activity that drive the poem. Conscience might be deliberately different in a different dream, or might look different to a maturing dreamer. What is Conscience? That depends upon who is describing him and when. The poem is not driving toward conceptual coherence, where we can finally determine Langland's theory about the various figures represented in the personification allegory. Instead, *Piers Plowman* is dramatic all the way down. The energy of the poem comes from Langland's art in depicting how particular signs function in particular discourses at particular moments.

These are some of the ideas I want to illustrate in this chapter by discussing a sampling of authoritative figures: Holy Church (Passus I),

Anima (Passus XV), and Need (Passus XX). But I want also to work on the idea, perhaps more important for my purposes, of Langland's "textuality." The authoritative figures in *Piers Plowman* are primarily interpreters. They do not just give commands that they expect to be unquestioningly obeyed, but instead they explain why the commands they give are appropriate. What I mean by calling them "authoritative," precisely, is that they interpret experience to us through arguments that seem to make some sort of claim on us to believe in or to do certain things. I am arguing that Langland, as a medieval intellectual obsessed with texts, interprets interpretation on the model of textual hermeneutics. That is, he understands that anyone who interprets is performing activity analogous to the activity of construing a text. For Langland, whoever interprets reads the world like a book. I want to show in the cases of these three authoritative figures how *Piers Plowman* construes their interpretive activity on the model of textual hermeneutics. That means, in terms of critical methodology, finding patterns in the discourse of the three figures that correspond with characteristic patterns of textual hermeneutics.

But it is important to note that I am not making the Coleridgean move. I am not, that is, looking for a finished doctrine of textual hermeneutics that will explain and evaluate all the interpretive activity of these three figures. The premise of this book is that textual hermeneutics itself remains as problematic for Langland as is anything else he talks about. In fact, textual hermeneutics enters the picture in three different ways in the three passages I will analyze, and each authoritative figure poses his or her own characteristic hermeneutic problems. At the same time that Langland is implicitly evaluating the discourse of these three figures by means of dramatic irony, he is also implicitly interrogating the characteristic processes of textual hermeneutics.

It is a fair question why I choose in this chapter to discuss these three authoritative speakers—Holy Church, Anima, and Need—and no others. Since I am not arguing that successive discourses in *Piers Plowman* approach dogma as a limit, I perceive no dogmatic progression in the speeches of these three figures. In another chapter, I will argue that there is a progression of a sort in the poem—but not of *this* sort. On the one hand, considered only in terms of the content of their discourses, these three figures are just a sampling from the beginning, the middle, and the end of the poem.

On the other hand, considered in terms of the figures' dramatic interactions with the dreamer, their discourses constitute important moments in the dreamer's own narrative. The encounter with Holy Church encourages the dreamer to seek his own salvation through self-justification—not so much, perhaps, because of Holy Church as because of the dreamer's own predisposition. But in any case, the encounter becomes the initial stimulus for the long futile quest for Dowel. The encounter with Anima represents the crisis in the dreamer's narrative, where he begins to free himself from the self-destructive game of self-justification. And the encounter with Need occurs when the dreamer finally begins to grasp the reason why all human activity (in his case, in particular, hermeneutic activity) fails to produce a satisfactory resolution: it is because need is the fundamental structure of human being and, in an important sense, is itself the image of God in humans.

I must postpone the arguing of these points. But the three authoritative speakers of this chapter are not *just* a sampling. I hope by my discussion here to lay the groundwork for the later argument about the dreamer's narrative.

Holy Church

THE OPENING MOVES

Holy Church assumes pride of place among the dreamer's many instructors. As I have already mentioned, it is unclear who is talking in the first two lines of Passus I: "What this mountaigne bymeneth and the merke dale / And the feld ful of folk, I shal yow faire shewe." Is this only the obtuse dreamer, presumptuously donning the mantle of the preacher? Or does Langland himself put his head into the poem, as Piers does later? And by the latter hypothesis, since Holy Church interrupts immediately, is Langland telling us that he will explain everything by letting Holy Church talk? That is, does Langland himself give more or less unqualified endorsement to everything Holy Church says?

Considerable critical debate surrounds these and related issues. Some critics take Holy Church very seriously, and argue that the rest of

Piers Plowman only amplifies the lessons she tries to teach. Others argue that Langland more or less severely critiques her rhetoric, if not her doctrine. Mary Carruthers, for example, writes, "[H]er speech makes no apparent difference either to [the dreamer's] understanding or to that of anybody else in the poem. There could be no more dramatic indication of what the poem sees as the failure of the orthodox rhetoric of the Church" (35). For more on this point, see the Bibliographical Essay that follows. In this chapter, I want boldly to stake out a middle ground, and argue that Holy Church's statement is not definitive, but neither is her perspective completely relativized or superseded by subsequent statements. Although *Piers Plowman* offers many perspectives that are different from that of Holy Church, and that are apparently no less valid on their own terms, the poem never gets beyond the problems posed by Holy Church's discourse. As James Simpson notes, "In one sense, *Piers Plowman* is a remarkably consistent poem, which never moves far from a central problematic, concerning the relations of justice and love. In Passus I Holy Church states this theme" (246).

Preacherlike, Holy Church points to the dreamer's experience apparently to elicit his invitation to her to instruct him: "Sone, slepestow? Sestow this peple— / How bisie they ben aboute the maze?" (5–6). As I mentioned in the last chapter, the dreamer's first question to Holy Church betrays his own obsession: "what [may] this [be] to meene?" (11). Intellectual that he is, the first thing he wants is an interpretation of his own experience. But in another sense, Holy Church has already set him up to ask this question by placing him in the position of a disciple or student with respect to the authoritative commentary she is prepared to offer. She controls the terms of the discourse. Apparently, then, she agrees with the dreamer that the first order of business is to interpret experience.

It is perhaps easy to overlook, but the first line of Holy Church's answer to the dreamer's question already offers an interpretation, and furthermore an interpretation that turns out to be decisive for the whole discourse. She names God with the name of *Truth*: "'The tour up the toft,' quod she, 'Truthe is therinne . . .'" (12). It is an important question, and a deep question, what Holy Church means by *Truth*. She obviously means a great deal by it. Answering the question has been perhaps the major preoccupation of critics who have addressed Passus I. But I want to refocus the argument slightly, and ask why Holy Church, in particular, names God with this name as opposed to other possible names that the poem gives God elsewhere. Why not *Love* right away, for example, since Holy Church herself gets around to this name of God later? Why not *Grace,* as in XIX.209, or *Kynde,* as in IX.26 and elsewhere? Why not a more sharply focused antonym for Wrong, who lives in the "castel of care" (61ff.)—for example, *Rightwisnesse,* who in Passus XVIII as one of the Daughters of God has equal status with Truth? Why not just *God* or *Crist,* after all?

Obviously, in one sense these questions are frivolous. But I want to emphasize that to call God by the name of *Truth,* whatever Holy Church might mean by *Truth* in all the fullness of the term, already makes an interpretive choice. Moreover, the choice is dramatically appropriate to Holy Church, because she conceives herself essentially as the custodian of truth. That last *truth* is written lowercase, as referring to propositional truth. But propositional truth, as I shall argue, is not only a type of but a precondition for proper relationships among human beings and between human beings and God. Her custodianship lends Holy Church her meaning to herself. As a dramatic character in the poem, she interprets herself as the custodian of the truth—that is her story, and for her it is the whole story.

The discourse of Holy Church can be read—and in fact most often is read—as a steady enlarging, a kind of extended definition, of the concept of "truth," until the concept contains enough to begin to seem at least minimally adequate for human talk about God. This centrifugal movement begins immediately. Holy Church does not really hit her stride as a preacher until the dreamer recognizes her and finally asks what she considers to be the right question: "tel me this ilke— / How I may save my soule" (I.83–84). At that point she launches into a sermon explicitly about Truth; most of what I have to say will be about that sermon. But the opening moves of Passus I, in which Holy Church and the dreamer work out their relationship and home in on the ostensible subject of Passus I, are not negligible. Holy Church fences with the dreamer, as it were, parrying his awkward questions in order to redirect the discourse toward her central concern. But the very awkwardness of the questions suggests that Holy Church's agenda, the enlarging of the concept of truth, is not without its internal problems.

Holy Church first attempts to adumbrate the concepts of *mesure* (19, 35) and *reson* (22, 25) under the concept of truth. God as Truth has constructed an ecology, as we might say nowadays, in which all the things human beings need—"vesture" (23), "mete" (24), "drynke" (25)—are available in sufficient quantities:

> . . . he highte the erthe to helpe yow echone
> Of wollene, of lynnen, of liflode at nede
> In mesurable manere to make yow at ese . . .
>
> (17–19)

Everything works well as long as we "do noght out of reson" (25). The concept of propositional truth entails the notion of an orderly economy of worldly goods and human behaviors, precisely in the sense that we believe we can construct true propositions about what is "reasonable" and "measurable." Since we can truly say, or think that we can say, what is reasonable and measurable, it must be the case that the world is rational and mensurable. Holy Church illustrates such true propositions by means of the exemplum of drunken Lot and his "wikked dede" (31) of incest.

It is hard not to hear a faint satirical note in the rhetorical expansion of the Lot story. Here is another preacher getting carried away again by the preacher's favorite obsessions, which Holy Church shares with, for example, Chaucer's preaching Pardoner. There is no particular reason to think that the dreamer has special problems with drunkenness or lechery, but drunkenness and lechery always preach well. Holy Church is also turning the discourse from explaining Providence abstractly to making a claim: namely, that her position as custodian of truth warrants her influencing human behavior. She begins with a description of the ecology, and ends with advice: "I wisse thee the beste" (42). There are many levels on which the dreamer might challenge her claim. Why should *she* get to tell him how much to eat and drink, especially since, as it soon develops, he does not even know who she is? Even if we agree that the world is rational and mensurable, who gets to decide what to call reasonable and measurable?

But the dreamer does not directly challenge Holy Church on the ob-

vious ground of the source of her authority. Instead, in what is for me
one of the truly wonderful moments in the poem, he says,

> A madame, mercy, . . . me liketh wel youre wordes.
> Ac the moneie of this molde that men so faste holdeth—
> Telleth me to whom that tresour appendeth.
>
> (43–45)

On the one hand, the challenge is indirect. He is a little afraid of her: "I
was afered of hire face, theigh she fair weere" (10). But line 43, followed
by that *Ac,* slides very easily over into sarcasm, as in Chauntecleer to
Pertelote: "Madame, . . . graunt mercy of youre lore. / But nathelees. . . ."

On the other hand, the challenge is subtle and tempting—even phar-
isaical, as Holy Church's choice of the answering Scripture (Matthew
22:21) hints. It is not obvious at all, on the premise of an orderly ecology
where everything we need is provided, why there could be or should
be a money economy, and especially why some people should have
vast quantities of money and some people (for example, the dreamer
himself) should have none at all. And if anyone can see how Holy
Church's answer counts as an adequate response to the question the
dreamer really seems to be asking, that reader is more acute than I am.
That we should give Caesar Caesar's due, and give God God's due, and
should use our money in accordance with our reason and natural intelligence, is doubtless good advice; but it neither helps us know what to do
in any particular case, nor explains how money should be distributed in
order to achieve social justice. In fact, if Holy Church's were an adequate response, it would be unnecessary for Langland to keep revisiting
this issue throughout the poem, as he indisputably does. Christ's answer
to the Pharisees was adequate because the Pharisees were not asking an
honest question. Christ exposed their hypocrisy. Holy Church's answer
to the dreamer is not adequate because at some level the dreamer, impertinent and even hypocritical as he might be, is asking an honest question.

The challenge illuminates the dreamer's character in another way as
well. Like all intellectuals, he is supposed to be above mundane concerns
for money, but (again like all intellectuals) he seems sometimes to talk
about very little else. First, he wants, in general, to know what things
mean (I.11). Second, he wants social justice, which he tends to analyze,

at least at this stage of the poem, in terms of the distribution of wealth. Mixed with the potential sarcasm, the unruly disciple's impertinence, and the serious philosophical questioning is a kind of anxious and even agonized grasping at an opportunity, perhaps, to understand the suffering caused by social injustice. The dreamer's question, like some of the dramatic lines in the Prologue, contains potential for comedy and serious reflection all at once. The longer we look at the lines, the more they appear like one of those optical illusions that are first one thing and then another. Part of what Langland shows his readers here, in this paradigmatically Langlandian passage, is how our own interpretive activity gets swept up in the interpretive currents moving through the conflicting discourses of the text.

The unhelpfulness of Holy Church's response to the question about money—possibly an example of what Carruthers calls "the failure of the orthodox rhetoric of the Church" (35)—seems to motivate the dreamer's next question: "That dongeon in the dale that dredful is of sighte— / What may it bemeene, madame, I yow bineseche?" (59–60). His line of inquiry about social justice so far has produced only scriptural quotations and clichés. Why does the dreamer not pursue the question about money? Is he silenced by the authority of the gospel, afraid of appearing to challenge God's own words, overawed by *latinitas?* Or is the dreamer, somewhat patronizingly, now abandoning what he thinks is a dry well? As he suspected all along she would be, Holy Church seems unhelpful on the subject of money. But she did better before, when she was interpreting the scene of the dream. At least she provided a specific answer about the meaning of the tower. So now the dreamer asks her to do the same for the donjon.

He asks, that is, another question about *meaning,* as if he is developing the hypothesis that this authoritative figure is good at interpreting experience abstractly but not necessarily at dealing with practical affairs. This tension adds bite to his later petitions that Holy Church will "kenne me kyndely on Crist to bileve" (81) and will "Teche me to no tresor, but tel me this ilke— / How I may save my soule" (83–84). Having discovered that his interlocutor is Holy Church, who is supposed to help him toward salvation, the dreamer falls victim to his own preconceptions about her. He talks as though salvation is first of all an intellectual matter divorced from considerations of *tresor,* a word that by this time already resonates with all the issues of social justice. The dreamer believes as an article of orthodox faith that he is to get to heaven through the Church, and he has observed—or so he thinks—that the Church has little helpful to say about social justice and much to say about what things mean. Thus, in accordance with his own predisposition, the dreamer assumes that salvation must be a matter of hermeneutics. Holy Church immediately attempts to correct the dreamer's mistake by employing the metaphor of Truth itself as a *tresor* and by defining truth as entailing truthful speech acts and other good actions in the world: "whoso is trewe of his tonge and telleth noon oother, / And dooth the werkes therwith" (88–89). Later I will have a great deal more to say about the dreamer's intellectual development. But although the dreamer perhaps misinterprets Holy Church by separating thought from action or *intellectus* from *affectus,* he is not being a complete fool about himself. As the poem develops, it will be necessary for the dreamer to work through his own tendency as an intellectual to overvalue interpretation at the expense of action. Being who he is, he cannot simply set aside his obsession with meaning and proceed on his pilgrimage. Being who he is, he must follow the path of his pilgrimage through the difficult byways of textual hermeneutics.

Holy Church's answer to the dreamer's question about the donjon is interesting in a couple of ways. First, she interprets the opposite of Truth not as Falsehood, as one might expect, but instead as Wrong, who is the *father* of Falsehood (63–64). The suggestion is that for Holy Church the concept of Truth contains considerably more than the notion of propositional truth—as if Truth, in parallel with Wrong's fathering of Falsehood, produces propositional truth but is not exhausted by it. The point here is the point I made before: Holy Church understands herself as the custodian of propositional truth, and so she defines everything in terms of propositional truth. From where she stands, Truth is the most accurate name of God, who is the necessary condition for the possibility of propositional truth.

The second point of interest is Holy Church's quick listing of Bible stories (65–68) to illustrate the operations of Wrong in the world. This list is apparently what gets the dreamer's attention, especially: "Thanne hadde I wonder in my wit what womman she weere / That swiche wise wordes of Holy Writ shewed" (71–72). Is the dreamer merely slow on the uptake? Holy Church has already provided exegeses, with Latin quotations, of the Lot story from Genesis and the passage in Matthew where Jesus dodges the Pharisees' stratagem. Does Langland portray the dreamer as having a frivolous mind that picks up one thing and then another more or less at random, and that is only now getting around to wondering about what has long been obvious in the conversation? I read the effect rather as cumulative. The true test of literacy for the dreamer is not whether someone can quote a Latin tag like Chaucer's Pardoner "To saffron with my predicacioun," but instead whether someone can quote appropriate authority for *every* point, and especially whether someone seems to have a comprehensive view of the Bible such that New Testament and Old Testament can be used to illuminate each other. That is what happens, though in a muted way, in Holy Church's list. Old Testament events (the Fall, the murder of Abel) are read as types of New Testament events (Judas's betrayal of Jesus) so as to explain the presence of evil in the world as the work of the Tempter. The dreamer recognizes literacy where he recognizes the movement between parts and whole that defines the hermeneutic circle.

There is a hint, not unequivocal, that female literacy surprises the dreamer. There is a great deal to be said about the gender of the authoritative figures in *Piers Plowman.* I will not say much here, beyond pointing out that Holy Church is a woman, among other reasons, presumably because Latin *Ecclesia* is feminine, and literacy for a medieval *litteratus* means literacy in Latin. But that line of reasoning does not work everywhere. Anima in Passus XV is male, for example. But Latin literacy is particularly at issue in Passus I, since Latin literacy is one basis upon which the Church claims its authority as custodian of propositional truth. Where there is literacy, there is authority—at least for the dreamer. He begins to suspect that he might have been making a fool of himself in interrogating this figure, and so it belatedly occurs to him to find out who she is. This psychological movement implied in the dreamer's dramatic interactions with Holy Church is an instance of Langland's recursiveness: the dreamer interprets Holy Church's interpretive activity, while Langland shows us how the dreamer's own interpretive activity causes him to evaluate authoritative claims on the basis of his own understanding of textual hermeneutics.

The dreamer does not recognize Holy Church. It seems, both to her and to us, that he should recognize her: "thow oughtest me to knowe" (75). Langland employs this same device elsewhere. For example, the dreamer has to ask Thought to identify himself (VIII.72), although Thought seems to represent at least in part the dreamer's own thought. The same pattern is repeated with Ymaginatif (XI.439) and with Anima (XV.14–15). The device seems to signify a reflective turn on the part of the dreamer. He becomes consciously aware for the first time of something that has always been an intimate part of his life but that has so far been transparent to him. Following this thread, we might conclude that Holy Church in Passus I represents the Church *as it functions in the individual's life:*

> I underfeng thee first and the feith taughte.
> Thow broughtest me borwes my byddyng to fulfille,
> And to loven me leelly the while thi lif dureth.
>
> (76–78)

This is the Church as cultus and not the Church seen *sub specie aeternitatis.* The barn called Unity in Passus XIX, for example, is perhaps more like the Church seen *sub specie aeternitatis.*

This critical moment in Passus I, therefore, seems to correspond to the dreamer's awakening to an important fact about the Church. The dreamer has been working under the hypothesis that his interlocutor is someone who explains what things mean. Until now, he has apparently thought of the Church as the agent that shapes the course of his moral life, but he has not necessarily thought of the Church as an interpreter. Thus he does not at first recognize his interlocutor as Holy Church. The moment of recognition represents the reflective turn in which the dreamer grasps that cultus implies interpretation, that the Church by shaping his life is also interpreting experience to him.

The observation seems elementary, but its implications are world altering for the dreamer. Until now, his dialogue with Holy Church, though sometimes perhaps impertinent, has remained within the relatively comfortable bounds of orthodoxy. The dreamer's side of the conversation so far has not indicated that he is especially worried at the moment about his personal salvation—for him, this conversation is just two Christians sitting around talking. Now the dreamer, recognizing orthodoxy as an interpretive system, also recognizes the possibility of questioning its bounds. From the dreamer's perspective, the rest of the poem is a response to this intellectual earthquake. The salvation of his own soul suddenly becomes an *issue* for him: "Thanne I courbed on my knees and cried hire of grace, / And preide hire pitously to preye for my synnes" (79–80).

Part of his agenda here, no doubt, is to make amends for his earlier impertinence. But the sudden poignancy of his rhetoric suggests that something genuinely shocking has happened. The abyss yawns for him when he suddenly realizes that Holy Church, the transparent medium in which he has swum all his life, can be construed as an interpreter. As an intellectual, someone who takes responsibility for interpretation and for questioning interpretations, he suddenly realizes that he has all along been confronting a moral responsibility that places everything about him in peril. Characteristically, he addresses that issue by seeking intellectual understanding from authoritative commentary, agonizingly trying to shift the responsibility for his own salvation to Holy Church in the very moment when he realizes that Holy Church's interpretive activity requires him as an intellectual to question it: "tel me this ilke— / How I may save my soule" (83–84). It is, of course, not that easy—as the rest of the poem shows.

THE SERMON ON TRUTH

After this long preliminary, I finally come to the core of Holy Church's discourse. Holy Church's rhetorical fencing with the dreamer seems deliberately designed to prepare him, and us, to receive the long sermon on Truth, which modulates into the complementary sermon about Love. I want to look closely at the rhetorical movement of this sermon, which on its surface seems very strange. I believe that the rhetorical movement of her sermon implies a habit on the part of Holy Church of construing the social organism as if it were a text. In one sense, that is just what we should expect, since the Church is directed by the clergy, and the clergy are by definition those who read. What is maybe more interesting is the way the rhetorical movement of the sermon implicitly poses all or virtually all of the major problems that drive *Piers Plowman,* in such a way as to suggest that all of those problems are at base problems in hermeneutics.

When I say that the rhetorical movement of Holy Church's sermon is strange, I mean primarily two things. First, it is strange that she immediately quotes the text *Deus caritas* to support her theme that "Whan alle tresors arn tried, . . . treuthe is the beste" (85–86). It is not that this choice of texts cannot be explained. Much if not most of the critical commentary on Holy Church's sermon has been directed precisely at explaining the relationship between Truth and Love. Much of this explanation is illuminating and satisfactory. But the mass of this critical commentary is itself evidence that Holy Church's choice of text needs explaining. As Joseph Wittig puts it, "The meaning of these lines is neither instantly clear nor straightforward" (*Revisited* 61). The strangeness is not so much in the theological argument as it is in the rhetoric, in Holy Church's immediate production of the text *Deus caritas* as if it were the obvious choice to support her theme.

The second thing I find strange is the digressive movement of the part of Holy Church's sermon that talks about knighthood. Again, there are satisfactory explanations about how the theme of knighthood is related to the concept of Truth. But the impulse that critics feel to grind this passage finely in the mills of commentary is again evidence that the movement from Holy Church's ostensible theme into a discussion of feudal obligations at least *looks* digressive. The account of Lucifer's revolt allegorized as a feudal insurrection (111ff.) seems to have drifted a long way from the dreamer's question about saving his soul, even though Holy Church eventually returns to that question by advising that one not cast one's lot with Lucifer (128ff.). Again, the theological and exegetical framework is in place and is coherently connected up, but the rhetorical movement looks strange. I want to consider the implications of the rhetorical movement, because the drama of that movement is the technique by means of which Langland shows us—as opposed to telling us—that Holy Church reads the social organism as a text.

I want to start by examining how knighthood functions in Holy Church's sermon, and then to expand my discussion to the bigger question about Truth and Love. One of the strange things about knighthood in the sermon is the way its meaning shifts between what we might call "literal" and "figurative." Ultimately, I think, to construct a binary opposition between what is literal and what is figurative is a misleading way to talk about what Langland does in this passage and elsewhere. For Holy Church, ultimately, the propositions that truly articulate Truth—whether we would call them "literal" or "figurative"—are true. But at first approximation we might say that sometimes Langland seems to be talking "literally" about the functions of fourteenth-century knights, and sometimes he seems to be using the notion of knighthood "figuratively" to elucidate certain mysterious passages in Scripture.

We may ask, then, "What does knighthood signify to Holy Church?" Derek Pearsall's note on the passage in the C-text succinctly summarizes the orthodox answer: the ruling orders "are to serve and keep Truth by defending the land and administering justice. It is well to recognize here the medieval commonplace that the function of the political organization of society (i.e. the State) is moral, that is, the maintenance of Christian truth and righteousness" (47n). Kings and knights make the world safe for Christianity. That statement supposedly describes the state of affairs that exists (or should exist) in fourteenth-century Europe. Truth as a name of God—the definitive name of God from the perspective of Holy Church—is the principle of universal order, implying particular social structures.

It might appear obvious, then, that propositional truth, including the articles of the Christian faith, is only one aspect of the larger truth of social order that knights maintain. But propositional truth takes priority in Holy Church's exposition. Truth is the best treasure first of all in the sense that the good Christian is "trewe of his tonge and telleth noon oother" (88). Furthermore, the works of the good Christian are identified precisely as works that are in accord with propositional truth: "dooth the werkes *therwith*" (89; emphasis mine). Both Schmidt and Pearsall (46n) identify the gospel text in the background of line 90 ("He is a god by the Gospel") as John 10:34, Jesus' interpretation of a verse from the Psalms. In the gospel, the Jews are about to stone Jesus for blasphemy, because, as they say, he has called himself God. "Jesus answered them, 'Is it not written in your law, "I said, you are gods"?'" (RSV). Jesus asks, "If he called them gods to whom the word of God came (and scripture cannot be broken)" (verse 35), then does it follow that Jesus is blaspheming when he claims to be the Son of God? Jesus then asks to be judged by his works. A complicated intertextuality operates here, as is already signaled by the fact that Langland cites not John but Luke (91; see Pearsall's full and helpful note on the corresponding passage in C.86). But I want only to make the relatively simple point that in the gospel, Jesus explicitly connects being God-like with receiving propositional truth, and the whole discussion occurs in the context of the assumption that the ability to do good works depends upon accepting Scripture as propositional truth. Propositional truth is a larger issue than it might at first appear.

When Holy Church begins to cash out her doctrine in terms of social structure, she at least initially seems to draw on the theory of the three estates. But unlike the description of the first foundation in the Prologue, which begins with the King and Knighthood, Holy Church's foundation begins with the clergy: "The clerkes that knowen this sholde kennen it aboute, / For Cristen and uncristen cleymeth it echone" (92–93). Everybody claims to own the propositions that embody the truth, but only Christian clergy really do own them. Even virtuous pagans have something to say about good behavior, but they do not understand what ultimately makes good behavior good. Only the custodians of the articles of the Christian faith understand that. Holy Church, not surprisingly, justifies the social position of the ruling class in terms of their service to the clerical class. To enable the continuing exposition of Christian truth,

> Kynges and knyghtes sholde kepen it by reson—
> Riden and rappen doun in reaumes aboute,
> And taken *transgressores* and tyen hem faste
> Til treuthe hadde ytermyned hire trespas to the ende.
>
> (94–97)

The scriptural context of the term *transgressores* is interesting. The term comes from James 2:9 (Langland, ed. Pearsall 47n). There is perhaps an ironic undertone. In James, the *transgressores* are specifically those who "show partiality" (2:9, RSV), and James 2 begins by rebuking those who treat a "man with gold rings and fine clothing" better than they treat a "poor man in shabby clothing" (2:1–4). Rebuking the rich (in large measure, the knightly class) for ignoring the poor is one of Langland's favorite activities; and we might also remember the ambiguous passage in the first foundation of the Prologue (23–24), where there might be a hint that the characteristic function of the ruling class is to overdress. If Langland is reminding us of that passage and if he is drawing on the scriptural context of the term *transgressores,* he might be hinting that knights are most likely to offend in the very point they are most responsible for policing. In any case, Holy Church presumes an essential connection between propositional truth and social justice.

Here Holy Church takes her interesting and apparently digressive turn. In both Schmidt's edition and the Kane-Donaldson edition, the next line (98) reads, "For David in hise dayes dubbed knyghtes." *Because* David dubbed knights, fourteenth-century knights have the duties that have just been specified. Even in these editorial orderings, it looks as though Holy Church has gotten distracted from answering the dreamer's question about his soul, and even from explaining why Truth is the best treasure, and has lapsed into a scriptural justification for the existence of the first estate.

The B manuscripts, though, all place lines 100–103 after line 97, and lines 98–99 after 103 (Schmidt 19n and 365). This ordering emphasizes even more strongly the apparently digressive turn. In the manuscripts, Holy Church first finishes her analysis of the duties of knighthood ("And that is the profession apertly that apendeth to knyghtes," and so on—100–103), briefly mentions David and his knights as scriptural forebears of their fourteenth-century descendants (98–99, 104), and then jumps straight into the account of Lucifer's rebellion (105ff.). It is as though the pressure to provide learned scriptural exegesis pushes Holy Church further and further back into sacred history, further and further apart from mundane experience, and further and further away from the issue at hand, namely, the salvation of the dreamer's soul. This is not an unusual thing to occur in a pulpit. The impulse that motivates the editorial emendations, perhaps, is at root the discomfort caused by the apparently digressive movement. The emendations aim at integrating the mention of David and his knights, at least, more closely into the argument about the duties of fourteenth-century knights.

In any case, Holy Church proceeds with a kind of double-edged exposition. On the one hand, she is implicitly justifying feudal social structures in terms of scriptural precedents. Because David dubbed knights, and ultimately because God created orders of knights, there has been established an eternal pattern that should be replicated in any good system of social organization. On the other hand—and this is the point I want particularly to pursue—Holy Church is interpreting scriptural texts by appealing to fourteenth-century notions of knighthood. The angels are not "literally" knights. To compare the orders of angels with knights is to use the concept of knighthood "figuratively" so as to help human beings understand some of the more mysterious things that Scripture says. As Anna Baldwin puts it, Langland "used treason as an image of disobedience to God" (*Government* 76).

In particular, Holy Church's exegesis of the Latin quotation from Isaiah portrays Lucifer's revolt as a treasonous rejection of feudal obligations and as a spurious claiming of territory: *"Ponam pedem in aquilone, et similis ero Altissimo"* (119). The quotation enters *Piers Plowman* by way of a complicated intertextuality. In his note on the quotation in the C-text, Pearsall (48n) points out that the quotation, whose source is ultimately Isaiah 14:13–14, arrives via Augustine's commentary on Psalm 47 and, possibly, another intermediary text. The same quotation appears again at B.XV.51a, in the passage where Anima scolds the dreamer for wanting to know everything. The point in Passus XV seems to be somewhat similar to the point in Passus I: the dreamer in Passus XV, like Lucifer, fails to discriminate accurately between himself and God, and therefore is "oon of Prides knyghtes" (XV.50). That last phrase clearly uses the concept of knighthood "figuratively," and it anticipates the personification allegory of Passus XIX.338ff., where Pride appears as a military commander who attacks Unity.

At the point where Holy Church allegorizes Lucifer's revolt and quotes Isaiah, the C-text (C.I.111ff.) develops an apparently comic interlude based on the literal level of Holy Church's allegory. The dreamer wonders why anyone would choose to claim the north instead of the south, and Holy Church replies that she will refrain from criticizing the north, because she might possibly offend northerners. Either Holy Church and the dreamer are deliberately playing with the literal level of the allegory, or else the joke is on the dreamer for his dull literal-mindedness. That is, to get the joke, one must think of the dreamer as missing the metaphor. In either case, Langland is compelling attention to the fact that the idea of knighthood is being applied figuratively.

For Holy Church in this part of her sermon, then, knighthood functions as what we would call the "vehicle" of a metaphor. She uses the idea of knighthood to explain puzzling scriptural texts by connecting them with an institution of fourteenth-century society. Why does knighthood occur to her as the appropriate vehicle, and why does the vehicle not only carry her ostensible tenor but, for a time, completely carry away her discourse? Her discourse is about propositional truth and the more general Truth embodied in good social structures. I want to argue that for Holy Church the idea of knighthood is so intimately connected with the idea of propositional truth that the distinction between "literal" and "figurative" uses of knighthood blurs. Knighthood represents for Holy Church not only a social relation, but also a cognitive capacity necessary for arriving at propositional truth—namely, the power of discrimination or definition. The issue for my argument is the methodeutic principle by which Holy Church interprets, or, in other words, how Holy Church connects signs. Knighthood is for her simultaneously a sign of a particular kind of social structure and a sign of the cognitive capacity that makes that social structure possible.

In the discourse of Holy Church, what good knights do is to separate, to divide, to place within boundaries, to *define* in the etymological sense. The commentary tradition arising from the Pseudo-Dionysian *Celestial Hierarchy* all but makes this connection explicit. For example, Thomas Gallus in his commentary on Dionysius explains why certain images of human equipment are appropriately applied to the angels:

> Rods signify the power and prudence needed in order to rule one's subjects well and bring them to God, to guide with a sure hand whatever business has been laid on one by God, and bring it to a proper conclusion. For this is, or should be, the function of kings and judges who carry rods and sceptres. Lances and axes are the instruments of killing. They signify the power of separating out the wicked from the elect, or sin from a nature that is good, and of shrewdly discerning between good and good, good and better, and better and best, and of bringing one's activities to a successful conclusion. (Minnis, Scott, and Wallace 187)

It is of course tempting to link this particular passage, with its insistence on discriminating good, better, and best, with the "three lives" of *Piers Plowman:* Dowel, Dobet, and Dobest.

Kings and knights, furthermore, are to keep Christian truth "by reson" (94). *Reason* becomes a loaded term in *Piers Plowman,* although in Passus I the loading is unfinished. Line 94 therefore suggests numerous interpretations. But clearly one thing Holy Church means here by *reason* is cognitive discrimination. *Transgressores* are etymologically those who step across the line, who perform a "trespas" (97). Good knights must "tyen hem faste," must fix them in place to await a judgment rendered by Truth (96–97). One of Langland's etymological puns strikingly illuminates the intimate connection that Holy Church posits between social structures and propositional truth: "Til treuthe hadde ytermyned hire trespas to the ende" (97). Truth as judge should "determine" their trespass—set bounds to it, decide what the practical consequences of the crime are in terms of the damage done and the penalty to be assessed. Truth also, and simultaneously, should "term" their trespass—put a term or word to it. The pun as rhetorical device suggests that for Holy Church the two activities are the same. The knights' binding of the transgressors makes possible the construction of truthful propositions about them. As Judson Boyce Allen observes in his discussion of the Prologue, "The law and legal process are verbal procedures which render the world true by describing it" (279).

Bad knights, contrariwise, in the discourse of Holy Church are those who muddle boundaries and try to overturn hierarchies. Lucifer's lie is that he will be *"similis Altissimo"* (119), equal to the Highest—a major failure of discrimination. After the rebellion, God must "stable and stynte / And garte [to stekie the hevene] . . ." (122–23), and part of the restoration is to sort out the jumble of demons among the four elements, so that "Lucifer lowest lith of hem alle" (126).

So knighthood for Holy Church means to set bounds—literally, to maintain the borders: "Riden and rappen doun in reaumes aboute" (95). But this sort of activity is the exact analogue of what the clergy do when they distinguish the true from the false, the good from the evil, the saved from the damned. This activity of the knights is the exact analogue of articulating the propositional truth that everyone claims but that only the Christian clergy possess. To call the activities of the knights and the clergy "analogous" in fact puts it too weakly. The activities depend absolutely upon each other. Without the hermeneutic power of discrimination, knights could not know where the boundaries are that they are supposed to maintain; and without the social order maintained by knighthood, there would be no clear social categories about whom the Church could construct true propositions. For propositional truth to exist, for Holy Church to have something to be the custodian of, it must be possible cognitively to define the objects of knowledge, to fix meanings so as to differentiate one sign from another. Knighthood sustains the division of the social continuum into significant units, just as the hermeneutic capacity to discriminate different signs permits the analysis of a text. Whatever claim Holy Church can make to speak authoritatively about society, and thus to sort out the Babylonian cacophony, depends upon the possibility of dividing the social continuum into distinct classes. It is not strong enough to say that for Holy Church the social organism is one thing, and texts are another, and the social organism seems to be textlike in certain ways. Instead, for Holy Church the intelligibility of the social organism depends absolutely on its ability to be assimilated to the mode of being of a text, so that social truth is just propositional truth writ large.

If we take Holy Church at her word, all her hermeneutic activity here aims at the definition of Truth. She is giving a sermon, and in accordance with best fourteenth-century practice, she clearly states her theme several times: "Whan alle tresors arn tried, . . . treuthe is the beste" (85); "And enden as I er seide in truthe, that is the beste" (131); "Forthi I seye, as I seyde er . . . / Whan alle tresors arn tried, Truthe is the beste" (134–35); "Treuthe is tresor the trieste on erthe" (137); "Forthi I seye as I seide er . . . / When alle tresors ben tried, Treuthe is the beste" (206–7); "Now have I tolde thee what truthe is—that no tresor is bettre" (208). In fact, the repetition seems overdone enough to hint at a caricature of fourteenth-century preaching or else to indicate Holy Church's assessment of the limited attention span of the dreamer.

Be that as it may, John Alford might well take the passage to illustrate his principle that Langland normally "begins with a set of quotations, related to one another by theme and by verbal similarities," and then elaborates "upon their significance by means of dramatization, paraphrase, exempla, and so forth" ("Quotations" 89). That is, as scholars have already amply demonstrated, we can penetrate deeply into the theological issues implicit in the sermon by studying the scriptural texts containing the key words of the discourse—for example, *veritas, caritas, thesaurus*—and the relevant commentaries. The sermon looks very much as though it could have been composed by concordance, again in accordance with best fourteenth-century practice. My point here is that sermons thus composed by concordance depend upon the cognitive capacity of discrimination or definition that I have just been describing. A concordance is, simply put, a way of sorting, of dividing the continuum of authoritative texts into discrete units, with the purpose of defining the key terms thus isolated.

Let me go back to the beginning of the sermon: "Whan alle tresors arn tried . . . treuthe is the beste. / I do it on *Deus caritas* to deme the sothe . . ." (85–86). "When all treasures are tested, truth is the best." Schmidt translates the next line as "I ground my affirmation (that this is) truly to be judged (so) on the text *God is love*" (18n). The line is a little puzzling, largely because of the idiom *do it on.* The idiom occurs again, for example, in X.37—"I do it on God hymselve!"—where something like "call to witness" seems to be a reasonable translation. But the idiom in both of these passages, by means of the active *do,* stresses that the statement that immediately precedes the idiom is a performative utterance, a speech act that itself constitutes an action—in this case, the action of affirmation. "I affirm something, and I make that affirmation *(do it)* in *(on)* God or a scriptural text." This reading of the idiom might suggest a translation of line 86 slightly different from Schmidt's: "I affirm that truth is the best treasure, and I make that affirmation in construing the text *God is love* in order to judge what is true."

This reading might somewhat ease the obvious problem that I have noted before. It is at least not completely transparent why Holy Church makes this connection, how the thesis about Truth follows clearly and distinctly from the premise about Love. Making the theological connection might not be an impossible stretch, but it is a move requiring the flexibility of a limber first baseman. Pearsall puts it this way: "To love God, and to show a loving response to his love, is to obey his law and keep his commandments" (Langland, ed. Pearsall 46n). This jolt of apparent incoherence might at first look like a rhetorical tactic, creating the expectation that Holy Church will go on to flesh out the connection. But she does not. In fact, she does not get back to Love, and apparently has no intention of doing so, until she is prodded by the dreamer in line 138: "Yet have I no kynde knowynge, . . . yet mote ye kenne me bettre. . . ." My reading of line 86 does not necessarily imply that the proposition *God is love* is an immediate logical premise for the proposition *Truth is best.* In my reading, the rhetorical jolt remains, but it is perhaps possible to explain a little more economically how Holy Church has connected the ideas of Truth and Love.

The text *Deus caritas* comes from 1 John 4:8. It is immediately preceded by a statement implying that love is the principle that discriminates truth from error (Dunning, *Interpretation* 29–30): "By this we know the spirit of truth and the spirit of error" (1 John 4:6, RSV). What Holy Church seems to be saying here is that she affirms the thesis of her sermon in the very act of interpreting the text *Deus caritas* in order to judge what is true. She does not exactly assert that truth is best because God is love, although that is also a true proposition. Instead, she asserts that it is possible to make correct discriminations (that is, to see the truth) if one correctly interprets the text that says that God is love. If one understands this text when one attempts to apply it to situations in which discriminations are called for, then one loves in the sense that John means here, and one becomes God-like: "He is a god by the Gospel, agrounde and olofte, / And ylik to Oure Lord, by Seint Lukes wordes" (90–91). Not only does one discriminate correctly, but one is enabled to put together the passage from 1 John with other scriptural passages so as to understand all of the passages better. One construes the world as if using a concordance.

This is precisely the point the dreamer misses. When he demands that Holy Church teach him better, she is provoked to rebuke him for learning too little Latin (140–41)—presumably the Latin of the Vulgate that via a concordance of passages makes the connection between truth and love clear. A concordance would justify Holy Church's understanding of truth by sorting passages on the term *truth.* This sorting would turn up the passage in 1 John, collocating the terms *truth* and *love,* and fixing the term *truth* in its proper vicinity, which is the vicinity of the text

Deus caritas. As Holy Church stresses twice, she says whatever she says "by sighte of thise textes" (134, 206). The dreamer's failure to understand her is a failure of reading.

So, for Holy Church, understanding of Truth as best treasure results from discriminating truth and error. Discriminating truth and error is first of all a hermeneutic activity, an interpretation of authoritative texts via the particular methodology that underlies her sermon. Knighthood is only the replication of this hermeneutic activity on the social level, the social analogue of correct interpretation.

It is not dramatically surprising that Holy Church, as custodian of authoritative texts and true interpretations of them, construes the social world as a text, and particular social organizations as ways of interpreting that text. Nor is it surprising that she at least initially appears to be deeply invested in feudalism. That sort of social structure makes her notion of authoritative interpretation applicable to the social setting, by fixing social entities and relations and thus making it possible to construct true propositions about society. Old Testament feudalism, David's feudalism, depends upon making and keeping oaths: "David in hise dayes dubbed knyghtes, / And dide hem sweren on hir swerd to serven truthe ever" (98–99). In the manuscript ordering, the next line is "And whoso passe[th] that point is apostata in the ordre" (104) Holy Church's description of feudalism in heaven does not distinguish grammatically between God's creating the orders of angels and his teaching them the truth. That is, the verbs *knighted* ("knyghted tene"), *gave* ("yaf hem myght"), and *made* ("made hem archangeles") in lines 105–8 are grammatically parallel with the verb *taught* ("Taughte hem by the Trinitee treuthe to knowe") in line 109, as if to suggest that the dividing of the orders of angels in some sense *was* the teaching. A social structure that depends on keeping promises and recognizing hierarchy arises from and depends upon hermeneutic activity that makes accurate discriminations. Langland's move here suggests that for Holy Church, at least, all debates about social structure potentially slide into hermeneutics.

But, of course, Holy Church does not get the last word about either hermeneutics or social justice or truth itself. Certainly her conception of knighthood is qualified, if not undermined, by later passages. In Passus VI, for example, Piers reinstitutes knighthood as the institution that makes the world safe not only for Holy Church but also—perhaps pri-

marily—for the laborers (VI.24ff.). And then the knight in Passus VI
fails to deal satisfactorily with Wastour, so that Piers has to summon
Hunger. Also, Jesus himself appears as the lover-knight in Passus XVIII
and Passus XIX. Whatever knighthood might be said to mean in such
passages, it is not identical to what it seems to mean for Holy Church in
Passus I.

And in fact, in the second part of her sermon, Holy Church herself
undermines the remarks she made about Truth in the first part. She
seems to be rounding to a close, with three repetitions of her theme, in
lines 130–37, after the story of Lucifer's rebellion. But in the portrayal of
ideal knighthood and especially the excitement of recounting the war in
heaven, she seems to have forgotten to return to her primary text *Deus
caritas.* There is perhaps another satirical aside directed at the preacher's
penchant for getting distracted by material that preaches well. The
dreamer has a point. Holy Church has shown him how everything depends upon accurate discrimation, but she has not told him how to do
that trick. The secret of discriminating accurately, as it turns out once
one examines the scriptural context, is to understand the text she has
forgotten to talk about: *Deus caritas.* Holy Church's pique at the dreamer's question ("Thow doted daffe!"—140) perhaps results partly from
her own embarrassment at suddenly realizing that she has omitted half
her sermon.

It is possible and even natural to read the "kynde knowynge" (138)
the dreamer seeks as some sort of intuitive knowledge more or less opposed to the abstract intellectual knowledge that one might expect to
find in books. But it is not necessary to read "kynde knowynge" that
way. Certainly the concept is one of the most problematic in *Piers Plowman,* and like several other crucial concepts it seems to grow and develop and, perhaps, ultimately to remain open-ended. Mary Clemente
Davlin, for example, argues that Langland fuses in this concept the tradition of biblical "wisdom" with the "allegorical literary convention of
the goddess Natura" (5); thus, the concept becomes very broad indeed:
kynde knowynge is

> a genuine ME equivalent for the *gnosis* of Scripture and the Fathers, the loving
> knowledge of monastic and scholastic tradition; and thus this meaning, "wis-
> dom," is resonant with the other operative meanings of *kynde knowyng*—experi-

ential knowledge; intimate, loving knowledge; personal, thorough knowledge; knowledge as if by second nature; committed knowledge; connatural knowledge. (*"Kynde Knowyng"* 15)

It seems to me likely that Langland here wants to arouse the suspicion, at least, that the dreamer himself does not fully understand what he means by "kynde knowynge." In any case, I will have more to say in Chapter 3 about the dreamer's "kynde knowynge." But, for the moment, I want only to point out that "kynde knowynge" is not *absolutely* opposed to book knowledge. The first time Piers himself comes into the poem, for example, in Passus V, he says of Truth as a name of God that "I knowe hym as kyndely as clerc doth hise bokes" (V.538). Thus we have Piers's own word for it that the relationship a cleric has with books can be described at least metaphorically as "kynde knowynge." Possibly, then, for some people (intellectuals?) "kynde knowynge" comes at least initially through intimacy with texts or through reading the world as a text. The point is that in Passus I the dreamer is not necessarily rejecting scriptural exegesis as a satisfactory way for him to know. It is possible that he is merely pointing out that Holy Church's sermon is incomplete because of her glaring omission of exegesis of the chief text *Deus caritas.*

As I have said before, Truth and Love can be united in ways that are as theologically satisfactory as any theological explanations of Christian mysteries can be. But I want to pay attention rather to the metaphoric structure of Holy Church's sermon. At the great turn in line 140, where Holy Church begins preaching specifically about love, there is an interesting shift. Knighthood serves as the vehicle for Holy Church's discourse about truth. Her trope of truth is that knighthood represents the hermeneutic power of discrimination or definition. Her tropes of love, however, tend to be drawn from the realm of the feminine, the relative, and the commercial, as opposed to the realm of the masculine, the absolute, and the feudal. A tension thus springs up in the discourse that prefigures many of the unresolvable issues of the poem.

The sword of truth that David's knights swear upon, for example, is replaced by the needle of love, a feminine tool, specifically opposed to the heavy machinery of war, something made not to divide but to insinuate. Love is "portatif and persaunt as the point of a nedle, / That myghte noon armure it lette ne none heighe walles" (157–58). Men do

sew; there are "Taillours" in the catalog of occupations in the Prologue
(221). But women do the sewing in Piers's establishment on the half-
acre (VI.9ff.), and I think the opposition between the needle and the
armor is decisive. The lines about the needle also immediately follow
lines stressing not the male power of the Holy Spirit, but the physical
incarnation of Jesus in Mary's womb: love "hadde of this fold flessh and
blood taken" (155).

Heaven absolutely repels the rebel angels who hope that Lucifer will
replace God: "alle that hoped it myghte be so, noon hevene myghte hem
holde" (120). The line is echoed in the part of the sermon about love:
"hevene myghte nat holden it, so was it hevy of hymselve" (153). But the
second time the line occurs in the context of wordplay involving the relative concepts of heaviness and lightness. In her commentary on the
passage, P. M. Kean points out that weight (*pondus*) in Aristotelian phys-
ics is what "ensures that every body in the universe takes its appropriate
place" (360). Another way to put this is to say that the weight of anything consists precisely in its relation to everything else. What is heavy
in one environment is light in another, and there is no absolute division
between heaviness and lightness to correspond with the division between truth and falsehood.

Truth in the first part of Holy Church's sermon is the king who divides the angelic orders. Love in the second part of the discourse is not a
king or a knight, but "ledere of the Lordes folk of hevene, / And a
meene, as the mair is, [inmiddes] the kyng and the commune" (159–60).
Love, exactly unlike truth, perceives not differences but similarities. It
does not define, but instead smoothes over divisions; it does not discriminate but mediates. The trope of the mayor as intermediary is
drawn not from feudalism, but from the new urban money economy.

Still other tropes can be mapped into the opposition I have been
constructing. Truth wounds, as in the war in heaven; love heals, as in the
"triacle of hevene" (148), the "spice" (149), and the "leche of lif" (204).
Truth fixes in place, as when the knights "taken *transgressores* and tyen
hem faste" (96) or when God "garte [to stekie the hevene]" (123) or even
when, in the discourse on love, "chastite withouten charite worth
cheyned in helle" (188); but giving is "the lok of love that leteth out my
grace" (202). We might even contrast the "inorganic" structuring of

heaven and its orders of angels with the "organic" metaphors of love as the "plante of pees" (152) or the "leef upon lynde" (156).

It is hard to argue against love, and in fact this second part of Holy Church's sermon is one of the most sublimely lyrical passages in the poem. In one sense, its very beauty is the problem. The metaphorical structure of the passage undermines the surface structure of the argument. On the surface, Holy Church wants to establish that Truth and Love go together, that *Deus caritas* supports her theme "Truth is best." But the tropes, by creating this strong pattern of opposition, call into question whether the hermeneutics of definition, Holy Church's notion of authoritative, truthful interpretation, can coexist with the activities of love. The self-confessed inability of Dame Study to come to terms with Theology's mystical teachings about love (X.182ff.) perhaps constitutes a reprise of this theme in a different context.

By the time one works through Holy Church's discourse on Truth, uppercase Truth is more or less specifically connected via lowercase propositional truth with issues of textual hermeneutics. On the other hand, if one discounts the scriptural context of her text *Deus caritas,* Holy Church's discourse about Love does not explicitly connect Love with issues of textual interpretation. Just as there is a hermeneutics of definition, however, there is an opposing hermeneutics of mediation; this opposition can be mapped onto the rhetorical opposition in Holy Church's tropes. Holy Church does not explicitly reject the new money economy either, but because her hermeneutics of definition is implicitly at odds with the hermeneutics of mediation, critics read her sermon as plumping for feudalism. James Simpson, for example, argues that she adopts a "reactionary position with regard to the kind of society presented in the Prologue; she anchors her sense of theological truth and justice in specific social forms which can be described as feudal" (37). In the hermeneutics of definition, one divides and clarifies the parts. In the hermeneutics of mediation, one puts together separate parts into a coherent whole. The two hermeneutics are, more accurately speaking, two different moments in the hermeneutic circle.

Whether Holy Church herself is aware of that is open to question; that she confuses the dreamer by implying seemingly irreconcilable modes of interpretation is beyond doubt. Is interpretation, upon which everything seems to depend for Holy Church, a matter of sorting things out or a matter of putting things together? Truth seems to demand the former, Love the latter. The dreamer begins by asking Holy Church the hermeneutic question: "madame, what [may] this [be] to meene?" (11). In the course of Holy Church's sermon, Langland suggests by his puns on *meene* that there are two ways of "meaning." One kind of "meaning" is "making mean," in the Middle English not necessarily with any negative connotation: that is, making lesser, subordinating, what I have called sorting things out. God "means" this way when he sets the archangels "over his meene meynee" (108). The other kind of meaning is "being a mean," being in between, mediating, what I have called putting things together. The mayor "means" this way when he serves as a "meene" between the king and the commons (160). As custodian of propositional truth, Holy Church speaks strongly via the trope of knighthood for a hermeneutics of definition. As proponent of love, she implies the necessity for a hermeneutics of mediation, via a family of tropes rhetorically opposed to knighthood. The dissonance raises the disturbing political and theological question of whether Holy Church can still claim to speak authoritatively for a society based on the new money economy, since her notion of truth seems to rest on a hermeneutics of social reality that is fundamentally dependent on the vanishing feudal economy.

But the real issue here, as I have been arguing, is not political or religious but hermeneutic. Or rather, political and religious issues for Langland inevitably slide over into hermeneutic issues. Many of the recurring debates of *Piers Plowman* can be mapped onto the axis of the opposition between the two hermeneutics that contend in Holy Church's discourse: justice that divides the guilty from the innocent versus mercy that accepts the guilty as innocent; works that divide the deserving from the undeserving versus faith that treats the grasshopper and the ant alike; dogmatics that divides the heretic from the orthodox versus mysticism that unites God's children with him in a space where the strictures of orthodoxy are irrelevant; political "absolutism" that divides the social continuum into hierarchies versus "democracy" that aims at unifying the body politic by equitable distribution of power. Thus, although *Piers Plowman* might get beyond Holy Church's limited understanding of feudalism as a political phenomenon, it never gets beyond the hermeneutic problems posed by that understanding. Langland succeeds in Passus I in establishing his two main concerns, which are reflected in the dreamer's first two questions to Holy Church. His questions are about meaning and money, in that order. Both questions are ill formed, probably improperly motivated, and preliminary. But the first is a question about interpretation, and the second is a question about social justice. These issues, in various forms, obsess Langland throughout *Piers Plowman*. But a more important observation for me is that the structure of Holy Church's sermon shows how for Langland the two issues are really one, and that the one issue is the quest for a viable hermeneutic.

LADY MEED

The appearance of Lady Meed at the beginning of Passus II marks the beginning of a new movement in *Piers Plowman*. Lady Meed has proven to be problematic, to say the least, and I will not add much here to the welter of conflicting critical opinions. I do want to consider her episode briefly, however, insofar as it serves also to complete the episode of Holy Church. At the end of Passus I, Holy Church announces her intention to take her leave, and so her remarks about Lady Meed appear not as part of a set sermon, but as more extemporaneous and therefore perhaps more directly revealing of her inner necessities.

The first line of Passus II echoes the line in Passus I where the dreamer, finally realizing who Holy Church is, falls on his knees and asks for her grace: "I courbed on my knees and cried hire of grace" (I.79, II.1). Langland thus elevates the dreamer's first question in Passus II to the same level of rhetorical and dramatic importance as his earlier question about how to save his soul. This time he asks, "Kenne me by som craft to knowe the false" (4). Presumably, Holy Church has just explained how to know Truth through love. But the dreamer, characteristically, drops back a step. Not really understanding Holy Church's mystical discourse about Love, he wants to go back to the issue of intellectually discriminating the true from the false. The dramatic pattern here repeats that of the earlier dialogue where the dreamer asks about the meaning of his vision. He receives a clear label for the tower; but then he asks about money, and receives an answer that he is not ready to understand. Therefore, he goes back to the vision, and asks for a label for the donjon. Another earlier pattern is repeated here as well. Holy Church seems to be winding up her sermon in Passus I before she talks about love (I.134ff.), and she resumes her discourse—somewhat petulantly—upon prodding by the dreamer. At the end of Passus I, Holy Church at first seems to be taking her leave (I.208–9), but then remains to identify False, again at the request of the dreamer. At this point in his experience, the dreamer seems to be looking not for parables or mystical poetry, but for intellectual distinctions based on sharp binary oppositions. He is caught up in the hermeneutics of definition. Langland's satirical point seems to be that the Church tends to provide believers with various sorts of ecclesiastical discourse, and then to leave the believers in the lurch. Holy Church is an unexceptionable teacher in every way but in paying attention to what her pupils really need. But if believers do not get from the Church what they need, neither is that entirely the fault of the Church. The believers themselves tend to want the wrong kinds of things, and to be impervious to alternative discourses.

And even the dreamer's lust for intellectual understanding is soon forgotten. When he glimpses Lady Meed, he is carried away by the beauty of her clothes in a moment of folly and forgetfulness worthy of Bartholomew Cokes at the Fair: "Hire array me ravysshed, swich richesse saugh I nevere" (II.17). Ironically, the dreamer himself becomes one of the *transgressores* in James 2:9 whom the knights are supposed to tie up—one who "shows partiality" to those who are finely dressed. The violence of Holy Church's outburst against Meed seems justified, if for no other reason, because of the ease with which Meed succeeds in distracting her pupil from his moral reflections.

Holy Church's outburst sometimes sounds, again, petulant in tone: "I oughte ben hyere than [heo]—I kam of a bettre" (28). It is also conceptually muddy at the level of the allegory: Meed is the daughter of "Fals . . . that hath a fikel tonge" (25), but she is to be married to "Fals Fikel-tonge" (41); and later Theology seems to think that "Mede is muliere, of Amendes engendred" (119). The branches of Meed's family tree could perhaps be laboriously untangled in various ways, but my point is only that Holy Church's anger at Meed terminates in at least pedagogical murk. That is, even trying to talk about Meed begins subtly to corrupt Holy Church's essential function: custodian of clear propositional truths.

The Meed episode seems extraordinarily rich, in the sense that Meed can be thought to represent many different things, and can be connected in various ways to most of what happens subsequently in the poem. But if one reads the episode looking backward, as it were, as a completion of the episode of Holy Church, then I think that one will read Lady Meed much as Mary Carruthers does. Among all the things that Meed might (or does) represent, she represents a very powerful word (Carruthers 45–47, 63). Meed is, among other things, a *term* that occurs in various discourses to justify various kinds of behaviors. In the debate about Meed's betrothal to Conscience (III.120ff.), the issue is essentially what *meed* means—especially in Conscience's distinction between the two "manners" of meed (III.230ff.), which develops in the C-text into the notorious "grammatical analogy." Langland certainly in the event has failed to clarify the B-text by means of this analogy, if that is what he meant to do. But the point is that he looks to grammar to explain the nature of Meed. Meed is to be understood as a word is understood.

Considered as a word, Meed represents the antithesis of the kind of language Holy Church needs in order to make her claims of authority stick. It is tempting to hear one of Langland's bilingual puns in Meed's name: English *mede* and Latin *medium*—that which is in the middle, the mediating. As all the rascals ride to Westminster, in fact, we find "Mede in the middes" (II.185), and the cleric who comforts Meed in Passus III "Took Mede bi the myddel" (10). There might not be any other way to take her. She represents a structure of mediation. As such, she embodies the very ambiguity that underlies Holy Church's own sermon. Lady Meed bothers Holy Church so much because Meed, the personification of all that Holy Church hates, therefore represents what is repressed in Holy Church herself. Mediation cannot be all bad, because Holy Church herself expresses Love in metaphors of mediation. And yet it is not clear how the hermeneutics of mediation, played out on the level of social organization, can be consistent with the hermeneutics of definition that justifies feudalism and Holy Church's moral authority. Thus Meed can appear to be evil. Sometimes "bribery" seems a good translation. Certain things about her even associate her with Langland's apocalyptic themes. She is dressed like the Whore of Babylon (see Schmidt's note, 415; Robertson and Huppé 49–54). Langland's later description of

Antichrist's advent (XX.53–55) recalls things Conscience says about Meed (III.140), and critics have identified her with earthly "tresor" (Alford, "Design" 37) and with the institution of maintenance (Baldwin, *Government* 24–38).

On the other hand, Meed defends herself by arguing that the world cannot work without money: "No wight, as I wene, withouten Mede may libbe!" (III.227). Theology thinks Meed can be good if only she has the right husband—that is, when *mede* refers to the just hire of the laborer (II.119ff.). Conscience himself distinguishes between "mesurable hire" (III.256) and "mede mesurelees" (246). He objects to meed taken "To mayntene mysdoers" (247), or meed taken by priests for singing masses (252–54). The interesting word here is *measureless,* not least because the word recalls the structure of Holy Church's argument that attempts to subsume the concept of "measure" under the concept of "truth." Conscience argues that there is something that some people call "meed" that does not truly match services rendered, and this meed corrupts as spin doctoring corrupts. Conscience's argument with Theology seems to be strictly over terminology: Theology is willing to use the word *mede* to refer to measurable hire, and Conscience is not. But the argument is not a quibble, for all the reasons that Holy Church would give to substantiate her implicit claim that propositional truth—a matter of words—is inseparable from social justice.

Not surprisingly in this context, critical opinion is divided on the question of whether Meed is *inherently* evil. But to argue about the inherent nature of Meed might be a mistake in the first place. Langland's point might be precisely that Meed is not *inherently* anything. The violent repulsion that Holy Church feels for Meed comes from the impossibility of fixing the term in fourteenth-century discourse. Meed thus has the potential to become the antithesis of everything that matters to Holy Church. Meed can become a floating signifier, the representation of something as a medium of exchange where no value has in fact been exchanged, and where the value that ought to attach to the human relationships mediated by money in fact attaches to the money itself. As Carruthers puts it, Lady Meed "epitomizes the semantic looseness and ambivalence which is the image of the False" (45).

When Lady Meed quotes *"Honorem adquiret qui dat munera"* (III.336),

Conscience sarcastically replies with the other half of the verse: *"Animam autem aufert accipientium"* (350). Conscience compares Lady Meed to the woman who read *"omnia probate"* and forgot to turn over the leaf to read *"Quod bonum est tenete"* (338ff.). "Try everything" sounds like an expression of strict pluralism or even nihilism, a maxim for life in a world of floating signifiers, whereas "hold to what is good" is a maxim for life in a world neatly sorted out by the hermeneutics of definition. The debate is, of course, on the simplest level a debate about Latin literacy, about who gets to interpret authoritative texts, and about how to turn in the hermeneutic circle (Meed, line 332: "I kan no Latyn? . . . Clerkes wite the sothe!"). But the deep danger of "mede mesurelees," the floating signifier, is its corrupting effect on the individual soul, and therefore on the social institutions that are supposed to place human souls in just and equitable relations. The episode of Peace and Wrong illustrates the danger. Peace sues for redress of the many outrages that Wrong has committed (IV.47–60). But Lady Meed smoothes things over with a present of gold, and Peace himself begs the King to have mercy on Wrong: Meed, he says, "hath maad myne amendes" (103). Overwhelmed by mediation, Peace has forgotten the principles that justified his complaint in the first place. We might say that he contradicts himself, or even that he cancels himself. Allegorically, if wrong goes unpunished, then peace cannot exist (compare Simpson 59).

Read as a commentary on the episode of Holy Church, therefore, the episode of Lady Meed throws certain ideas into sharp relief. First, the episode of Lady Meed confirms, without explicitly saying, that Holy Church's discourse constitutes a reading of the social organism as text. Holy Church's tropes of mediation become clearer in retrospect as interpretive moves in tension with the hermeneutics implied in her tropes of definition. Precisely when we look at the social organism as text, the phenomenon of the floating signifier becomes visible as such. Meed as word becomes a problem from the perspective of the interpretive system articulated by Holy Church. In that sense, then, the episode of Holy Church generates the episode of Lady Meed. Holy Church summons her demon opposite, thus more clearly defining herself.

Second, it seems clear that Holy Church is in fact failing to deal adequately with the new urban money economy. The cliché "Render unto

Caesar" is not by itself going to prove a satisfactory answer to the dreamer's questions, or to the reader's questions, about money and its relation to social justice. The failure here is primarily hermeneutic. Holy Church cannot clearly match her hermeneutics of definition with the hermeneutics of pure mediation implied in the semiotic system where money is the only signifier and sometimes the only signified. Here we have an example of Langland's recursiveness, in which the episode of Lady Meed counts as an interpretation not only of Holy Church's doctrine, but also of Holy Church's interpretive activity.

Third, the hermeneutic problem goes very deep, involving but also transcending Langland's satirical commentary on fourteenth-century society and the Church. The intellectual's lust for propositional truth gets in the way of understanding love, because the intellectual's focus on the hermeneutics of definition obscures the necessity for the other moment of interpretation, the hermeneutics of mediation. The dramatic interaction between the dreamer and Holy Church thus constitutes, among other things, Langland's interpretation of the dreamer's interpretive activity.

BIBLIOGRAPHICAL ESSAY 2.1

As I have already indicated, much of the critical debate about Passus I has to do with how definitive the discourse of Holy Church is. John Alford, for example, believes that her answer is *the* answer: "Here in a nutshell is the poem. 'How may I save my soul?'—this is the central question. 'Truth is best'—this is the answer, and virtually all of *Piers Plowman* is an inquiry into its ramifications" ("Design" 35). R. E. Kaske has argued that the speech of Holy Church provides the structural principle for the whole poem ("Holy Church's Speech and the Structure of *Piers Plowman*"). On the other hand, I have already quoted Mary Carruthers on the subject of the failure of Holy Church's rhetoric. Britton Harwood too is more interested in "what Holy Church may be leaving out" (5). Harwood's learned discussion of the dreamer's need for intuitive knowledge and of Holy Church's failure to provide it (5ff.) establishes theological and philosophical contexts for Langland's reflections on the nature and importance of propositional truth.

As is often the case, my own position is closer to Gillian Rudd's.

Rudd in a way takes the middle ground in this debate about Holy Church, arguing that this initial scene of instruction is an example of the "theme of lack of understanding between users of different discourses" that "recurs throughout the poem" (14). Rudd distinguishes "the divine, ontological *logos,* usually termed in Modern English 'the Word,' and the more everyday perception of language as an essentially human construct, . . . *verbum*" (6). From these two notions of the word come two discourses, which collide in the episode of Holy Church. Will speaks of treasure, for example, in the earthly signification, and Holy Church tries to lift the discourse into the realm of the *logos.* But Holy Church knows what she is doing: "[I]t is possible to regard this passage as the first, subtle introduction of the *via negativa* in which the very uselessness of words is exploited, as their inability to express the divine paradoxically creates an apprehension of it" (13). While I endorse Rudd's point about colliding discourses—indeed, that is perhaps the main point of my book—I do not follow Rudd all the way to the conclusion that Holy Church consciously and subtly leads the dreamer into the *via negativa.* The dramatic interactions that I have detailed seem to me to count especially against the conclusion that the dreamer actually gains an apprehension of the divine from the encounter. He gets in his own way too much. Furthermore, as I have suggested, I think that Holy Church in this particular moment of the personification allegory does not represent the Church *sub specie aeternitatis.* As she herself says, she is the Church as the dreamer ought to know the Church, the Church as *cultus* in an individual's life.

Clearly, though, what Holy Church says is very important; and it is possible that Langland expects his readers to understand things the dreamer does not understand. The concept of "truth" dominates the discourse of Holy Church. As Mary Clemente Davlin has pointed out ("Tower"), the architecture of the tower on the hill in the dreamer's vision would have been associated in Langland's time with the architecture of a church—thus it tells us a great deal about Holy Church that her name for the one who dwells in the tower is Truth. She is implying, on one level, that Truth is to be found in the Church. But one of the interpretive problems here is to explain how the different uses of *truth* in the language are related to each other. Edward Vasta connects heavenly truth with earthly truth by defining *treuthe* in the context of Holy Church's sermon as "the likeness between man and God resulting from the unanimity of their wills" (22). The *Deus caritas* text belongs with this complex of ideas because the text suggests the "doctrine of deification" given wide expression by the Cistercians: "In essence, this doctrine teaches that through a conformity of man's will with God's, man becomes like God and is thereby deified" (27). James Simpson distinguishes three types of truth: literary, theological, and social (17–38). In the theological sense, truth is "the most profound existential reality," and this sense is related to another sense of truth "which implies conformity with the standards of that reality" (28). In the "earthly sphere," Holy Church "sees the defence of 'truthe' as essentially the enactment of justice," which is the job of kings and knights (29).

John Alford gets at the notion of "truth" in a way more congenial to my project here. Alford argues that "Langland accepts implicitly the medieval identification of language and nature and treats the evidence of grammar with utmost respect" ("Grammatical" 754). Holy Church means by *truth* "primarily fidelity or obedience" (756). For Langland, truth "is not only the political virtue par excellence—governing the relation between king and subject, master and servant, and the like—but it is also the fundamental principle of grammar. Like society, speech depends upon *fidelitas,* each constituent part observing its proper relation to the others" (756). Thus the propositional truth that Holy Church guards is necessarily entailed in theological and political truth. Or, as Daniel Pigg puts it, Holy Church "has a hierarchical and interconnected conception of truth in society. The presence of truth in the world generates the concept of society" (35).

My reading differs from Alford's, however, in my suspicion that Holy Church's notion of propositional truth, as dependent upon her hermeneutics of definition, might ultimately stand in tension with her notion of love. Simpson, in fact, implies something similar. He describes the passage in the sermon about Love as "mysterious," and says that it "suggests the radical potency of love by describing Christ's incarnation in unfamiliar, paradoxical poetic images"; but "if this is what Truthe can tell about love, then its metaphorical density suggests that Truthe, or justice, contains meanings which are not open to rational analysis" (28–29). With the mention of "rational analysis," we come to the nub of the issue. Rational analysis should refer to the exercise of the faculty of reason, and reason for Langland should mean, as Alford has argued, two things: (1) the "eternal law as manifest in the *lex naturalis,*" and (2) the human faculty that apprehends that order ("Reason" 206). Rational analysis is what Holy Church aims at in her position as custodian of propositional truth; and rational analysis on the social level is precisely what knighthood makes possible in the feudal system. Where is love in all of this? If the truth of love is beyond rational analysis, then Holy Church will not be able to perform her definitive function of constructing true propositions about love. And there is also a hint that she will prove unqualified to comment authoritatively on the new urban money economy.

It is debatable whether the things I find strange about Holy Church's discourse are in fact strange, or even whether they are meant by Langland to seem strange. Siegfried Wenzel analyzes Holy Church's discourse as a medieval sermon. Medieval sermons, often generated from concordances and preachers' commonplace books, often depend on complex intertextuality involving not only scriptural passages whose connections are not obvious, but also commentaries on those passages. Intellectual leaps that seem excruciatingly strange to twentieth-century readers, then, might have seemed quite normal to fourteenth-century audiences. Considerable critical energy has gone into making Holy Church's sermon seem less strange, by retracing the lost connections between ideas. Some of the clearest work of that sort remains that of T. P. Dunning on the A-text. As I have already mentioned, Dunning explains how *Deus caritas* is connected to the thesis "Truth is best" through 1 John 4:6–8 (*Interpretation* 29–30). He also argues via a learned discussion of medieval ideas about knights and angels that the passage about knighthood is not digressive: Holy Church "has just set up before the Dreamer the ideal of truthfulness in word and simplicity in work—the ideal of the just man in the Middle Ages" (31), and "the primary purpose of kings and knights is to help the righteous man to lead a life in justice and truth" (34). To show that all of these ideas can eventually be connected by intertextual analysis, however, is not the same as showing that the *rhetorical* movement of the poem is not digressive or jolting.

Clearly there are points to be gotten from Holy Church's sermon. It is just that the dreamer does not always get them, and we as readers have to restore connections more or less laboriously. I am arguing, again, not from the exegetical tradition, but from the dramatic interactions that I believe I detect between the dreamer and Holy Church.

For me to get into the question of editorial emendation at B.I.98ff. would certainly be to play the fool who rushes in where angels fear to tread. To argue that Kane-Donaldson and Schmidt should have let the ordering of the lines in the manuscripts stand, because that ordering more obviously indicates a digressive movement and therefore more clearly supports my interpretation, would seem embarrassingly circular. But to adopt the order of the Z and A manuscripts, as Schmidt does, with the notation that "on balance" this order "is preferable" (365), *could* conceal an equally embarrassing circularity. *Why* preferable? If the reason has anything to do with the rhetorical coherence of Holy Church's argument, then the editorial decision has been made on the basis of a presupposition that Langland is trying to depict coherence. I am far from qualified to question this or any other editorial decision. But I do want to note in passing that such interpretive issues immediately get snarled in the incredibly tangled nest of textual problems that makes a hypertext edition of *Piers Plowman* seem the only reasonable alternative for postmodern scholars of Langland.

Finally, I wish to offer a few words about Lady Meed. This episode has attracted more than its share of commentary and controversy, and I cannot summarize the entire critical tradition here. Most critics who talk about Meed, as I have indicated, want to settle whether she is good or bad. Critical opinion on this question runs the gamut from Robertson and Huppé's discussion of Meed as the Whore of Babylon (49–54), through A. G. Mitchell's treatment of Meed as morally neutral, to David Benson's argument that, although Meed is evil from "any purely rational perspective" (197), nevertheless she prefigures Christ in her "human warmth and indiscriminate generosity" (205). This critical approach is not inherently unreasonable, but is, I think, misdirected. If the whole episode of Lady Meed is in fact about how a term functions in discourses of justification, then we will not be able to determine an inherent nature for Meed.

In her article exploring the pitfalls of treating Meed as an allegory either of a particular medieval woman (Alice Perrers) or of medieval female agency, Stephanie Trigg observes that "the allegory demands to be decoded in medieval 'historicist' terms, which have the uncanny effect of presenting the attitudes that sustain them as immune from historical change" (26). Trigg is worried because treating Meed as any one thing, whether a person or an idea, risks affirming patriarchal essentialism, "the sex/gender system of Western patriarchy with its attendant stereotypes and decorums of, and questions about, femininity (and masculinity)" (26). I am worried because I think Meed is first of all a word, and words, especially the big words, rarely mean only one thing.

I have already quoted Mary Carruthers, who thinks of Meed as a powerful word, and who points out that *mede* is already a pun in Middle English: it can refer either to bribery or to a just reward (45ff.). Other critics who tend to focus on Meed as a term include James Simpson, who provides an interesting discussion of how Meed's semantic ambiguity functions to drive the development of the personification allegory (40–49), and Pamela Raabe, for whom Meed represents a poor signifier—Meed is "a greatly dissimilar similitude for spiritual meed" (31), and since "all earthly things, including people, are relative truths and possess only a secondary reality as imitations" (29), Meed's failure to signify properly cuts her off from reality. To be real, for things and people as for words, is to signify. As floating signifier, Meed strictly speaking has no reality of which good or evil could be predicated.

Puns are thick on the ground in the passages I have been discussing, particularly in the Meed episode. The possibility of punning depends upon dispersed reference, the ability of "the same word" to refer to different things. Langland thus reminds us that we have not yet escaped from Babylon. Carruthers's point about the pun on *mede* is already a point about how dispersed reference can cause confusion with serious social consequences. Mary Clemente Davlin (*Game of Heuene*), P. M. Kean, and A. V. C. Schmidt (in both *"Lele Wordes"* and *Clerkly Maker*) present extended treatments of Langland's punning.

James Hala offers an especially detailed and impressive reading of punning in the Meed episode. Hala says that the pervasive punning suggests the morally neutral nature of Meed—in the Christian context, her "immoral neutrality" (119). She is a whore, as words can turn into whores. A central pun in the episode is on *tail/tale*. Langland means "to enlighten an audience concerning the dangerous polysemy of all language," where "all words are in a sense puns since they are capable of radically different uses (or usages)" (99). The rhetoric Langland portrays, "founded upon the polysemy of all human language, is a kind of divining rod that points either to Truth or falsehood, depending upon who is holding it" (100). "For a poet attempting to explicate the uses and abuses of this rhetoric, the pun becomes the principal trope" (101). The nature of Langland's project, then, explains why Meed's significance cannot "be understood in terms of a static, finite concept such as cupidity or bribery" (101). She is an "unattached signifier," a *"bele parole"* as opposed to *"lele wordes,"* a *"signum"* without a *res"* (102). Hala's approach explains how Holy Church's commitment to propositional truth in a sense generates Lady Meed as Holy Church's own shadow, and how both episodes look back to the Babylonian confusion of the Prologue.

Anima

INTERPRETIVE FRUSTRATIONS

Passus XV of Langland's B-text is the second longest passus, and it represents one of Langland's characteristically frustrating performances. Here the dreamer meets Anima, or "Soul," who discourses abundantly on the corruption of the clergy. The initial frustration, as I have mentioned before, is that Anima in Passus XV is not the same as Anima elsewhere in the poem. In Latin and in Passus IX (lines 6, 16, and 23, for example), Anima is feminine, whereas in Passus XV he is masculine. In Passus IX the feminine Anima is silent, whereas in Passus XV the male figure is nothing if not loquacious. Anima in Passus IX is Anima as Wit conceives of her, according to the way Wit interprets the world. Malcolm Godden traces the two medieval theories of the soul that give rise to these differing conceptions of Anima (117–18); readers are left to decide which conception Langland endorses, or whether he endorses either.

In Passus XV, Anima, like bishops (XV.40–43), has many names. The whole soul is called *Anima* only in the Latin following line 39. The dreamer is invited to choose the name by which to call this instructor:

"now thow myght chese / How thow coveitest to calle me, now thow knowest alle my names" (38–39). Significantly, the dreamer does not choose, but allows all of the names to remain open possibilities. This grabbag of names creates another potential frustration: as a dramatic character in the personification allegory, Anima is aptly described by Elizabeth Kirk as "colorless yet chameleonlike" (159). Also in Passus XV, of course, the dreamer names himself: "my name is Longe Wille" (152). The name Will corresponds with the faculty of the soul that in Passus XVI–XVIII of the C-text, as Liberum Arbitrium, takes over both the list of the soul's names and the dramatic functions corresponding with Anima's functions in the B-text. At some level, then, Passus XV of the B-text seems to be about names and naming.

Another frustration is that Anima seems to have an obsession, or at least a hobbyhorse. He discourses at enormous length on the subject of clerical corruption. In a pattern that recalls the dreamer's interactions with Holy Church, the dreamer tries to nudge Anima back into channels that run more in the direction of the dreamer's own concerns. When Anima talks about the grief attendant upon the death of almsgivers, Anima mentions charity in passing:

> Ac for goode men, God woot, greet doel men maken,
> And bymeneth goode meteyyveres, and in mynde hem haveth
> In preieres and in penaunces and in parfit charite.
>
> (146–48)

There is perhaps an interesting pun here on *bymeneth:* those who benefited from the charity of the dead almsgivers both "lament" and "signify" those benefactors in their prayers—as if by giving alms we mystically unite our personalities with the personalities of our beneficiaries, whose lives then come to stand for our own. I believe that this idea of the Christian community turns out to be the most important idea of Anima's discourse. But the dreamer, as someone who periodically needs alms and who has the intellectual's pathological fascination with money, is more interested in the subject of almsgiving itself: "'What is charite?' quod I tho" (149). The dreamer jumps in as if seizing the chance to deflect Anima from his harangue. Anima responds at some length. But the discourse on charity fails to attain escape velocity. Anima falls inexorably back into the bottomless pit of clerical corruption.

Godden describes (maybe a little unhelpfully) the rhetorical problem I am trying to articulate: Anima's speech, Godden says, "is a rambling speech covering a variety of issues, and Langland is clearly at times speaking in his own voice, forgetful of the nature of the supposed speaker" (117). This response seems to me to overlook the dramatic interactions between the dreamer and Anima, making the dreamer into an obtuse Platonic interlocutor whose only function is to relieve the monotony of the Socratic exposition. But as I have said before and will say again, I think there is more to the dreamer than that. The dreamer here at least exhibits persistence. At the beginning of Passus XVI, he insists again that he wants to know what charity is: "Ac yit am I in a weer what charite is to mene" (XVI.3). This line in context sounds like a gentle rebuke: "All of what you have said is very interesting and valuable, but you have not yet answered my question." We might remember the dreamer's earlier rebuke (as I read the passage) to Holy Church (I.138–39) for failing to connect her text *Deus caritas* with her theme. The dreamer's persistence pays off this time, and he gets what he wants—not in the form of discourse from Anima, but in the form of his vision of the Tree of Charity.

Be all of that as it may, even if we read a subtler dreamer with an agenda and something of an edge, the interpretive problem remains. It is hard to pry Anima away from gnawing at the bone of his favorite subject. But why should this particular figure, Anima, be so obsessive about clerical corruption? If not a dead horse—Langland's horses seem never to die—this topos is at least well thrashed by this point in the poem. Clerical corruption and related themes appear, for instance, in the Prologue (for example, 58–67, 78–111); in the discourse of Holy Church (I.195–203); off and on throughout the episode of Lady Meed (for example, allegorically in the appearances and frequent mentions of Simony, in the clergy who comfort and confess Meed in III.3ff., in Conscience's and Reason's speeches in III.142–52 and IV.119–25); in the confessions of Wrath (V.135–66) and Sloth (V.416–22); throughout Passus X (the passus perhaps most reminiscent of Passus XV), mingled in the satirical speech of Dame Study (17–136) and prevalent in Clergy's discourse on Dobest (258–329) and the dreamer's presumptuous reply (371–475); in the satire on the friars in XI.54–83; in the blast at avaricious and ignorant priests in XI.281–318; in the dreamer's reflections in XIII.7–13; and in the dramatic portrayal of the Doctor at the feast of Clergy in Passus XIII. We may also oppose to these passages Ymaginatif's great defense of clergy (XII.64ff.). One might have hoped that Anima, as the combined powers of the human faculties distributed earlier in the allegory, would have found a more original or apposite topic, or at least would have made more obvious progress.

A related question is why Langland himself should want to insert a new and extended grumble on an old topic at just this point. If one credits the rubrics in the manuscripts, a major division comes here: the end of Dowel and the beginning of Dobet (Schmidt 246n). But as with most matters concerning the structure of *Piers Plowman,* critics disagree about dividing the poem here. In the "Introduction" to his edition, Schmidt argues for a major division, on the grounds that the episode of Haukyn in Passus XIV seems to conclude a movement (Schmidt xxxiii–xxxiv), and Kirk says that Anima "provides the conclusion to *Dowel* and the beginning of *Dobet,* and . . . stands in much the same relation to the later *Dowel* as Imagination to the earlier and Holy Church to the landscape of the Prologue" (160). As I have indicated, I think there is much to be gained by looking at the episode of Anima as in some sense refiguring the episode of Holy Church. On the other side, Robert Worth Frank puzzles over whether Dobet really begins at the beginning of Passus XV (*Scheme* 78–79), and John Alford apparently denies that Dowel ends with Passus XIV ("Design" 51–52). Without getting any further into this controversy, I want only to point out that the controversy itself is a symptom of critical frustration at trying to determine exactly how Anima's discourse on clerical corruption is supposed to advance the presumed argument of the poem.

I want to get at these interpretive frustrations, as usual, by assuming that the best description of the poem is as the locus of colliding interpretive systems, so that what any apparently authoritative figure preaches is always to be understood as an index of that particular figure's nature and compulsions. The poem is dramatic. "Soul" here is not necessarily or not only Langland's own soul, but is instead a particular picture of the nature of the human soul, a picture that performs a dramatic function in the "plot." Anima interprets as he does because of what he is, and not because he is serving as "a convenient mouthpiece for Langland's most sustained diatribe against the evils of his age" (Schmidt xli).

Primarily, I want to continue here the main argument of this book, namely, that Langland as a fourteenth-century intellectual is obsessed with written texts to the point that for him the quest for salvation becomes inseparable from the quest for a viable hermeneutic. I would ease some of the interpretive frustrations I have identified by looking at Passus XV as being somehow about *reading*: that is, about the construing of texts, and the construing of the world as if it were a text.

THE ONTOLOGICAL QUESTION

Let me begin with what might be called the *ontological* question of Passus XV. From the perspective of the soul as pictured here, what is there? There is, first (and this means first in terms both of logical priority and of rhetorical presentation), the activity of the soul itself. And what is the mode of being of the soul? The soul as pictured in Passus XV seems to be in fact a set of functions or a system of relations. Anima has many names, depending upon what he is doing:

> The whiles I quykke the cors . . . called am I *Anima;*
> And whan I wilne and wolde, *Animus* ich hatte;
> And for that I kan and knowe, called am I *Mens,* "Thoughte" . . .
>
> (23–25)

And so on. The activity of the soul is characterized by *intentionality*—that is, in all of these activities the soul has an *object,* and the nature of the soul is determined (named) according to the nature of the object. The soul quickens the body, it wills or knows something or other, it senses what people say, it loves God and his creatures, and so on.

Even the conscience, which we tend to think of as a "feeling" or quality inhering in the substantial soul, is here (as normally in the poem) a broader intentional faculty, according to the medieval understanding of conscience. It is the faculty that chooses among good and bad actions: "whan I chalange or chalange noght, chepe or refuse, / Thanne am I Conscience ycalled, Goddes clerk and his notarie" (31–32). The metaphor of conscience as clerk and notary seems to suggest simultaneously that God causes the world to be written as a text for the human soul to construe (the conscience as witness of God's creative acts), and that the human conscience constructs the soul as a text for God to read (the conscience as recorder of human ethical decisions). Through the faculty of conscience, the human text is written in the act of reading the divine text. The conscience is not just a feeling, but the name for the human faculty of interacting intentionally (interpretively) with situations.

The last clause in the list appears to be an interesting exception to this general rule about the names of Anima: "whan I flee fro the flessh and forsake the careyne, / Thanne am I spirit spechelees—and *Spiritus* thanne ich hatte" (35–36). This sounds a little like the substantial Cartesian soul, or even like a ghost. On the other hand, the Latin quotation that comes almost immediately afterward, and that Anima is presumably translating, defines the soul rather as a function, and etymologically: "*dum spirat, Spiritus est*" (39). Anima's translation actually reverses the Latin. The Latin says that the soul is called spirit "while it breathes," whereas Anima's translation says that the soul is called spirit after it leaves the flesh, or perhaps at the precise moment of leaving the flesh—that is, at the moment of death or postmortem. Anima seems to reserve the name *spirit* to refer to something hypothesized but impossible to experience on earth: the soul as "speechless," beyond human language, which means, by definition, removed from human experience. As far as possible experience goes, the soul is always characterized by intentionality, which turns out to be inseparable from the linguistic capacity. We can hypothesize, but cannot experience or describe, the soul as existing apart from the body.

In general, the picture of the soul here is not that of the substantial Cartesian soul, but rather a picture of a reality that acquires a determinate nature for humans only as a pole of some relation with some intentional object. As implied in the word *sotil* (XV.12), the soul itself is not subject to direct inspection (Simpson 172n). To put it crudely, our consciousness is at any given moment just what we happen to be thinking about then.

But to picture the soul this way is to picture it as having a mode of being very like that of a grammar. A grammar, strictly speaking, constitutes a set of relations that is instantiated only in actual words that stand in those relations. Where there are utterances, *subject* and *predicate* and *object* are real names for words; but apart from utterances, these grammatical categories have no determinate nature. One may persuade oneself that this is true by trying to define the grammatical categories without providing examples. On the other side, words apart from these grammatical relations cannot be *construed*. Without syntax there are no sentences, but only strings of disconnected virtual signs, just as there could be no meaningful or even coherent human experience apart from the unity of the various human faculties—if sense did not connect with reason did not connect with will, and so on.

The description of the soul as a grammar rests on a more fundamental assumption about grammar. If the soul in its activity of knowing resembles a grammar, that is because grammar reflects the reality to be known. This account of grammar is not a modern invention. John Alford has shown how widespread the notion was in the Middle Ages, appearing not only as a metaphor in poetry and preaching ("Grammatical" 729–30), but also as serious epistemological and moral philosophy (736–50). As Alford says, "The prevailing view is expressed by John of Salisbury: 'While grammar has developed to some extent, and indeed mainly, as an invention of man, still it imitates nature, from which it partly derives its origin. Furthermore, it tends, as far as possible, to conform to nature in all respects'" ("Grammatical" 736; John of Salisbury quoted from *Metalogicon,* trans. Daniel D. McGarry [Berkeley, 1962], 39). Alford observes that "[t]he pattern is set by St. Augustine," whose immense authority grounds the position that "[a]lthough language is manmade, God has nevertheless established a profoundly real as well as conventional relation between certain words and things, just as he has brought about a real and not coincidental relation between certain historical events, mystically joined, as a sign to the thing signified" ("Grammatical" 737). Similarly, in his discussion of how John Wyclif's "theory of real being depends fundamentally on language," Jesse M. Gellrich talks about the "venerated medieval premise that language and nature obey the same laws" (*Discourse* 86–87).

It is worth quoting at this point from Jeffrey Huntsman's discussion of the medieval "speculative" grammarians, called *Modistae* because their studies

> centered on the several manners or *modes* of language and thought, [where] the word *modus* . . . had its basic meaning "way" or "manner": thus it refers to a process of relation, not a category of being. (82–83)

[The Modistae] concerned themselves with the functional categories of language, its abstract forms and relations. (85)

These philosophical grammars attempted to achieve a level of explanation that was ... ultimately applicable to the organization of the world in general. For this reason, [this] type of philosophical grammar was called speculative grammar, ... for it attempted to mirror the structure of the universe. (64)

Two points here are particularly interesting to me: first, the notion of grammar as relational and therefore necessarily involving intentionality; and second, the idea that the structure of grammar reflects the structure of reality, including the reality of the human soul. Thus, as Robert Myles puts it, "In the Middle Ages the nature and structure of reality as a metaphysical description became a semiological description" (66). In her discussion of Dowel, Dobet, and Dobest as grammatical infinitives, Anne Middleton says something that could apply equally well to Langland's treatment of Anima:

Grammar reflects the structure of mind, but, more important, the relation of concepts in the human mind corresponds to relationships of real entities in the universe, to what eternally is. . . . In the sense in which Langland invokes it, grammar provides one of the least unreliable explanatory models by which he can overcome the tendency of personification allegory to distort what it seeks to explain. ("Infinites" 185)

I am arguing that in Passus XV grammar becomes an explanatory model for the understanding of the human soul, and therefore for the world that the soul defines itself in encountering.

For example, Anima, being grammarlike, defines charity also as like a grammar. Charity, like Anima himself, seems to have no determinate nature of his own. Many of Anima's "definitions" of charity are negative definitions: "Charite ... ne chaffareth noght, ne chalangeth, ne craveth" (XV.165); "Corseth he no creature, ne he kan bere no wrathe" (171); "Of rentes ne of richesse ne rekketh he nevere" (177). Charity appears in any walk of life: "I have seyen hym in silk and som tyme in russet" (220); even "in a frere frokke he was yfounden ones" (230). His reality consists in his relations to his fellow Christians. The same sort of idea is expressed in this passus and later in Passus XVI by the tree image: here by the image of the priests as the "roote of the right feith to rule the peple" (100) and by the Tree of Charity in Passus XVI. The tree is Langland's vehicle for expressing what we would call "organic unity." The social organism is like Yeats's chestnut tree: "Are you the leaf, the blossom, or the bole?" ("Among School Children," lines 61–62). The answer is that the question makes no sense, that we cannot tell the dancer from the dance. The clergy as clergy have no meaning apart from their relation to the social organism within which they serve.

THE EPISTEMOLOGICAL QUESTION

The point is that Anima tends to construe the social organism, where charity must be instantiated or not, as repeating in macrocosm Anima's own grammarlike nature. Here is another way of reading the world like a book, a different way of doing the same thing Holy Church did. This hermeneutic is not just an egoistic predisposition on Anima's part, but an epistemological necessity of his nature. Here is the *epistemological* question of Passus XV: How do we know? We know objects only intentionally, as objects of consciousness, and we know ourselves only as reflexes of those intentional objects. As the dreamer himself tells Anima in a strange and strangely moving passage of this passus, "Clerkes kenne me that Crist is in alle places; / Ac I seigh hym nevere soothly but as myself in a mirour" (161–62). The syntactic ambiguity of the line neatly balances the dreamer's problems and possibilities. Is he saying, as apparently in the source of the mirror metaphor in 1 Corinthians 13:12, that he has *never* seen Christ truly in this world, but *instead* has seen him only by dim reflection as one sees oneself in a mirror? In other words, should there be a comma after *soothly* in the Middle English? Or is the dreamer saying, as Schmidt's punctuation suggests, that the *only* way he has ever seen Christ truly is by looking to the reflection of Christ in the dreamer's own soul? Langland seems to be commenting on a latent ambiguity in the scriptural passage: we do not see Christ clearly *in enigmate,* but nevertheless we see him. Is that a good thing or a bad thing? The dreamer is not sure what to think; neither are we. But from Anima's perspective, one's understanding of salvation depends on the proper understanding of one's own consciousness. If the soul is like a grammar, then the world the soul construes through its various faculties must necessarily appear as a grammar as well. One knows God by knowing oneself, and in particular by knowing oneself in the study of how language functions (Myles 66).

Therefore, I am inclined to read as profound and resonant Anima's apparently tossed-off remark that grammar is "the ground of al" (371). It is not just that one has to learn Latin to read significant books, but that one must understand how grammar works in order to construe oneself and the world. Ultimately, the salvation of the heathen and the Jews depends on their ability, literally, to *construe grammatically* the relevant clauses of the Creed, as Langland puts it at the end of the passus: they "Konne the first clause of oure bileve" already (607), and must be taught "litlum and litlum" the clauses that refer to the Second and Third Persons of the Trinity, "Til thei kouthe speke and spelle . . . / And rendren it and recorden it" (609–10). Reading here is first of all just what we would call "reading," that is, construing a written text, but it is also, for Anima at least, a type of a particular way of being-in-the-world, a way of understanding oneself (and what is not oneself) that leads to salvation.

And here, finally, is the explanation for Anima's obsession with the clergy. The clergy are, essentially, the ones who read—the ones who understand grammar as a way of knowing. As such, their activity from Anima's perspective is the definitive human activity, the construing of the human soul, and therefore the world intended by that soul, as text. The proper performance of that activity is the way to salvation, and the corruption of that activity is the essence of sin. To put it quite simply: from Anima's perspective we cannot know ourselves as we are in ourselves, but only as we are in relation to God and God's other creatures. We can learn to construe ourselves this way without actually knowing how to read, but the paradigm of this relational mode of knowing is the knowledge of grammar. That fact explains Anima's obsession with the clergy, whose special province is the knowledge of grammar. From Holy Church's discourse, the dreamer concludes that to be saved he must "do well," and he attempts unsuccessfully to think through the idea of "doing well," without submitting to the discipline of the *litteratus*. Anima encounters the dreamer when the dreamer has run out his string of attempted self-justification, and Anima's advice is to learn to read—in the deepest sense of "reading."

THE ETHICAL QUESTION

And so now we broach the *ethical* question of Passus XV. The first sign of tension between the dreamer and Anima appears when the dreamer acknowledges that he wants to know why bishops and Anima have so many different names. Anima responds,

> . . . "now I se thi wille!
> Thow woldest knowe and konne the cause of alle hire names,
> And of myne, if thow myghtest, me thynketh by thi speche!"
>   "Ye, sire," I seide, "by so no man were greved,
> Alle the sciences under sonne and alle the sotile craftes
> I wolde I knewe and kouthe kyndely in myn herte!"
>
> (44–49)

Anima rebukes the dreamer, and launches into a satire against the corrupt clergy who use their learning to feed their covetousness. It is worth paying close attention to what the dreamer actually wants: he wants to *collect words,* to know the "cause," presumably the etymology, of "alle hire names" (45). He aspires to lexicography. It is possible to read Will's failing here as the desire to know all causes *tout court*—that is, to know all sciences "in terms of the causal logic of earthly knowledge" (Carruthers 125), as Will himself seems to be saying in line 48 (so also Robertson and Huppé 178). But the point appears to me rather to be precisely that Will confuses science with lexicography. His assent to Anima's initial formulation of his desire implies that he believes he will know all the sciences once he has mastered their respective jargons.

The evil that lurks behind this apparently innocent wish is the desire to appear learned by knowing big words. Big words alone are like expensive clothes on hypocritical priests, like the snow on the dunghill or the whitened wall of the sepulcher: "Ye [b]en enblaunched with *bele paroles* and with clothes" (XV.111–15). The Doctor of Passus XIII is perhaps the most fully developed example of this particular form of clerical corruption. Typically, the dreamer finds the Doctor unendurably irritating precisely because the Doctor shares the dreamer's own besetting sin of intellectual pride. As Gillian Rudd points out, the Doctor's gluttony is also a gluttony of words, and "[o]ver-indulgence in food is clearly linked with abuse of knowledge" (104). The connection between food and knowledge seems to go deeper for Langland than the merely metaphorical, as Jill Mann has argued: with Langland's images of eating and drinking, as with other allegorical images, "the material world is not merely a vehicle for expressing the immaterial, but on the contrary contains the heart of its meaning and its mystery" (27). Langland continues working the connection in the many passages in Passus XV that express clerical activities as eating or feeding; for example, the passage in which birds bring food to the anchorites (305); or lines 458ff., which develop the etymologically based notion that converting the heathen is like tilling the soil, and then explain how the clergy should feed their flock as the man in the parable fed his guests, or as cows feed calves milk, or as farmers feed their capons.

The gluttony of words, the lust to collect words without concern for wisdom, leads to another of the dangers of clerical corruption: ignorant priests, who know just enough Latin to sound out individual words from a written text, might "overhuppen . . . in Offices and in Hourcs" (385), reducing the liturgy to a gabble of words, abstracting from the syntax that gives the words their sacramental power.

Anima implies one way of reading, therefore, that is corrupt and sinful—reading as mere accumulation of words, text as mere context for increasing vocabulary, learning for the sake of appearing learned. This is textual hermeneutics as *cupiditas,* for Anima the source of clerical corruption and the disease that strikes at the root of the tree:

> Right so persons and preestes and prelatis of Holi Chirche
> Is the roote of the right feith to rule the peple;
> Ac ther the roote is roten, reson woot the sothe,
> Shal never flour ne fruyt, ne fair leef be grene.
>
> (99–102)

The social analogue of this way of reading is the behavior of the clerics who misuse their learning to get rich. Mohammed deluded his followers by training a dove to eat grain out of his ear, and pretending that he was receiving heavenly instruction (396ff.). The heathen are made susceptible by their fascination with a mere physical sign masquerading as a miracle. From Anima's perspective, understanding of salvation comes not through direct interpretation of ambiguous physical signs, but from the matching of works and words:

> Right so rude men that litel reson konneth
> Loven and bileven by lettred mennes doynges,
> And by hire wordes and werkes wenen and trowen . . .
>
> (475–77)

On the other hand, corrupt "Englisshe clerkes a colvere fede that Coveitise highte" (414). The Word sown by the Sower enters their ears, but
goes no deeper; instead, they misappropriate their knowledge of words
to get money, feeding the birds that Jesus identifies in his interpretation
of the parable as the Evil One (Matthew 13:19). The horror of the image
here is that it becomes a blasphemous parody of receiving the inspira-
tion of the Holy Spirit.

But what is the alternative? One alternative to covetousness on the
level of the social organism is clear enough: it is the way of the ascetic.
Anima returns again and again to such figures as antitypes of the corrupt
clergy: Antony and Egidius (272); Paul the hermit and Paul the Apostle
(286, 290); Peter and Andrew, described as poor fishermen (292); Mary
Magdalene in her solitude (294); Dominic and Francis, Benedict and
Bernard (420–21). Ultimately, Anima proposes disestablishment of
clerical endowments (563), in a passage that James Simpson calls a "radical proposal for reform, the most concrete in *Piers Plowman*" (179). But
obviously the way of the ascetic is not the only way. Charity himself, for
example, is not a beggar, but "in riche robes rathest he walketh" (228);
and even kings can be charitable (223–24). I think a clue can be found in
a line that is, again, about asceticism: "It is ruthe to rede how rihtwise
men lyvede"—note how Anima has learned this by *reading*—"How thei
defouled hir flessh, forsoke hir owene wille" (532–33). The key is the
forsaking of one's own will, the dispossession of the self that allows the
center of one's universe to be occupied by Christ. Thus Charity himself,
as Haukyn has not quite learned to do in the preceding passus (XIV.49),
subsists on *Fiat-voluntas-tua* (179), and his vocation in the laundry—a work
of purging—produces a *Cor contritum et humiliatum* (194).

And, in fact, everything depends upon will. Anima tells the dreamer
of Charity,

> . . . by colour ne by clergie knowe shaltow hym nevere,
> Neither thorugh wordes ne werkes, but thorugh wil oone,
> And that knoweth no clerk ne creature on erthe
> But Piers the Plowman—*Petrus, id est, Christus.*
>
> (209–12)

To the extent that this passage can be read as anything other than mystical, it appears to be a statement of the Augustinian principle that *caritas*

or *cupiditas* is determined by the direction of the will. The passage illustrates a particularly irritating mannerism of Langland's, by which he causes an authoritative figure apparently to contradict himself. Anima, quoting the authoritative passage (Pseudo-Chrysostom—Schmidt 252n) that contains the image of the priesthood as the root of the tree, has implied earlier that good clergy produce a flourishing Church: *"de templo omne bonum progreditur. . . . Si sacerdocium integrum fuerit, tota floret ecclesia"* (118) ["all good comes out of the temple. . . . If the priesthood has integrity, the whole Church flourishes"—Schmidt's translation 252n]. Is Anima saying now in lines 209–12 that clergy can neither tell the difference between charity and covetousness, nor help anyone else to do so? If one knows charity only through one's own will, and if clergy can neither know others' wills nor through words or works direct others' wills toward charity, then how, exactly, are clergy supposed to function in the Body of Christ? E. Talbot Donaldson, for example, worries over this problem considerably in attempting to rationalize some of Langland's revisions in the C-text (Donaldson 194–95).

Perhaps this apparent tension can be eased a little. As Anima sees it, the soul is like a grammar. That means that we can know only ourselves, and we can know ourselves only as knowers. As a system of intentional relations, we are to ourselves just whatever we happen to be conscious of at any given time. But, on the other hand, we are never conscious of anything absolutely as it is in itself. We are conscious of it only as it is known to us. In terms of the grammatical analogy, the syntax of a sentence does not exist in isolation from the words that can make it up, just as the soul does not exist except in relation with its intentional objects; but, on the other hand, isolated words have no determinate sense without the syntax in which they are situated. The "same" word means something at least a little different in every sentence where it appears.

The implication is that when I know charity, I in some sense become charity. I become the one whose consciousness is filled with charity. But just to *intend* charity in one of the many ways I might do that is not necessarily to *know* it. Not every thought I might have about charity is salvific. I might think of charity as a bad idea, or I might think of charity as a means of advancing my interests, and so on. In such cases, I exemplify *cupiditas* as a misdirection of the will. To know charity, to think salvifically, I must not only think of charity, but I must think Christ's own thoughts about it. I must become as Christ is when he wills my will, so as to allow my will to be dispossessed by his. And since only Christ knows my will, according to Anima, this dispossession of my will is paradoxically also the only way for me to know myself. Part of the significance of the Incarnation is that by becoming human, God enables human beings to know him, and therefore themselves, in the way that human beings are capable of knowing. When God becomes fully human, it becomes conceivable that I should know myself as he knows me. The passage in Langland perhaps alludes again to 1 Corinthians 13:12, the verse containing the mirror metaphor, where Paul talks about knowing as one is known: "then I shall understand fully, even as I have been fully understood" (RSV).

The proper articulation of the function of the clergy, then, is not to say that clergy judge other persons' wills. It is a natural mistake to think that is what clergy do, and the Pope (*Petrus*) must do that—presumably with "apostolic discernment" (Robertson and Huppé 183) in direct communion with Christ—in order to carry out his duties as the Vicar of Christ and head of the Church on earth. But a more accurate articulation is to say that clergy help other persons in various ways to perform the definitive human activity of construing one's own soul as though it were a grammar, of understanding one's soul as achieving its reality only through its right relation to God and his creatures. This activity can in a very deep sense be described as reading. Clergy as readers teach us to read; but our wills turn the epistemological tool to use, and our wills are inscrutable to ourselves and to all others but Christ.

READING AS ETHICAL ACTION

But what about reading in its narrower sense, namely, "that which we do with written texts"? If the social analogue of good reading is to understand one's right relation to the social organism through the dispossession of the self, then what is good reading narrowly construed? It would be, it seems natural to conclude, to allow the dispossession of the self by the sacred texts—to allow the texts themselves to define one's experience, as opposed to "mastering" or getting power over the texts for all the various selfish purposes for which we might want to use them. Throughout *Piers Plowman,* the dreamer or various authoritative speakers

obviously try to master the sacred texts—Scripture, liturgy, patristics—
in the most ruthless way. As Anne Middleton says, "The problem of
knowledge in the poem exerts pressure on its form when it is raised on
the field of contention between two actors for whom knowledge is power," so that an episode "reaches its point of explosion, turning discourse
to context, not over the meaning of words, but over doing things with
words" ("Narration" 106).

But blessed is the man, says Saint Bernard, *"qui scripturas legit / Et verba
vertit in opera"* (XV.60–61) ["who reads the Scriptures and turns (its)
words into works"—Schmidt's translation 248n]. Turning words into
works means, first, giving the words a syntax, construing them in sentences that make truth claims and moral claims and thus become capable of determining thoughts and actions. This sort of reading means also
seeing oneself not as mastering the text, but as mastered by it. As
Schmidt puts it, grace "comes through the words of God, given in Scripture and ritually embodied in the Liturgy"; in the *"divine* 'use' of words"
the words "operate sacramentally, enacting that which they signify"
(*Clerkly Maker* 109). Passus XV makes dramatic sense in the poem if we
regard it as preparing for a crisis in a process of coming to understand
reading, the moment at which the dreamer as surrogate for the author
begins to understand that there must be another way of reading, a relation to the sacred texts other than mastering them. The hermeneutic
that Langland seeks, as it turns out, cannot in itself guarantee salvation,
but it can perhaps at least free him from the compulsion to master texts
that seems to drive his poetic activity.

Perhaps this is one reason why Anima has no tongue or teeth: sym-
bolically, he lacks the teeth to chew over the sacred texts, unlike the gluttonous Doctor of Passus XIII or some corrupt clerics who "gnawen
God with the gorge whanne hir guttes fullen" (X.57). The tongue, similarly, as I mentioned above in my discussion of the Prologue, is the or-
gan by means of which human beings pridefully dominate others—thus,
the tongue in the exegetical tradition is the appropriate locus of punishment for Babylonian pride. Anima is "sotil" (XV.12) in many ways—
some might think, at this point, entirely too subtle in my reading—but
one clear way in which he is subtle is that he is hard to get hold of, that
he appears indeterminate. Because his nature is to become the other

pole of his relationship with whatever he intends, his nature seems to depend crucially upon his situation. The dreamer first questions Anima's Christianity (14–15), apparently because anything this indefinite seems fundamentally at odds with any meaningful notion of orthodoxy: "as it sorcerie were" (12).

I will have more to say about Haukyn later, since I read him as a surrogate of the dreamer and of Langland himself. But, for now, consider the end of Passus XIV. At that point, Haukyn has learned all too thoroughly the lesson of Patience:

> "So hard it is," quod Haukyn, "to lyve and to do synne.
> Synne seweth us evere," quod he, and sory gan wexe,
> And wepte water with hise eighen . . .
>
> (XIV.322–24)

The lesson is necessary, but it leaves the Christian nowhere to go. Patience deconstructs itself. The one problem that Patience cannot overcome is the problem of the recognition of one's own sin. Our own sin is the one grief that we cannot accept patiently. The dreamer, for once nonobtuse, gets the point: he catches Haukyn's grief, and it nearly drives him mad. At the beginning of Passus XV,

> . . . after my wakynge it was wonder longe
> Er I koude kyndely knowe what was Dowel.
> And so my wit weex and wanyed til I a fool weere . . .
>
> (1–3)

The dreamer cannot even imagine what it would be for him to "do well," since he understands himself as *essentially* sinful. Patience can take the dreamer no further, because the lesson of patience is premised on the notion of the self as essentially sinful—there is no escape for Haukyn from his paralyzing grief, because to cease to be sinful would be to cease to be himself as he understands himself.

Anima's picture of the soul, then, offers a way out. It is significant that at the beginning of Passus XVI, the dreamer, apparently much comforted, thanks Anima for *Haukyn's* sake: "For Haukyns love the Actif Man evere I shal yow lovye" (2). By picturing the soul as a grammar, Anima removes the specter of a soul inexorably defined by its own sinfulness. The picture of a soul determined by its relations opens the possibility of right relatedness, of a syntax of salvation. And, in fact, in Passus XVI, the dreamer is allowed a new vision of Piers Plowman—not through strenuous interpretive effort, but because he swoons for joy in a "love-dreem" (XVI.18–20).

But perhaps more significant, in Passus XVI the dreamer encounters the text of the gospel, which breaks into the allegorical dream of the Tree of Charity through the speech of the Holy Spirit, in one of the most astonishing and beautiful moments of the poem (XVI.90). Alford, for example, describes the moment this way: "[T]he whole agitated scene suddenly collapses into the serenity of the Annunciation. The allegorical explanation of the Redemption thus gives way to the literal story in the gospels" ("Design" 53). In the turn from allegory to gospel narrative, the course and the pretensions of the poem itself have suddenly been disrupted and displaced by the sacred text. I shall have more to say in the next chapter about this crisis. But my immediate suggestion is that Langland is showing the reader poetically what it might mean to read charitably, by surrendering control of his poem to the gospel text. For the fourteenth-century intellectual, pursuing salvation is essentially connected with pursuing a viable hermeneutic. The episode with Anima constitutes a necessary moment in the process by means of which the dreamer, as surrogate of the author himself, finally begins to break free temporarily from the apparent cacophony of conflicting interpretive systems, and, himself a reader, begins to comprehend what good reading might really be.

BIBLIOGRAPHICAL ESSAY 2.2

The interpretive frustration with which I began this discussion of Anima is the frustration attendant upon trying to say exactly what Anima is at this point in the poem. Mary Carruthers says that he is "all the major characters of the preceding passus, appearing here in a different form"; this form is the "root form of the various functions it embodies, which . . . are seen here in their essential, integrative relationship" (124–25). For James Simpson, similarly, Anima "represents the achievement of a reintegrated soul" (173). Teresa Tavormina says that Anima and the corresponding Liberum Arbitrium of the C-text "provide recapitulatory closure to the intellectual and moral quests of the Third and

Fourth Dreams" (112). The bother here is that such a reintegrated soul should turn out to be primarily a satirist of clerical corruption. Considering the poignant and personal issues that fill the long middle of the poem, beginning with the dreamer's encounter with Thought, it seems somewhat anticlimactic to say that clerical corruption—a given in the poem since early in the Prologue—turns out to be the most nutritious food for the reintegrated soul's rumination. After all, it is the dreamer who prods Anima to discourse upon charity, the other great subject of Passus XV. (Simpson's reading might in fact provide a plausible response to this bother, which I will get to in a moment.)

Reading Anima as the reintegrated soul in a sense avoids the question of what Anima is like. On the one hand, we deduce what Anima is like from our knowledge of the various faculties that have appeared earlier in the allegory. On the other hand, if we concentrate on the dramatic portrayal of Anima, and conclude that he seems "colorless yet chameleonlike," as Elizabeth Kirk says (159), then the philosophical question of Anima's mode of being thrusts itself forward again. Kirk analyzes the mode of being of God and the soul in terms of the categories of "activity" and "passivity": "Not only does the list of Anima's names put man's ostensibly 'active' and ostensibly 'passive' qualities on a footing of parallelism, but Anima goes so far as to define God's own nature—his sheer act—as involving a mode of response to man that man can only call passivity" (166–67). I am arguing, among other things, that the category of "relation" offers a better way to talk about Anima than do the categories of "activity" and "passivity." But I share Kirk's sense that Anima's dramatic portrayal in Passus XV needs attention. Failing to question Anima's "colorlessness" naturally leads to Schmidt's conclusion that Anima is only Langland's "convenient mouthpiece" (xli). Such an interpretation of Anima seems to me to have the disadvantage of making it rather difficult to explain, for example, how Anima's discourse effects the remarkable movement from the "carnal" to the "mystical" (xxxiii–xxxiv) that Schmidt himself sees in Passus XV. And that observation obviously touches on the critical debate about how Passus XV is supposed to fit into the rest of the poem—a debate that I have already sketched above.

The problem of the nature of Anima bleeds over into the problem of the nature of charity. In my argument, Anima portrays charity as grammarlike because Anima is grammarlike. Both figures, then, exhibit the puzzling relational mode of being that makes them so hard to characterize definitely. Britton Harwood analyzes this situation differently. Anima

> takes a series of concepts—being indifferent to clothing, being patient in adversity, and so on—and constructs the semblance of a person. For Anima, charity is a genus of such acts. . . . While charity as a genus is really a second-intentional term used in simple supposition for other abstractions, Anima treats it as an incomplex, a subject known evidently at the same time one knows evidently that the subject acts in a certain way. A subject is known like that, however, only in an intuitive cognition. (18)

This process (like many things) leaves the dreamer confused (18). Whether one reads charity as more like a pseudoperson constructed of abstractions or more like a grammar would ultimately depend upon one's sense of the whole poem: that is, is *Piers Plowman* "about" pursuing personal knowledge of Christ, or is it "about" pursuing a viable hermeneutic? I would like to say, of course, that the difference in the two readings in the last analysis is only a difference of emphasis.

Part of the difficulty of getting a handle on Anima is, of course, Anima's supposed rhetorical incoherence. There are various approaches to this problem. I have already mentioned Malcolm Godden's approach, which is to admit that Anima's speech is "rambling," and to conclude that the rhetorical incoherence arises at least in part from the intrusions of the authorial voice (117). Robert Worth Frank focuses on the problem posed by the rhetorical seesawing between the themes of clerical corruption and charity. His solution is to place charity at the center of concern, and to treat the satire on clerical corruption as arising from Anima's conviction that people need examples of the practice of charity, which clergy are failing to provide (*Scheme* 84–85). Lawrence M. Clopper's solution falls out, as it were, from his overall project of demonstrating Langland's Franciscanism. The "Wanderer," as Clopper calls him, a surrogate for Langland, has been living a mendicant life—though he is concerned about his own confusion over the question of what constitutes "a legitimate mendicant life" (*Songes of Rechelesnesse* 257–58). Then,

Anima's speech—Wille's understanding—is not just a sermon on Charity but a charitable sermon. It describes the functions and obligations of regular and secular clerics and bishops and in so doing defines the role of friars and of Wille. The sermon thus is outwardly directed toward a reformation of clergy and, consequently, of society, but also inwardly directed since Wille reveals to himself what his life is to be, what his role is. (260)

Simpson, as it seems to me, provides a more cogent explanation of why the themes of charity and clerical corruption are necessarily connected in Langland's own thought. Simpson points to the tree images in XV.96–102 and XVI.4–9. In the first of these, "the moral health of individual Christians . . . is dependent on the moral health of their root, which is the institution of the Church." In the second, "the source of moral health lies in individuals themselves" (174). But "[t]hese two images are not contradictory: charity is both the source and the product of the Church as it is conceived by Langland," so that "[i]f he is to treat charity, then he must necessarily treat the subject of the Church also" (174–75). But Simpson's interpretation does not directly take up the problem of why, in the dramatic interaction of the poem, the dreamer must keep dragging Anima back to the topic of charity and away from the topic of clerical corruption, or—the problem I am most interested in here—why *Anima,* in particular, should be the allegorical personification who is especially obsessed by clerical corruption. I believe, however, that Simpson might argue that the soul, now reintegrated (173) and therefore newly capable of judging accurately, must address the problem of clerical corruption anew because of the essential connection between the Church and the moral health of individuals.

Much of the scholarly work that I have cited before on medieval ideas of language as an epistemological tool forms the background also of my discussion of Anima. In general, I might say with Gillian Rudd that "the literary perspectives and the dialogues between the discourses of knowledge, language and authority and how they are used, . . . form the centre of interest for this particular reading of *Piers Plowman*" (43). Mary Carruthers and Pamela Raabe, though they occupy opposite poles in the critical debate about Langland's attitude toward language, both start from the premise that language is a central concern of the poem: "*Piers Plowman* is an allegory which devotes its primary energies to redeeming its own *littera*" (Carruthers 4–5); the paradoxical truth of the Word of God "has been embodied in every allegory in the poem, each requiring readers to read the whole ambivalent Truth of all God's texts: the text of the poem, of humankind, of society, and of the cosmos" (Raabe 167). Robert Myles's work on "Chaucerian realism," which I have already cited several times, is particularly helpful in connecting theories of grammar with theories of intentionality. Myles makes the connection this way, in a passage I quoted in the preceding chapter: "A shared medieval and modern presupposition, and one that is due to a direct filiation, is the linguistic model of intentionality: all structures that operate intentionally may be understood to operate as language operates" (37). Further, "The principle upon which *intentio* operates is love, desire, or passion. Will is the motor which leads to subsequent action and knowledge" (42). Burt Kimmelman's discussion of Langland's place in the development of the literary persona is also relevant. Kimmelman shows how fourteenth-century philosophical and theological debates about language connect with notions of the human person implied in Langland's creation of his dreamer as literary persona (*The Poetics of Authorship in the Later Middle Ages*).

Brian Stock's learned chapter on "Language, Texts, and Reality" (326–454) discusses the relationships in the eleventh and twelfth centuries between literacy and philosophical and theological thought. For the period of his concern Stock provides a precise articulation of the notion I am fumbling toward here when I say that medieval intellectuals were obsessed with texts. There might be other dimensions to the notion in the late fourteenth century, when poets, at least, seem to have reflected on the implications of widespread vernacular literacy and the concomitant possibility of a new kind of "private" reading. In his exploration of *The Canterbury Tales,* for example, Donald R. Howard proposes that Chaucer was in on the invention of a "new attitude toward reading," "the real heart of humanism," in which reading "becomes a voyage of exploration, writing a creation of worlds, often interior worlds, in which the reader travels" (66). This new sort of reading is close to what we would call literacy today, as opposed to the competence in Latin grammar distinctive of Stock's medieval *litteratus.* The danger of the new sort of literacy is maybe best illustrated by the cartoonish dreamer of the *Hous of Fame,* who is so wrapped up in his books that he does not know what is going on with his nextdoor neighbors (lines 649–59). In part, *Piers Plowman* is a satire on the "bookish" intellectual—sometimes blatantly so, as with the figure of the Doctor in Passus XIII; and sometimes more subtly, as with the intellectual pretensions of the dreamer himself.

My description of grammar as relational is tangled in a complex way with the line of thought Anne Middleton pursues in her reflections on XIII.128–30, the grammatical metaphor of the infinitives *Dowel, Dobet,* and *Dobest.* She says that the grammar of these three terms "suggests that Langland coined them in an attempt to show intellectual or spiritual relationships in their essential, changeless aspects, independent of the temporal circumstances into which they may be translated" ("Infinites" 171). Langland attempts, that is, to "purify allegorical language," to "make human language eschatologically adequate, valid beyond the narrow base in the world and experience upon which the terms of its metaphors rest" (172). One possible interpretation, at least, is that Langland means to show by the failure to locate Dowel under such presuppositions that it is impossible to purify allegorical language, and that if our quest for Dowel depends upon such a purification, then we are doomed. We must find another way to look at the way grammar works in the soul—possibly, Anima's relational way—that does *not* require separating spiritual relationships from the "temporal circumstances into which they may be translated." Indeed, only when we understand how spiritual relationships are constituted by temporal circumstances will we understand the real sense of the quest for Dowel.

Myles explains how language as epistemological model gives a sense to the notion of locating God's image in the human being: "The epistemological model for the relation of *human* thought, word, and referent, understood as an intentional act or 'dede,' was analogically based on an analysis of the intentional relation of created reality to *God's* 'thoughts' and 'words' and the 'referents' these thoughts create. Man is *imago Dei,* but God, in a sense, is *imago hominis*" (69). A systematic treatment of the idea of God's image in man as this idea appears in *Piers Plowman* is available in Barbara Raw's "Piers and the Image of God in Man." Harwood identifies the premise that grounds the dreamer's project of achieving "kynde knowynge" of Christ: "Belief in Christ as a person was often thought to require the knowledge of oneself as a person. In one of the classic dilemmas of epistemology, one cannot know what is not oneself" (7). For Harwood, the "abstractness that necessarily arises with literacy" stands opposed to the "kynde knowynge" that is the object of the dreamer's quest (20). My own reading of *Piers Plowman* suggests rather that the point of Langland's poetic activity is precisely to find a sounder understanding of literacy.

Need

NEED AS A WORD

The dreamer's encounter with Need opens the last passus in *Piers Plowman*. The meeting constitutes a famous crux because of the difficulty of determining the valency of Need's instruction. Is Need orthodox, morally neutral, or diabolical? Antichrist enters the poem right on the heels of Need (XX.53), but later in Passus XX Need seems to be giving Conscience good advice about the friars (232ff.). Need in some ways seems to round out the overall structure of the poem by taking up again the same themes that Holy Church introduces in Passus I. As Robert Adams says in his summary of the evidence presented by Need's "defenders," "[W]hat Need says about the three things that men hold 'in comune' . . . echoes Holy Church's statement of the same commonplace (1.17–26); and just as she moved from this topic to its corollary, the necessity for temperance, so does Need in the later dialogue. According to this view, Need acts as a principle of *mesure*" ("Need" 275). Adams himself, as Need's prosecutor, dissents from these opinions and associates Need with the lying "noonday demon" of "perverted temperance" (301). But Need in a way also balances Lady Meed. As Meed's rhyming opposite, Need depicts an economy based on the distribution of goods according to basic necessities. In such an economy, money would be not only unnecessary but also inherently deceptive. Where the rule is that goods must be distributed as they are needed, the whole concept of "medium of exchange" that justifies the monetary system falsifies the nature of economic relationships. I should get what I need regardless of whether I have something of supposedly equal value to exchange for it—

even if I have to steal what I need. Or, more accurately, if I have genuine need, then there is no such thing as "stealing." The concept of "stealing" itself depends upon the premise that I may properly acquire goods from others only by offering something of equal value in exchange. Need's economy bypasses that premise. So if we look at *Piers Plowman* as exhibiting some sort of circular structure whereby Need is supposed to remind us of Lady Meed, then all the difficulties we have in evaluating Lady Meed also get involved in our attempts to interpret Need.

The move that I and some other critics make to ease the interpretive problems with Lady Meed is to regard her as a word, a term that figures in different ways in different discourses. I will argue here that a similar move might help with Need. Need, like Meed, behaves like a word. But Langland does something different with Need. Lady Meed's downfall is that, try as she might, she fails to control the terms of the discourse through which she is judged. Langland's point with her is precisely that the concept of "meed," like money itself, is infinitely slippery. Money belongs to whoever has it. Lady Meed's name is not just her property, but also the property of Conscience, of Reason, of the King, of her minions, and of anyone else who can turn her name to the ends of some particular discourse of justification or vilification. Thus in common parlance she ends up a whore (IV.166).

Need, at least as Langland portrays him in Passus XX, is made of sterner stuff. He does control the terms of his discourse. In fact, as I will try to demonstrate, most of his discourse consists precisely of an attempt to marshal the crucial terms of self-justification under his banner. With Lady Meed, Langland shows what happens when a term slides so much throughout various discourses that it finally seems to signify nothing at all. With Need, on the other hand, Langland shows what happens when we in fact construe human experience from the perspective of a single term of self-justification. Thus I will argue that the episode of Need also has important affinities with the episode of Anima. That is, Need is relational in the same way that the functions of the human soul are relational in Passus XV. Need, as a term, functions in Passus XX as the central word in a language that interprets human experience in a certain way. The Anima episode interprets on the model of a grammar both the soul and the world that soul inhabits; the Need episode with blunt economy interprets everything on the model of a single relation, the relation that Langland names "need." But in both episodes the underlying model is textual hermeneutics. With Anima, we understand ourselves and our experience via the epistemological model provided by grammar; with Need, we understand ourselves and our experience via the epistemological model provided by a rhetorical structure of self-justification dependent upon a single value term. For Anima, we are what we are because of the relations we are capable of assuming with God and with other human beings. For Need, we are what we are simply because we need.

The Need episode is odd in that it is a waking episode. The dreamer normally meets allegorical figures in his dreams, and Need certainly looks like an allegorical figure. Then Need appears again within the dream that follows, in accordance with the more usual pattern. Is Need in the waking episode the same as Need in the dream? And, if so, why does Langland so blatantly and uncharacteristically introduce the same allegorical figure both while the dreamer is awake and while the dreamer is asleep?

There might be a clue in a parallel passage in the C-text: namely, the so-called autobiographical passage in C.V. where Will argues with Reason and Conscience about the course of his own life. Reason and Conscience are both important allegorical personifications at various other points in the poem, and clearly they do not always mean just the *dreamer's* faculties of reason and conscience. But in the autobiographical passage, it makes sense to say that they do represent, among other things, what the dreamer might call "his own" reason and conscience. Most often in *Piers Plowman* the dreamer is dreaming, and already by the conventions of the allegorical dream vision the human faculties are dramatized, placed over against the narrating consciousness as interlocutors. But sometimes even when we are awake, it makes sense to say—we often do say—that we "debate" with our own reason and conscience, as Will does in the C-text. The metaphor makes sense, however, only in the context of self-justification. If I am trying to make tricky judgments about social justice in general, for example, I might say that my reason is debating with itself perhaps, but not that "I" am debating with my own reason. I perceive my reason and conscience as separate from myself only when I am concerned with evaluating my own behavior—when I seem to want to think or do something that my reason and conscience seem not to approve of. Strictly speaking, I debate with my own reason and conscience when they are at odds with my will. When I am awake and not dreaming allegorical dreams, I dramatize my other faculties and "debate" with them only in such situations of attempted self-justification. In such situations, I do not need the conventions of the dream vision in order to perceive reason and conscience as somehow separate from myself. To debate with my reason and conscience is already to dramatize them, and to acknowledge that both of these faculties are transpersonal. There is no sense in which "my" reason and "my" conscience "belong to" me alone. If they did, there could be no debate between us. My reason and my conscience are specifically the faculties that connect me with what is normative beyond the realm of my private experience.

I want to argue that something parallel is happening in the episode of Need in the B-text. That is, the idea of Will's self-justification is crucial in the Need episode, and dramatizing Need while in a wakeful state corresponds to the dreamer's acknowledgment that Need too is transpersonal—is not *just* "his own" need. Need is not, for example, just the name of a category of the dreamer's private, prelinguistic feelings such as hunger, cold, thirst, and so on. But, on the other side, it does make sense to talk about "one's own" need in the same way as it makes sense to talk about "one's own" reason or "one's own" conscience. Need is not *only* an ethical concept subsuming a particular subset of human behaviors, or another name for destiny or fate. The task for the dreamer consists of matching what he wants to call "his own" need with the abstract structures of rational justification based on the transpersonal concept of need.

Will's own particular life is being called into question. Need rebukes Will for failing to use the argument from temperance to justify appropriating food, clothing, and drink—just as other people in the preceding passus have used arguments from the other three cardinal virtues to justify taking advantage of their fellow Christians in various ways. Will is supposed to "excuse" himself "That thow toke to lyve by, to clothes and to sustenaunce, / Was by techynge and by tellynge of *Spiritus Temperancie*" (6–8). And at the end of his argument, Need stresses as the *logical* conclusion ("Forthi") that because Christ was needy, one who imitates him need not be ashamed of neediness: "Forthi be noght abasshed to bide [*bydde* in some manuscripts] and to be nedy, / Sith he that wroghte al the world was wilfulliche nedy . . ." (48–49). This stress on self-justification provides the clue about what Need means here.

In fact, this strange mode of being that is exhibited by Need, this hovering between the personal and the transpersonal, corresponds to the mode of being of a word. I can meaningfully talk about "my word for that," or "my use of a word," or "what I mean by that word," or "what the word suggests to me." Such a view of words can even be carried to the extreme of Lewis Carroll's Humpty Dumpty, who gives the words their wages so that they mean exactly what he wants them to mean. There is catachresis. But of course the extreme is impossible to sustain, and catachresis is possible only against the background of the communal understanding of the language. Words are ultimately not private property. Like the grammars that provide their syntax, words are relational, in that they are signs whose signification depends upon the propositions in which they appear and by which they are connected with the things they signify.

Need can be dramatized, then, as a personification in a dream vision, as later in Passus XX. But when the dreamer first encounters him, Need also makes sense purely as the key term in a particular rhetorical structure of justification. That the dreamer is awake when he first meets Need is Langland's way of suggesting that the dreamer conceives of Need first as a word, a term with both private and public applications. That is, one can talk about justifying oneself by the "argument from need" that argument is what Need articulates—and then one is talking about Need more or less as a rhetorical topos, a word in an argument from whose application certain other words are thought to follow logically. At the beginning of Passus XX, the dreamer consciously and without the intervening scrim of the dream vision encounters Need as a word. Aware of himself as physically needy in the waking world, he realizes that certain actual behaviors that he might perform in that world might be justified by means of the argument from need.

NEED AND THE CARDINAL VIRTUES

As I have suggested before, Need is the name of a relation. To say that one "needs" food is to say that one stands in a certain relation to something edible. But Need is a relation of incompleteness. If one really *needs* food, then one is incomplete without it. On the physical level, for example, we might say that without the food that one needs, one starves—is already less than oneself, is becoming even less oneself, and ultimately, in the old meaning of the word *starve,* will cease to exist at all. There are of course needs other than the physical. Every person needs. But to say that one needs already implies that this *one,* this person who needs, is not just a simple substance. Simple substances, being complete in themselves, cannot need. The person who needs is defined by a relation between a presence and an absence, a needy now and a projected completeness. The *I* who needs is the *I* who is, by definition, incomplete—not fully itself. In Anima's picture of the human soul in Passus XV, when I say that I love something, the *I* who loves is defined as one pole of the relation. What I am depends upon what I love, and the soul itself at that moment is the grammar of the relation, the verb of the proposition. Similarly, for Need, the human person is always just that which is involved in the relation of needing, a relation between something I do not yet have and something that I have not yet become.

The crucial move in justifying oneself by the argument from need, it turns out, is to connect the concept of need with the four cardinal virtues, starting with the virtue of temperance. Practicing temperance, to put it crudely, means not taking too much of anything. When one is hungry and needs food, for example, what one needs is not some particular apple, but any edible thing that is *enough. Enough* is, by definition, what one needs. Too much is what one does not need. "Enough," like "big" and "small," is a relative concept. This is how the virtue of temperance becomes logically implicated with need.

The structure of the argument by which Need apparently justifies stealing is interesting. When Need accosts Will, he calls Will a "faitour" (5), a word connoting, among other things, a liar. *Faitour* and the related noun *faiterie* and verb *faiten* are normally used in *Piers Plowman* to apply to people who get money under false pretenses, especially false beggars (for example, Prologue 42, II.183, VI.121, X.38, XI.92). Will interprets the term as an insult: Need "afrounted me foule" (5). But if Need's intention is to justify even stealing as a way of acquiring the bodily necessities, what, exactly, would be wrong with *faitynge,* if that would accomplish the same end? We might answer, as I have already suggested, that Need in fact does not mean to justify stealing, but instead means to argue that the concept of stealing itself has no application for anyone who lacks the necessities in the economy Need postulates. But, then, how is *faitynge* morally different, exactly, from getting one's dinner "by sleighte" (14), which Need clearly excuses?

Langland's point must be that Need's insult is directed primarily not at what Will does to get his dinners, but at what Will thinks about it. That sort of critique belongs to the interior debate that I am arguing occurs here. From the perspective of Need, everyone has the *right* to the necessities of life. Will implicitly lies to others when he lacks the courage to assert his right, and instead tries to wheedle or flatter—he tacitly consents to the premise that he has no right to the necessities, and thus must lie, cheat, or steal in order to acquire them. He allows himself to be coopted by the big lie of "exchange" that drives the money economy. But a more serious problem is that Will lies to himself. He is apparently ashamed to be called a *faitour,* and ashamed to perform the activities that seem to justify the accusation. But he lacks the gumption to do anything about his situation. He is ashamed because he thinks of himself as being better than he acts, but he is too slothful to claim his own redemption. Especially here, my reading of the Need episode finds a point of tangency with that of John Bowers (159). Bowers in general portrays Will as a victim of *acedia,* and points out that Need does little more than remind Will of things he has heard already—thus illustrating the morally ambiguous faultiness of Will's faculty of memory. I think Need does more than recite old lessons, but I agree that the emphasis here is on Will's interior problems. If Will is to lay claim to the presumably *good* reasons that Need provides to justify Will's life in the world, Will must overcome the cowardice and sloth that are the *real* reasons for his current thought and behavior. Will is a *faitour* because he thinks of himself that way. If Will really thought of himself as justified by need, then he would not be ashamed of his behavior. This would be first and primarily an interior change in Will. To bring about this change, Will needs Need.

What Need provides, again, is a structure of rhetorical justification which, could Will only avail himself of it, would relieve Will of the necessity of feeling ashamed of himself. Here I need to analyze that rhetorical structure in some detail. The point is to show how Need marshals all four cardinal virtues by deriving them, as it were, from the notion of need itself. Need begins with temperance:

> Coudestow noght excuse thee, as dide the kyng and othere—
> That thow toke to lyve by, to clothes and to sustenaunce,
> Was by techynge and by tellynge of *Spiritus Temperancie*,
> And that thow nome na moore than nede thee taughte . . . ?
>
> (6–9)

The syntax is elliptical. If we read the lines as an attempt to justify stealing, we might fill out the sentence this way: "Could you not excuse yourself, that [the fact that] you took [things] to live by was by the teaching of temperance?" But then the argument would seem a little strange. How does this work? How do I practice temperance by taking things from you? I could say that I am ensuring that I do not have too little, and at the same time I am helping you to practice temperance by ensuring that you do not have too much. But this is not the usual way of talking about temperance. Usually, I say that I am practicing temperance when I rein in my own impulses and keep *myself* from having or feeling or doing *too much* (that is, more than *enough*), as in Passus XIX:

> The seconde seed highte *Spiritus Temperancie*.
> He that ete of that seed hadde swich a kynde,
> Sholde nevere mete ne meschief make hym to swelle;
> Ne sholde no scornere out of skile hym brynge;
> Ne wynnynge ne wele of worldliche richesse,
> Waste word of ydelnesse ne wikked speche moeve;
> Sholde no curious clooth comen on his rugge,
> Ne no mete in his mouth that Maister Johan spicede.
>
> (XIX.283–90)

And Need in fact at once turns the argument into this more familiar path: "that thow nome na moore than nede thee taughte" (XX.9). It seems less strained, then, both syntactically and logically, to complete the ellipsis as Pearsall (362n) suggests in his note on the corresponding line in the C-text: "Could you not excuse yourself, that [what] you took to live by was by the teaching of temperance?" The lines stress *how much* the dreamer takes. That is, one practices temperance not in the act of taking things, but in the restraint of not taking more than one needs. Temperance excuses not the taking itself—which needs no excuse in the economy of Need—but the manner of taking.

The structure of rhetorical justification, very precisely, is this: one can justify taking things from others only so long as one practices the virtue of temperance, but one can practice the virtue of temperance only insofar as one has need. As Robertson and Huppé phrase it, "Only in a condition of Need can the bounds of temperance be determined" (228). Temperance is logically defined in terms of need. Thus *temperance* as a term in arguments of justification has a special rhetorical relation with the term *need*. The appeal to temperance is at bottom the same as the appeal to need, because the appeal to temperance always implicitly entails the appeal to need. That is why, in the interpretive system where Need is the central word, temperance is the chief of the cardinal virtues:

> So Nede, at gret nede, may nymen as for his owene,
> Withouten conseil of Conscience or Cardynale Vertues—
> So that he sewe and save *Spiritus Temperancie.*
> For is no vertue bi fer to *Spiritus Temperancie* . . .
>
> (XX.20–23)

I will postpone for a moment the discussion of the connection between Need and Conscience, since these two figures interact allegorically in the dream vision that follows. But Need's point about temperance here is precisely that, if Need is the central term of justification, then justification in terms of the other cardinal virtues requires extra rhetorical steps, whereas justification by temperance already essentially involves justification by need. Whenever I am practicing temperance, I am acting from need; and when I justify myself by the argument from temperance, I have gone as deep as I can go or need to go within Need's universe of discourse.

Need demonstrates this rhetorical hierarchy by showing how the other cardinal virtues fail to justify until they are further connected with Need itself. Interestingly, Robertson and Huppé argue that in Passus XIX the cardinal virtues are perverted "through a lack of temperance" (228). Here, Need says,

For *Spiritus Fortitudinis* forfeteth ful ofte:
He shal do moore than mesure many tymes and ofte,
And bete men over bittre, and som body to litel,
And greve men gretter than good feith it wolde.

(25–28)

One cannot justify oneself by arguing only that one has practiced fortitude. One must also show that one has practiced it in accordance with
the precepts of need: that one needed to practice it, and that one practiced it when one needed to.

As for *Spiritus Iusticie,* he "shal juggen, wole he, nel he, / After the kynges counseil and the comune like" (29–30). This statement, like the later statement about prudence, is maybe more cryptic than it looks at first.
The spirit of justice does not always get to act purely according to its
own will, but must judge "wole he, nel he." On the surface, it sounds as
though the spirit of justice does not always judge justly. The point seems
to be something like this: in the give-and-take of politics, one cannot always (if ever) make decisions that can be justified purely on principles of
justice. One has to consider vested interests, power relations, and all the
other social and political realities. If one is going to justify political decisions, one will ultimately have to appeal, as we say, to "necessity"—to say
something like, "The decision was of course not completely just, but it
was the best decision possible under the circumstances." Making such
judgments is the only way to *practice* the virtue of justice in the world,
and so rhetorical justification of practice in terms of justice ultimately
requires a complementary justification in terms of need.

Similarly,

. . . *Spiritus Prudencie* in many a point shal faille
Of that he weneth wolde falle if his wit ne weere.
Wenynge is no wysdom, ne wys ymaginacion . . .

(31–33)

Lines 31–32 are syntactically difficult. I paraphrase as follows: "The spirit of prudence will err in many cases in thinking that something or other
would happen if his wit did not intervene to prevent it." In other words,
practicing prudence is not in itself good. In fact, one can waste a good
deal of time hypochondriacally scheming about how to avoid some ca-
tastrophe that is not going to happen anyway. We can always imagine

more evils than are sufficient to the day. Therefore, to the justification by prudence must be added the justification by need. One's practicing of prudence is not virtuous if it turns out to be jejune. At least, this is how things look from the perspective of Need.

It is worth noting that with all four of the cardinal virtues, the concern of Need is not so much with the abstract interpretation of the virtues, but instead with practicing the virtues in an imperfect world—a world with poverty, violence, entrenched patterns of social injustice, and constant worry. From the perspective of Need, to be human is to be needy. Humans are needy because they inhabit an imperfect world and yet are called on to practice the perfections of the cardinal virtues. Practice of the virtues in the world is a matter of needing, an attempt to match a needy now with a projected perfection.

So far, I have argued that Need is carefully constructing a rhetorical hierarchy of justification, and that Need does this by showing how the four cardinal virtues look when interpreted from the perspective of Need as the central hermeneutic principle. The four cardinal virtues, moreover, especially when they appear formally attired in their Latin names, suggest a learned (literate) pattern of self-justification. The cardinals in the Prologue have care of the cardinal virtues (Prologue 103) and therefore of the election of the pope at least in part because of their "lettrure" (Prologue 110). In the establishment of Unity in Passus XIX the cardinal virtues are the seeds corresponding to the words sown by the Sower of Matthew 13 (XIX.277ff.), words which, though Jesus spoke them aloud to his disciples, are for us written words. In one way of looking at it, then, Need's discussion of the cardinal virtues almost takes the shape of an exercise in school rhetoric, an analysis of the hierarchical relationships among value terms that tend to appear in learned arguments of justification.

NEED, CONSCIENCE, AND THE FRIARS

Considering Need as the chief term in a structure of self-justification might also ease some of the apparent difficulties that arise when Need appears for the second time in Passus XX, at 232ff. Here Need becomes part of the dreamer's dream. In the more familiar mode of the personification allegory, the issue is no longer the dreamer's attempt to match his own needs with the abstract concept of need. Need here talks

about the friars, not the dreamer. Given all of the "antifraternal" satire
in the poem, there is of course a satirical backblast at the dreamer, a hint
that the dreamer himself might be well qualified to fill the space in
Need's new discourse that the friars currently occupy. But Need here, if
he is a term of justification, is the term apprehended in its more abstract, generalized extension. Need counsels Conscience not to give the
friars "cure of souls" (233, 237), but instead to "Lat hem be as beggeris, or
lyve by aungeles foode!" (241).

At least three puzzles present themselves. First, what does it mean to
say that Need counsels Conscience—especially in light of the earlier
waking passage, where Need asserts that in dire circumstances Need
may operate "Withouten conseil of Conscience or Cardynale Vertues"
(21)? Second, why should Need at first encourage the dreamer to excuse
his own behavior, and then later be so hard on the friars? As Lawrence
M. Clopper puts it, "If Nede in the waking moment is a counselor to
theft, . . . then how are we to regard the Nede in the vision who counsels
Conscience *not* to give the friars cure of souls?" (*Songes of Rechelesnesse* 98).
Do all the arguments from need not apply equally well to needy friars?
And third, a related question, to what extent does the passage about the
friars throw a dubious light on Need's earlier advice to the dreamer? Is
Langland alluding already at the beginning of Passus XX to the argument of the friars, satirized ubiquitously in antifraternal literature, that
the friars are more perfect than others because they live a Christ-like
life of voluntary poverty (see, for example, Chaucer's *Summoner's Tale*)?

As to the first question, it seems reasonable to say that Need can operate without counsel of Conscience precisely in the sense that rhetorical justifications based on the argument from need do not have to mention conscience at all. In fact, the argument from need often serves
precisely as a means of abstracting from issues of conscience. If I genuinely need something in order to survive, the argument goes, then I am
justified in taking it, no matter what my conscience might say. Whether
this line of reasoning is theologically sound is a deep question that was
debated in the Middle Ages and is still debated now, and much depends
on what one thinks the conscience is, exactly. Langland is making a
statement not about absolute theological truth, but about how terms
function in arguments. On the other hand, it makes sense to say that

Need can counsel Conscience, in the sense that one issue that the human conscience must deal with in many particular situations is the issue of need. Even in the more limited context of the rhetoric of self-justification, in discussing the distribution of goods it is hard to imagine an appeal to conscience that does not entail also a discussion of who needs what.

Now let me take up the issue of Need and the friars. At the very end of the poem, Conscience in a legal metaphor recognizes explicitly the function of Need as a term in a self-justifying argument. The friars "for nede flateren / And countrepledeth me, Conscience" (384–85). The friars, as the ones who undermine the validity of the confession, form the primary tone in the sour note that ends *Piers Plowman*. Conscience wishes "that freres hadde a fyndyng" (384), apparently because if friars were given a living, they would not be able to confuse people so easily by perverting the argument from need to serve their covetousness. Here the term *need* is once again reminiscent of *meed: need* has by the end of the poem become a slippery term of unclear reference that can therefore be perverted to serve anybody's ends.

These observations might clarify the dramatic interaction in the scene where Need advises Conscience. Unity is besieged by Antichrist and the Deadly Sins, and corrupted priests have almost brought "Unitee and holynesse adown" (227). Conscience calls upon the clergy for help: "Help, Clergie, or ellis I falle / Thorugh inparfite preestes and prelates of Holy Chirche!" (228–29). The friars answer the call. Presumably, the friars mean to take up the slack created by corruption in the ranks of the regular parish clergy. But "for thei kouthe noght wel hir craft, Conscience forsook hem" (231). That is, it develops that the friars do not know how to keep people out of deadly sin; and when one does not know how to do one's job, it is impossible to be *conscientious* about it—a term whose etymology captures nicely what is going on here. If I am incompetent at my work, I soon begin to find other ways of justifying my existence. Once justifying my activities—as opposed to doing my job— becomes my first priority, conscience is effectively banished from my economy. Whatever I do is, by definition, justifiable; the issue is only to find the most effective rhetoric to justify it. This is a well-documented psychological process prevalent in our own time among politicians, bureaucrats, and college administrators. Precisely at this point, where the work of the friars has been thus separated from the dictates of Conscience, "Nede neghede tho neer" (232). That is, the term *need* begins to enter into the friars' arguments of self-justification. Arguments from the friars' neediness begin to crowd into the rhetorical space where their activities as confessors are being debated, thus displacing arguments about the central issue of whether the friars are in fact keeping people out of deadly sin. And these are not only arguments about whether hunger or thirst justify particular friars' begging on particular occasions. They are primarily arguments about the friars' special worthiness as a class because they imitate the neediness of Christ.

At this point the argument from need ironically turns on the friars. Need suddenly materializes in the rhetorical space formerly occupied by debates about saving souls. Conscience is able to deduce from this appearance ("Conscience he tolde"—232) that the argument has become an argument about "coveitise" and not about "cure of soules" (233). The friars' flattery of rich penitents is generated not from their genuine need, but from their wanting "to fare wel" (235), to have more than enough. But Need himself, as Langland portrays him in the opening lines of Passus XX, is essentially connected with the virtue of temperance. Self-justification by the argument from need is available only so long as there is genuine need. The argument from need, strictly applied, implies that if being needy in itself justifies (as the friars might say, because Christ was needy, and we should imitate him), then one should obviously remain needy: as Need himself says, "Lat hem chewe as thei chose, and charge hem with no cure!" (237).

The argument from need gives the friars two choices: "Lat hem be as beggeris, or lyve by aungeles foode!" (241). In the first case, they will be genuine mendicants, and their begging can be justified in terms of need. They will, admittedly, have the same temptations all mendicants have— "lomere he lyeth, that liflode moot begge" (238)—but at least any flattering lies they tell will not drag penitents down with them.

The second choice is to live by "angels' food." I believe that Need alludes here to the exegetical tradition surrounding Psalm 77:24 (RSV 78:24), which takes the *panem angelorum* to refer to the manna in the wilderness, thence to the body of Christ as incarnation of the divine

Word preached to the world by the apostles, and thence to the Real Presence in the Eucharist. Ambrose, for example, commenting on the relevant passages in this psalm, says,

> [I]t is a marvelous thing that God rained manna on the fathers, and they were fed by daily nourishment from heaven. Therefore, it is said: "Man has eaten the bread of angels." But yet all those who ate that bread died in the desert, but this food which you receive, the "living bread, which came down from heaven," furnishes the substance of eternal life, and whoever eats this bread "will not die forever"; for it is the body of Christ. (22–23)

The *Glossa Ordinaria* says, "Significat panem qui de caelo descendit, qui est cibus angelorum: quem, ut manducaret homo, *Verbum caro factum* (*Joan.* 1), qui per nubes evangelicas pluitur toti mundo" (PL 113.969) ["It (the manna) signifies the bread that comes down from heaven, which is the food of angels—which, in order that man should eat it, *The Word was made flesh* (John 1), who through the evangelical clouds rains on the whole earth"]. And from Peter Lombard, *Commentarium in Psalmos:* "manna, quo significatur panis angelicus, scilicet Christus . . . significat panem qui de coelo descendit, id est Christum, vel corpus Christi, qui est vere cibus angelorum" (PL 191.732) ["the manna, by which is signified the angelic bread—that is to say, Christ—signifies the bread that came down from heaven, that is Christ, or the body of Christ, which is truly the food of angels"]; also, "*Et mandavit nubibus desuper* [verse 27], id est praedicatoribus; *et januas coeli aperuit:* januae coeli sunt praedicatores, quibus intratur in coelum, vel Scripturae sacrae" (PL 191.732) ["*He had commanded the clouds from above,* that is, the preachers, *and opened the doors of heaven:* the doors of heaven are the preachers, by whom entrance is gained into heaven, or the sacred Scriptures"]. If earthly neediness is meritorious in itself, as the friars are apparently attempting to argue, then the friars should be willing to await whatever manna falls, and to subsist on the sacraments—living, like the apostles they say they imitate, by preaching the Word.

"Conscience of this counseil tho comsede for to laughe" (242), perceiving how a strict application of the argument from need turns the tables on the corrupt friars. The strict application also points to a solution, which is not, interestingly, one of Need's suggested alternatives. Conscience, in a passage that repeats Kynde's instructions to the dreamer

(208ff.) and anticipates Conscience's words at the end of the poem, invites the friars into Unity, and tells them,

> . . . ye shal have breed and clothes
> And othere necessaries ynowe—yow shal no thyng lakke,
> With that ye leve logik; and lerneth for to lovye!
>
> (248–50)

That is, the friars should spend more time loving, and less time inventing arguments of self-justification. When they have "necessaries ynowe," the whole structure of specious arguments about their worthiness collapses. This is not one of Need's alternatives, because in Conscience's economy of sufficiency Need is strictly speaking not an issue. The question of need simply disappears—as a strict Conscience might prefer, having noticed how the term *need* shows a tendency to become as slippery as Lady Meed herself in contexts of self-justification.

NEED AND LOVE

Thus I believe that it is possible to read Need consistently throughout Passus XX, in waking and in dream, as a term that anchors various arguments of self-justification. This reading has important implications for an understanding of the character of the dreamer, who at this point in the poem has the name Will, and might seem to be growing closer and closer to the implied author himself. Will meets Need while Will is wandering "by the way, . . . awaked, / Hevy chered . . . and elenge in herte" (1–2), not knowing "wher to ete ne at what place" (3). Will might even be wondering not only *where* to eat, but actually *whether* to eat—whether he is justified in accepting any food that he might be given. Waking, goaded by misery of body and spirit, perhaps literally wondering whether he should passively starve, Will encounters a word that seems to have the capacity to serve as a hermeneutic principle to interpret to him his own current experience. The word *need* seems to hold out to him a possibility of self-justification, a possibility of which he has not had the courage or psychological energy to avail himself. As I have often said, Will is an intellectual, with the intellectual's virtues and flaws. To be an intellectual meant to Langland, and still means in the West, to be obsessed with texts, and therefore with the normal rhetorical structures of self-justification. It is something of a mystery why we intellectuals, in the midst of physical and spiritual pain, should consider rhetorical justification important, why the texts that we can imagine ourselves producing about our experiences should sometimes seem more important to us than the experiences themselves—but nevertheless it is so. The appeal to Need involves a deeply personal concern for Will, but it is not personal in the sense of elevating his private aches and pains to be his sole moral standard. That seems to be exactly the mistake people make about need when they fall victim to Antichrist, in the dream that immediately follows the waking episode:

> Antecrist cam thanne, and al the crop of truthe
> Torned it [tid] up-so-doun, and overtilte the roote,
> And made fals sprynge and sprede and spede mennes nedes.
>
> (53–55)

Already in this passage the meaning of *need* begins to slide into something altogether less edifying. Will's waking encounter with Need is personal rather in the sense of arising from an intellectual's passion to interpret his experience through words arranged in a hierarchy of self-justification.

But justifying ourselves to ourselves and to our fellow human beings by the use of rhetorical commonplaces is not the same as being justified before God. Indeed, such attempts at rhetorical self-justification often get in the way because they are at base self-flattering. It becomes necessary to ask how any interpretive system interprets God, who is finally outside of all human interpretive systems. What sort of talk about God and the sinner's relationship to him is possible in the interpretive system where Need is the central hermeneutic principle?

Need makes the transition to talk about God via the Latin proverb *Homo proponit et Deus disponit* (33a). Human beings can only "propose," or suggest, interpretations of reality; God "disposes," or creates and sustains, the ultimate reality that is at the limit of all human interpretations. The C-text changes the *disponit* to perfect-tense *disposuit*. The change is odd, since the present-tense form is the more usual—appearing also in the other occurrence of the proverb in the C-text (C.XI.306–7)—and since *disponit* is a rhyme, whereas *disposuit* is not. This might be one of Langland's grammatical tropes: God in the C-text "has disposed," is *perfect,* is complete as human beings are not complete. Human beings "propose" out of their incompleteness and need; God, who has founded all human interpretations, is himself always beyond them. God "*governeth alle goode vertues*" (34; emphasis mine), first in the theological sense of grounding the possibility of human goodness, but also in the grammatical sense of founding the possibility of the rhetorical hierarchies within which the names of the virtues function.

The metaphor of God as "governing" the names of the virtues in the grammatical sense suggests an answer to the question of how Need interprets God. Need himself, as the central term in a rhetorical structure, has been arguing that Need also "governs" the names of the cardinal virtues—that is, that the names of the virtues are subordinated to Need in arguments of self-justification. I want to propose that the lines in which Need talks about his relationship with God be taken quite straightforwardly: "[God] governeth alle goode vertues; / And Nede is next hym" (34–35). That is, literally and proximately, Need is next to God—is, in fact, in Need's interpretive system the name of Jesus, who "meketh" (35; contrary to Schmidt, I read *meketh* here as reflexive, as also in V.69—where the pronoun, however, is expressed), and who is "as lowe as a lomb, for lakkyng that hym nedeth" (36). This lamb is the Lamb of God. In this reading, the lines about the philosophers who "forsoke welthe for thei wolde be nedy" (38–39) do not look backward to function as an illustration of the principle articulated in line 37 ("nede maketh nedé fele nedes lowe-herted"). Instead, the lines look forward to function as an earthly analogy for the Incarnation: just as philosophers give up earthly wealth, so God gives up his "grete joye *goostliche*" (40; emphasis mine), in a spiritual signification, as opposed to the philosophers' renunciation of literal wealth. By the Incarnation, God is given the name of Need.

Langland presents Need as the central word in an interpretive system, as having the peculiar mode of being of a word that hovers between private and transpersonal reality. In the language where Need is the central word, God himself takes on in Jesus the mode of being of a word— not the divine Logos itself (though that Word of words makes human language possible), but instead the human word that is the human interpretation of God. As Mary Carruthers says in her discussion of Augustine's doctrine of signs, "Christ is the true significator of all language, just as He is the source of all understanding"; Augustine develops the "analogy between the rational mind [composed of memory, understand-ing, and will] and the Trinity," where the "mind's understanding is par-ticularly the image of Christ, as Wisdom and as the Word. . . . The Word is thus the significator of the inner word, which is the mind's un-derstanding" (16). We are back to one of the founding metaphors of An-ima's epistemology in Passus XV: namely, the metaphor of the mirror in which human beings see God, though darkly, represented in their own mental processes. God is also represented, though darkly, in the names that human beings give him. God as he is cannot be talked about, be-cause God is the ultimate reality at the limit of all human chains of in-terpretation. But Jesus, precisely because he can be interpreted as Need, can be talked about, can enter into the structures of rhetorical justifi-cation centered on Need—in particular, all justifications including the cardinal virtues.

Jesus, as Need, is the self-imposed incompleteness of God. God "cam and took mankynde and bicam nedy" (41), as if the *differentia* that distinguishes humanity from divinity is precisely neediness. Need in-vokes scriptural authority for his interpretation of Jesus: "So he was nedy, as seith the Book, in manye sondry places" (42). Jesus says on the Cross,

> Bothe fox and fowel may fle to hole and crepe,
> And the fissh hath fyn to flete with to reste,
> Ther nede hath ynome me, that I moot nede abide
> And suffre sorwes ful soure, that shal to joye torne.
>
> (44–47)

As Robertson and Huppé (228–29) point out, this passage draws on a complicated scriptural and patristic tradition, and is not as strange a speech in the medieval context as it might initially appear to a modern reader. Jesus stresses here his homelessness in the world that he creat-ed—the process, the in-betweenness, the imperfection, the incomplete-ness, that neediness implies. Following this speech comes Need's "For-thi" (48), the "therefore" that signals the conclusion of his argument. Need has been teaching Will how Need as a hermeneutic principle makes it possible to introduce the name of Jesus into rhetorical struc-tures of self-justification. We can be Christ-like in that we can be needy. We participate in God's love when we interpret ourselves as yearning and incomplete—not when we believe that we can say we "do well." Jesus is for us, strictly speaking, the relation between God as interpreted—the God who needs—and the human beings who also need.

At this point I want to turn briefly to two texts very distant from *Piers Plowman*. One of them, an ancient text, could have influenced Langland only very indirectly. The other, a modern text, could not have influenced Langland at all. But I think both texts can inform a reading of the Need episode. I want to use these texts to help me articulate the implications of Langland's argument for an understanding of human and divine love.

In Plato's *Symposium*, Socrates tells a myth of the origin of Love. The myth follows an exemplary Socratic demonstration that love is a relational term—that is, that love is always love *of* something that the lover lacks. In the myth, then, the mother of Love is Need. The passage is in *Symposium* 203b. The word in Greek is πενίσ, which is translated as *Need* by Michael Joyce in the *Collected Dialogues* in the Bollingen Series (555), and as *Poverty* by Walter Hamilton (82). Robert Worth Frank distinguishes between *need* and *poverty* in Langland (*Scheme* 113–14), but both senses seem to have been present in the Greek term. Greek has a related agent noun πένης, meaning a day laborer or a poor man—the noun which, interestingly enough, might be the noun of choice in ancient Greek to identify Piers himself. Socrates' point—my point—is that Love springs from Need, and therefore is always needy, desiring something that it lacks. Transposing Socrates' argument to Langland's context, we would read that God's love for human beings is a manifestation of his need, the self-imposed incompleteness of the Incarnation. Need's interpretation of God is that God loves us because he needs us, and so we understand him best through our own need, by identifying our neediness with the neediness of God incarnated in Jesus. Need is what human beings can share with God.

Andrew Galloway, as it seems to me, arrives by an entirely different route at a very similar conclusion about Langland's theology. Galloway analyzes Langland's representations of the Trinity, and concludes that God the Father needed to be incarnated in the Son in order to gain experience of human suffering. In Galloway's narrative of the dreamer, as in mine, the dreamer finds the usual "clerical" ways of gaining knowledge unsatisfactory (143); the dreamer needs, instead, what Galloway calls "experience": "Suffering pain as a human being among human beings, social suffering and experiences, is the primary means for intellectual and spiritual growth" (144). Ultimately, Galloway suggests, "the experience of suffering the world and suffering in the world constitutes the *imago Dei* in human consciousness" (146).

But why does God need our suffering, according to the interpretation of Need? Charles Sanders Peirce, in the last of a series of five papers published in the *Monist* from 1891 to 1893, discusses his doctrine of "Evolutionary Love," or, in a typically ugly Peircean coinage, *agapism*. A passage near the beginning of his essay interests me here: "[T]he love that God is, is not a love of which hatred is the contrary; . . . but it is a love which embraces hatred as an imperfect stage of it . . . yea, even needs hatred and hatefulness as its object. For self-love is no love; so if God's self is love, that which he loves must be defect of love" (353). Peirce is concerned to show that the universe evolves not by "absolute chance" or by "mechanical necessity," but by the "law of love" (362). This seems to me very close to what Need is saying in Langland's poem. Need, like Peirce, interprets the universe as evolving, yearning toward its perfection. Transposing this idea to Langland's context, we might say: God's love needs our sin as its object, as the imperfect stage of itself; and we interpret God's love this way when we adopt Need as our hermeneutic principle. We understand and to some degree participate in the love of God through our neediness, by interpreting ourselves as incomplete. By desiring for ourselves and others the perfection we lack, we love ourselves and others as incomplete versions of what we might evolve to be. We become need, a relation between an incomplete now and a projected completeness. To that extent, we share God's thoughts and God's need. By giving Jesus the name of Need, we understand how human beings may love by needing. We interpret ourselves this way, paradigmatically for the intellectual, when we attempt to justify ourselves by appealing to our need that is like the need of Jesus.

That appeal is of course exactly the appeal the friars try to make, and so Langland characteristically has it both ways. On the one hand, the episode of Need constitutes one of the profound statements in the poem about the nature of divine love and the possibility for human understanding of and to some degree participation in that love. On the other hand, arguments from need can, and somehow always do, go wrong. The term, like any term, slides into perversions of itself. Rather than turning the exercise of rhetorical self-justification into a salvific discipline, the term more typically helps us oil the logical machinery of Hell. I think, then, that we might sometimes miss the point when we dispute whether the speech of Need represents Langland's final opinion, or whether the implications of the speech can be made to square with orthodoxy, or whether the poem finally comes to rest on a hard but final answer to every question that can be posed about human behavior on earth—the answer of need. All of these questions are interesting and important, and I believe that Langland wants us to think hard about all of them. But I also believe that it is a mistake to assume that a book that would answer all such questions would be the last book that would need to be written about Langland. Langland lets the lightning strike with a moment of brilliant illumination, and then the darkness floods back in. The hermeneutic quest remains a quest, now and always in *Piers Plowman*.

BIBLIOGRAPHICAL ESSAY 2.3

The episode of Need has always been one of the more problematic passages in a poem that sometimes seems virtually a pastiche of problematic passages. S. S. Hussey, for example, identifies the passage as one of the puzzling "insertions" in the poem (1). Britton Harwood provides a quick summary of some opinions about the passage (216). As I have hinted, most of the critical energy expended on the passage has been directed toward attempting to determine Need's moral valency. Most critics read the passage with the hermeneutics of suspicion, finding less there of redemptive value than I do. Malcolm Godden sees Need as "the culmination of the series of commons, brewer, lord and king" but argues that the speech of Need "has rather a special status, between the two visions, as well as a special complexity, because it concerns what for Langland was the crucial case: a reduction of the divine spark to earthly needs by the Church itself, and more particularly the corruption of an ideal which had meant a great deal to Langland within and outside his poem: the eremitic values and life exemplified by Patience" (164). Robert Worth Frank says that Need's argument "makes need the sole principle of morality," where "Need is primarily the lack of food, drink, and clothing" (*Scheme* 113). Harwood cites Robert Adams on the ethical neutrality of Need, and says that Need's argument leads to the conclusion that the law "must be suspended so that this physical suffering might end" (133). James Simpson also regards Need's arguments askance: "Whereas the powerful can manipulate intelligence, courage and justice, the poor, and Will in particular, are being encouraged to manipulate temperance" (223). Mary Carruthers (159–60) and Pamela Raabe (137) make similar connections. Carruthers believes that the error in Need's argument is that "by his appeal to temperance, he is using a moral concept to justify a nonmoral necessity" (161). Carruthers and Raabe are in general strongly at odds about Langland's attitude toward language (see Bibliographical Essay 1), and they respectively stress Langland's themes of the corruption and the ambivalence of language. It seems maybe a little strange, then, that they should both severely critique the argument of Need in philosophical and theological terms—as if Langland might have thought there existed some uncorrupted, nonambivalent language from the perspective of which to judge Need's argument. My project is rather to try to get inside the perspective from which human experience appears when we attempt to justify ourselves by the argument from need. As Carruthers says, in an aside that could almost be my motto here, "From one point of view, Need's argument is not vicious; it is merely the argument of Need" (162).

Lawrence M. Clopper's discussion of Need shows how it is possible to interpret Need's counsel subtly and yet without suspicion. Not surprisingly, given the thesis of his book, Clopper thinks that Need is a friar. Need's rhetoric, Clopper argues, is the rhetoric of the Franciscan reformists (93–99)—and, therefore, in a sense, Need speaks for Langland himself, who "directs his text to a special audience—the Franciscans—in order to call them to reform" (*Songes of Rechelesnesse* 19). Clopper's is the most thoroughgoing attempt I know of to read Langland's own mind and purpose (as it turns out for Clopper, a very Franciscan sort of mind and purpose) from the texts and contexts of *Piers Plowman*. Clopper's book persuades me that Langland knew Franciscan texts and took them very seriously; I am not as ready as Clopper is to infer from that premise that we know Langland's mind and have identified his purpose. In my reading of *Piers Plowman*, it is more important to notice the contending of texts than it is to try to tease out a single strand from the complex intertextuality to identify with Langland's own intention.

Anyone who thinks seriously about the episode of Need must be deeply indebted to the splendid article by Robert Adams ("The Nature of Need in *Piers Plowman* XX"), who comes as close as anyone could expect on historicist principles to providing a "final word" on the episode. Adams's approach, like Clopper's, is different from mine, and it is certainly the more natural approach. Adams, like Clopper, attempts to decode Langland's text by reading it against other texts that might have influenced it, in order to arrive at some fairly stable determination about what Langland thought about Need. Adams's method is implied in the metaphor that controls his article, the metaphor of a trial in which Need's conviction is ultimately secured on the basis of a single "clue," the decisive text that provides the key for decoding Langland:

> [T]he motive for Need's remarks is hardly transparent, even when viewed from the proper literary, historical, and theological perspectives. Only one truly definitive clue to Need's role exists; but it is not one that would have been any more obvious to most of Langland's contemporaries than to us. So long as this clue remains undiscovered, we are in a rather precarious position; we must convict Need, if at all, on evidence largely circumstantial—guilt by association with characters who themselves are guilty mostly by implication. (281)

The clue, the "ultimate source for the Need episode" (283), turns out to be Gregory the Great's *Moralia in Job*—specifically, Gregory's commentary on Job 41:13b, "faciem eius praecedit egestas"—and a number of texts related to Gregory's. Furthermore, Adams argues, Langland's reflections on the Apocalypse and the coming of the Antichrist in Passus XX are indebted to "the treatise through which Gregory's discussion . . . may have first come to his attention": namely, the *Liber de Antichristo*, a "thirteenth century anti-mendicant work from the circle of William of St. Amour" (296). After Adams's article, it is hard not to accept that in the Need episode Langland was thinking about Gregory's commentary on Job and about the *Liber de Antichristo*, among other texts. But it remains possible to believe—or so I think—that Langland's point about Need is not necessarily the same as Gregory's point or the point of the *Liber*. Apart from the nontrivial question of who knows more about the texts Langland alludes to (I stipulate that Adams knows far more than I do), the issue here on the theoretical level is precisely the issue of methodeutic principle. Adams's methodeutic principle is that the exegetical tradition should form the primary control on interpretations of the Need episode. My methodeutic principle is that the primary control should be the dramatic and rhetorical structures in Langland's text that function to show the reader how interpretation happens.

My debate with Adams—or Clopper, for that matter—is not, however, simply the old debate between the formalist and the historicist. I have tried in all the arguments in my first chapter to explain why things are more complex than that. I, of course, would prefer to say that my reading includes Adams's and Clopper's readings, in the sense that I am prepared to believe that Langland wanted at least some of his readers to think about all of the things Adams and Clopper mention—without, however, thinking of Langland's text as a respectful translation of Gregory's thought or of Franciscan reformist thought. My approach agrees more with Harwood's, in assuming that "Langland wrote *Piers* not in order to teach but to find out" (4). On the other hand, I am less ready than Harwood is to argue that Langland represents himself even in the last passus as having found out.

Another issue in the Need episode is the issue of the relation between the dreamer and the author. I will have more to say about this relation in Chapter 3. Here, the issue is connected with the question of waking and dreaming. When the dreamer, having been given Langland's own name Will, acts in the waking world, as opposed to the world of dreams, is he somehow closer to Langland himself? Carruthers cites the Need episode in remarking on the "fluidity" of the relationship between waking and sleep, which "has a serious purpose, as it gradually merges dream with waking life, casting into doubt the ordinary perceptions of reality" (22). E. T. Donaldson (199–226) discusses at length the biographical implications of the so-called autobiographical passage in C.V (in Donaldson's numbering, C.VI), which, as another waking episode where the dreamer talks with personifications that appear also in dreams, I have connected with the Need episode. John Bowers challenges Donaldson's identification of Will with Langland himself, and argues for a more complex relationship between the persona and the poet (165–89). Bowers, somewhat like Carruthers, argues that the point of the waking episode is to confuse "the boundaries between dream and reality. . . . Is it any wonder that Will has become so distraught when his dreams impinge upon the nightmare of this world, affording him no escape?" (159). I believe that the distinction between Will and Langland might ultimately be unfathomable for us, and perhaps was unfathomable for Langland himself. Perhaps Langland wrote his poem, in part, in an attempt to know himself. Interpreting the world, as I have argued, is essentially a matter also of interpreting oneself. Neither process of interpretation achieves closure in *Piers Plowman*.

CHAPTER 3

THE DREAMER
AND PIERS

So hope y to haue of hym þat is almyghty
A gobet of his grace, and bigynne a tyme
That alle tymes of my tyme to profit shal turne.

(C.V.99–101)

Private Symbols and the Narrative

In one sense, the dreamer and Piers Plowman are the only private symbols in the poem. That is, we do not know who or what the dreamer is until Langland portrays him, and we do not know what allegorical significance to attach to Piers before the experience of the poem itself—or, if the truth were to be told, even after reiterated experiences of the poem. As John Bowers says of Piers, "[N]o one can say clearly or indisputably who he is or what he symbolizes" (34). All the other allegorical personifications are already firmly established cultural entities, and Langland uses or subverts their established meanings to whatever ends he happens to be pursuing at the time. Obviously, we can look at other dream visions to see what dreamers tend to be like, and we can locate other literary plowmen to help us conceive what Langland's audience might have expected of Piers. But such activities of contextualizing seem less decisive for interpretation than do explorations of the Deadly Sins, for example, or of the *vis imaginativa,* or of the particular texts Langland quotes. This is not to say that we always quickly determine what Langland means by examining medieval notions of this or that. It is to say that we do often quickly determine an answer to the question, "What is Langland talking *about?*" But that is exactly the question that is not easily answered with the figure of the dreamer or the figure of Piers himself.

In the criticism of *Piers Plowman,* the problem of the dreamer fragments into several related issues. First and fundamentally, is the dreamer in any sense a coherent ego, or is he himself already a collection of fragments? This is the problem of the "interior Babel" that I have already discussed, and it is the problem articulated most sharply by David Lawton in a passage I have already quoted: the dreamer's "consciousness is itself plural and split: necessarily so, for it is constituted by the discourses that divide it. If truth cannot be seen as single or stable, the seeker cannot be either" (4). Second, is the dreamer a purely dramatic character completely different from his creator, or a surrogate for Langland himself, or even an actual representation of Langland himself told retrospectively? Any or all of these, at different points in the poem? Depending upon how we answer such questions, we will see the dreamer alternately as bumbling fool or witty interrogator, incredibly naïve or excruciatingly subtle; and we will find in Langland's work a critical problem exactly parallel to the problem of Chaucerian irony. To what extent, that is, does the dreamer speak for Langland himself? Third and finally, does the dreamer make progress? Is there an overarching narrative in the poem? Does the "step" of each passus represent movement to another stage of a continuing journey, or is it only one more step in a random walk?

There are parallel problems with Piers. First, the Plowman is not a stable symbol. He is at various times a laborer, a pilgrim, a good man, Jesus, Peter, and the pope. Second, depending upon what we think Piers stands for at any particular time, we might assign him more or less authority. He asks for lessons from Hunger in Passus VI (210–11), but he gives lessons to the child Jesus in Passus XVI (104). The priest questions Piers's authority in the "pardon scene" (VII.135–36), but at the end of the poem Conscience goes in search of Piers as if Piers were the ultimate authority (XX.381ff.). Third and finally, is there in any sense a "development" in the meaning of Piers Plowman? Is there an increasingly profound understanding of the symbol, an accruing of meanings around a coherent though perhaps ineffable center, or only a jostling of incommensurable discourses each of which abuses Piers according to its own compulsions?

For me, the operation of Piers as a mysterious symbol is one of the features that lends what is after all a highly intellectualized and satirical poem a genuinely dreamlike quality. That is, there is a kind of inexplicable strangeness in the fact that a laborer can contend with a priest over Latin texts (VII.131ff.); or in the fact that the dreamer swoons in a "love dream" at the very mention of Piers's name (XVI.18–19), after Piers has been more an absence than a presence in the poem for eight passus; or in the fact that although Piers himself has constructed the landscape of Passus XIX, he silently disappears from it in Passus XX and again becomes the absent object of a quest. Piers operates, that is, exactly like the private symbol of a dream—as a signifier invested with a surplus of meaning for the dreamer, so that the dreamer himself understands neither why the symbol has such power for him nor how to explain its power to anyone else.

I believe that this is the crucial fact about the symbol of Piers Plowman: Piers means more to the dreamer than the dreamer can say, and more than the dreamer can encompass intellectually. Gillian Rudd's reflections are especially helpful here. In Rudd's reading of the pardon scene, Piers "fragments his own identity," so that

> the original Piers disappears. In order to even begin to fulfill his potential Piers must fragment or deconstruct and break down his identity into a plurality of possible identities. The same may be said of the language or poetic discourse of the poem itself. The search for the one transcendent signifier (Truth) in a fixed and readily defined form (the tower or shrine) is abandoned and instead a process of exploration is begun which investigates the way one's notion of what knowledge is, or ought to be, affects not only one's language but also the way one seeks to acquire such knowledge. (222–23)

As Rudd points out, the unquestioned belief in the existence of the "transcendent signifier" makes possible the quest for meaning that results in the fragmentation of Piers and of all the other provisional signifiers in the poem.

Even though I have argued that postmodern categories of thought prove useful in analyzing *Piers Plowman,* here is one respect in which Langland is not a postmodern thinker. At least, Langland does not think like contemporary American pragmatists such as Richard Rorty, who sees "vocabularies as instruments for coping with things rather than representations of their intrinsic natures" (193). The horns of the dilemma, as Rudd points out, are nihilism, on the one hand, and submitting to a single authoritative discourse, on the other. If all discourses are equally valuable, then there is nothing to choose among them other than the power of the enforcing authority. But the ultimate reality at the limit of all discourses checks our errors and explodes the authoritative discourses that block inquiry. We avoid the dilemma

> precisely by the acknowledged existence of a transcendental signifier, since this relieves the need or the call for a definition of such an ultimate "truth" silently supporting or lying within the text, and allows the attention to shift to the text itself. . . . The "founding subject" in a Christian text is the *logos* which provides the assurance of the existence of a final meaning, an ultimate Truth. The text and audience are thus relieved from trying to discover or define this Truth. Any quest within the text is therefore a search for, or exploration of, the possible ways of expressing this Truth; the status of that Truth itself is not questioned. (Rudd 223)

Langland's thought perhaps has more affinities with the pragmatism of Charles Sanders Peirce—or, as Peirce eventually termed it, "pragmaticism." Human consciousness is interpretive and fallible, but at the limit of all interpretations—at the limit of all the chains of signs that constitute human consciousness—is the reality that endures. This reality, which for Langland is God himself, has many names in *Piers Plowman*. As Mary Carruthers puts it, Piers is "the *figura* within time, . . . the vehicle through which the ineffable is articulated within the limitations of human experience" (170).

The nature of self-conscious interpretation, therefore, is to be aware of itself as stretching toward a limit that it never reaches. At any given moment, we have some notion of what might be at that limit—without, however, a sense of having grasped it. The "figure remains implicit, a dimly perceived, distant prospect" (Carruthers 171). We have direction without completion, a vector, as it were. As in the quotation from the C-text at the beginning of this chapter, interpretation always stretches toward the "not-yet" that is going to make sense, presumably, of all the "up-to-now." This "not-yet," so far ungrasped, nevertheless will be continuous with our present experience, and so we have at least some vague apprehension of the general shape it must take. Any interpretation that is aware of itself as such is a gesture. It includes a component of absence or provisionality. By awareness of itself as "only" interpretation, the interpretation admits that it is not, after all, identical with what it seeks to comprehend. Piers is in one sense a sign of God. But that does not distinguish Piers from any of the other signs in the poem. All signs in human consciousness, directly or indirectly, are signs of God. More precisely, I want to argue that Piers is the dreamer's private symbol for what the dreamer feels is missing in his understanding—the dreamer's projection of what he needs to understand in order to represent reality accurately to himself. As an intellectual, the dreamer is always asking himself, "What would I need to understand in order to grasp the reality that I dimly sense at the limits of my current understanding?" At times, the dreamer seems to think it would be sufficient for him to understand what it is to be a good laborer or a good man. Later, it seems necessary to him to understand Jesus, or Jesus' vicar on earth. Piers is the interpretive act that is always receding, always just beyond the dreamer's horizon. The dreamer can only guess at the nature of what he knows he does not grasp but believes he needs to grasp; and these projections, changing as the dreamer's understanding changes, constitute the portraits of Piers in the poem. To put it quite starkly, the dreamer as intellectual is in search not of mystical union with God, but of a definitive or at least satisfying interpretation of God. Whether the dreamer *ought* to want what he wants is another question, and whether he has any choice about wanting it is perhaps a third question. Nevertheless, the dreamer in *Piers Plowman* is not the only intellectual who ever wanted an interpretation of God. The space that is always opening in the poem between God himself and our embarrassingly inadequate interpretations of him is the space occupied by the symbol of Piers.

The implication of this reading is that the dreamer and Piers are reciprocally determining, two sides of a coin, and that progression in the dreamer's understanding, if any, may be read off the changes in the dreamer's understanding of Piers. We will know the dreamer by knowing what he thinks he needs. This is another way of saying that we will know the intellectual by knowing what the intellectual wills to know. In this chapter, I want to look closely at the passages in the poem that detail the dreamer's relationship with Piers. The point here, as everywhere in this book, is not to give a "reading" of *Piers Plowman* in terms of some single theme or story, but to show how the fragmented, perhaps even embryonic, narrative of the dreamer serves not to supersede the authoritative commentaries it incorporates or to provide moral directions like a proto—*Pilgrim's Progress,* but instead serves recursively to show that autobiographical narrative itself is an open form—that configuring one's life as a particular kind of story does not constitute salvation, and that the conflict of interpretations does not end with the dénouement of the autobiography.

I will argue, nevertheless, that there *is* a narrative of the dreamer, through which Langland attempts to articulate the complexities of the intellectual's spiritual development. Because the narrative is inconclusive, *Piers Plowman* also critiques the pretensions of narrative to provide the definitive interpretive system for an understanding of the human self. But for narrative to be critiqued, there must be enough in the poem for the rudiments of narrative to be recognized as such. The develop-

ment I shall follow is simple but often subterranean. It surfaces and becomes visible, I shall argue, precisely at those points in the poem where
the dreamer's relationship with Piers is at issue.

In brief outline it goes like this. The dreamer of the first five passus,
until the startling moment at V.537 when Piers first puts his head into
the poem out of nowhere, wants to know "How I may save my soule"
(I.84). Sloth, intellectual pride, downright dullness, and a predisposition
to wrangle with authoritative figures obstruct him—as I have argued in
my analysis of the dreamer's interaction with Holy Church in Passus I.
But he also has an extraordinary talent for getting hold of the wrong end
of the stick. His question about saving his soul, while it sounds sincere
and harmless enough, is like the tiny error in the launching of the rocket
that multiplies into a miss of a million miles. As David Mills says, "He
does not seek in a spirit of humility but in a spirit of speculative curiosi-
ty" (209). The point is, precisely, that he himself cannot save his soul. In
theological terms, he cannot justify himself. In long retrospect from
much later in the poem, Holy Church's answer might even seem to hint
at the problems implicit in the dreamer's question: "Whan alle tresors
arn tried, . . . treuthe is the beste" (I.85), so that "tho that werche wel as
Holy Writ telleth" may be "siker that hire soule shul wende to hevene"
(I.130–32). While the answer may be completely satisfactory from the
perspective of Holy Church, who claims to be the agency of salvation for
those who believe and behave as she tells them to, nevertheless the answer anticipates the whole snarl of later arguments about faith and
works, Augustinianism and Pelagianism, that fill the middle of the
poem. Thus Holy Church herself, perhaps unwittingly, encourages the
dreamer in his initial mistake of thinking that some sort of self-
justification might be possible.

The dreamer observes evil at work in Passus II–V. The dreamer's
plea to Holy Church is of a piece with his desire for self-justification:
"Kenne me by som craft to knowe the false" (II.4). The false is that
which one must recognize and avoid. Lady Meed proves subtle and at-
tractive, but ultimately helpless before those who see through her. The
Deadly Sins are comical and are often unconvincing in their protesta-
tions of repentance. In one way, evil in this part of the poem, being ex-
ternalized, is not taken seriously enough. The genre of satire makes evil

laughable or repulsive, and therefore apparently easily avoidable. The satirical mode thus fosters the dreamer's illusion that evil is something "out there," that intellectual distinctions between the true and the false are more or less easily made, and that the making of such distinctions leads naturally to good works and therefore self-justification.

The first vision of Piers, then, in this context appears as the dreamer's first attempt to conceive good at work in the world. Given that the poem begins with the cacophony of the earthly city conceived in terms of social classes and occupational groups, it is not surprising that good is construed here in terms of good labor within the social organism—that Piers is first of all the laborer who works in accordance with the will of Truth. That is what the dreamer thinks he needs to understand at this point: how to labor well within the social organism. To do that would constitute self-justification.

But something strange happens. The vision overleaps its own premises. Piers's establishment is challenged first by the wasters and then by the priest. Piers tears the pardon and changes his way of life, and the dreamer does not understand.

I want to argue that this is the moment that begins the rising action in the dreamer's narrative. The dreamer needs to understand why Piers tears the pardon, and that is something that the dreamer will not be equipped to understand until he has experienced the long educative middle of the poem. It is not something he can be told about from within the perspective of any particular interpretive system, but instead something—like love—that must be experienced to be understood. The dreamer's initial vision of Piers as the good laborer within the social organism contains within it the seed of its own overcoming, its *Aufhebung* in another vision that Piers also represents but that currently lies over the dreamer's horizon. I will argue that Piers signals by the tearing of the pardon the deconstruction of a whole system of thought that centers on the ultimately stifling and self-defeating notion of self-justification. With respect to the long middle of the poem, at least, I can agree with Anne Middleton's eloquent statement:

> The belief that one may win heaven by works alone is everywhere for Langland the original and final delusion of mankind, yet it is so very tenacious, and so very reasonable—especially to those who care as deeply as Langland does about

civil virtue—that it always in this poem requires a violent shock to dislodge. Every major reversal in the poem witnesses to the power of this delusion. ("Making" 254)

The dreamer spends Passus VIII–XIV catching up with Piers, in the long middle throughout which Piers is absent except by hearsay. When the dreamer is ready, through his identification with Haukyn the Active Man, to understand the impossibility of self-justification in the continually renewed state of sin, then Anima by defining the soul as relational leads the dreamer to the new vision of Piers as the guardian of the Tree of Charity and the landlord of *Liberum Arbitrium* (XVI.16).

That is, the dreamer has moved. At first, he believes that all he needs to understand is how to work well in the world, so that he will be self-justified. Now, he believes that he needs to understand how to foster charity in himself, so that he will stand in proper relation to his fellow human beings and to God. As I suggested in my earlier discussion of Anima, I read the vision of the Tree of Charity and the subsequent introduction of the gospel narrative as the crisis in the dreamer's own narrative. Here the dreamer begins to free himself not only from the disease of self-justification, but also from the intolerable itch to master texts that until now has been his primary symptom.

As the gospel narrative increasingly absorbs the dreamer, Piers increasingly comes to resemble Jesus in his human nature. Anima anticipates the development: "Piers the Plowman—*Petrus, id est, Christus*" (XV.212). Piers teaches the human Jesus "lechecraft" (XVI.104); Jesus on Palm Sunday is "semblable to the Samaritan, and somdeel to Piers the Plowman" (XVIII.10); Faith explains that Jesus will joust in Piers's armor, *"humana natura"* (XVIII.23); and in Passus XIX the dreamer confuses or conflates Piers with Jesus:

> . . . sodeynly me mette
> That Piers the Plowman was peynted al blody,
> And com in with a cros bifore the comune peple,
> And right lik in alle lymes to Oure Lord Jesu.
>   And thanne called I Conscience to kenne me the sothe:
> "Is this Jesus the justere," quod I, "that Jewes dide to dethe?
> Or it is Piers the Plowman! Who peynted hym so rede?"
>   (XIX.5–11)

What the dreamer now believes he needs to understand is the human nature of Jesus. Finally, however, this desire translates into the more limited, less mystical, but perfectly orthodox desire to understand Christ's representative on earth, the head of Christ's Church (XIX.183ff.). This is what Piers represents at the last moment when he is actually present in the poem, when he returns once again and for the last time to his symbolic plow: "Now is Piers to the plow" (338).

This moment represents the resolution of the dreamer's own narrative, which of course turns out already in the last lines of Passus XIX but especially in Passus XX to be no resolution. The dreamer might in fact have arrived painfully at the knowledge he needs. It might even have been the knowledge he had all along, if he had only paid attention to his own nature, his *kynde:*

> "Counseilleth me, Kynde," quod I, "what craft be best to lerne?"
> "Lerne to love," quod Kynde, "and leef alle othere."
> "How shal I come to catel so, to clothe me and to feede?"
> "And thow love lelly, lakke shal thee nevere
> Weede ne worldly mete, while thi lif lasteth."
> And there by conseil of Kynde I comsed to rome
> Thorugh Contricion and Confession til I cam to Unitee.
>
> (XX.207–13)

The first of the quoted lines looks back to the dreamer's requests to Holy Church: "yet mote ye kenne me bettre / By what craft in my cors it [truth] comseth" (I.138–39), and "Kenne me by som craft to knowe the false" (II.4). The dreamer still has not taken sufficiently to heart Holy Church's advice to pay attention to the "kynde knowynge" in his own heart that teaches him to love (I.142–44). But at least the dreamer finally seems ready to entertain the notion that intellectual discrimination is not sufficient "craft" for salvation. He still sounds a little grudging, however, in his acceptance of Kynde's counsel, and he still cannot shake his concern for the distribution of worldly goods. The resolution might be true and good and perfectly orthodox, but it is not satisfying. It does not solve for the dreamer the intellectual and social problems that he poses for himself—at least, not in the form that he has posed them, a form that seems difficult or impossible for him to get beyond. Meanwhile, the Deadly Sins are attacking Unity, and false confessors are undermining believers' hard-won knowledge of how to deal with their sins. History—even sacred history, which anticipates the advent of the Antichrist—resists narrative resolution until the day of the "dredful dome, whan dede shulle rise / And comen alle bifore Crist acountes to yelde" (VII.188–89). Finally, then, Piers in the poem is what he has always been, the needful understanding that is absent, the object of the continuing quest of Conscience (XX.381ff.). And finally, then, the dreamer is not different in any important way from Langland or from any other sincere Christian. He arrives where everyone must arrive who wants to be in the will of God.

In the remainder of this chapter, I mean to trace in more detail the narrative structure I have just outlined. For the most part, however, I will proceed not by following the dreamer's pilgrimage in all its details, but instead by paying close attention to the places where the dreamer's interactions with Piers are most obviously at issue. If Piers is, as I have suggested, the dreamer's private symbol for the dreamer's projection of what he needs to understand, then the dreamer's narrative will be most visible not in the various discourses that he serially assumes and discards, but in the reference points where Langland shows us the dreamer's interpretive activity at white heat, as it were—the moments at which the dreamer sets for himself the direction of his own interpretive will.

The Pardon

THE PREPARATION

Piers's first speech is one of those deeply resonant sayings that occasionally pierce the clutter and cacophony that constitute the normal background. Piers, having suddenly "putte forth his heved" out of nowhere into the middle of the blundering rout of would-be pilgrims, says that he knows Truth "as kyndely as clerc doth hise bokes" (V.537–38). Piers has found the way to Truth's "place" by "Conscience and Kynde Wit" (539)—that is, presumably, without formal study. His relationship with Truth is one of long-term service as Truth's laborer (540–49).

What is especially interesting here is the suggestiveness of the simile Piers chooses. By comparing his knowledge of Truth with a clerk's knowledge of books, Piers simultaneously suggests that book knowledge is in some sense the definitive epistemological model, and yet that his own knowledge is in at least some sense beyond or at least outside that model. The vehicle of the simile—a clerk's knowledge of books—is *like* Piers's knowledge of Truth, not identical with it. More precisely, Piers's knowledge is like a clerk's knowledge in one particular respect: Piers knows Truth "as kyndely" as a clerk knows books. Clearly Langland means his readers to think of all the times in the poem when the dreamer querulously complains that he lacks "kynde knowynge" (for example, I.138; VIII.57, 110; and elsewhere). As Mary Clemente Davlin puts it,

> The comparison ("as clerc doþ hise bokes") shows that *kyndely* cannot mean "innately," since clerks are not born with a knowledge of their books, but gain it by the experience of learning. However, the same comparison sets Piers apart from clerks by implicitly contrasting the object of his knowledge (Truthe) with the object of theirs (books). Piers seems to have little learning, . . .
>
> Lines 542–53 suggest that Piers's knowledge of Truthe is intimate, practical and personal. (*"Kynde Knowyng"* 13)

That is, when the intellectual dreamer attains to Piers's knowledge of Truth, if the dreamer ever gets so far, that knowledge will seem in one sense familiar and continuous with the dreamer's current experience. The dreamer will know Truth in exactly the same way that, as an intellectual, he knows the texts that are nearest and dearest to his thought. And that knowledge is natural or "kyndely" in a profound way. Not only does long meditation on texts render them so familiar that it is impossible to distinguish between the text itself and one's own interpretive activity, but also it finally appears that texts are profoundly in harmony with the mind's "natural" way of understanding human experience. The world reads like a book, even for the illiterate. Because human experience itself is a virtual text, Piers knows that the pilgrims with the help of Grace can "see in thiselve Truthe sitte in thyn herte" (V.606), without the intellectual's necessary detour through texts.

But, of course, Piers does take a long detour through texts. The allegorical pilgrimage he describes in V.560 and following actually makes texts into *topoi,* into places. The scriptural verses listing the Ten Commandments become a ford (567) and a field (572–74), stumps (576–77) and a hill (580). The Court of Truth described in lines 585 and following makes sense only as a verbal artifact, an abstraction apprehended as the continuation of a long tradition of allegorical texts. And in the startling return to the human heart where Truth ultimately resides, the landscape Piers describes turns out to have been the interior landscape. That is, the texts he alludes to have become constitutive parts of the mind itself, the objects that literally construct mental "space." That kind of thing too is what happens to the clerk who lives long enough with his books.

So in his first speech Piers establishes what he symbolizes for the dreamer, but neither the dreamer nor the reader can articulate any final definitive meaning for the symbol. What the dreamer needs to understand, or so he thinks, is the life of good labor within the social organism. If he could only grasp that, he thinks, he might stand a chance of solving the intellectual problems posed by the Babylonian confusion of the Prologue. And with those problems solved, he thinks—mistakenly—that he will be able to save his soul. At this point, then, Piers represents what the dreamer thinks he needs to know. On the one hand, because he is an intellectual, the dreamer can project the general shape that knowledge must take for him. It will "feel" like book knowledge, like the knowledge an intellectual has of the texts that have most intimately formed that intellectual's mind. On the other hand, the dreamer is not yet in possession of that knowledge. The Commandments and the Court of Truth are to the dreamer as yet only the allegorical verbal abstractions Piers presents, not the concrete "places" of the mind with which Piers is intimately familiar as everyday features of his interior landscape. Piers's family is symptomatic. His wife "Dame Werch-whan-tyme-is" (VI.78), his daughter "Do-right-so-or-thi-dame-shal-thee-bete" (VI.79), and his son "Suffre-thi-Sovereyns-have-hir-wille-: / Deme-hem-noght-for-if-thow-doost-thow-shalt-it-deere-abugge; / Lat-God-yworthe-with-al-for-so-His-word-techeth" (VI.80–82) constitute a comic catalog that grows sillier and sillier. We cannot apprehend these names, Piers's intimates, as people or as anything other than verbal abstractions. The dreamer and the reader cannot think as Piers thinks, but the dreamer, at least, believes that he needs to.

In the dreamer's and reader's initial experience of Piers, then, Langland shows us a fundamental moment of the hermeneutic process: the moment wherein we think we know in a general or abstract way what we are looking for, but understand that our reach exceeds our grasp. For the imperfect dreamer, Piers represents the perfected understanding, the life lived in the world confidently and wholeheartedly. Piers as the perfected self is never grasped except in a dream, is always at the limit of the interpretive acts that intend him. The analogue in interpreting a text, perhaps, is the moment in which I say I know what the words mean and can even paraphrase them intelligently, but cannot yet relate the text meaningfully with my own life. Langland's point seems to be that in the long run there is no shortcut through abstract knowledge of texts. Instead of just parroting texts like a sluggish pupil, I must laboriously learn to relate the texts to my own life. Every time I do that, I find that each text reveals another horizon. Piers, the constantly changing symbol, represents this receding margin of understanding in a hermeneutic process that remains forever open-ended.

THE TEARING

So much has been written about Piers's tearing of the pardon that it seems hopeless to take everything into account in a book that is small enough to be held in one hand. In the Bibliographical Essay below I will mention the scholarly and critical essays that have most influenced my own reading. But as is the case elsewhere in this book, I believe that what I have to say about the pardon scene is more eclectic than original. Scholars of Langland will find scattered about in my reading like *disjecta membra* things that others have said in aid of cogent and coherent interpretations of this scene. What everybody agrees on, of course, is the structural importance of the scene to any reading of *Piers Plowman* that sees in the poem anything more than a jumbled pile of ideas. Critical practice since John Lawlor seems to support his dictum that "[t]he hinge upon which the poem turns is the Pardon" (298). Unfortunately, agreement stops there.

I will proceed on the following assumptions. First, I assume that the pardon from Truth is "valid." That is, the term *purchased* in the statement that Truth "purchaced hym a pardoun *a pena et a culpa*" (VII.3) suggests Christ's purchase of salvation for repentant sinners by his death on the Cross (Carruthers 72). Truth's pardon is "valid" in the sense that God has graciously provided an economy (which might like God its author also be named "truth" or ultimate reality) that allows sinners to do good works, to have those works counted as good, and to have their sins erased as if the sins had never been. The two lines from the Athanasian Creed in the written pardon are "ywriten right thus *in witnesse of* Truthe" (VII.110; emphasis mine). That is, the lines from the Creed merely describe the providential economy that allows for the performing of good works and the erasure of sin. The written pardon bears witness to the nature of ultimate reality, as opposed to creating a new reality by its drafting. As a legal document, it is "evidential," not "dispositive" (see Stock 42). The written document describes a genuine pardon, but not a new one that gets anybody off any hooks that Christ's sacrifice has not already provided for.

Second, I assume that the priest misinterprets the pardon. He implies that one should expect the kind of pardon that pardoners say they purvey, a dispositive pardon in the narrow sense, a document that releases sinners ex post facto from the temporal consequences of particular though unspecified sins. Thus, he "kan no pardon fynde" (VII.111) in the lines of the Creed, which because of false expectations now come to sound more like a threat.

Finally, I assume that Piers understands the pardon correctly. Therefore, the change in Piers after he tears the pardon is not a complete change of life, but a change of orientation: the "intensive adverbs" in "swynke noght so harde" (VII.118) and "so bisy be na moore" (119) "indicate not a total repudiation of physical labor but a de-emphasis of that . . . dimension of 'plowing' in favor of the spiritual plowing 'Of preieres and penaunce'" (Adams, "Pardon" 406).

Each of these assumptions would attract disagreement. Each of the assumptions impinges on one or more of the hotly contested issues in the interpretation of the pardon scene, which itself is the most hotly contested episode in the poem. Nonetheless, critics can be found who do agree with some or all of the assumptions. Nor are the assumptions pulled out of the air. What textual evidence there is for the assumptions, though it may appear thin to some, is suggested in what follows. But my main problem here is that, given the lack of consensus, some sort of simplifying assumptions seem necessary in order to proceed at all. Without some assumptions, no attempt to trace the dreamer's narrative would ever get past the pardon scene.

But even with these simplifying assumptions, the two major interpretive problems in this scene remain relatively unmitigated: first, what
does Piers mean by tearing the pardon; and second, how is the speaker's
(Langland's?) interpretation (VII.144ff.) of the dream to be taken?
What would the general premises of this book—that Langland connects
signs as if he were interpreting a text, and that he means to show recursively how one "goes about" textual hermeneutics—imply in connection
with these venerable problems?

To understand how the pardon is to be interpreted, it is necessary to
consider how it functions in the dramatic situation the poem sets up.
This is Langland's most obvious point about interpretation in the pardon scene: he shows that the meaning of a text for any interpreter is
likely to depend crucially upon the interpreter's understanding of the
function of the text in the social situation. In the drama of the poem,
the pardon from Truth comes with a message that Piers is to "taken his
teme and tilien the erthe" (VII.2)—no doubt with Langland's customary puns on *team/theme* and *till/tell,* so that Piers already exceeds his role as
the good laborer and shadows the scriptural sower. But Piers is to "holde
hym at home" (5), not to lead the pilgrimage to the Court of Truth as he
had promised in VI.6. Truth sends the message and the pardon apparently in response to something that has gone before: "Treuthe herde
telle herof, and to Piers sente" (VII.1). Robert Adams remarks the ambiguity of the *herof;* I think Adams has it about right when he reads the
herof as functioning on at least two levels:

> [G]race surely remains a key issue. The problem for the loyal folk has been
> to pursue a specifically religious life (the pilgrimage) while nevertheless coping
> with the time-consuming duties of ordinary daily life (the plowing). Insofar as
> that issue is at stake, Truth's pardon provides a merciful deliverance from the
> seemingly contradictory demands posed by these two obligations.
>
> Of equal importance, however, the contents of the pardon address the nar-
> rower issue of justice raised at the end of Passus 6 . . . , where wasters . . . enjoy
> a free ride on the backs of honest laborers. Truth's pardon mercifully redresses
> the apparent injustice of the natural cycle by transcending it rather than repeal-
> ing it. Now winners and wasters alike are confronted with the certainty that
> their behavior will entail appropriate final consequences. ("Pardon" 415)

I would like to focus on the second of these two functions. That is, the
pardon is at least in part a response to the breakdown in the social order

based on labor that is instituted by Piers on the half-acre. That break-down is evidenced by the repeated refusal of the wasters to work except under the harsh management of Hunger.

In short, Piers as the good laborer can envision a good society based on labor, but ipso facto he cannot see how to deal with the marginal figures who either cannot or will not labor. Piers's own relation with Truth is based on labor, and in his role as laborer he has trouble conceiv-ing any other possible relation with the providential economy. His anger at the lazy laborers is "pure tene" (VI.117), where *tene* connotes also "suf-fering" (as, for example, in VI.133). What upsets Piers is that those who will not work undermine what the good laborer understands as the providential economy. Ultimately, Piers's good society has no solution to the problem. The courteous knight can resist aggression and protect Piers, but he cannot make wasters willing to work. The threat that "thow shalt abigge by the lawe" (VI.166) comes to nothing: on the one hand, labor laws in fact do not work in practice; but, on the other hand, the problem is the more fundamental problem of the reformation of the will. Until the will of the wasters is reformed, wasting will go on as long as feast succeeds famine.

And the problem turns out to be more uncomfortable and personal for the good laborer than we might suspect at first. Piers's own state-ment to the lazy laborers is suggestive:

> "Now, by the peril of my soule!" quod Piers al in pure tene,
> "But ye arise the rather and rape yow to werche,
> Shal no greyn that here groweth glade yow at nede,
> And though ye deye for doel, the devel have that recche!"
>
> (VI.117–20)

There is a disturbing hint in the oath of line 117 that the health of Piers's own soul is bound up with his ability to deal properly with the wasters. If he cannot make them work, he must decide whether to feed them or to let them starve—literally, whether to send them to Hell. This moral dilemma seems to be the point of Piers's colloquy with Hunger. After Hunger masters the wasters, "Thanne hadde Piers pite" (VI.199). Though Piers is well aware that when Hunger is gone, "thei wol werche ful ille" (204), nevertheless they are "my blody bretheren, for God boughte us alle" (207). The commercial image here looks ahead to Truth's "purchasing" of the pardon in the opening lines of Passus VII. Piers asks Hunger "how I myghte amaistren hem and make hem to werche" (VI.211). The inescapable implication is that the good laborer has some sort of moral responsibility with regard to his fellow human beings, even those whose misdirected wills seem to exclude them from the providential economy of labor.

When we try to assuage our liberal guilt nowadays by occasionally putting in a stint at the local soup kitchen, we always wonder how much we are contributing to the delinquency of the homeless by making it possible for them to continue to survive without working, or even to persist in a dangerous and self-destructive drug habit. Lawrence M. Clopper says, "[I]mproper support of able-bodied beggars would seem to make one complicit in their sins . . . ; the giver of alms . . . enables a life of idleness that will result in the false beggar's damnation" (*Songes of Rechelesnesse* 146). This seems to me very like Piers's problem as the good laborer: the inability to conceive of human beings outside an economy based on labor, and therefore the inability to render wasters intelligible to ourselves. If we support those who are outside the economy, how do we avoid undermining the economy ourselves? As Jill Mann puts it, the "question of whether Piers is perverting justice and nature if he gives food to those who do not work" is a problem "of more than local interest, since it forms part of the larger problem of how mercy can be exercised without undermining justice" (30).

The advice of Hunger is just what we might expect, and the part of it that Piers specifically endorses (VI.274) is helpful at least for the good laborer: we can work better and will be generally healthier if we do not eat too much (256ff.). We learn this empirically, from dealing with our own appetites. But Hunger is a little more ambiguous about Piers's moral problem. Our own experience of hunger teaches us that it is cruel to allow our fellow human beings to go hungry; but at the same time we know that in general human hunger must be satisfied through labor. Piers is not sure, then, "Of beggeris and of bidderis what best be to doone" (203). Hunger seems to distinguish two categories: beggars who are capable of working, and beggars who are not because they have been injured either by "Fortune" or by "any manere false men" (218–19). The first category can be prevented from starving but encouraged to work by being fed dog food and horse food (214). The sins of those in the second category are God's business and not ours: "Theigh thei doon yvele, lat thow God yworthe" (225). Hunger quotes Luke: *"Facite vobis amicos de mammona iniquitatis"* (227a).

Exactly at this point in Hunger's discourse, Piers sharply articulates the problem of the wasters not as an abstract social issue ("what best be to doone . . . ?"), but instead as a problem of his own personal salvation: "'I wolde noght greve God,' quod Piers, 'for al the good on grounde! / Mighte I synnelees do as thow seist?'" (228–29). Hunger's answer is interesting. On the one hand, it might be interpreted as contradicting Hunger's earlier injunction to give food to the lazy: *"Piger pro frigore* no feeld wolde tilie— / And therfore he shal begge and bidde, and no man bete his hunger" (235–36); *"servus nequam* hadde a mnam, and for he wolde noght chaffare, / He hadde maugree of his maister for everemoore after" (238–39); "And he that noght hath shal noght have, and no man hym helpe" (244); "Kynde Wit wolde that ech a wight wroghte" (246). On the other hand, we might argue that Hunger is speaking anagogically in these passages, and so the passages do not contradict his earlier advice about Piers's proper behavior on earth. But the point is rather that Hunger's speech is a direct answer only to *Piers's question* about what Piers (the good laborer) should do. That is, the speech functions dramatically to show what Hunger teaches the good laborer about the salvation of the good laborer's soul. Hunger teaches the good laborer to labor for himself and others. Apparently, Hunger teaches the waster something different. Ultimately, when we interpret the social organism in terms of labor, we *do not know what to say* to or about the wasters.

Hunger's answer to Piers's question about sin, therefore, essentially evades what has gradually become the real issue of Passus VI. Reminding the good laborer what he personally must do is not the same as rendering intelligible the human behavior that falls outside the providential economy as the good laborer understands it. After Hunger has spoken, the dreamer is in some ways not much further along with respect to his large projects of understanding his vision of the earthly city and knowing what he can do to save his soul. The dreamer has proposed to himself in the symbol of Piers as the good laborer a solution to social injustice and personal salvation. But this symbol turns out to present unforeseen problems. To analyze the social organism in terms of labor leaves some of our "blody bretheren" on the margins, and leaves good laborers wondering what their moral responsibilities are with respect to these marginal figures. The real issue has become whether Piers as the symbol of the good laborer can provide the adequate interpretive system the dreamer thinks he needs. Would we really understand human experience fully if we only could manage to understand what it is to be a good laborer?

In the dramatic context, therefore, the pardon sent from Truth is a response to this problem. The pardon reconfigures the problem by reassuring Piers that there is a providential economy, that, as Jill Mann says, justice is "naturally 'built in to' the world" (29). Truth's injunction to Piers to stay home and till the earth is on one level an injunction to have faith in the ability of the providential economy to deal with sin. But it is also a warning that to construe the providential economy under the symbol of human labor, while clarifying some things, will always leave other things unintelligible. The inability of Piers, even with Hunger's help, to know clearly how to treat beggars is only a particular instance of the human inability in general to know what good works are—that is, the inability to apply Truth's pardon, the clauses of the Athanasian Creed, to life as it is lived on earth.

Piers and his "heires" (VII.4) and "alle that holpen hym" (6) might do well enough to trust Truth, living the life of the good laborer without intellectual certainty even about some of their own actions. But the priest forces the issue of self-justification. This issue, already implicit in Piers's question "Mighte I synnelees do as thow seist?" (VI.229), finally usurps the dreamer's attention entirely and casts him into the long middle of the poem, temporarily exiling the dreamer from Piers as the dreamer tries unsuccessfully to work out his own salvation through the limited powers of his own intellect. The dreamer understands some things about Piers. He understands, for example, that there is such a thing as good labor in the world. But in reflecting on his own private symbol of what he needs to understand, the dreamer is brought up against some things that he does not yet understand about Piers. The dreamer does not yet understand, for example, that self-justification in terms of labor is an intellectual and spiritual dead end. Piers, I will argue, does understand that. The dreamer's private symbol transcends the use the dreamer planned to make of it, goading the dreamer on to the next stage in his understanding. After the pardon scene, as Anne Middleton says, Piers "becomes the absent beloved, always sought and never recovered—yet engendering all the while a personal narrative of uncommon power and amplitude" ("Narration" 109). The dreamer takes a long time to catch up to the surplus in the meaning of his symbol—to understand what Piers as good laborer already understands—but the dreamer eventually gets there.

As he did earlier with the wasters, Piers experiences "pure tene" in his interaction with the priest. After the priest, with the dreamer looking over his shoulder, examines the documentary pardon and pronounces that "I kan no pardon fynde" (VII.111), Piers "for pure tene pulled it atweyne" (115). Piers experiences "pure tene" also on a later occasion. In Passus XVI, when the devil begins stealing the fruit of the patriarchs and the prophets as they drop off the Tree of Charity, Piers

> . . . for pure tene, that a pil he laughte,
> And hitte after hym, happe how it myghte,
> *Filius* by the Faderes wille and frenesse of *Spiritus Sancti* . . .
>
> (86–88)

Especially in this last passage, *tene* connotes not only anger but suffering, and connects Piers's emotion directly with Christ's struggle on the Cross that is allegorically represented by Piers's action. This pattern seems to suggest more than Langland's desire to portray Piers as irascible. In the case of the wasters and the devil, at least, what seems especially to upset Piers is whatever tends to undermine the providential economy. The wasters undermine the temporal economy of good labor on earth, and the devil attempts to undermine the spiritual economy by which God has eternally provided for the salvation of good souls. In both cases, there is perhaps a reminiscence of Jesus' anger at the money-changers in the Temple (Matthew 21:12–13; Mark 11:15–17; Luke 19:45–46).

If I am going to hold to the assumptions with which I began this discussion, then Piers's *tene* cannot be directed at Truth or at the pardon itself, which Piers understands to be valid. The priest's behavior, then, must be the target of Piers's dramatic gesture. It is worth asking how the priest might be seen as similar to the other targets of Piers's anger. How is it that the priest undermines the providential economy?

I find Anne Middleton's reflections on the pardon scene most helpful at this point. Middleton argues that the priest's "sole challenge is not to the meaning of the text but to its public power and performative kind, its *genre*: it is not, he declares, a pardon" ("Narration" 108). The priest challenges the pardon because Piers possesses it. The priest's concern is "to assure that interpretation and the public proclamation of Christian truth shall be made only by those with the literacy and learning to do it correctly" (107). Piers correctly understands the priest's challenge as a challenge to Piers's own authority, and so Piers "destroys the object that called forth this interference from the sanctioned and traditional magisterium" (108).

Middleton goes on to draw conclusions that I cannot as wholeheartedly accept, but I think her insight into the dramatic interaction in this scene is crucial. The priest believes that latinity confers authority: "thi pardon moste I rede," as if he expects that Piers cannot read it; "For I shal construe ech clause"—a small display of technical jargon—"and kenne it thee on Englissh" (VII.105–6). And later the priest seems simultaneously annoyed and condescending when he discovers that Piers knows a little Latin: "'What!' quod the preest to Perkyn, 'Peter! as me thynketh, / Thow art lettred a litel—who lerned thee on boke?'" (131–32). The "Peter!" here is ironic; like the oath with which Piers himself enters the poem (V.537), it reminds us that Piers himself ultimately represents Saint Peter and his successors the popes, the very custodians of literacy on earth. When Piers refuses to make the appropriate gestures of intellectual submission, the priest grows downright nasty and sarcastic: "'Were thow a preest, Piers,' quod he, 'thow myghtest preche where thow woldest / As divinour in divinite, with *Dixit insipiens* to thi teme'" (135–36). The priest, then, insists on reserving to himself the authority to decide what counts and what does not count as a pardon.

What would count for the priest, presumably, is the type of dispositive document that the Church commonly calls a pardon. Although he might have the formal theological training that Piers lacks, the priest's commitment to the jargon of the ecclesiastical bureaucracy blinds him to the deeper meaning of *pardon* that makes Truth's document a valid witness to the providential economy of salvation. Piers justly calls the priest "Lewed lorel!" (137).

But how does the priest's way of thinking undermine the providential economy? Why should he provoke Piers's "pure tene"? I think there might be a couple of answers to these questions. First, the priest undermines the providential economy by not being a good laborer himself. In the brief but intense dramatic interaction with Piers, the priest shows himself to be concerned more with preserving his own prerogatives than with getting the work done. It is more important to him to maintain his authority than it is to save souls. In this way, he is exactly similar to the wasters who might work to fill their bellies, but who will not work like Piers to serve Truth. The priest is also similar to the devil in Passus XVI, who takes souls not because he wants to save them, but because he wants power over them.

But perhaps a more interesting answer is that in the priest's twisted way of thinking the concept of pardon ultimately entails self-justification. What the priest is willing to call a "pardon" is a dispositive document that looks to past sins and erases their temporal consequences. As James Simpson points out, the words of the pardon from Truth have "practical force" only if they *precede* the act of sin. If they are read after the act of mortal sin, they do not absolve the sinner from that sin or pardon him from the penance pertaining to it" (73). What the priest is willing to call a "pardon" is, literally, a piece of paper that someone could show in an ecclesiastical court to demonstrate effective innocence. Such a notion of pardon makes sense only in contexts of self-justification, contexts where one says, either to others or to oneself, "I'm O.K." One might even imagine, as the dreamer does, dragging along a "pokeful of pardon" (VII.192) on doomsday to prove one's worthiness of admission to heaven. To entertain such a notion of pardon is to assume that self-justification is somehow possible. Otherwise, the notion would be completely empty.

Piers, on the other hand, recognizes the futility of attempting self-justification. Even the good laborer sometimes does evil. The good laborer's good deeds are activated, and the good laborer's sins erased, by the grace of God. I am not making Langland into a strict "Augustinian" here, or questioning recent critical wisdom that describes Langland as "semi-Pelagian" in his theology of grace (for example, Adams, "Pardon" 369). The issue between "Augustinianism" and "Pelagianism" is not whether God is gracious, but how God's grace operates. I am only suggesting that Piers, unlike the priest, understands that to try to reduce our relationship to God to legalistic terms so that we can feel self-justified before God is a spiritual dead end. As Piers tears the pardon, declaring independence from the dark side of ecclesiastical authority that wants to gain power over him instead of trying to save his soul, Piers quotes from the psalm: *"Si ambulavero in medio umbre mortis / Non timebo mala, quoniam tu mecum es"* (VII.116–17). The word *mala* echoes the clause of the Athanasian Creed quoted as the second clause of Piers's pardon: *"Qui vero mala, in ignem eternum"* (110b). Piers's point seems to be that he need not fear the evils alluded to in the pardon—by implication, the evils that he himself, as human being, is bound to fall into even though he does good—because God is with him. Not, that is, because Piers has some document that justifies him. To accede to the priest's notion of pardon would be to fall into the trap of self-justification: someone—presumably, the priest—would have to provide Piers with documentary evidence that could function in legal or quasi-legal contexts to demonstrate that Piers's sins were erased. Wanting such a thing is just not the right way to think about our relationship with God. The tearing of the pardon is the dramatic gesture by means of which Piers rejects the futile enterprise of self-justification—without, however, damaging the providential economy of pardon that already existed before the documentary pardon bore witness to it.

It is always tricky to read the B-text in the light of the revisions of the C-text, because the C-text in places seems to be an entirely different poem in terms of its valencies and balances. But if one assumes that Langland in the C-text at least sometimes means to *clarify* the B-text, it is initially hard to see how the C revision might count as a clarification of the pardon scene. After the priest's translation of the pardon in the C-text, instead of tearing the pardon, Piers "jangles" with the priest, and the dreamer awakes (C.IX.294–95). A more inconclusive—even disappointing, in comparison to the drama of the B-text—conclusion to the vision could hardly be imagined. Nevertheless, in my reading of the B-text it is possible to see the C revision as a clarification in one sense.

Piers's gesture in the B-text is obviously ambiguous at least, as witnessed by, if nothing else, the large body of critical controversy about the scene. The C revision, on the other hand, deliberately stops short of providing any clues about what Piers thinks of the priest's pronouncement, other than to suggest that Piers somehow finds the pronouncement debatable. In my reading of the B-text, as will develop, the dreamer does not understand Piers's gesture. The dreamer's private symbol has suddenly and dramatically transcended the dreamer's current understanding of it. It will take the dreamer a long time to catch up with Piers. For the reader to understand what Piers is thinking at this point—for the reader to understand more about the dreamer's private symbol than the dreamer himself understands—admittedly requires the kind of heavy interpretive inference that I am indulging in here. In the C-text, maybe, Langland elides the problem, withholding clues about Piers's thoughts so that the reader's developing understanding of the symbol of Piers remains closer to the dreamer's own understanding. So one might say that Langland in his revision "clarifies" the B-text in the sense that he makes it clearer that the dreamer's understanding of Piers is incomplete.

The B-text, however, invites or even commands the reader to read Piers's mind in his gesture. In my reading, the tearing of the pardon demonstrates Piers's anger at the second breakdown in the economy of labor he has instituted on the half-acre. The first rock upon which the economy breaks is the unregenerate wills of the wasters who fall outside the economy, and the second rock is the clergy who corrupt the economy from within. The pattern is repeated, for example, at the end of the poem, where Unity is assaulted from without by Antichrist and the Deadly Sins, and corrupted from within by the false friars. Just as the wasters prey on the productivity of the laborers who support them, the priest reinforces and preys on the good laborers' natural desire for self-justification. Human beings profoundly want to justify themselves to themselves and to others, and it is very easy to let this desire become the most important motive for good labor in the world. When we become absorbed in the various activities of "doing good," it "feels as though" we are being unselfish, and we easily forget that we are acting as we do in the first place because we want to feel good about ourselves and because we want to extort from others the admission that we are doing good. Corrupt clergy encourage us not to examine our motives, not to question whether the game of self-justification is the game we should be playing. Corrupt clergy want us to play that game, so that they can maneuver us into the position of trying to justify ourselves by more or less thoughtlessly doing whatever those with moral authority over us say we should do. It is a scam, and it undermines the providential economy from within by exploiting the tendency of fallen humans to do the right thing for the wrong reason.

Piers reacts to the scam when he tears the pardon. The priest's argument shifts attention from Christ's sacrifice to self-justification, turning Piers's economy on the half-acre into a kind of parody of the providential economy. In this parody, the pardon would be the dispositive document the priest apparently expects it to be. By destroying the central symbol in the parody, Piers reorients himself and his followers so that they perceive the economy of good labor correctly, perhaps for the first time—as with Moses' smashing of the tablets of the Law, a scriptural passage to which the tearing of the pardon has been compared (see, for example, Carruthers 70; Harwood 154, 227; Justice, *Writing and Rebellion* 123). The priest's move has clarified the situation and perhaps moved Piers to another level of understanding. Self-justification is not the name of the game. If Piers had before been working unreflectively, assuming with childlike faith that his sins were taken care of because Truth was pleased with his work, the priest's move makes Piers aware of how easily that unreflectiveness can be taken advantage of or lapse into smugness. By assuming that Piers should expect a dispositive pardon, the priest drives home to Piers the real implication of human sinfulness—namely, that the desire to justify oneself is futile and ultimately self-destructive.

Piers's response is precisely to shift into the mode of *contrition:* "Of preieres and of penaunce my plough shal ben herafter" (VII.120). Piers will not stop laboring entirely, but he will make sure that his concentration on good labor does not distract him from the most important fact about himself—namely, that even as the good laborer he is a sinful human being. The labor itself and its results are not the important things: "We sholde noght be to bisy aboute the worldes blisse: / *Ne soliciti sitis,* he seith in the Gospel" (126–27). Sin is the important thing: "That loveth God lelly, his liflode is ful esy: / *Fuerunt michi lacrime mee panes die ac nocte*" (124–24a). Piers's response to the premise of the priest's argument is to change orientation, to focus not on his sense of worthiness as a good laborer ("I . . . do what Truthe hoteth. / For though I seye it myself, I serve hym to paye"—V.548–49), but instead on his sense of unworthiness that is the proper posture with respect to Truth's genuine pardon and the promises of the Creed. Piers thus rejects the authority of the priest precisely at the point where the priest wants to determine the orientation of Piers's own soul. Priests cannot function as magical engineers of salvation for believers. The priest wants Piers to ask the same question the dreamer asks Holy Church, with the same implications: that salvation is a matter of self-justification and that the authoritative speaker gets to say what counts as self-justification. "How may I save my soul?" Piers declines the game. He turns from allowing all of his attention to be usurped by his worldly labor, with the concomitant reliance for salvation on potentially corrupt literate specialists. The priest wants to argue with Piers on the basis of Piers's qualifications as a *litteratus,* but Piers dismisses the priest with a scriptural quotation: *"Eice derisores et iurgia cum eis ne crescant"* (VII.138a). The point seems to be in part that arguing about whether one is justified is not only a waste of time, but potentially destructive to the economy of good labor itself. The dreamer, characteristically, misinterprets what he has heard: "The preest and Perkyn apposeden either oother" (139). A more accurate description, as it seems to me, is that Piers is *refusing* to get caught in a self-justifying argument with the priest. It is not necessary to choose between a reading of the pardon scene as ecclesiastical satire and a reading of the scene as expressing Piers's profound care about his own salvation. Characteristically, Langland does both. The priest's error, not his warning, provokes Piers's reaction—and the priest's error is, at base, his belief that self-justifying argument somehow leads to salvation.

Earlier, Piers has interpreted the social world in terms of labor and has constituted the intersubjective interior world in terms of authoritative texts. Now a new hermeneutic is required. Labor as interpretive principle breaks down because of those who cannot be made to work, and the intersubjective world of texts breaks down because of the self-serving misinterpretations of corrupt clergy. Piers as the dreamer's symbol of the good laborer suggests that interpreting the world from Piers's perspective leaves as residue the problem of coming to grips with one's own sin. Piers then disappears from the poem for a long time, until the dreamer catches up with him and learns to understand the implications of his own symbol. By that time, Piers will have become something different, because the dreamer's projection of what he needs to know will have altered.

THE DREAMER'S INTERPRETATION

The voice that speaks after the first vision of Piers is, again, problematic. At first, we seem to hear the dazed dreamer of the conventional genre, recounting his jumbled thoughts in the moment of his awaking:

> And I thorugh hir wordes awook, and waited aboute,
> And seigh the sonne in the south sitte that tyme.
> Metelees and moneilees on Malverne hulles,
> Musynge on this metels a my[le] wey ich yede.
>
> (VII.140–43)

Immediately, however, Langland modulates into a retrospective voice, and the distinction between the dreamer and Langland himself seems to blur: "Many tyme this metels hath maked me to studie / Of that I seigh slepynge—if it so be myghte" (144–45). Then this ambiguous speaker discourses on the validity of dreams, in a passage that, though it seems to come to the opposite conclusion, is somewhat reminiscent of Chanticleer's treatise on this subject to Pertelote: "I have no savour in songewarie, for I se it ofte faille" (149). And yet he thinks that after all there might have been something in what the priest said (148, 168). This speaker's unclear and inconclusive line of argument, setting Cato against the Bible (150–52), makes us suspect that some irony lurks in the passage, especially since most of *Piers Plowman* itself is composed of accounts of dreams. Finally, the argument issues in the generic advice of lines 196 and following, advice which Langland or any other author of his time might as well claim, which sounds completely orthodox, and which is completely unhelpful in thinking through any of the intellectual problems posed in the just-concluded vision:

> Forthi I counseille alle Cristene to crie God mercy,
> And Marie his moder be oure meene bitwene,
> That God gyve us grace here, er we go hennes,

> Swiche werkes to werche, the while we ben here,
> That after oure deth day, Dowel reherce
> At the day of dome, we dide as he highte.

That is, these lines speak the language of theological compromise, balancing mercy and justice, grace and works, in such a way as to evade the whole issue of self-justification. They sound like an attempt to articulate something that both an Augustinian and a Pelagian could subscribe to, because each could read the lines with different emphases. Rosemary Woolf's discussion of various ways of handling the "paradox" of the "relationship of God's justice to His mercy" in medieval literary and theological works is instructive (66ff.).

Being inclined to believe that there is a narrative of the dreamer, that the priest misinterprets the pardon, that the dreamer is to some degree fooled by the priest, and that Langland is more often ironic than is always appreciated (especially about his own intellectual pretensions), I read lines 140 and following of Passus VII as a speech of the dreamer, who is nevertheless a persona representing Langland himself at an earlier stage of theological understanding. We are to hear that odd dissonance of two voices, speaking the same words but with radically different tones, that is characteristic of some of the most exquisitely ironic passages in Chaucer, where the voices of "Chaucer-pilgrim" and "Chaucer-author" merge, intertwine, and jar with each other in innumerable subtle ways. Here as elsewhere in *Piers Plowman,* the indeterminacy of voice is one of Langland's techniques for showing us how the human person itself is as deeply ambiguous as the discourses that constitute it.

What is perhaps most striking about the dreamer's response to his dream is the way Piers vanishes from the dreamer's reflections after the first cursory mention:

> Many tyme this metels hath maked me to studie
> Of that I seigh slepynge—if it so be myghte;
> And for Piers the Plowman ful pencif in herte,
> And which a pardon Piers hadde, al the peple to conforte,
> And how the priest inpugned it with two propre wordes.
>
> (VII.144–48)

The remainder of the dreamer's reflections in Passus VII are devoted to the question of what the priest meant in the dream. There is no apparent attempt to determine what Piers's gesture or his subsequent words might have meant, even though it is clear to the dreamer that Piers and the priest "apposeden either oother" (139). In my reading, this vanishing of Piers corresponds to the dreamer's awakening to the fact that his initial projection has proved inadequate. Piers as the symbol of the good laborer does not do the hermeneutic work the dreamer thought the symbol would do. It is not going to be sufficient for the dreamer to understand what it is to be a good laborer in the world, because the pardon scene, in the dreamer's understanding, drives home to the dreamer that he does not know what it means to "do well." The dreamer can no longer think he is sure of what he needs to know. Piers vanishes over the dreamer's horizon, leaving the dreamer struggling with the issues posed by the priest and the pardon.

The dreamer as intellectual typically tries to sort things out in terms of authoritative texts. He opposes Cato and the Bible, and apparently awards priority to the Bible: "Ac for the book Bible bereth witnesse" (VII.152). It is interesting, however, that the *for* in line 152 never receives its syntactic completion:

> Ac for the book Bible bereth witnesse
> How Daniel divined the dremes of a kynge
> That was Nabugodonosor nempned of clerkes . . .
>
>   (152–54)

The dreamer is distracted into the biblical narratives of Daniel and Joseph, and the logical conclusion of the *for,* when it comes, is perhaps rather lame: "Al this maketh me on metels to thynke" (168). That is, the dreamer never actually *says outright* that he believes the Bible rather than Cato. He says only that the contradiction occasions much reflection for him. There is a moment when we have to wonder whether the dreamer, as well as failing to deal with Piers's gesture, also misunderstands the priest: the dreamer reflects on "how the preest preved no pardon to Dowel, / And demed that Dowel indulgences passed" (169–70). But this is at best an inference on the dreamer's part from what the priest actually said in the dream; and, if my reading of the pardon scene is correct, the inference is far from accurately describing the priest's agenda. The priest would not have wanted to prove that doing well is superior to pardons. He would have wanted to suggest rather that the Church's documentary pardons are superior to what Piers offers. Does the dreamer completely misunderstand his own dream? Or does he subtly cut through the priest's corrupt agenda to get at the real heart of the issue, using the priest's statements as a mere occasion to talk about what he himself, looking over the priest's shoulder at Piers's pardon, has seen as the real intellectual problem? Who is talking here?

The dreams in the Bible are *prophetic* dreams, and the dreamer uses this fact to hint at a possible solution to the theological problem of the validity of documentary pardons from the pope:

> . . . Dowel at the day of dome is digneliche underfongen,
> And passeth al the pardon of Seint Petres cherche.
>   Now hath the Pope power pardon to graunte
> The peple, withouten penaunce to passen into [joye];
> This is oure bileve, as lettred men us techeth:
> *Quodcumque ligaveris super terram erit ligatum et in celis* . . .
> And so I leve leelly (Lordes forbode ellis!) . . .
>
> (172–77)

The *Now* (174), I believe, should be read adversatively: "My dream, like the biblical dreams, might accurately prophesy about what is *going* to happen on doomsday; but I believe in accordance with the orthodoxy taught by the clergy that right *now* on earth the pope's pardons are valid too" (see Woolf 66). But the "other voice" here, the ironic voice, seems to turn up its volume: "*Nowadays,* in these wretched times, people seem to think that they can get pardon from corrupt popes. And of course, heaven forbid that *I* should say anything different!" Finally, the dreamer's tactic is just to lump everything together: "pardon and penaunce and preieres doon save" (178), where the dreamer tacitly adopts Piers's own solution, "preieres and penaunce" (120), along with the priest's "pardon." The formula of prayers, penance, and pardon is no doubt comprehensive, but it does little to solve the intellectual problem that the dreamer is ostensibly working on here: that is, whether pardons are better than prayers and penance. As usual, the dreamer proves subtler in articulating problems than in solving them. Like the very last lines of the passus, these lines exhibit the language of theological compromise, a straining to state the unexceptionable, to have one's doctrinal cake and eat it too. But the reflections issue in the confident and even scathing sermonizing that critics have come to associate with "Langland's own voice": "Forthi I rede yow renkes that riche ben on this erthe" (182); "I sette youre patentes and youre pardon at one pies hele!" (195).

My point is that the voices speaking in dissonance at the end of Passus VII show the dreamer floundering, trying to reconcile dogma with experience, trying to find the discourse that defines him, while Langland looks on, commenting ironically on his struggles with his own intellectual problems. The dreamer has lost his tenuous grip on Piers, the symbol the dreamer thought he was about to understand, and Piers has temporarily vanished beyond the dreamer's horizon. With the vanishing of Piers, the whole question of the nature of the human person revives with renewed poignancy. It is not going to work simply to define the human person as the good laborer, because to do so immediately implies the question, "What is good labor?" That is, "What is it to do well?" Because the dreamer is an intellectual, the priest who challenges Piers's authority undermines not only Piers's economy of labor, but the internal economy of the dreamer himself, who thinks that now he must be able to define "Dowel" in order to save his own soul.

The dreamer is thus confused on several levels. First, he hypostatizes Dowel, making the verb (a relation) into a noun (a substance), assuming that Dowel is some thing to be known "objectively" as an object, as opposed to some relation to be known pragmatically by living certain practices (see Carruthers 84–85 and Simpson 135). Second, the dreamer seems still to be trapped in the priest's game of self-justification. The dreamer wants to know what Dowel is, so that he can justify himself to himself, to other people, and to God. That is, he thinks at some level that he can save his own soul. He has missed Piers's point so completely that he seems temporarily incapable even of reflecting upon what Piers might have meant by tearing the pardon.

But the dreamer's case is not hopeless. Piers, after all, as I am arguing, is the dreamer's own private symbol. There is more in the symbol than the dreamer himself consciously understands at the moment, but the dreamer is at least dimly aware of where his problem lies. I believe Langland makes this clear in the waking episode where the dreamer meets the friars, at the beginning of Passus VIII. The dreamer's misdirected quest for Dowel falters apparently because he cannot find any person who always "does well." He is looking for "what man he myghte be" (VIII.5), but "Was nevere wight as I wente that me wisse kouthe / Where this leode lenged" (6–7). Surely, the problem is not that the dreamer never finds anyone who does anything good, but instead that he never finds anyone who has *persisted* ("lenged") in doing good. Maybe a little smug about his ability to argue "as a clerc," with the technical term *contra* (VIII.20), the dreamer disputes the friars' claim that Dowel lives with them, because

> . . . *"Sepcies in die cadit iustus.*
> Sevene sithes, seith the Book, synneth the rightfulle,
> And whoso synneth," I seide, "dooth yvele, as me thynketh,
> And Dowel and Do-yvele mowe noght dwelle togideres."
>   (VIII.21–24)

Typically for the *litteratus* he is imitating, the dreamer proceeds in disputation by applying logical categories to authoritative texts. As James Simpson points out, "Will's argumentative procedures are drawn directly from the dialectical models of university debate, as we might expect in a vision which is about the education of the soul" (108). As elsewhere in *Piers Plowman,* it is hard to know here how to take the dreamer. Is Langland portraying him as the presumptuous naïf whose intellectual pride renders him incapable of hearing the friars' good advice? Or is the dreamer himself the ironist who sees through the friars' own pride? But in either case the root problem is the problem of sin: How can Dowel coexist with sin? And since every human being is sinful, how can any human being exemplify Dowel? And if no human being can do well, how can anyone be saved? The dreamer does not say that he is thinking specifically of his own sin here, but the promptness of his challenge to the friars suggests that the problem of sin is deeply personal to him and never far from his mind. That is, he is tangled in the confusing nest of problems surrounding the central issue of self-justification. He is not yet capable, as Piers is, of dramatically freeing himself from that nest of problems in a gesture corresponding to the tearing of the pardon, but at least the dreamer has some dim intimation that corresponds to Piers's understanding that sin is the problem, that the hermeneutic of labor needs to be replaced or at least supplemented by a hermeneutic of sin.

Elizabeth Kirk's reading of the pardon scene in the A-text has interesting affinities with the argument I am pursuing here:

> Paul continually reminds the Romans that what brings transformation about is a psychological event within each man which corresponds to and depends on the crucifixion of Christ, in which the resentment of the righteous man at Christ's claims, superseding his whole view of human responsibility, destroys him; and this "death," the Atonement, is what releases man from bondage just as in history God acted, man destroyed what he sent, and that destructive act transformed man. But Paul makes no attempt to explain this doctrine; he assumes it, and the A poet does not explain it either. Instead, he has Piers enact an analogous psychological sequence whereby man vents his resentment at God's transcendent superiority on God's immanent manifestation of himself (the pardon) by destroying the manifestation, thereby releasing its energies. (94)

What is most interesting to me in Kirk's reading, however, is her assertion that Langland in the B-text is "substituting for this scene the kind of historical reconstruction and analysis of the Incarnation, Crucifixion, Harrowing of Hell, and Resurrection, with its accompanying intellectual analysis"; this new material becomes the "climax" of the B poet's "differently oriented drama" (94). This line of argument seems to me to correspond to my own notion that through the long middle of the B-text the dreamer is in a sense catching up to the theological understanding that Piers already illustrates in the pardon scene, so that the new "climax" of the poem in the B-text is the crisis of the dreamer's own narrative. Kirk, however, places the crisis in the dreamer's narrative earlier than I do, characterizing the dreamer's terror at Scripture's sermon on *"Multi"* and *"pauci"* (XI.107ff.) as the "turning point" where the dreamer finds himself experiencing "precisely what happened to Piers when Truth sent him a pardon": "The moment that came to the good man at the end of his resources comes now to his antiself, and he feels what Piers must have felt when the pardon was translated" (130).

This time, however, "the stages which lead a man from the desire to be justified in his own right . . . to the relationship between his will and the realities within and without, . . . will be clearly dramatized" (130).

G. R. Owst places *Piers Plowman* in the context of the contemporary sermon literature, explaining the ideal of social justice based upon good labor that Langland might have heard articulated from the pulpit. Janet Coleman provides a fairly full treatment of the fourteenth-century theological context of *Piers Plowman*. Robert Worth Frank's reading of the pardon scene (*Scheme* 19–33) is still very illuminating, and although Frank's reading is not identical with mine, our readings overlap in several crucial respects. Two of the most influential articles on the pardon scene and its function in the poem in relation to Langland's theology are those of Denise Baker ("From Plowing to Penitence: *Piers Plowman* and Fourteenth-Century Theology") and Robert Adams ("Piers's Pardon and Langland's Semi-Pelagianism"). Baker provides an "Augustinian" (as opposed to "Nominalist") reading of the scene, and Adams, as his title suggests, identifies Langland as consistently constructing a "semi-Pelagian" position. Both of these scholars provide summaries of various critical opinions. In Adams's later excellent discussion of "Langland's Theology," Adams reiterates his point about Langland's semi-Pelagianism in the pardon scene (95–97). Lawrence M. Clopper reads Piers as "the *idiota* before his persecutor, the *rusticus simplex* who is the *sapientia* evident in the plowmen and apostolic men. . . . He is the personification and manifestation of the *vita apostolica*" (*Songes of Rechelesnesse* 195). In general, my own critical methodology and my assumptions about *Piers Plowman* are inconsistent with the attempt to define any particular theological position so as to use its tenets as a rule for interpretation of the poem. I am arguing that one thing *Piers Plowman* does is to show the impossibility of extracting a comprehensive or completely satisfying theology from the conflict of authoritative texts that constitutes the substance of the poem.

Britton Harwood's reading of the pardon scene is one of the more subtle in a family of interpretations proceeding from the assumption that Piers himself experiences some sort of conversion. Piers has sought Truth through the moral conscience and "kynde wit" alone, and he is disappointed in the result: "Between the time Piers holds out his 'par-

doun' and then destroys it, God the void becomes for him God the enemy. His 'tene,' surely ambiguous, is likely some resentment at Truth who
has not paid. Piers walks 'in medio vmbre mortis.' But his 'tene' may also
be sorrow and anger with himself, for the priest's 'no pardon' may give
voice to much doubt suspended in Piers's mind" (155). The essential difference between any reading of this type and my own reading is that
Piers for me is not a separate, self-subsistent character in the poem, but
instead is the dreamer's own private dream symbol of that which is just
beyond the dreamer's current understanding. Piers represents many different things, precisely because the dreamer's understanding is constantly changing. It is less accurate to speak of Piers's "conversion," then,
than it is to speak of a new development in the dreamer's understanding. It would be better to say not that a character named Piers is converted, but instead that a symbol unfolds its latent meanings.

Although I read the function of the pardon scene differently from
James Simpson in crucial respects, his analysis seems to me especially
acute and helpful. Simpson offers two explanations for Piers's tearing of
the pardon. First, much as Anne Middleton in the passage that I have
already quoted, Simpson believes that Piers "is tearing not at the words
of the pardon itself so much as the paper document upon which they
are written—at 'pardon' as it is normally understood" (74). Simpson's
stress on what Donald R. Howard might have called the "paperness" of
the pardon reinforces M. E. J. Hughes's point about the image of the
document in *Piers Plowman*. Hughes points out that documents as paper
are "morally neutral and can be the carriers of truth or falsehood equally" (130–31); "because documents are morally and linguistically neutral,
they raise the question of the capacity of any linguistic structure to carry truth," and Langland plays on every "layman's deep-rooted fear that,
when the small-print is analysed, an apparently watertight document
becomes worthless" (131). Thus the scene contributes to Langland's ecclesiastical satire. Second, Simpson argues that Piers tears the pardon
"not only as a satiric act, but also as an act of profound anxiety before
the strictness of the Old Law. He tears not only at the paper of the pardon, but also in anxious protest at the spirit of the words, despite their
evident and unassailable truth" (76). In other words, Simpson stresses,
as I have stressed, the impossibility that human beings will justify

themselves by works (see especially 82–83). (I might prefer the word *care* where Simpson puts *anxiety;* the best word, no doubt, is Langland's own *tene,* with its connotations of worry, anger, and suffering.) Simpson's discussion seems especially illuminating when he places Augustinianism and Pelagianism, and the concepts of "condign" and "congruent" human merit, within the context of fourteenth-century economic developments (75–85). By this route, Simpson arrives at the same conclusion about Langland's theology as Robert Adams does: Langland might best be described as a "semi-Pelagian" (93). Simpson dissents, however, from Adams's implication that we can already detect Langland's semi-Pelagianism for sure in the pardon scene (85–86n).

John Bowers's chapter on "The Poet as Worker" (191–218) talks about poetry as labor. Pamela Raabe's reading of the creative act of the poet as repeating in a limited, human sense the creative act of God (139ff.) is also relevant here: Raabe says that "Will himself . . . as both the human will and the poet's faithless persona, is bound in dissimilar similitude to the faithful narrator who is also the voice of God. Like God, Langland strives to approach Unity through multiplicity and plenitude in his poetic cosmos" (168). Bowers reads *Piers Plowman* as a poem about sloth, the besetting sin of the dreamer and of Langland himself. Although I have not talked much about poetry as labor, I believe that the activity of writing poetry does become implicated in Langland's critique of the attempt to justify oneself by performing good labor. We would be God-like if we could justify ourselves by the good labor of writing poetry, but we cannot. I suppose I tend to stress intellectual pride more than I stress sloth. Certainly the dreamer is lazy and prefers not to work either physically or, at some points, mentally. But the more dangerous side of his sloth is the near-despair that results from his not knowing how to justify himself—his tendency to give up. This part of sloth comes from the premise that one *ought* to be able to justify oneself; and that premise is rooted, in my reading of the poem, in the intellectual pride of the *litteratus.*

The Long Middle

I read the long middle of the poem as the rising action in the dreamer's narrative, the complication of the conflict sharply defined by Piers's tearing of the pardon. I would articulate the narrative action not as "the dreamer's quest for Dowel," in which the dreamer's desire to know Dowel would be in conflict with everything that stands in the way of that knowledge. That is how the dreamer himself might articulate his own narrative. But the dreamer is wrong. Instead, the narrative is about "the dreamer's struggle to become like Piers," in which the conflict is between the dreamer's desire for self-justification and his gradually increasing understanding that this desire itself is a spiritual dead end. One thing that makes me read the poem this way is the verbal patterning by means of which Langland toward the end of the long middle begins to reinsert Piers into the poem as a symbol. This happens at the points where the dreamer, after his laborious but for him unavoidable detour through literary education, begins to understand what Piers meant by tearing the pardon, and thus begins to be ready to reinterpret Piers as something more than the good laborer who defines salvation in terms of doing well in the world.

For example, in Passus XIII the dreamer sees clearly in the person of the gluttonous Doctor a conclusive demonstration of the disturbing truth that a literary education does not necessarily make a good person. The Doctor, having been soundly insulted by the dreamer, provides at Conscience's request a short and maybe somewhat surly definition of Dowel, Dobet, and Dobest. Immediately thereafter, Conscience asks Clergy to comment, and Clergy's uncertainty implicitly criticizes the Doctor's offhand pronouncement:

> "I have sevene sones," he seide, "serven in a castel
> Ther the lord of lif wonyeth, to leren hym what is Dowel.
> Til I se tho sevene and myself acorden
> I am unhardy," quod he, "to any wight to preven it.
> For oon Piers the Plowman hath impugned us alle . . ."
>
> (XIII.120–24)

Clergy goes on to give the famous definition of Dowel and Dobet as "two infinites" (128). But his language is interesting because it echoes the dreamer's language in Passus VII, the passus where Piers last appeared in the poem. Langland erects a neat symmetry. In Passus VII, the dreamer says of Piers's pardon that "the preest *inpugned* it with two propre wordes" (VII.148; emphasis mine), and talks about how the priest "*preved* no pardon to Dowel" (169; emphasis mine). In Passus XIII, Clergy admits that Piers "impugns" the pronouncements of the learned, and that Clergy himself cannot "prove" his definition of Dowel. In fact, as it develops, Piers himself will "come and preve this in dede" (XIII.133)—as opposed to proving it in words—according to Conscience.

Another such echo occurs at the beginning of Passus XV, the passus of Anima, which in my reading prepares for the crisis in the dreamer's narrative by preparing him to understand the vision of the Tree of Charity. At the beginning of Passus XV, the waking dreamer seems to have reached some sort of low point:

> Ac after my wakynge it was wonder longe
> Er I koude kyndely knowe what was Dowel.
> And so my wit weex and wanyed til I a fool weere . . .
>
> (XV.1–3)

The dreamer, in the midst of spiritual anguish, refuses to pay proper respect to important and wealthy people (5–9), and so he cannot get ahead in the world. I believe the lines refer back to VII.125–26, where Piers, having torn the pardon and having entered the mode of contrition, says, "but if Luc lye, he lereth us be fooles: / We sholde noght be to bisy aboute the worldes blisse." The dreamer, that is, with much pain, has at long last gotten to the point where Piers arrived in Passus VII. Whereas before the dreamer understood the passage from Luke only abstractly, now he fully understands through his own physical and spiritual anguish what it means to be a "fool" in the world. He is ready at last to understand the meaning already implicit in his own private symbol of the good laborer, the meaning that will broaden that symbol far beyond what the dreamer at first conceived to be contained in it.

Finally, the dreamer in Passus XV and XVI seems obsessed with the idea of charity. He asks Anima, "What is charite?" (XV.149), and says that he would "travaille" to see the Tree of Charity "twenty hundred myle, / And to have my fulle of that fruyt forsake al other saulee" (XVI.10–11). Charity, Anima says, grows in a garden that is called the human heart, and "*Liberum Arbitrium* hath the lond to ferme, / Under Piers the Plowman" (XVI.16–17). This complex of ideas is reminiscent of the dreamer's conversation with the friars in Passus VIII that began

his misdirected quest for Dowel. What the dreamer does not understand in the friars' exemplum, precisely, is how Dowel as "charite the
champion" (VIII.46) keeps human beings from falling into deadly sin,
and how charity is connected with God's "yeresyyve to yeme wel thiselve— / And that is wit and free will" (52–53). The dreamer reports, "I
have no kynde knowyng" (57). In Passus XV and XVI, therefore, Langland suggests that the dreamer is ready to try again to understand charity and free will, in terms of another, perhaps deeper and more satisfying,
symbol of Piers that both takes up and replaces the earlier vision.

Because Piers is an absence throughout the long middle of the poem,
the long middle will receive relatively short shrift in this book. Scholars
more learned and thorough than I am have placed this part of *Piers Plowman* in its context by examining in detail medieval notions of the human
faculties and literary education. I think especially of the work of Joseph
Wittig ("Inward Journey"); A. J. Minnis; and, more recently, Britton J.
Harwood and Ernest N. Kaulbach. My limited objective here is only to
sketch quickly and in outline the intellectual process by means of which
the dreamer laboriously achieves his own version of the insight that
Piers expresses in tearing the pardon: namely, the insight that the game
of self-justification is self-destructive.

At the same time, however, I want to advance the big thesis of this
book by describing the dreamer's intellectual process as hermeneutic.
That is, as I have said before, *Piers Plowman* construes not only the social
organism but also the human self on the model of a text. The point is
most obvious in the middle of the poem in the fact that education is
construed there as *literary* education, the remaking of the self as a *litteratus*. As James Simpson says, in the third vision of the poem (Passus
VIII–XII) Langland "invokes the discourses of education—those discourses which train the soul to analyse and resolve the theological question of 'dowel,' or works" (92). To become educated means, in practice,
to remake the self as a text. The self is construed as text through the "inorganic" separation of the soul into its various faculties, by means of
Langland's personification allegory. Although human beings are familiar
with the experience of "being at odds with ourselves," we normally do
not apprehend our faculties as neatly separated from each other. The
separation of the faculties into different bodies in the personification allegory makes it possible—necessary—to apprehend them first one at a

time and then as parts of a structure. To apprehend the faculties analytically and hierarchically, as the allegory treats them, is already to consider
them as they would necessarily be treated in a book: spatially and abstractly. As Gillian Rudd puts it, the figures in this section of the poem
are "predominantly concerned with acquiring knowledge by means of
deduction and definition. They are interested in knowledge as *scientia*"
(73). All of this happens because "Will himself is determining the forms
which his search takes. While he perceives the cognitive challenge presented by the pardon, he immediately thinks of that puzzle as an intellectual one, a problem in definition" (Carruthers 89).

But beyond that, the personification allegory operates here as elsewhere to cause us to consider the persons of the allegory *dramatically*.
That is, like Holy Church, Anima, and Need, the faculties become, each
for his or her fifteen minutes of celebrity in the poem, authoritative
speakers whose interpretations of human experience are driven by their
own natures. So it turns out not to be a very fruitful exercise, for example, to collect all the various definitions of Dowel, Dobet, and Dobest in
the hope that somehow the cumulative wisdom of the human faculties
will suggest some essential core that corresponds with "Langland's
definition." The point here, again, is that interpretation is going on.
Langland shows us, and slowly the dreamer comes to realize, that the attempt to define *Dowel* founders on the same problem that creates the
Babylonian cacophony: namely, the problem that definition happens
only within the boundaries of some language, some particular interpretive system, and all interpretive systems are provisional, limited by the
needs and compulsions of the interpreters who make and use them. The
attempt to isolate what any particular human faculty can tell us about
Dowel by isolating that faculty the way a medieval encyclopedia (or
modern psychology text) might do is already to adopt an interpretive
system. To read human experience like a text—to place our best epistemological bet—entangles us already in the hermeneutic problem that
human texts are made possible only by the provisional interpretive systems that generate them.

Broadly speaking, the dreamer thinks that he is on a quest to find
Dowel. As I have said, I think the dreamer is mistaken about his own
narrative. His real problem is not to locate Dowel, but instead to cure
his malady of self-justification. But the metaquestion, so to speak, that

comes up again and again in the long middle of the poem is an epistemological question: "How do we know what something is?" Different
interpretive systems produce different answers to that question, and in
the long middle Langland shows us, among other things, that it is impossible for human beings even to ask what something is without already having some preconceptions about the general form of the answer.
The dreamer tries on various ways of asking the question. One way of
separating the faculties of the human soul, in fact, is to say that wherever
we have a distinct way of knowing what something is, there we have a
distinct faculty. Langland is therefore also showing us the implications
of various ways of interpreting (that is, analyzing) the human soul.
Against the background of the extensive scholarly commentary that already exists on the long middle of *Piers Plowman,* I want to focus more or
less sharply on the epistemological issue. Thus I hope not only to sketch
the dreamer's intellectual process, but at the same time to continue an
implicit argument that what *Piers Plowman* "goes about" is textual hermeneutics.

THE FACULTIES AND LITERARY EDUCATION

After his unsatisfactory and inconclusive dialogue with the friars, the
dreamer falls asleep and meets Thought (VIII.70ff.). The dreamer
finds in Thought some resemblance to himself "A muche man, as me
thoughte, lik to myselve" (70)—but has to be told who Thought is:
"'What art thow,' quod I tho, 'that thow my name knowest?'" (72).
When the dreamer learns that his interlocutor is Thought, the dreamer
expects that Thought will be able to tell him "Where that Dowel
dwelleth" (77). But Thought's discourse fails to satisfy the dreamer, who
makes his habitual complaint about lacking "kynde knowynge," and
Thought himself seems to agree that the dreamer's question has not
been answered:

> "Ac yet savoreth me noght thi seying, so me Crist helpe!
> For more kynde knowynge I coveite to lerne—
> How Dowel, Dobet and Dobest doon among the peple."
>   "But Wit konne wisse thee," quod Thoght, "where tho thre dwelle;
> Ellis woot I noon that kan, that now is alyve."
>
>   (109–13)

And Thought and the dreamer lapse into "Disputyng" (115). Apparently, what Thought fails to do is to locate an actual earthly exemplar of Dowel for the dreamer to see and touch. Wit is the faculty that is supposed to explain whether Dowel "be man or no man" (127).

This dramatic interaction suggests that Thought represents something like the semiotic system that underwrites the connection of ideas in the human consciousness—loosely speaking, the structure of meanings that determines our processes of mental association, our characteristic ways of proceeding from sign to sign in the chain of signs that constitutes our consciousness. John Lawlor's phrase is telling: after the dialogue with the friars, "[i]t is time for the Dreamer to search the universe of discourse. We therefore resume the dream-sequence, and encounter first of all Thought" (90). *Thought* here means something fairly close to what we mean by it when we talk about the "thought of Plato" or the "thought of Marx." What determines the way we associate ideas might in some cases be arcane or even repressed; to be able to understand even our own system even abstractly might require effortful introspection or psychoanalysis. But even though we are normally so absorbed in the chain of signs that we do not pay attention to the principle that links those signs together, we can often recognize ourselves in someone else's description of how our minds work, and we can turn our gaze inward so as to thematize our own processes of association. At that point, we might actually ask ourselves questions like the following: "What sort of associations would I normally make in this situation? What would my normal way of thinking suggest about the present subject of my thought?" It makes sense, then, for the dreamer to find Thought similar to himself without actually recognizing Thought at first, and for the dreamer to expect Thought, once recognized, to illuminate the problem the dreamer is currently working on.

It also makes sense that Thought cannot provide satisfactory knowledge of Dowel. From the perspective of Thought as the semiotic system underwriting the connection of ideas, the answer to the question "How do we know what something is?" is quite simple. We know what something is by paying attention to everything we associate it with, by locating it, as it were, as a node in the n-dimensional graph of associations through which we think about the world. What the dreamer ultimately wants, however, is not to know what he *thinks* about Dowel, but what Dowel *is*. The dreamer's request to Thought to teach "Where that Dowel dwelleth" (VIII.77) indicates that the dreamer himself is a little confused on this point. Thought can teach the dreamer where Dowel lives inside the dreamer's own semiotic system, but cannot teach the dreamer how Dowel does outside "among the peple" (111). If the dreamer does not already know of an actual exemplar of Dowel to associate with his concept, the only knowledge of Dowel that Thought can provide is abstract and verbal.

Thought apparently thinks that Wit can help, and that Wit is the only thing that can help—or at least, that Wit is an essential faculty for making progress in this world toward understanding where Dowel lives (112–13). This is a decisive moment for the dreamer. His own thought, that is, maps the world in such a way that it seems to him that knowledge beyond knowing one's own mental processes must necessarily come through the agency of human intelligence. In the dreamer's picture of the world, human intelligence is an analytically separate faculty that is also somehow transpersonal. The dreamer's first step outside his own head, as it were, is already deeply intellectualized. He thinks the intellectual's way of knowing is the only way—and so, for him, it is. This move takes the first step onto the slippery slope of literary education, since for a medieval intellectual the paradigmatic way of developing the natural intelligence was to become a *litteratus*. The move is a symptom of how far the dreamer is from Piers's gesture in the pardon scene. The dreamer wants to believe that his intelligence can somehow procure objective knowledge of good action in the world, as a first and necessary step toward the dreamer's being able to perform good action and thus justify himself to himself and to God.

Whatever else the term *wit* might imply in the context of medieval thought, in *Piers Plowman* Wit is also the faculty that understands experience by means of understanding causes and effects. By the faculty of Wit, we know what something is by knowing how it arose. Wit's allegory of Dowel (IX.1ff.) depends on the primordial allegory of the "castel that Kynde made of foure kynnes thynges" (IX.2), where Kynde as a name of God (28ff.) is "creatour of alle kynnes thynges" (26). Kynde is not himself a "kind," but the creator of "kinds." That is, by generating the natural kinds, God also renders his creation intelligible to the human mind by causing along with his creatures the possibility of their classification. Human nature (also "kynde," in Middle English), and hence the nature of doing well, is to be understood in terms of God's creation of the human body and soul: "that is the castel that Kynde made, *Caro* it hatte, / And is as muche to mene as 'man with a soule'" (49–50). To be true to our *kynde* as created by *Kynde* is to be *kynde* to our fellow humans: "Allas that a Cristene creature shal be unkynde til another!" (84).

Wit's genetic preoccupation also explains his concern for marriage and the laws regulating human sexual behavior:

> Trewe wedded libbynge folk in this world is Dowel,
> For thei mote werche and wynne and the world sustene.
> For of hir kynde thei come that confessours ben nempned . . .
>
> (108–10)

And, on the other hand,

> . . . fals folk and feithlees, theves and lyeres,
> Wastours and wrecches out of wedlok, I trowe,
> Conceyved ben in yvel tyme, as Caym was on Eve.
>
> (119–21)

Of the offspring of Seth: "some, ayein the sonde of Oure Saveour of hevene, / Caymes kynde and his kynde coupled togideres" (127–28), eventuating in the punishment of the Flood (129ff.). "I fynde, if the fader be fals and a sherewe, / That somdel the sone shal have the sires tacches" (147–48). Nor should people marry for money: some "For coveitise of catel unkyndely ben wedded," and "careful concepcion cometh of swiche mariages" (157–58). Besides, "It is an uncomly couple, by Crist! as me thynketh— / To yeven a yong wenche to an[y] olde feble" (162–63). Human beings arise bodily on earth through sexual intercourse, and Wit explains good and evil human behavior on the basis of the lawful and the illicit, the good and the bad sexual acts that produce human bodies.

Wit's epistemology also accounts for his obsession with time and with times: "[Tyn]ynge of tyme, Truthe woot the sothe, / Is moost yhated upon erthe of hem that ben in hevene" (99–100); "Whan ye han wyved, beth war, and wercheth in tyme" (184). Time for Wit is constituted by the sequence of causes and effects. That is, to say that there is time is to say neither more nor less than that causes precede effects. We understand the temporal nature of life on earth through understanding how some things give rise to other things. Thus to waste time or to do things at the wrong time means precisely to set in motion a chain of cause and effect that eventuates in temporal evil.

And this is precisely the point at which Dame Study attacks Wit. She accuses him, essentially, of wasting time:

> . . . *Noli mittere,* man, margery perles
> Among hogges that han hawes at wille.
> Thei doon but dryvele theron—draf were hem levere . . .
>
> (X.9–11)

Study's discourse operates on more than one level. On the one hand, there is considerable comedy here in her portrayal of the genuine scholar's professional jealousy of the successful charlatan. Those of us who inhabit the ivory tower are often known to deplore the state of the body politic whenever people seem to be taking too seriously the pronouncements of the pundits and the so-called public intellectuals. People should be paying more attention to us, who are the genuine article; and incidentally, we are the ones who should be getting paid the big money to make the big pronouncements. But, on the other hand, Study makes a serious philosophical point. How can Wit know whether he is wasting time to instruct the dreamer, until he knows what use the dreamer will make of his advice? There is more to knowing what something is than to know where it came from. Wit might be an unimpeachable source; but if the dreamer or someone else misuses his discourse, Wit is reduced to the somewhat lame defense of the artilleryman whose shot has gone awry: "Well, it was all right when it left here."

Study's criterion for determining the real nature of anything seems to be not genetic like Wit's, but instead teleological. Instead of inquiring into the causes of things, she must wait to see how something turns out before she knows what it is. That notion of study makes sense on the most superficial level: we still use the word *study* to mean something like "consider all the ramifications," in a process that might include, but is not limited to, considering the history of any subject. Even to say that I "study" *causes* of any phenomenon implies already that there is some controversy about the causes, that I cannot just *name* the causes and attain general agreement, but that I have to consider the ramifications of the various theories.

Study attacks Wit's epistemology clearly but indirectly, and in an interesting way. She trenchantly satirizes the half-learned "heighe men etynge at the table" who "Carpen as thei clerkes were" and "leyden fautes upon the fader that formede us alle" (X.103–5). These would-be clerks in fact make the mistake of inquiring into causes, into the "why" of God's Providence. "Why wolde Oure Saveour suffre swich a worm in his blisse . . . ?" (107). "Why sholde we that now ben, for the werkes of Adam / Roten and torende? Reson wolde it nevere!" (113–14). Then, they quote scriptural passages in support. This last argument against the doctrine of original sin goes directly counter to Wit's argument that the son tends to inherit the father's faults. Dame Study is not without subtlety. She satirizes the disputatious lords at the point where they contradict Wit, but she does not satirize them for the opinion they express. Instead, she satirizes them for daring to express an opinion at all on a subject about which they know only enough to be dangerous: "For alle that wilneth to wite the whyes of God almyghty, / I wolde his eighe were in his ers and his fynger after" (124–25). Dame Study therefore succeeds in showing how Wit might be correct in his conclusions, and nevertheless completely wrongheaded in his epistemology. To know what Dowel is means not to understand where human nature comes from, but instead to understand how Dowel turns out in the individual human life:

> And tho that useth thise havylons to [a]blende mennes wittes
> What is Dowel fro Dobet, now deef mote he worthe—
> Siththe he wilneth to wite whiche thei ben alle—
> But if he lyve in the lif that longeth to Dowel . . .
>
> (131–34)

Wit's reduction to silence comes not only because of embarrassment at his ignorance and his shame at being lectured by his own wife, but literally because he "bicom so confus he kouthe noght loke" (138). Dame Study has caught Wit in a contradiction. By his own premises, he cannot be sure that he himself is not indulging in what is for him the worst sin, the sin of wasting time.

Of course, no human faculty can be sure of predicting the future—of knowing how things will turn out—even though study no doubt gives us a better chance of doing so than does our unaided natural intelligence. Dame Study has an ambiguous attitude, for example, toward astronomy, geometry, geomancy, and alchemy—all of these sciences considered, apparently, as sciences of prediction. She acknowledges them as her children, but says she "founded hem formest folk to deceyve" (216–17). From Dame Study's perspective, nevertheless, we make our best guesses about what things are not on the basis of where they have come from, but on the basis of where they seem to be going. Wit's epistemology does not allow him to be sure that he is not casting his pearls before a swinish dreamer, but Dame Study sends certain "tokenes" (218) to serve as a "signe" (170) to Clergy and Scripture that they are not wasting their time. When the dreamer asks for a "tokene" (158), Dame Study first describes a *way of life,* in a passage reminiscent of the allegorical pilgrimage detailed by Piers in Passus V: "Aske the heighe wey . . . hennes to Suffre- / Bothe-wele-and-wo"; "ryd forth by richesse"; "the likerouse launde that Lecherie hatte— / Leve hym on thi left half"; "Til thow come to a court, Kepe-wel-thi-tunge . . ." (159–65); and so on. Then the dreamer must demonstrate that he has already to some degree seriously taken up the path of study, by telling Clergy and Scripture what Dame Study *is*— that is, from her perspective, what she has *done*: she has set Clergy "to scole" (170) and has written the Bible for Scripture (171); "Plato the poete, I putte hym first to boke; / Aristotle and othere mo to argue I taughte" (175–76); she has written grammar and contrived all the crafts (177–81); and so on.

   Dame Study's own limitation surfaces in her comments about Theology, the science that "hath tened me ten score tymes" (182). She says, "It is no science, forsothe, for to sotile inne" (185). I take this line to mean that the subtlety that is the deepest part of Dame Study's nature, her insistence on considering all the ramifications of everything in order to assess how everything will turn out, is unsuited to the nature of this science itself. Dame Study is suggesting that what she does best is the very thing that obstructs her in her understanding of theology. In a speech reminiscent of the dreamer's own earlier meditation on the validity of dreams (VII.149ff.), Dame Study contrasts the advice of Cato with the teachings of Theology. "In oother science it seith—I seigh it in Catoun" (191) that we should beguile the beguilers, lie to the liars, "And

so shaltow fals folk and feithlees bigile" (195). This sounds like a good
outcome; and by Dame Study's normal premises, what turns out well is a
good thing. But Theology

> . . . kenneth us the contrarie ayein Catons wordes,
> For he biddeth us be as bretheren, and bidde for oure enemys,
> And loven hem that lyen on us, and lene hem whan hem nedeth,
> And do good ayein yvel—God hymself it hoteth . . .
>
> (198–201)

Dame Study concludes, "Forthi loke thow lovye as longe as thow durest,
/ For is no science under sonne so sovereyn for the soule" (207–8). The
dreamer has already heard advice very similar to this from Holy Church,
in Passus I (142ff.). Dame Study's words might serve to caution the
dreamer in the path on which he has embarked, by suggesting that all
the science he accumulates will be meaningless if he does not learn to
love. But her subtlety also teaches Dame Study that in one sense, the
dreamer does not have a choice about the path he takes to love. She
knows who the dreamer is by projecting his journey along the direction
he has already chosen. She knows him as an intellectual who must em-
bark on the difficult and perhaps ultimately frustrating path of literary
education. His immediate destination, then, is the world of the educational establishment and of the written texts that construct that world:
"Tel Clergie thise tokenes, and to Scripture after, / To counseille thee
kyndely to knowe what is Dowel" (218–19).

Clergy, which I translate roughly as "literary learning," knows what
something is by knowing what authorities have to say about it: "It is a
commune lyf . . . on Holy Chirche to bileve" (X.232); also,

> Austyn the olde herof made bokes,
> And hymself ordeyned to sadde us in bileve.
> Who was his auctour? Alle the foure Evaungelistes;
> And Crist cleped hymself so, the [Gospelleres] bereth witness . . .
>
> (243–46)

Not even clerks can explain the mystery of the Incarnation, but nevertheless "thus it bilongeth to bileve to lewed that willen dowel" (247–
48). We are not to consult our human capacities of understanding, but
to believe unquestioningly what the clergy tell us to believe. Dobet, in
turn, is "to suffre for thi soules helthe / Al that the Book bit bi Holi

Cherche techyng" (251–52); and Dobest is "to be boold to blame the gilty, / Sythenes thow seest thiself as in soule clene" (258–59). In effect, Dobest is what priests are supposed to do, and so Clergy's definition launches him into a satirical attack on corrupt priests. Scripture, as Clergy's wife (X.151–52), is not just the Holy Scriptures, but authoritative writing in general, and therefore is the patroness of the texts to which the magisterium of the Church presumably refers in providing authoritative answers to all human questions: "I nel noght scorne . . . but if scryveynes lye" (331); "Poul preveth it impossible" (335); "Salamon seith also" (336); "Caton kenneth us" (337); "patriarkes and prophetes and poetes bothe / Writen to wissen us" (338–39); "the Apostles bereth witnesse" (340). From Scripture's perspective, to know what anything is means to know what authoritative texts have to say about it. There are no epistemological surprises here.

At precisely this point, the dreamer becomes more loquacious and disputatious than he has yet appeared to be at any other point in the poem. He begins a long running debate with Scripture (and others), which might be broadly characterized as a debate about faith and works and baptism and predestination. He directly contradicts Scripture, perhaps even more fiercely than he contradicted the friars in Passus VIII: "'Contra,' quod I, 'by Crist! That kan I repreve'" (X 343) And he turns Scripture's own methods against her, arguing on the basis of authoritative texts: "preven it by Peter and by Poul bothe" (344); Solomon "demed wel and wisely, as Holy Writ telleth" (381), but his and others' "werkes, as Holy Writ seith, was evere the contrarie" (395); as for the carpenters who worked on Noah's ark and yet were drowned, "the culorum of this clause curatours is to mene" (408); the Bible tells of many who did evil and yet were saved, such as the thief crucified with Jesus (413), Mary Magdalene (421), King David (422), and Paul the Apostle (423); the words of Solomon (429), of Christ (441–42), and of David (448), as reported in the Bible, can be adduced to argue for the dreamer's thesis, as can the sermons of Saint Augustine (453). In a passage whose irony is reminiscent of the Wife of Bath's marshaling of authorities to undermine authority, the dreamer shows us that a little learning is a dangerous thing.

Thus, by the normal route of medieval literary education, the dreamer has come again from another direction into the heart of the hermeneutic problem—the Babylonian cacophony that exists because presumably authoritative discourses seem to contradict each other. He expresses the disgust and despair of the tyro in the discipline who has just begun to perceive what a difficult and tedious process learning really is, and how uncertain its rewards are:

> "This a long lesson," quod I, "and litel am I the wiser!
> Where Dowel is or Dobet derkliche ye shewen.
> Manye tales ye tellen that Theologie lerneth,
> And that I man maad was, and my name yentred
> In the legende of lif longe er I were,
> Or ellis unwriten for some wikkednesse, as Holy Writ witnesseth:
> *Nemo ascendit ad celum nisi qui de celo descendit.*
>   "And I leve it wel, by Oure Lord, and on no lettrure bettre."
>   (371–77)

The dreamer characteristically homes in on one of the dangerous ways of thinking about the doctrine of predestination, the interpretation that suggests that since I can do nothing to effect my own salvation, I need not worry about whether I am doing good or evil. For the dreamer, this rejection of worry amounts to a rejection of literacy:

> *"Ecce ipsi idiote rapiunt celum ubi nos sapientes in inferno mergimur"*—
> And is to mene to Englissh men, moore ne lesse,
> Arn none rather yravysshed fro the righte bileve
> Than are thise konnynge clerkes that knowe manye bokes,
> Ne none sonner ysaved, ne sadder of bileve
> Than plowmen and pastours and povere commune laborers . . .
>   (455–60)

There is already considerable irony in the dreamer's method of proving that the *idiotae*—that is, the illiterate—are more likely to get to heaven than the *litterati* are. (See Stock 28–30 on the connotations of *idiota* in medieval Latin; see also Clopper's discussion of the term—*Songes of Rechelesnesse* 85ff.) The dreamer supports his thesis with an authoritative Latin quotation:

> The doughtieste doctour and devinour of the Trinitee,
> Was Austyn the olde, and heighest of the foure,
> Seide thus in a sermon—I seigh it writen ones . . .
>   (452–54)

In spite of what the Latin quotation says, what counts for the dreamer himself is what he sees written. In spite of himself, he is an intellectual. But he is an incompletely educated intellectual. Langland might, in fact, be laying the irony on thicker by making the dreamer misquote Augustine (see Schmidt's note on line 455—page 448 of Schmidt's edition).

Perhaps even more telling is the dreamer's earlier speech. Although he says he rejects literacy, he apparently conceives of his own salvation in terms of being written in a book (374–76), and he decides what to believe on the basis of "lettrure" (377). Whether he is aware of it or not, he cannot free himself from the intellectual's obsession with texts. His own compulsions will require him to follow up the path he has set himself upon, even though he might take detours of many years' duration. Scripture's rebuke to the dreamer at the beginning of Passus XI bites in just this way: *"Multi multa sciunt et seipsos nesciunt"* (XI.3). Not only does the dreamer's intellectual pride obstruct his understanding of Scripture's lessons, but he fails to understand the crucial thing about himself— namely, that his intellectual's obsession with texts will ultimately require him to come to terms with Scripture, and that there is no easy rejection.

In one sense, the dreamer is doing the right thing. He is temporarily abandoning his quest for understanding of Dowel. He has persuaded himself that doing well is not in itself a ticket to heaven. But if the dreamer is doing the right thing, he is doing it for the wrong reasons. First, to wash one's hands of the educational enterprise at the first moment when one perceives that one will have to struggle for a lifetime with apparently contradictory texts evidences intellectual sloth. Second, the dreamer thinks he is giving up on self-justification because self-justification is useless. That much is correct. He knows *that* self-justification is useless—ironically, he knows it only abstractly, through the book learning he ostensibly rejects. But he has not yet come to understand *why* self-justification is useless. That is, he has not yet come to a full understanding of the significance of his own sin. He has not yet taken on his own pulse the measure of his own desire for self-justification. The dreamer falls victim to exactly the intellectual error he says he rejects. He knows what he knows abstractly, because he has read books; and that knowledge blocks his inquiry into its own application to the dreamer's life.

After the dreamer's long sojourn with Fortune in the "lond of long-

ynge and love" (XI.8), the interaction with the friars that gets him back
on track, as it were, has interesting parallels with Piers's interaction with
the priest in the pardon scene. The dreamer has entrusted the care of
his soul to the friars, under the assumption that they will provide easy
penance and dispositive pardon. As Coveitise of Eighes says,

> Go confesse thee to som frere and shewe hym thi synnes.
> For whiles Fortune is thi frend freres wol thee lovye,
> And fecche thee to hir fraternitee and for thee biseke
> To hir Priour Provincial a pardon for to have . . .
>
> (XI.54–57)

The lines describe exactly the sort of relationship between laity and
clergy that the priest tries to foist on Piers in the pardon scene, the relationship that the dreamer's spiritual sloth has allowed him to accept tacitly for "fourty wynter and a fifte moore" (47). The dreamer becomes
suspicious of the friars, however, when it turns out that they are more
interested in confessions and burials than they are in baptisms (71ff.). In
a somewhat dim and distorted reflection of Piers's tearing of the pardon, the dreamer rejects the friars' self-seeking assumption of authority:
"roughte ye nevere / Where my body were buryed, by so ye hadde my
silver!" (73–74). The dreamer hesitates to perform the dramatic public
gesture of satirizing the friars—not so much because he is uncertain
about his conclusions, but rather because he is afraid that they will use
their learning to make him look like a fool: "'They wole aleggen also,'
quod I, 'and by the Gospel preven: / *Nolite iudicare quemquam*'" (89–90).
The dreamer has the intellectual's fear of being embarrassed in public
disputation. Lewte encourages the dreamer to go ahead and "reden it in
retorik to arate dedly synne" (102), but only if the dreamer is reporting
"Thyng that al the world woot" (101). Lewte, who seems to represent
here the proper fulfilling of one's social function, hints at a possible theological justification for writing satirical poetry—but only if the dreamer
does not take it upon himself alone to render public judgment: "Though
thow se yvel, seye it noght first" (104). The poet is not to get into intellectual disputes, but only to translate into "rhetoric" what everybody already agrees about.

     Scripture affirms what Lewte says—"He seith sooth" (107)—and be-
gins preaching on the theme that many are called but few are chosen

(111ff.). The connection between Lewte's speech and Scripture's text is perhaps not immediately clear. But I think there is a decisive clue in the repetition of the word *pryvé*. Lewte tells the dreamer, "No thyng that is pryvé, publice thow it nevere" (105), whereas in Scripture's sermon the porter "plukked in *Pauci* pryveliche and leet the remenaunt go rome" (114). As Peter Goodall says, "[T]he principal meaning of 'pryvetee' in Middle English is a secret, arcane knowledge" (9). Scripture's text emphasizes, that is, the impossibility of human knowledge about who is saved and who is not. Thus we should hesitate to make judgments. But the other side of the coin is that we cannot be certain about ourselves either. The dreamer takes the sermon personally to heart: "I took ful good hede" (111). Having conceived of his salvation as already determined by inclusion in the Book of Life, the dreamer has suddenly begun to consider the possibility that his name is *not* there. From the first theological danger of the doctrine of predestination, the dreamer rebounds immediately into the other danger, the danger of crippling despair:

> Al for tene of hir text trembled myn herte,
> And in a weer gan I wexe, and with myself to dispute
> Wheither I were chose or noght chose . . .
>
> (115–17)

The word *tene* here connects this passage with Piers (Simpson 121–22), and the dreamer's reaction looks like a dwarfish imitation of Piers's own turning inward to a consideration of his own sin after he has rejected the priest's notion of self-justificaion. The dreamer, hindered by sloth and intellectual pride, is repeating in his own fumbling way the same pattern that Piers has established.

It is not clear who is speaking in lines 153 and following of the B-text—or, for that matter, in the corresponding lines of the C-text (XII.87ff.). Schmidt's punctuation of the B-text attributes the lines to Trajan. Pearsall's note to the lines in the C-text suggests that the speaker might be Rechelesnesse, whom Pearsall identifies as "an aspect of the dreamer's consciousness" (203n). I believe there are strong arguments that the speaker is in fact Scripture.

In the first place, to attribute to Scripture the speech in lines XI.153–318 (including lines 170–71, where Scripture paraphrases Trajan) continues a rhetorical pattern that Langland has already firmly established. Scripture tends to use the rhetorical tactic of affirming all or part of what her interlocutor has said, and then going on to use the affirmation to help her make whatever point she is working on. Sometimes her tactic actually works like a concession in debate. Maybe Langland's point is that Scripture, as writing in general, already contains all of the arguments and counterarguments we can think of. In Passus X, for example, when the dreamer contradicts Scripture's claim that rich men will have a hard time getting into heaven, he argues from the premise that everyone who is baptized is "saaf, be he riche or povere" (X.345). Scripture concedes the dreamer's point, in part: "That is *in extremis* . . . amonges Sarsens and Jewes" (346). Scripture later seizes the rhetorical initiative from Lewte by affirming Lewte's point about judging: "'He seith sooth,' quod Scripture tho, and skipte an heigh and preched" (XI.107). When the dreamer more or less desperately appeals to the mercy of God, Scripture concedes his point:

> "That is sooth," seide Scripture; "may no synne lette
> Mercy, may al amende, and mekenesse hir folwe;
> For thei beth, as oure bokes telleth, above Goddes werkes . . ."
>   (XI.137–39)

She is then immediately and impolitely interrupted by Trajan: "Ye, baw for bokes!" (140). Line 153, therefore, might seem to continue the pattern. Scripture retakes the initiative by conceding Trajan's goodness, incorporating him into the sermon she has been delivering, but at the same time insisting again on the importance of books—as we might expect of Scripture: "Lo! ye lordes, what leautee dide by an Emperour of Rome / That was an uncristene creature, as clerkes fyndeth in bokes" (153–54).

Besides the rhetorical pattern, the speech in lines 153–318 extends themes and images that have previously been important to Scripture. Scripture began her debate with the dreamer by satirizing the rich (X.331ff.), and here the burden of the sermon is to praise poverty. Scripture begins her sermon in Passus XI with the parable of the feast (111ff.), and another parable involving a feast is picked up in lines 189 and following. Scripture's concern at the beginning of Passus XI with the dreamer's knowing himself sounds something like the insistence of the speaker in line 229a that *"Melius est scrutari scelera nostra quam naturas rerum."*

Finally, the speaker of lines 153–318 is obsessed with the issue of textual correctness—so much so that the speaker at one point even becomes aware of having been distracted by that obsession from the main theme of poverty: "This lokynge on lewed preestes hath doon me lepe from poverte" (317). The problem with "lewed preestes" is that a priest is "a goky, by God! that in his gospel failleth / Or in masse or in matyns maketh any defaute" (307–8). The ignorant priest who skips over portions of the liturgical text is compared to the "goky" who puts "fals Latyn" or "peyntcd parentrelynarie, parcelles overskipped" in a charter, thus making it "chalangeable" (303–6). The lines look back to the dreamer's image of the charter, from which he tries to derive comfort in his fear of damnation: "may no cherl chartre make, ne his c[h]atel selle / Withouten leve of his lord no lawe wol it graunte" (XI.127–28). By raising the specter of false charters in court and false priests with cure of souls, the speaker of lines 153–318 puts the dreamer back on the hook of personal responsibility that he thought he had wriggled off; and the speaker conceives of clerical corruption in terms of corruption of texts. Throughout the long speech, there are many other references to books and writing as authoritative sources of knowledge: "The legende *sanctorum* yow lereth more largere than I yow telle" (160); "the book blissed of blisse and of joye: / God wroughte it and wroot it with his on fynger" (167–68); "In the olde lawe, as the lettre telleth" (204); "lakke no lif oother, though he moore Latyn knowe" (213); "some wordes I fynde writen, were of Feithes techyng" (225); "Salomon seide, as folk seeth in the Bible" (269); "as Luc bereth witnesse" (272); "as seith the Book" (275); "As David seith in the Sauter" (278).

The notion that Scripture speaks lines 153–318 seems important not because the point is obvious or undebatable, but precisely because Langland's text does seem to leave the identity of the speaker vague. Line 319, spoken by the dreamer, is curious: "Ac muche moore in metynge thus with me gan oon dispute. . . ." It is not immediately clear how the speaker of 153–318 is disputing with the dreamer. If Scripture is the speaker, then the lines could count as a continuation of the dispute over the salvation of the rich begun in Passus X (343ff.). On the other hand, the proximal dispute in the text is the dreamer's dispute with himself about whether he is saved: "in a weer gan I wexe, and with myself to dispute / Wheither I were chose or noght chose" (XI.116–17). On one level, the disputes are the same as far as the dreamer is concerned. He wants to know whether his baptism is sufficient for salvation, or whether he must also exhibit the patient poverty that Scripture praises. As I read lines 153–318, Langland is deliberately vague about the speaker, because the dreamer is debating not only with Scripture but with himself. Reche-lesnesse, who gets many of the corresponding lines in the C revision, is something of an alter ego of the dreamer. The dreamer is the "oon" who is disputing with himself; but he is also at this point the "oon" whose thinking has been informed by Scripture. He says, "with me gan oon dis-pute," almost as if he has internalized Scripture to the point that her dis-tinctiveness is not completely clear to him, not completely separate from his own dream thought.

Lawrence M. Clopper's conclusion about the problem of the speaker in this passage seems not so very far from my own, though Clopper and I arrive at the conclusion (and move beyond it) by very different routes. Clopper wants

> to read the entire discourse from the meeting with Clergye until Wille awakens from the Inner Dream as an internal monologue in which positions in the de-bate are personified as speakers: Clergye, Scripture, Trajan, and so forth. Read-ing the section as an interior monologue conforms well with the whole action of Dowel since passus 8–12 describe a peregrination through the faculties of Wille's mind. The identity of the speaker of the passage that begins at line 154, therefore, is less important than the function of the speech. (*Songes of Reche-lesnesse* 221)

The dreamer's consciousness, as is inevitable for the intellectual, is formed by literary education—by writings. To dispute with himself is to dispute with Scripture, to confront with each other the apparently conflicting authoritative texts that have formed his mind. The dreamer's apparently facile rejection of Clergy and Scripture in Passus X has not taken. Because he is an intellectual, his path ultimately lies through Scripture itself. Because he is a poet, his path lies also through poetry. As Elizabeth Kirk says of the dreamer's later defense of his "makynge"

(XII.16), "Writing the poem is his 'werke,' not his play, his only means of finding out what he has to know. His defense is not that his way of life is defensible—every attempt to reconcile it with traditional morality has failed—but that it is essential to him, that no other experience will bring him 'kynde knowynge'" (141–42).

At this point in the dreamer's narrative comes his vision of "Myddel-erthe" (XI.323) and an encounter with Reason. The dreamer's en-counter with Reason might initially seem to set us all the way back to the beginning of Passus IX, because here the dreamer, like Wit earlier, seems primarily concerned with the "engendrynge of kynde" (XI.335). And here, as with Wit earlier, Kynde is a name of God (XI.325). But there is a radically different emphasis in Passus XI. Whereas Wit at-tempts to understand everything in genetic terms, Reason stresses that we do *not* understand certain things, precisely because their causes are hidden from us: "For is no creature under Crist can formen hymselven" (XI.387). Reason is self-limited, and the conclusion is that we must suf-fer what we do not understand: "Holy Writ . . . wisseth men to suffre" (382). To worry about how God has made the world, as the dreamer wants to do, is to meddle in what does not concern human beings: *"De re que te non molestat noli certare"* (393). Ymaginatif, at this point unnamed, ex-plains the proper relation between Reason and Clergy, human intelli-gence and learning, and uses the concept of suffering to rebuke the dreamer's presumption:

> "Haddestow suffred," he seide, "slepynge tho thow were,
> Thow sholdest have knowen that Clergie kan and conceyved moore
> thorugh Reson;
> For Reson wolde have reherced thee right as Clergie seide."
>
> (411–13)

The proper function of Reason is to support Clergy, not to undermine it. Both teach, by different routes, the lesson of human limitation. Nei-ther, therefore, can coexist with pride: "right so ferde Reson bi thee— thow with thi rude speche / Lakkedest and losedest thyng that longed noght the to doone" (418–19); "Pryde now and presumpcion paraven-ture wol thee appele, / That Clergie thi compaignye ne kepeth noght to suwe" (421–22).

The vision of Reason's operation among earthly creatures comes after Scripture's sermon on patient poverty. The vision contains a lesson appropriate to the moment, which the dreamer, characteristically, misses. God, as Kynde, means to help the dreamer to apply Scripture's theme to his personal life, by teaching the dreamer to love God through observing the rationality of God's creation. As Ymaginatif says, reason supplements learning. Love is what would make patient poverty possible:

> . . . sithen cam Kynde
> And nempned me by my name, and bad me nymen hede,
> And thorugh the wondres of this world wit for to take.
> And on a mountaigne that Myddelerthe highte, as me tho thoughte,
> I was fet forth by ensaumples to knowe,
> Thorugh ech a creature, Kynde my creatour to lovye.
>
> (XI.320–25)

The purpose of God's creation is not to provide a puzzle for human understanding to solve, but instead to stimulate human love. The dreamer's drive for intellectual mastery is misdirected.

Ymaginatif, as the faculty of purposes, explains all of this to the dreamer. (See Kaulbach 7ff., whose approach to the poem is nevertheless very different from mine, as explained in Bibliographical Essay 3.2, below.) Like the Kantian (and Coleridgean) faculty of imagination, Langland's Ymaginatif unifies. But he unifies experience by placing it within a narrative of salvation. My understanding of Ymaginatif, then, seems to me not so very far from that of John Lawlor, who says that imagination in the poem should be conceived as "the capacity to profit from experience" (113), and that in the encounter with Ymaginatif "[w]e begin to make sense of experience" (115). That is, Ymaginatif is concerned with how the various disparate moments in human experience function to bring human beings to God. Ymaginatif is concerned with instrumentality, with the uses of historical and psychological entities and events. He first admonishes the dreamer about how Reason and Clergy *would* have been useful (XI.411ff.). Modern popular psychology tends to treat shame as a debilitating and useless emotion to be discarded as quickly as possible; but Ymaginatif explains how even shame has its use (423ff.). In identifying himself to the dreamer, Ymaginatif renders intelligible as spiritual warnings all the apparently random afflictions of human life: "thow hast ben warned ofte / With poustees of pestilences, with poverte and with angres" (XII.10–11).

Ymaginatif's use of the peacock is characteristic. The dreamer in the vision of Reason had mentioned the peacock as one item in a long list of curiosities:

> . . . some briddes at the bile thorugh brethyng conceyved,
> And some caukede; I took kepe how pecokkes bredden.
> Muche merveilled me what maister thei hadde,
> And who taughte hem on trees to tymbre so heighe . . .
>
> (XI.357–60)

The dreamer wants to know all about the peacock, in order to scratch his itch for pseudoscientific knowledge of the creation—that is, to understand God intellectually. Ymaginatif, on the other hand, postulates another use for the peacock. He reminds the dreamer that the dreamer wanted "of briddes and of beestes and of hir bredyng knowe" (XII.218), and insists that "Kynde knoweth the cause hymself, no creature ellis" (225). The use of the peacock and the peahen is not as scientific curiosities. Instead, "of briddes and of beestes men by olde tyme / Ensamples token and termes" (235–36), and the peacock and peahen serve as a moral example: "proude riche men thei bitokneth" (239).

Ymaginatif, then, unifies human experience by projecting its uses for salvation. The main point of his discourse has to do with the uses of clergy or learning, as Dame Study has anticipated in her satire against the pseudolearning of the charlatans who delight in arguing about things that are beyond human understanding: "Ymaginatif herafterward shal answere to youre purpos" (X.117). Learning is a necessary supplement to natural human intelligence ("kynde wit"). Natural human intelligence tries to do what the dreamer tried to do with the peacock: namely, to understand it. "Ac kynde wit cometh of alle kynnes sightes— / Of briddes and of beestes" (XII.128–29), and

> [Olde] lyveris toforn us useden to marke
> The selkouthes that thei seighen, hir sones for to teche,
> And helden it an heigh science hir wittes to knowe.
>
> (131–33)

But, on the other hand,

> Patriarkes and prophetes repreveden hir science,
> And seiden hir wordes ne hir wisdomes was but a folye;
> As to the clergie of Crist, counted it but a trufle . . .
>
> (137–39)

The dreamer needs the lesson at this point, having made, as it seems, all of the mistakes that it is possible for an intellectual to make: attempting to understand the totality of human experience with the unaided human intelligence; rejecting the tedium and struggle of literary education and thereby denying the deepest part of himself; failing to understand how profoundly his own intellectual problems are tied to the texts that have formed his mind; proceeding as though intellectual understanding were at least a necessary and maybe also a sufficient condition for salvation; and throughout it all, continuing to lust unreflectively for an impossible self-justification in terms of some unimaginable argument.

Ymaginatif's type of clergy is a written text, presumably from the "Olde Lawe" (XII.73), in the "caractes" (78, 88, 91) that Christ wrote in the dirt when the woman was taken in adultery (John 8:3–9): "Holy Kirke knoweth this—that Cristes writyng saved; / So clergie is confort to creatures that repenten" (82–83). But this is the Old Law interpreted through the love of Christ: "clergie for Cristes love, that of clergie is roote" (71). Like the Eucharist, which depends for its efficacy on the clergy, Christ's writing was good for the repentant and bad for the evil:

> For Goddes body myghte noght ben of breed withouten clergie,
> The which body is bothe boote to the rightfulle,
> And deeth and dampnacion to hem that deyeth yvele;
> As Cristes caracte confortede and bothe coupable shewed
> The womman that the Jewes broughte, that Jesus thoughte to save . . .
>
> (85–89)

Clergy does not *justify* the repentant sinner, but *comforts*. Line 88 admits of a double reading: "Christ's written character comforted [the woman] and also ["bothe"] showed [the Jews] to be blameworthy"; or "Christ's written character comforted [the woman] and showed both [the woman and the Jews] to be blameworthy." That is, there is no question of self-justification for the party of either part. The dreamer has been looking for the wrong result from literary learning. At the end of Passus XII, Ymaginatif in fact suggests that the point of the story of Trajan is the same and is valid whether the story is true or not: "And wher it worth or worth noght, the bileve is gret of truthe, / And an hope hangynge therinne to have a mede for his truthe" (288–89). What we get is not a rhetoric of self-justification by means of which to argue our way into heaven, but instead a *hope* that God will reward the good works he has made possible. Ymaginatif quotes at this point part of the same line from the psalm that Piers quoted upon tearing the pardon: "*Si ambulavero in medio umbre mortis*" (291). Piers finishes the line: "*Non timebo mala, quoniam tu mecum es*" (VII.117). Ymaginatif's partial quotation sounds like a reminder of the earlier vision (Simpson 92), an echo of the absent Piers, and hints that the dreamer is perhaps getting closer to understanding what Piers understood earlier: that human beings are protected from evil, if they are, not by their ability to justify themselves, but only because God is with them. Ymaginatif's conclusion from the story of the woman taken in adultery in fact tries to steer the dreamer away from futile attempts to judge human behavior: "*Nolite iudicare et non iudicabimini*" (XII.89a). Since we are sinful, avoiding judgment is our only hope; and we avoid judgment not by seeking to justify ourselves, but instead by being charitable toward others.

Ymaginatif defines Dowel in terms of faith, hope, and charity:

> Poul in his pistle . . . preveth what is Dowel:
> *Fides, spes, caritas, et maior horum* . . .
> Feith, hope and charitee—alle ben goode,
> And saven men sondry tymes, ac noon so soone as charite.
> For he dooth wel, withouten doute, that dooth as lewte techeth . . .
>
> (XII.29–32)

What something is, for Ymaginatif, is determined by its use for salvation. To do well is to perform one's function within the social organism. That Ymaginatif criticizes the dreamer because "thow medlest thee with makynge—and myghtest go seye thi Sauter" (16) suggests that it is difficult for the dreamer to construct a narrative in which his verse making can be seen as functioning to save him. His somewhat lame (and again, self-justifying) response is that he occasionally needs recreation (20ff.). What the dreamer needs to learn is the operation of charity in

the world. What he might begin to suspect as a result of his colloquy
with Ymaginatif is that charity is not a matter of self-justification
through good works. The text with which Ymaginatif ends, *salvabitur vix
iustus* (278ff.), is not about self-justification, but instead about how hard
it is to be saved even if one is just. Ymaginatif uses, perhaps even strains,
a text to show that good works do not justify, but they might comfort
through the hope that subsumes all of the apparently random events of
human experience under a narrative of salvation. From the perspective
of Ymaginatif, that comfort is what the dreamer should expect from
learning.

PATIENCE, THE FEAST, AND HAUKYN

As I and others have already suggested, the figure of the Doctor at
the feast of Conscience shows learning turned grotesque and cancerous.
The dreamer observes what he himself might be in danger of becoming
and is repelled by the spectacle. Patience becomes his chief instructor
throughout this section of the poem, because once the intellectual re-
signs his project of intellectual mastery of human experience, there is
apparently nothing left to do with life except to put up with it and suffer
through it—to be *patient* both in our modern sense of the term and in
the etymological sense. The dreamer is of course not especially patient,
but at least Patience is able to restrain him somewhat. "Pacience parceyved what I thoughte, and [preynte] on me to be stille" (XIII.86);
"And I sat stille as Pacience seide" (99).

There is an interesting implication in the way the dreamer, taking
the advice of Patience, questions the Doctor about Dowel: "'What is
Dowel, sire doctour?' quod I; 'is Dobest any penaunce?'" (103). The
dreamer clearly does not seriously expect to get an intellectually satisfying answer, as he has sometimes expected when he has questioned one
of his other instructors about Dowel. His intention, instead, is to em-
barrass the Doctor, because the Doctor's way of life is so dissonant with
any possible definition of doing well. The dreamer no doubt acts in part
from intellectual pride, and certainly not from charity and forbearance:
"I shal jangle to this jurdan" (84). But at least temporarily, he by implication frees himself from his obsession with intellectual understanding
(that is, verbal definition) of Dowel and begins to conceive of Dowel as

a way of life. He does not expect the Doctor to be able to define Dowel, and that is because the Doctor does not live that way.

At exactly this point in the narrative of the dreamer, Piers Plowman begins to be heard of once again after his long absence. Clergy (among other things, the dreamer's own learning), all of whose implications the dreamer has laboriously worked through in his process of literary education in Passus IX–XII, confesses his own uncertainties, and says,

> . . . Dowel and Dobet arn two infinites,
> Whiche infinites with a feith fynden out Dobest,
> Which shal save mannes soule—thus seith Piers the Plowman.
>
> (XIII.128–30)

Whether or not one accepts all of the conclusions of Anne Middleton's well-known article on Dowel and Dobet as two grammatical infinitives (see also Mills 198–99), it seems correct to say that the terms in this passage do not function like normal personification allegory. They are "not referential, but purely formal. As Clergy's analogy shows, they order the progressive form of the search for perfection, rather than characterize its object" ("Infinites" 171). If doing well is an "infinite" process, perpetually incomplete, then the desire for self-justification makes no sense. Since one never actually completes the process of doing well, one can never point to a list of good deeds that warrant one's admission to heaven. Clergy, therefore, cannot give the dreamer what the corrupt priest implies he can give Piers in the pardon scene: that is, an authoritative true judgment of works that will allow the sinner to feel self-justified. Piers's proclamation that Dowel is an "infinite" can be read as a less dramatic but equally radical restatement of what Piers means by tearing the pardon.

The debate of Clergy and Conscience is instructive. When Conscience decides to become a pilgrim with Patience, Clergy offers what he conceives of as a better deal:

> I shal brynge yow a Bible, a book of the olde lawe,
> And lere yow, if yow like, the leeste point to knowe,
> That Pacience the pilgrym parfitly knew nevere.
>
> (186–88)

Conscience replies,

> For al that Pacience me profreth, proud am I litel;
> Ac the wil of the wye and the wil of folk here
> Hath meved my mood to moorne for my synnes.
> The goode wil of a wight was nevere bought to the fulle:
> For ther nys no tresour therto to a trewe wille.
>
> (190–94)

In "proud am I litel," Conscience implies that the danger of intellectual pride lurks behind the desire of the learned to know "the leeste point" of the law. This intellectual pride is of course one of the dreamer's besetting sins. Conscience's speech looks back to the pardon scene, in that the decision to reject learning clears space for the salutary desire "to moorne for my synnes," just as Piers's rejection of the priest's authority led Piers to prayers and penance (VII.120). In its concentration on the importance of will, Conscience's speech also looks forward to Anima's assertion in Passus XV that charity can be known "Neither thorugh wordes ne werkes, but thorugh wil oone" (XV.210; see my discussion of this passage, in the preceding chapter). Therefore, Conscience whispers in Clergy's ear, "Me were levere, by Oure Lord, and I lyve sholde, / Have pacience parfitliche than half thi pak of bokes!" (XIII.201–2). Clergy is not so sure: "Thow shalt se the tyme / Whan thow art wery forwalked, wilne me to counseille" (204–5).

Conscience and Clergy, however, seem to come to some sort of accommodation. First, Conscience concedes that learning can refresh the weary pilgrim: "That is sooth" (206). But Conscience proposes a division of labor in a cooperative effort to transform the world:

> If Pacience be oure partyng felawe and pryvé with us bothe,
> Ther nys wo in this world that we ne sholde amende,
> And conformen kynges to pees, and alle kynnes londes—
> Sarsens and Surre, and so forth alle the Jewes—
> Turne into the trewe feith and intil oon bileve.
>
> (207–11)

Clergy agrees, apparently understanding Conscience's point for the first time:

> That is sooth . . . I se what thow menest.
> I shall dwelle as I do, my devoir to shewe,

And confermen fauntekyns and oother folk ylered
Til Pacience have preved thee and parfit thee maked.
(212–15)

World-transforming missionary activity depends upon the perfecting of
Conscience, whereas Clergy's function is to minister to the converted.
Although their functions are different, however, they must work as a
team. Conscience's thinking here, as he says, is inspired by Patience: "the
wil of the wye" (191). Patience has defined Dowel, Dobet, and Dobest as
"*Disce, . . . doce; dilige inimicos*" (137ff.), respectively. Patience's definition is in
harmony with Piers's proclamation, in the sense that learning, teaching,
and loving are all "infinites." They are activities, ways of doing life, as
opposed to particular deeds. Clergy accepts teaching as his "devoir," and
Conscience takes on the more difficult but necessary task of pursuing
perfection—loving the enemies of Christians, patiently loving the warring nations and the hostile pagans in order to convert them.

The allegory here can and should be read on a very general level, but
I want to apply it more particularly to the dreamer's situation at this
point in the poem. The dreamer has laboriously worked through his
own experience of literary education, and has painfully learned the limitations of learning itself. Learning cannot provide him with what he
wanted namely, an intellectual understanding of human experience
that would enable him to know what it means to do well in the world.
The dreamer wanted this knowledge because he thought it was a necessary first step to his ultimate goal of self-justification. He is beginning
to understand dimly that the quest was misconceived. On the other
hand, he has also found out that for him, at least, as an intellectual,
there is no easy rejection of the texts that have in the most profound
sense formed the self he wanted to justify. Following Fortune through
the land of longing provides a fascinating and long-lasting distraction,
but finally the dreamer has to come to terms with the texts that still
have the power to terrify him. The dreamer's conscience will need the
sustenance of learning as he tries to learn to love. Scripture is still at the
banquet, serving up the nourishing dishes that the Doctor passes up,
and upon which Patience and the dreamer must subsist (XIII.37ff.,
46ff.). But these dishes of Patience are the substance of penitence: "*Agite
penitenciam*" (48); "*Miserere mei, Deus*" (53a); "*Confitebor tibi*" (54); "*Cor contritum et humiliatum*" (58). The intellectual understanding now foreground-

ed is not the understanding of what it is to do well, but the opposite. It is the understanding of one's own sin. The passage anticipates Conscience's later definition of Dowel, Dobet, and Dobest in terms of the three parts of the sacrament of penance: contrition, confession, and satisfaction (XIV.16–22).

Like Piers's attention in the pardon scene, the dreamer's attention begins to shift toward the issue of dealing with his own sin. This feels to the dreamer like "patience," like postponing the gratification of judging others, or of justifying oneself (which turns out to be intimately connected with judging others negatively), or of achieving a sense of intellectual mastery over authoritative texts or over the experiences those texts shape. Confronting one's own sin also feels like patience in the other sense, patience as suffering. This suffering through patient poverty—including bodily poverty as conducive to the crucial poverty of spirit—is to issue, through some process as yet mysterious to the dreamer, in the way of life described as love (caritas). The way of life called love, and not intellectual knowledge of good action in the world, becomes with increasing explicitness the new object of the dreamer's quest. Piers Plowman, as the dreamer's private symbol of what the dreamer thinks he needs to know, can no longer be thought of merely as a symbol of the good laborer. Increasingly, it becomes important to the dreamer to grasp the relation between Piers and charity.

The episode of Haukyn the Active Man recapitulates and intensifies unbearably for the dreamer the dreamer's own idealized first image of good action in the world. Although Haukyn, like most common laborers, is apparently illiterate (XIII.248), he is associated with the dreamer by his clothing, if by nothing else: Haukyn is "Yhabited as an heremyte, an ordre by hymselve" (285), just as the dreamer was first dressed "In habite as an heremite unholy of werkes" (Prologue 3). With the line about the dreamer's clothes, Langland already in the third line of the poem connects clothing with "works," just as the filth on Haukyn's coat will be connected with Haukyn's sins. With the line about Haukyn's "habit," Langland suggests that the sinfulness of the laborer ironically isolates him from the very community within which he thinks to labor. In both lines, Langland seems to pun on Latin habitus. Haukyn clearly thinks of himself as doing what Piers first represented to the dreamer—

namely, laboring within the social organism under Piers himself as the paradigm of the good laborer:

> I have no goode giftes of thise grete lordes
> For no breed that I brynge forth—save a benyson on the Sonday,
> Whan the preest preieth the peple hir *Paternoster* to bidde
> For Piers the Plowman and that hym profit waiten . . .
>
> (XIII.235–38)

The lines apparently refer to the "daily bread" clause in the Lord's Prayer. The luster of good labor is already somewhat dimmed for Haukyn by the fact that one cannot necessarily expect appropriate earthly rewards for performing it.

Haukyn also finds himself caught on the same theological hook that snared the dreamer in the dreamer's meditations on the pardon scene. Haukyn says that the pope's pardon should "lechen a man" (254), because "he hath the power that Peter hymself hadde" (255). On the other hand, sometimes it seems that the pope's pardon does not work:

> Ac if myght of myracle hym faille, it is for men ben noght worthi
> To have the grace of God, and no gilt of the Pope.
> For may no blessynge doon us boote but if we wile amende . . .
>
> (256–58)

Here Haukyn falls again into the tangled brambles of the old debate between Augustinianism and Pelagianism. In short, he recapitulates the very issues that surfaced in the debate between Piers and the priest in the pardon scene. Although the healing of the pardon Haukyn describes is clearly on one level allegorical, Haukyn nevertheless remains in part stubbornly stuck at the literal level. He wants to ask the pope to send him "under his seel a salve for the pestilence, / And that his blessynge and hise bulles bocches myghte destruye" (249–50). Haukyn looks for a pardon with quasi-magical efficacy—a notion of "pardon" much like the priest's in the pardon scene, the notion that Piers rejects. If Haukyn had such a pardon, he says,

> . . . thanne wolde I be prest to the peple, paast for to make,
> And buxom and busy aboute breed and drynke
> For hym and for alle hise, founde I that his pardoun
> Mighte lechen a man—as I bileve it sholde.
>
> (251–54)

It is hard not to hear a pun on *prest*—not only "prompt," but also "priest." That is, if pardons were what Haukyn wants them to be, and if he had such a pardon, then it would confer on him the quasi-magical authority that is his misguided notion of priesthood. Then he himself could consecrate the elements of the Eucharist, and dispense healing according to the belief system that he is currently operating under.

Thus in Haukyn Langland presents a completed picture of what it would be to accept the symbol of the good laborer, with all that implies, as the central hermeneutic principle for interpreting one's experience and living one's life. If Piers were really only what the dreamer projects him to be in Passus V–VII, then Haukyn is what the dreamer, and every other sinful laborer, would turn out to be. Labor is not in itself salvific. Living and laboring in the world inevitably soil one's coat: "'I have but oon hater,' quod Haukyn, 'I am the lasse to blame / Though it be soiled and selde clene'" (XIV.1–2). At the very moment in which he implicitly admits the impossibility of justifying himself, Haukyn is still trying to get out from under any blame. Haukyn's anguish is precisely that his own sin will not allow the self-justification that he thinks he desperately needs. He himself recognizes the problem already when he rationalizes the failure of the pope's "myracle" (XIII.256). The appropriate response to that recognition is Piers's response in the pardon scene—that is, to turn one's attention to dealing with one's own sins.

Conscience offers Haukyn the orthodox comfort of the constantly renewed sacrament of penance (XIV.16ff.). Penance is itself imaged as labor in a laundry: contrition "shal clawe thi cote of alle kynnes filthe" (17), confession will "wasshen it and wryngen it" (18), and satisfaction will "beten it and bouken it" (19). The passage anticipates Anima's later image of the laundry work of charity itself (XV.186ff.). But Patience offers, in a way, a deeper response. By proffering the *"Fiat voluntas tua"* (XIV.49), Patience implies that the real difficulty is that we already think too much in terms of labor, in terms of getting our worldly livelihood; and such thinking gets in the way of our dealing directly with the central problem of human life, which is our own sinfulness. The answer is patience itself, to accept patiently whatever God sends. Patience repeats, that is, the change of orientation that is the response of Piers himself in the pardon scene. Patience says, "We sholde noght be to bisy abouten oure liflode" (XIV.33), in a line that echoes Piers himself: "Ne aboute my bely joye so bisy be na moore" (VII.119); "We sholde noght be to bisy aboute the worldes blisse" (VII.126). And Patience reiterates the very same biblical texts that Piers alludes to: *"Ne soliciti sitis"* (XIV.34a and VII.127); and *"Volucres celi Deus pascit"* (XIV.34a), translated by Piers in VII.129–30 as "The foweles in the feld, who fynt hem mete at wynter? / Have thei no gerner to go to, but God fynt hem alle."

Haukyn, naturally, is dubious about such advice: "Whoso leveth yow [either], by Oure Lord, I leve noght he be blessed!" (XIV.36). There is some question in my mind about Schmidt's emendation here, which supplies the *either* from a variant tradition (see the textual note on page 393 of Schmidt's edition) and thus suggests that Haukyn's speech is addressed to both Conscience and Patience. Haukyn's *yow* might be merely the plural of respect addressed to Patience, as also in XIV.277, and his objection seems more apposite to the advice of Patience alone. Haukyn as laborer should more easily understand Conscience's imaging of penance as labor. Be that as it may, Haukyn's worry is something else that links him with the dreamer. Even at the very end of the poem, the dreamer is still unable to shake his obsession with getting his livelihood. In Passus XX, after Kynde has counseled the dreamer to enter Unity and to learn to love, the dreamer asks, "How shal I come to catel so, to clothe me and to feede?" (XX.209).

But Patience's discourse gradually begins to penetrate Haukyn's confusion. Haukyn, indeed, seems to leap ahead of Patience and to cut to the heart of the issue when he asks, "Where wonyeth Charite?" (XIV.97). Patience has mentioned love (for example, 47, 59a), but his discourse has not been specifically about charity. Haukyn's subsequent question almost sounds as though he has been listening in on the dreamer's own discourse at the end of Passus XIII (422ff.), where the dreamer is concerned that the rich provide charity to the deserving poor. Haukyn asks, "Wheither paciente poverte . . . be moore plesaunt to Oure Drighte / Than richesse rightfulliche wonne and resonably yspended?" (XIV.101–2). Patience questions whether such a rich person in fact exists: "Ye—*quis est ille?* . . . quik—*laudabimus eum!*" (103). The response suggests that Haukyn has as yet a rather narrow and superficial understanding of the true spiritual nature of charity. But Haukyn's questions anticipate the dreamer's own growing obsession with charity, evidenced, among other places, in the dreamer's subsequent interrogation of Anima (XV.149, XVI.3). If charity, and not labor, is the essential thing, and if Patience is putting forward patient poverty as the strait gate to charity (and also, incidentally, as a kind of hermeneutic opposite to the principle of labor itself), then what one needs to know is the connection of patient poverty with charity: "What is poverte, Pacience, . . . proprely to mene?" (XIV.275). From Haukyn's perspective, which construes the world in terms of labor, what Patience says at first seems counterintuitive.

After Patience's discourse, however, which causes Haukyn to confront his own sin, Haukyn finds Patience's interpretation of human experience all too persuasive. Furthermore, it has ceased to be a purely intellectual issue for Haukyn. At first, like someone in the early stages of therapy, he more or less cheerfully admits his problems, treating them as a matter of considerable intellectual fascination both for himself and others:

> "By Crist!" quod Conscience tho, "thi beste cote, Haukyn,
> Hath manye moles and spottes—it moste ben ywasshe!"
> "Ye, whoso toke hede," quod Haukyn, "bihynde and bifore,
> What on bak and what on body half and by the two sides—
> Men sholde fynde manye frounces and manye foule plottes."
> (XIII.314—18)

Later, he tries to excuse himself by pleading extenuating circumstances: "I am the lasse to blame" (XIV.1). Finally, however, under the tutelage of Patience, Haukyn experiences fully the anguish of the sinner who cannot stop sinning:

> "Allas," quod Haukyn the Actif Man tho, "that after my cristendom
> I ne hadde be deed and dolven for Dowelis sake!
> So hard it is," quod Haukyn, "to lyve and to do synne.
> Synne seweth us evere," quod he, and sory gan wexe,
> And wepte water with hise eighen . . .
> (XIV.320—24)

This is the point where anyone must arrive who sets out to find Dowel in order to achieve self-justification by means of labor in the world.

Haukyn, who actually lives as the dreamer would live if the dreamer ever succeeded in ordering his life according to the principle of good labor in the world as he understands it, is doing the best he can do. It is not good enough. The dreamer's first projection of Piers, as the symbol of the good laborer, has failed decisively. Whatever Piers represents, it is not to be exhausted in the notion of good labor within the social organism. By means of the dreamer's relationship with literary education, which has been to him like a difficult marriage, the dreamer has come finally to see himself in the figure of Haukyn. The dreamer would be Haukyn, if the dreamer were to live under the dispensation he initially proposes to himself. He arrives laboriously and discursively at the same place where Piers arrived immediately and intuitively when the priest challenged the pardon: through the long middle of the poem the dreamer understands by the experience of warring texts, the experience definitive for him as an intellectual, that the game of self-justification is futile and self-destructive.

Patient poverty might be the proper mode of life for the dreamer, if he wants "kynde knowynge" of charity. But Patience in itself is no more the ultimate answer than any other hermeneutic principle that the dreamer has so far encountered. Patience, as I have argued in the preceding chapter in my discussion of Anima, ultimately deconstructs itself. We must be patient in all suffering *except* the suffering attendant upon the recognition of our own sin. We must attempt to do something about our sin. All that Haukyn can learn about his sin from Patience is that it is an occasion of acute and constantly renewed suffering. As Britton Harwood says, Patience is "ultimately less virtue than pain; and he inscribes the fact of pain into the poem" (103). The dreamer himself, as I have argued before, catches Haukyn's anguish:

> Ac after my wakynge it was wonder longe
> Er I koude kyndely knowe what was Dowel.
> And so my wit weex and wanyed til I a fool weere . . .
>
> (XV.1–3)

In the biblical sense (as for Piers in VII.125 and also for Conscience in XX.74), it is a good thing to be a fool. But because he is still searching for a hypostatized Dowel, the dreamer still worries that he cannot do good labor in the world. He worries that he is barred forever by his own essential sinfulness from making any progress in his search. Being a fool hurts. His pain prepares the dreamer for a new projection of what he needs to know, a new notion of Piers. Having, as it were, caught up with the real problem presented in the pardon scene—the problem of the impossibility of self-justification, with all that implies—the dreamer is ready for the new understanding of the human soul that, as I have argued, Anima provides. By defining the soul as grammarlike, as relational, Anima gives the dreamer a new way to think, a way that potentially breaks him out of the dead end where Haukyn is stuck. It is significant that the dreamer thanks Anima for *Haukyn's* sake: "For Haukyns love the Actif Man evere I shal yow lovye" (XVI.2). But the dreamer is also clearly talking about himself.

BIBLIOGRAPHICAL ESSAY 3.2

Understandably, a great deal has been written about medieval theories of the human faculties, in an attempt to understand exactly what Langland might have meant by Thought, or Wit, or Ymaginatif. Much of this material is extremely helpful. On the other hand, one of the premises that drives my book is the premise that Langland is a highly *original* poet. That means, among other things, that we do not necessarily know everything that Langland thought about the different human faculties just by knowing how the standard medieval sources treated them. It would be more accurate to suppose—or so I am arguing—that Langland himself was more or less constantly struggling to understand the faculties, and more or less constantly revising his own understanding of them according to the demands of whatever discourses he was involved in. What happens with these psychological terms in the reader's mind is much like what happens with Dowel, Dobet, and Dobest in the text. Many attempts—all of them more or less unsatisfactory, at least to me—have been made to isolate some essential core of meaning for Dowel, Dobet, and Dobest. Nevill Coghill's early attempt, for example, is one of the more thoroughgoing: Coghill argues that Piers himself represents successively the three grades of the good life. T. P. Dunning's work is another good example. Dunning sees the three "Do's" as blending "two traditional concepts: the three stages of the soul's progress in the love of God, and the three objective states of life—the active life, the religious life and the life of prelates" ("Structure" 274). But Mary Carruthers's discussion of the scholarly activity directed at defining the three "Do's" is more instructive. As she concludes, the "process of continual definition suggests that the sign itself is being tested, explored, even stretched to the limits of its conceptual significance. In a very real sense Dowel is a word in search of a referent" (10). And it is the same way for us with the names of the faculties themselves, by Langland's recursiveness that makes us as readers repeat the dreamer's interpretive activity. The study of standard medieval sources, however, is never useless; such study alerts modern readers to the possible range of the concepts Langland was engaging.

When I make statements about what Thought, or Wit, or Ymaginatif means in *Piers Plowman*, then, I do not want to exclude other possible meanings that other scholars or critics have identified. It is the old story of the blind men and the elephant. I am reading the poem in a particular way, and I am therefore emphasizing certain aspects of Langland's personifications that I think are suggested by the dramatic structure of the poem. Other readings will emphasize other aspects, and will perhaps find better warrant in the standard medieval sources. The argument about what Langland "finally" meant by any of these terms is not an argument that I am competent to engage, and is anyway an argument whose premise I question.

Some of the more helpful treatments of medieval theories of the human faculties include John Alford's "The Idea of Reason in *Piers Plowman*," James Simpson's brief but lucid discussion of the Aristotelian and Augustinian schemes of psychology (94–110), and A. J. Minnis's exploration of "Langland's Ymaginatif and Late-Medieval Theories of Imagination." James M. Dean's discussion of Wit's obsession with "genetic wickedness" (209) and the "untyme" of Cain's conception is helpful (205–12). There is also the valuable article by Joseph Wittig that I have already mentioned ("Inward Journey"). Wittig's article is a model of thoroughgoing historical scholarship, in which Passus IX–XII are read in the light of "the traditions of 'monastic,' moral psychology" ("Inward Journey" 211). Wittig concludes that such a reading "reveals a poet who, far from thrashing about indecisively for truth, firmly controls his fiction, a poet who is quite separable from his *persona,* and who deliber-

ately manipulates the misadventures of that *persona*" (279). Furthermore, Wittig argues, "traditional elements are selected and bonded into
a network of perspectives which give the dreamer's progress temporal
and ontological moorings in a universal context" (280). Without in any
way minimizing the importance of the methods of historical criticism, I
would only point out that conclusions of the general form of those
Wittig reaches are, in some sense at least, already implicated in the
premises from which historical criticism begins. To hypothesize that the
clue for decoding the poem is contained in some coherent historical
tradition is already to assume that the poem is to be understood as pos-
sessing a unifying theme in the Coleridgean sense. The tradition becomes coherent precisely because Langland himself has "selected and
bonded" certain elements from it—whereas, as Britton Harwood puts
it, "the vernacular does not supply the poet with a stock of unambiguous psychological terms and the poet's milieu furnishes the critic with
no single, received psychology" (31). That is, Wittig's more or less purely
historical approach takes the tradition of moral psychology as a control
on interpretation of Langland's poem, selecting from that extremely
complex tradition what makes Langland's poem seem coherent. If Augustine can read everything in the Old and New Testaments as somehow enjoining *caritas* or condemning *cupiditas,* we should not be sur-
prised that Wittig can read everything in *Piers Plowman* as harmonizing
with the monastic tradition of moral psychology—where the tradition
is treated, in part, as the set of passages that define a Coleridgean unity
for Langland's poem.

One might make corresponding comments about the methodology
adopted by Lawrence M. Clopper in his book *Songes of Rechelesnesse.* Clopper's book makes an instructive comparison with Wittig's article, because Clopper finds everywhere in *Piers Plowman* themes, images, and
modes of thought that associate Langland not with monasticism, but
with the tradition of Franciscan reformism. Is Langland more a monk
or more a friar? If one were disposed to critique Clopper's procedure (I
am not so disposed), one might say that Clopper, like Wittig, has
worked by a process of selection. But instead of selecting from a complex tradition those passages that make the poem a Coleridgean unity,
Clopper selects as definitive (authoritative, "authorial") those passages

from a complex poem that match the presumably unified tradition. The case of monasticism versus Franciscanism is a case in which I, lacking Wittig's or Clopper's familiarity with the primary sources, am incompetent to render judgment. What is interesting for my purposes, however, is the fact that the jury is still apparently out—that the poem in its complex intertextuality is capable of supporting two such different readings.

Ernest N. Kaulbach's strategy might seem to avoid the argument that might be aimed at Wittig. Instead of selecting elements from a complex tradition, Kaulbach argues that a particular cluster of specific texts are in fact the very texts that underlie the psychological theory expressed in *Piers Plowman:*

> Avicenna's prophetic psychology of the "vis imaginativa" came to the Christian and Latin West by way of Toledo; but the "Augustinisme Avicennisant" [Etienne Gilson's term—Kaulbach 87], peculiar to Will's prophetic ascent in the B-text of *Piers Plowman*, originated in England. From *Worcester MS Q 81* (possibly) and *F 57*, we surmise how the "vis imaginativa secundum Avicennam" was baptized into the concepts and terms of St. Augustine's "imaginatio," how an English "Augustinisme Avicennisant" originated, and how the PP-poet revived the deliberative and prophetic psychology of the "vis imaginativa secundum Avicennam" in the B-text, after 1366. (107)

Kaulbach carries out a detailed, point-by-point comparison of the psychological theory implied in *Piers Plowman* with the theory expounded in the particular manuscripts he suggests might have been available to the author of the poem:

> If *Worcester MS Q 81* was at Worcester in the fourteenth century, the PP-poet had at his disposal sufficient tracts to convert the "vis imaginativa secundum Avicennam" into the Christian Ymaginatif of the B-text. Since the anonymous tract in *Worcester MS F 57* was at Worcester in the fourteenth century, at least one copy of the tract links "Augustinisme Avicennisant" to the environs of the Malvern Hills, and the other two copies of the tract link the invention of "Augustinisme Avicennisant" to thirteenth-century England. If the PP-poet conceived the B-text of *Piers Plowman* near the Malvern Hills after 1366, then he had nearby, in at least one of the two Worcester mss, the means to conceive Ymaginatif's deliberative functions and prophetic powers, and to convert this Avicennan hypostasis to Christian prophecy. (107–8)

Clearly, then, Kaulbach cannot be accused of selecting from the many texts of a complex tradition just those elements that support a particular way of unifying the poem. On the other hand, Kaulbach's procedure does share with Wittig's the assumption that once the relevant tradition or the relevant texts have been identified, the tradition or the texts will serve as a key for the unambiguous "decoding" of Langland's text. This assumption is of course directly opposed to the assumption I make in this book that Langland means not to expound doctrine, psychological or otherwise, but instead to show his readers the agony of the struggle to understand how words relate to experience. The doctrines of any particular tradition, or the particular texts he has read, are in my view things Langland struggles with—not things he merely passes on.

I do not mean to caricature Wittig's or Clopper's or Kaulbach's procedure, which is certainly as rationally consistent as my own. It at first might seem possible to read the issue here as just another manifestation of the old argument between historical criticism and formalist criticism. Do we look for answers to our interpretive questions in the historical context, or in "the text itself" (whatever that means)? Because nobody escapes the hermeneutic circle, all I can say about that question is that it is naïvely posed. For a fuller explanation of this point, see my discussion in Bibliographical Essay 2.3 of Robert Adams's article on Need. Adams's procedure, in fact, seems especially similar to Kaulbach's, in the attempt to locate a particular text or texts that will allow one to "decode" *Piers Plowman*. I mean only to point out that Wittig's or Clopper's or Kaulbach's or Adams's procedure (again, like my own) rests upon certain assumptions about the nature of authorship, the nature of texts, and the nature of the human person. But the assumptions underlying the historicist approaches of these critics happen to be precisely the ones that I think Langland critiques in the act of "doing hermeneutics" in *Piers Plowman*. With Wittig and others, I want to say that Langland is not the same as his persona. But neither does Langland ultimately claim to have meaningful intellectual advantage or moral authority over his persona or over anyone else. Langland (and we as intellectuals) have been that persona at certain times, and we all at our best share some of the foibles of the persona at his most foolish. As far as what really counts for salvation, all of us intellectuals are in the same boat.

Presumably, Wittig would aim an equally pointed critique at my assumptions. In his recent book on Langland, Wittig says,

> A recurrent strain in Langland criticism is the notion that the poem is a quest for some kind of knowledge or understanding and that Langland, or his speaker and dreamer, is wrestling with intellectual problems and searching restlessly for their solutions. I believe this to constitute a fundamental misunderstanding of the poem.
>
> Someone undertaking behavior modification in order to lose weight does not face intellectual conundrums. The problem is not a "knowledge problem," but an "attitude problem" and a "behavior problem." I argue that, similarly, the dominant "problems" *Piers Plowman* confronts are not problems of knowing but problems of willing and doing. (*Revisited* 31–32)

What Wittig describes as a "fundamental misunderstanding" is in fact my understanding of the poem. Probably Wittig and I are not talking about exactly the same set of "intellectual problems"; and probably I am not as ready as Wittig is to separate "knowing" from "willing and doing"—at least in the case of an intellectual. But the real issue here is not whether historicism or formalism is the "correct" approach to the poem. The real issue is not even whether medieval Catholicism as represented by Langland can speak helpfully to modern Christians. (I believe it can.) The real issue is a matter of what different readers want from texts. I think it is possible to maintain that *Piers Plowman* can provide both what Wittig wants and what I want, and I think it is possible to think so without descending into strict relativism. But such a conclusion depends upon a long theoretical argument that is not the business of this particular book.

Britton Harwood's learned and intelligent reading of the long middle of the poem provides an interesting supplement and corrective for Wittig's reading, on the one hand, and for my own reading, on the other. Harwood, who is doing what he calls "formalist historicism" (ix), looks closely at the way Langland actually uses the psychological terms in the poem, and tries to match those uses with various authoritative definitions. Harwood's method issues in succinct definitions of the faculties: for example, Thought is "the rational soul *qua* abstractive" (54); Wit, being "distinguished by the discovery of means to an end," is to be associated with "the ancient faculty 'ingenium'" (59); Study is "the teaching

voice, equivalent in modern terms to the auditory memory" (66); Clergy
is "the corpus of beliefs invoked by Study" (70); Ymaginatif is "the faculty for making similitudes" (85). It is hard to deny that the meanings
Harwood identifies are among the meanings that were available for
Langland, and that these meanings are in some sense present in the
poem. It is perhaps easier to question the assumption that any one of
these terms ultimately has unitary meaning for Langland. Like so many
other things in *Piers Plowman,* the profound questions about the nature of
the human faculties are up for grabs. The faculties look different from
the perspectives of different interpretive systems.

   M. Teresa Tavormina's extended discussion of Wit's discourse is instructive in this regard. Tavormina traces Langland's revisions from A to
C, with the assumption that Langland's thought was evolving and that
he was attempting to clarify Wit's discourse in the successive versions of
the poem. Tavormina takes Wit, then, as an authoritative speaker on
such themes as "(1) social obligations and vocations; (2) word and work
in the human family"; and "(3) law and love as the basic principles of doing well" (105). She therefore questions James Simpson's interpretation,
which she characterizes as suggesting "that Wit's speech is irrelevant to
Will's needs at this point in the poem, since Piers has already given Will
the example of abandoning marriage and work in the world" (102). (At
this point, Tavormina cites Simpson 112.) The issue here, as it seems to
me, is the usual issue of context. Against which context is Wit's discourse to be read? Wit clearly gives (at least some) good advice, and
Tavormina reads his discourse against the background of the social history of medieval married people who were trying to live a good life in
the world. Simpson reads Wit's discourse against the symbol of Piers as
representing a greater perfection. I am contextualizing the symbol of
Piers himself by making Piers a private symbol dependent on the narrative of the dreamer as *litteratus.*

   Thus I share Simpson's sense of the limitations of the authoritative
discourses in this part of the poem. Simpson argues that the third vision
of the poem (Passus VIII–XII) functions in part to deconstruct "two
genres, each of which claims authority for itself: satire; and academic debate" (128). Whereas in the first vision of the poem Langland "adopts
the genre of satire and exploits it for its most authoritarian potential . . . ,
without questioning his own role as a satirist," here Langland is "deeply

reflexive about his own poetic practice" and about what is implied in blaming others (131–32). And the "vision as a whole does recognise the clear limitations of academic discourse as it proceeds through the institutions which promote such discourse" (133–34). Simpson sees the movement from the third vision (the faculties, Passus VIII–XII) to the fourth vision (the feast, Passus XIII) as a movement from the "academic treatment of scriptural texts (associated with the universities) to a more inward, reflective consideration of Scripture, drawn from monastic traditions" (144). This more "inward" consideration is expressed in metaphors of "eating" texts (compare Savage). This reading is consistent with Simpson's interpretation of the fourth vision as the crisis in the dreamer's narrative: the fourth vision represents "a *transitus*, a Passover from the Old Law to the New" (165). I want to affirm Simpson's conclusion that in general the function of this section of the poem in the dreamer's narrative is to lead up to a new understanding of *reading*. I suppose that when I locate the dreamer's crisis later, in the vision of the Tree of Charity, I am betraying my own disposition to lean a little more toward the Augustinian end of the theological scale. That is, entering into the proper relation to a text, like all good works, is not something that can be accomplished by human effort. Instead, it is something that must be given, as the gospel is given out of nowhere, as it were, during the vision of the Tree of Charity. So whereas my reading of the long middle of the poem is very similar in spirit to Simpson's (Simpson reads the "inner dream" of Passus XVI as a "compressed version of action found in the larger vision in which it is enclosed"—191), ultimately I analyze the dreamer's narrative differently. If I were to push my own premises about Langland to their logical conclusions, I would argue—as I do not have space to do here or historical competence to do anywhere—that although Langland might have had a theological position of his own for which *Piers Plowman* provides some evidence, it is a mistake to try to read the poem as existing in order to articulate an Augustinian, or a Pelagian, or a semi-Pelagian position. The poem exists, I am arguing, in order to show the activity of textual interpretation at white heat as the intellectual grapples with these theological questions. We are all Augustinians or Pelagians or semi-Pelagians, alternately, depending upon which discourse has taken us up at any particular moment.

Piers and Jesus

THE TREE OF CHARITY

Anima's "organic" metaphors of the clergy as the root of the tree (XV.96ff., 118ff.) and of the Tree of Charity (XVI.4ff.) support his relational epistemology in which the world and the soul itself are construed as grammar. What something is depends on its relation to everything else in the providential syntax of salvation. Charity, for Anima, is to be understood through the tree considered not only as type or antitype of the various significant biblical trees, but also as primordial symbol of organism. The new epistemology projects a new understanding of Piers: the Tree of Charity

> . . . groweth in a gardyn . . . that God made hymselve;
> Amyddes mannes body the more is of that stokke.
> Herte highte the herber that it inne groweth,
> And *Liberum Arbitrium* hath the lond to ferme,
> Under Piers the Plowman to piken it and to weden it.
>
> (XVI.13–17)

There are unmistakable echoes here of Piers's first establishment in Passus V–VII. There, Piers says that the end of the pilgrimage to Truth will be when each pilgrim sees "in thiselve Truthe sitte in thyn herte" (V.606); and Truth's pardon is for those who work on Piers's half-acre under Piers's direction or on his behalf: "alle that holpen hym to erye, to sette or to sowe, / Or any [man]er mestier that myghte Piers availe" (VII.6–7). In Passus XVI the crucial term has changed from *truth* to *charity,* with the dreamer's change in orientation from an overriding concern with self-justification and social justice to a concern for dealing with his own sin. The labor being done in the allegory of the Tree of Charity is not economic functioning within the social organism, but instead the individual labor of free will in cultivating charity in the individual's own heart. As Anima's relational epistemology has helped the dreamer understand, charity is not a matter of an objective calculus of words and works, but instead a matter of the direction of the will:

> . . . by colour ne by clergie knowe shaltow hym nevere,
> Neither thorugh wordes ne werkes, but thorugh wil oone,

> And that knoweth no clerk ne creature on erthe
> But Piers the Plowman—*Petrus, id est, Christus.*
>
> (XV.209–12)

Anima's statement suddenly and startlingly opens the symbol of Piers to signify far more than just the good laborer—without, on the other hand, canceling the initial approximation. Piers in one of his facets continues to signify the good laborer. But what the dreamer has come to understand through the long middle of the poem is that the meaning of Piers cannot be exhausted in terms of the concepts of economic function, social justice, or self-justification through works.

The dreamer's reaction to the bare name of Piers seems strangely excessive and especially dreamlike:

> "Piers the Plowman!" quod I tho, and al for pure joye
> That I herde nempne his name anoon I swowned after,
> And lay longe in a love-dreem . . .
>
> (XVI.18–20)

The swooning for joy represents an affective abdication of intellectual activity, a kind of opposite to the dreamer's angry rejection of literary learning that occurs at the beginning of the other "inner" dream when Scripture scorns the dreamer for lack of self-knowledge: "Tho wepte I for wo and wrathe of hir speche / And in a wynkynge w[o]rth til I was aslepe" (XI.4–5). After the inner vision of Piers, interestingly, the dreamer

> . . . awaked therwith, and wiped myne eighen,
> And after Piers the Plowman pried and stared,
> Estward and westward I waited after faste,
> And yede forth as an ydiot . . .
>
> (XVI.167–70)

That is, the dreamer has finally by a circuitous and embarrassing route become like one of the "idiots" (that is, illiterates—see Stock 28–30 and Clopper, *Songes of Rechelesnesse* 185ff.) who he himself told Scripture would be more likely than the learned to inherit heaven (X.455). What the dreamer, irredeemably an intellectual, nevertheless has in common with the illiterate is the need to understand Piers as the one who directs the will in the will's cultivation of charity. The dreamer emerges from the inner dream weeping, apparently—"wiped myne eighen"—just as he enters the dream through profound affective experience. He is weeping not only at the gospel narrative of the Passion, which he has just witnessed, but at his own sin. The gesture completes Haukyn's gesture at the end of Passus XIV: Haukyn "wepte water with hise eighen and weyled the tyme / That evere he dide dede that deere God displesed" (XIV.324–25). The dreamer is able to wipe his eyes and resume his pilgrimage because the new vision of Piers has somehow freed him from the dead-end game of self-justification.

The private symbol of Piers, I am arguing, is always filled with ineffable meaning for the dreamer because Piers always represents what is just over the dreamer's horizon, what the dreamer thinks he needs to understand but does not yet understand. At the beginning of Passus XVI, the dreamer has caught onto the fact that charity as right relation to God and to one's fellow humans is what is important, but he does not yet understand charity: "Ac yit am I in a weer what charite is to mene" (3). Again, this is a question about *meaning*—like the dreamer's first question to Holy Church in Passus I (I.11). Characteristically, the dreamer demands intellectual understanding of whatever it is that directs the will toward charity. In one sense, the dreamer's question is only the most recent in a long series of misunderstandings: "How may I understand the vision of the field of folk?" "How may I understand money?" "How may I know what is false?" "How may I save my soul?" "Where may I find Dowel?" Always, the dreamer as intellectual thinks that salvation will follow upon intellectual understanding. "What does charity mean?" The implication is that if the dreamer could only understand charity intellectually, he would be able to direct his will accordingly and reform his life.

In another sense, however, the dreamer's question must at least be a better question, or be more sincerely posed, than some of his earlier questions. Posing the question seems to open him to an experience of grace, the vision in which he actually sees Piers again and himself receives direct instruction. Although Piers seems accessible now only through the "joy" of a "love-dream"—that is, only when affective experience also figures in one's response to him—nevertheless it is fortunately not useless for the intellectual to try to understand Piers intellectually.

For the intellectual there is no other way; but the difficult thing is to come to understand exactly how intellect itself obstructs. That is the problem Langland is working on in this episode. In my reading, the episode of the Tree of Charity represents the crisis in the dreamer's narrative, a crisis prepared for by Anima's relational epistemology and resolved only through the repeated irresolution of the intellectual's continued attempts to construe the world through provisional encounters with authoritative texts.

Intellect obstructs precisely by doing what it ineluctably does, by attempting to construe. The reader of *Piers Plowman* too is necessarily always caught up in the processes of construction, by the very activity of interpreting the text. One of the things I mean when I talk about Langland's "recursiveness" is his technique of making the reader explicitly aware of the reader's own interpretive activity. Passus XVI provides what is for me the paradigmatic instance of that recursiveness, precisely at the moment of the crisis in the dreamer's own narrative. As the dreamer finds out what he needs to know about himself as intellectual, we also find out what we need to know about ourselves as intellectuals— that is, as interpreters of texts.

The episode of the Tree of Charity proceeds by means of a detailed, complex, and ultimately ambiguous allegory. Anima begins by labeling the parts of the tree, deliberately dissecting the organism apparently in order to analyze its functioning:

> Mercy is the more therof; the myddul stok is ruthe;
> The leves ben lele wordes, the lawe of Holy Chirche;
> The blosmes beth buxom speche and benigne lokynge;
> Pacience hatte the pure tree, and pore symple of herte,
> And so thorugh God and goode men groweth the fruyt Charite.
>
> (XVI.5–9)

The allegory is vastly extended by Anima's assertions that the tree grows in the human heart (14–15) and that it is cultivated by free will (16) whose landlord is Piers (17); by Piers's explanation of the three props that stand for the three Persons of the Trinity (25ff.); by Piers's equating of the different types of fruit with matrimony, widowhood, and virginity (67ff.); and by the identification of the fallen fruits with the patriarchs and prophets (81ff.). With every ramification in the allegory, interpretive questions proliferate. In what sense are married people, widows, or virgins identical with the "fruyt Charite"? Does charity exist only as instantiated in individuals, and does it not make sense to talk about it as a universal? If all the fruit is charity, why is some charity (virginity) better than other charity (matrimony)? How are the three props and the three Persons of the Trinity appropriately sorted among the three enemies: world, flesh, and devil? What does it mean that Piers himself shakes down the fruit (kills people?) so that the dreamer can taste it? Is that sort of destructive activity not more appropriate for the Fiend, who also steals the flowers of the tree? (In my reading, Piers as the principle that turns the will toward charity shows the dreamer the fruits of charity in the completed lives and deaths of the saints. But this is far from the only possible reading.) And so on.

I do not mean to suggest that it is foolish or useless to ask such questions and to attempt to answer them. Much interesting thought and commentary arises from such attempts. In fact, I want to suggest that Langland's point is precisely that *we cannot help* asking and attempting to answer such questions. That is what it means to read an allegory. To that extent, we share the dreamer's temperament and his obsessions. Of all the interesting things Piers tells the dreamer in his vision, the dreamer focuses, oddly, on the three props. Piers is talking about salvation and damnation, and the dreamer wants to know how three pieces of wood could be so similar (XVI.55ff.). In the comedy that often operates at the "literal" level of *Piers Plowman,* the dreamer's question perhaps suggests a certain triviality of mind. On the level of the theological allegory, he is fatally attracted to the very thing that he is not going to be able to understand intellectually—namely, the mystery of the Trinity. Piers knows what the dreamer is thinking and warns him off:

> ". . . the Trinite it meneth"—
> And egreliche he loked on me, and therfore I spared
> To asken hym any moore therof, and bad hym ful faire
> To discryve the fruyt . . .
>
> (63–66)

Piers conveys by his look "Don't ask"; and the dreamer, for once, takes the hint and redirects his attention to the main subject of the discourse, the fruit called charity. Piers is not telling the dreamer never to think or talk about the Trinity. He is suggesting only that this is not the time or the place to get distracted from the main issue by intellectual debates such as those Dame Study has described: "telleth thei of the Trinite" when they "dryvele at hir deys the deitee to knowe, / And gnawen God with the gorge whanne hir guttes fullen" (X.53–57).

But the seed is planted, and the dreamer spends a good deal of time in the subsequent episodes worrying at the mystery of the Trinity. The seed is also planted in the reader's mind. It is like asking a jury to disregard a telling remark that they have already heard. We cannot help worrying at the question of how the three props can be perfectly similar and yet different, nor can we help trying to assign each one of them to one particular Person of the Trinity. It is impossible for us to avoid such interpretive activity, for example, at the crucial moment when Piers picks up a prop to strike out at the devil:

> And Piers, for pure tene, that a pil he laughte,
> And hitte after hym, happe how it myghte,
> *Filius* by the Faderes wille and frenesse of *Spiritus Sancti* . . .
>
>   (86–88)

Piers's "pure tene" here recalls his reaction to the wasters (VI.117) and his tearing of the pardon (VII.115). Line 88 is ambiguous in seeming at once to say that the prop Piers selects is the one corresponding to the Son, and yet that all three props are somehow involved in the one. The line inevitably throws us into the mode of allegorical sorting out, of matching the elements of the *fabula* to the elements of the theological structure of thought expressed in the *fabula*. We as readers cannot help worrying at the allegorical meaning of the post—we are inevitably caught up in the explanatory movement of the discourse. Thus the sudden striking in of the gospel narrative is literally *astonishing*—it startles with its otherness and instantly sweeps away our pretensions to explain the allegory. The gospel narrative, in its surprising otherness, preempts our "normal" relation to discourse. We are not allowed to think that we are making sense (that is, making use) of the discourse. For a moment, at least, the gospel shocks us out of believing that discourse belongs to us. Instead, we are aware suddenly of belonging to it.

Langland, then, has caught us out. We as readers and intellectuals are doing exactly what Piers has hinted to the dreamer that he should not do. We are unwitting prisoners of our customary ways of interacting with texts, of trying to master them by means of intellectual understanding. The way out for the intellectual, as I have argued, also lies through texts. But instead of mastering texts, we must learn how to be mastered by them. In generic terms, we must substitute gospel for allegory—allegory, the genre in which we explain what we have mastered; gospel, the genre that destroys all of our pretensions to intellectual understanding. In line 90, the same thing happens to the dreamer and to the reader in a moment of close identification: "And thanne spak *Spiritus Sanctus* in Gabrielis mouthe" (90). The gospel narrative breaks into the poem not as something owned by the speaker or by the reader, but as a sudden rupture, an intellectual discontinuity suggesting the overmastering otherness of the biblical text. As Joseph Wittig says, "No attentive reader can miss the abrupt shift in tone and mode" (*Revisited* 127). In a sense, this critical moment in the dreamer's narrative represents something very like a replay at a metalevel of the tearing of the pardon. In tearing the pardon, Piers rejects the futile game of self-justification; in rupturing the texture of the poem itself, Langland rejects on his own behalf and ours the pretensions of literary learning to master authoritative texts.

Piers does not, strictly speaking, generate the gospel narrative, but instead is taken up into it. Jesus will joust in "*plenitudo temporis* tyme" for "Piers fruyt" (93–94). Meanwhile, Jesus as a child is already fit

> To have yfoughte with the fend er ful tyme come.
> And Piers the Plowman parceyved plener tyme,
> And lered hym lechecraft, his lif for to save,
> That though he were wounded with his enemy, to warisshen hymselve;
> And did hym assaie his surgerie on hem that sike were,
> Til he was parfit praktisour, if any peril fille;
> And soughte out the sike and synfulle bothe . . .
>
> (102–8)

Sickness and sin are mutually implicative doublets here. Piers, as the principle that directs the will to cultivate charity in the human heart, teaches the humanity of Jesus how charity may operate in a fallen world as "lechecraft." The stress on the "fullness of time" suggests that the practice of human charity, like sacred history itself, is a temporal process whose end is understood only in its fulfillment—that is, Piers teaches the humanity of Jesus the human way of perceiving divine truth. On this point, Britton Harwood quotes the *De gradibus humilitatis et superbiae* of Bernard of Clairvaux:

> [O]ur Savior . . . willed his passion in order to learn compassion; his misery, to learn commiseration. For, just as it is written of him, *Yet learned he obedience by the things which he suffered*, so also he learned mercy in the same way. Not that he did not know how to be merciful before, he whose mercy is from everlasting to everlasting; he knew it by nature from eternity, but learned it in time by experience. (Harwood 142)

Harwood summarizes: "Christ's compassion constitutes in part his sinlessness. Possible within time and history only because he learns from his own human nature the temptations to which other people are subject, his compassion—his 'curing himself'—flows from his Passion, his knowledge of Piers" (142). The relation between the dreamer and the gospel narrative is, for a moment and for a change, not a relation in which the dreamer attempts to master the text through intellectual understanding. The gospel is a bolt of lightning. Momentarily, both the dreamer and the reader, like Piers himself, are totally absorbed in its story.

THE LITURGY

But the moment of illumination does not last. The dreamer falls back from gospel into allegory, and Piers once again disappears from the poem for a time. The dream in XVI.167–XVII.352 that deals with Faith, Hope, and Charity—Abraham, Moses, and the Samaritan—is not barren. It contains some of Langland's most beautiful and moving poetry, and especially through the person of the Samaritan helps to move the dreamer toward readiness for the next stage in his understanding of Piers himself. As David Hale points out, the allegory in this section of the poem departs in many ways from the exegetical traditions surrounding the parable of the Good Samaritan, so as to open the normal clerical allegory to uses less rigid and static (131, 133). Nevertheless, what the dreamer is doing in this section of the poem is irritatingly typical of him. He is worrying at the mystery of the Trinity, from which Piers warned

him off. From that speculation, he nearly relapses into playing his old
tapes about faith and works. He says to Abraham and Spes,

> Youre wordes arn wonderfulle. . . . Which of yow is trewest,
> And lelest to leve on for lif and for soule?
> Abraham seith that he seigh hoolly the Trinite,
> Thre persones in parcelles departable fro oother,
> And all thre but o God—thus Abraham me taughte—
> And hath saved that bileved so and sory for hir synnes,
> He kan noght siggen the somme, and some arn in his lappe.
> What neded it thanne a newe lawe to brynge,
> Sith the firste suffiseth to savacion and to blisse?
> And now cometh *Spes* and speketh, that hath aspied the lawe,
> And telleth noght of the Trinite that took hym hise lettres—
> To bileeve and lovye in o Lord almyghty,
> And siththe right as myself so lovye alle peple.
>
>   (XVII.24–36)

The dreamer hopes, as earlier in the poem, that he can be saved just by
believing an impossible thing, without actually having to learn to love in
obedience to God's law. Part of what is going on here also is a submerged
debate on what are by now old questions in the poem: whether salvation
comes through knowledge of a person (or quasi-person, such as the allegorical Dowel) or through knowledge of texts (such as the Athanasian
Creed), and what the relation is between persons, on the one hand, and
texts, on the other. Abraham offers the dreamer "Thre persones,"
whereas Spes offers him the "lawe" and "lettres." It is left to the Samaritan to mediate the two positions: "thanne shal Feith be forster here"
(XVII.113) but "alle that feble and feynte be, that Feith may noght
teche, / Hope shal lede hem forth with love, as his lettre telleth"
(XVII.117–18).

The dreamer's obsession with the mystery of the Trinity follows the
rupture created by the intrusion of the gospel, just as his obsession with
Dowel follows the tearing of the pardon. Both obsessions ultimately
lead the dreamer to deeper understanding of himself, but neither obsession is intellectually fruitful in the way that the dreamer initially proposes. And something else links this dream of Faith, Hope, and Charity
with the pardon scene. The Athanasian Creed at its end contains mate-

rial familiar also from both the Nicene Creed and the Apostles' Creed, and it terminates in the clauses quoted in Piers's pardon from Truth. But most of the Athanasian Creed is devoted to a full articulation of the dogma concerning two central Christian mysteries: the Trinity and the Incarnation. The mystery of the Trinity is broached in the vision of the Tree of Charity. The mystery of the Incarnation is broached early in the vision of Passus XVIII: Faith says, after a hard look at the dreamer ("he preynte on me," line 21) reminiscent of Piers's hard look when the dreamer asks about the props representing the Trinity,

> This Jesus of his gentries wol juste in Piers armes,
> In his helm and in his haubergeon, *humana natura*.
> That Crist be noght biknowe here for *consummatus Deus*,
> In Piers paltok the Plowman this prikiere shal ryde;
> For no dynt shal hym dere as *in deitate Patris*.
>
> (XVIII.22–26)

Langland develops the dreamer's thought on these doctrines in turn: the Trinity in Passus XVI–XVII, and the Incarnation (which John Lawlor calls "Langland's central doctrine"—167) in Passus XVIII–XIX. Both times, the dreamer's speculation on mystery follows a vision of Piers himself, confirming a pattern—more accurately, a habit—by which the dreamer intellectually mulls over the meaning of his most recent projec-tion of Piers. As he assimilates the lessons of his visions—usually, the lesson that he has misunderstood something crucial—the dreamer pre-pares himself for the next stage in his own narrative, the widening of his intellectual horizons in such a way that Piers still remains just beyond them. The dreamer always apprehends the world as just a little more complex than he is currently capable of grasping.

It is noticeable that parts of the gospel narrative—most poignantly, the Passion—are told with some fullness not once, but three times: XVI.90ff., XVIII.36ff., and XIX.69ff. What is important in this pattern of repetition, in my reading, is the *mode* through which the narrative en-ters the poem. At first, the gospel narrative breaks in surprisingly, as I have argued. For a moment, it is just itself. It is gospel. Or at least I think Langland's technique of interrupting the allegory is meant to work that way. By this point in the poem, if Langland's technique works at all, it might seem almost miraculous that any authoritative text can be itself, can strike us with the freshness of something we have not yet tried to master for our own purposes. By a technique somewhat akin to the Russian Formalists' notion of "estrangement," Langland tries to make us as readers see the gospel as it is, or at least to understand that we have not done so up to now in the poem. We have tacitly cooperated with the dreamer's and the authoritative speakers' drive to master the texts they have encountered.

The second telling of the Passion narrative, associated also with a reappearance of Piers after the allegorical detour through Abraham, Moses, and the Samaritan, enters the poem by way of the liturgy. The dreamer

> Reste me there and rutte faste til *Ramis palmarum.*
> Of gerlis and of *Gloria, laus* gretly me dremed
> And how *osanna* by orgen olde folk songen,
> And of Cristes passion and penaunce, the peple that ofraughte.
> Oon semblable to the Samaritan, and somdeel to Piers the Plowman,
> Barefoot on an asse bak bootles cam prikye . . .
>
> (XVIII.6–11)

The scene seems to represent not the gospel narrative itself, but instead a liturgical reenactment in a church on Palm Sunday (Simpson 218). From this beginning, the poem temporarily modulates through the voice of Faith into a retelling of the Passion narrative, and then reverts to the words of the Nicene Creed, as the dreamer reports,

> What for feere of this ferly and of the false Jewes,
> I drow me in that derknesse to *descendit ad inferna,*
> And there I saugh soothly, *secundum scripturas* . . .
>
> (110–12)

The language here is interesting. The clause from the Creed is presented as literally a *topos,* a *place* to which the dreamer withdraws in fear and in darkness of mind. As opposed to a tool to be mastered to carry out human purposes, the text is a place of refuge. Again, though the dreamer's relation to the liturgy is different from his relation to the gospel, the crucial point seems to be that the dreamer does not think of the discourse of the Creed as "his own," but instead consciously thinks of himself as in some sense belonging to or even hidden within the text. The liturgy represents the ritual reenactment of the events narrated in the primary biblical text, where the point of the ritual is precisely to become absorbed in it, as opposed to trying to understand or master it through intellectual abstraction. Mary Carruthers points out that the "familiar echoes of the Creed not only signal the divine event which is about to occur but also associate Will with Christ in a figural relationship. This honor . . . completes the assimilative, unifying process which the Christ-knight brings about" (141).

Also, Passus XVIII ends with the Easter *Te Deum* (424) and the liturgical ritual of "creeping to the Cross," this time in the dreamer's autobiographical waking world:

> . . . men rongen to the resurexion—and right with that I wakede,
> And callede Kytte my wif and Calote my doghter:
> "Ariseth and go reverenceth Goddes resurexion,
> And crepeth to the cros on knees, and kisseth it for a juwel!"
>
> (427–30)

The feeling here is that of the ritual re-creation of sacred time, so that past and present, dream and waking, overlap momentarily. Ritual also enforces a sense of community, since everyone participates in unison, as it were. It is interesting that at this point, for the first time in the B-text, the dreamer evinces concern for his family, the human beings he should care for most (see Galloway 146). The first time the dreamer is attacked by old age, in the inner dream of Fortune, he seems worried mostly about where he is going to be buried (XI.60ff.). In Passus XX, however, when Elde assaults him and leaves him bald, deaf, and arthritic, he at least thinks of the consequences also for his wife:

> And of the wo that I was inne my wif hadde ruthe,
> And wisshed wel witterly that I were in hevene.
> For the lyme that she loved me fore, and leef was to feele—
> On nyghtes, namely, whan we naked weere—
> I ne myghte in no manere maken it at hir wille,
> So Elde and he[o] it hadden forbeten.
>
> (193–98)

The lines are ironic, but they also seem to embody an old husband's grudging affection. I take the lines much as Teresa Tavormina does, when she says that the passage "presents the past sexual bond between

Will and his wife with affection, wistful nostalgia, and a certain element of comic self-deprecation" (210). At least, the lines represent progress beyond the dreamer's earlier intellectual solipsism in which his personal bildungsroman was the only subject that seemed capable of holding his attention. It is shortly after this passage that Kynde gives the dreamer his final instructions: "Lerne to love, . . . and leef alle othere" (XX.208).

So what conclusions can we draw about the dreamer and Piers from all these observations? First, in my reading, the astonishing encounter with the gospel narrative has already begun to alter the dreamer's understanding of the symbol of Piers. After the gospel, the dreamer no longer conceives Piers vaguely as "that which directs the will to cultivate charity," but instead begins to think of Piers as representing the human nature of Jesus. Jesus is "semblable to the Samaritan, and somdeel to Piers the Plowman" (XVIII.10); Jesus will "juste in Piers armes," which are *"humana natura"* (XVIII.22–23); the dreamer is unable to distinguish between Jesus and Piers, and Conscience reiterates that Jesus fights in Piers's "armes, / Hise colours and his cote armure" (XIX.12–13). Having been given the human embodiment of charity in the gospel narrative, the dreamer now thinks he needs to understand Jesus' human nature, the part of Jesus available for human beings to imitate, and the fulfillment that subsumes everything that Piers has represented before: the good laborer, the absent lover, the agent of charity.

Second, this section of the poem illustrates a possible relation to texts other than the attempt to master them intellectually. To the extent that one becomes absorbed in the communal reenactment of sacred history through liturgical texts, one bypasses the futile desire for self-justification that seems to lurk behind most human attempts to understand sacred texts intellectually. The fact that the dreamer can find in the words of the Creed a place of refuge and a stimulus to affective experience, as opposed to an arena for intellectual debate, suggests progress in the dreamer's own narrative.

Finally, however, if the dreamer seems temporarily to have suspended his need for self-justification, Jesus himself protests entirely too much. It is instructive at this point to contrast Langland's poem with Dante's. In Canto IX of *Inferno,* the Heavenly Messenger appears to break open the gates of Dis and let Virgil and Dante into the lower regions of Hell. God's absolute power manifests itself in Hell as scorn. The Messenger rebukes the perversity of the devils, but does not attempt to explain to them why God's acts are just. Langland's Jesus, on the other hand, produces over seventy-five lines (XVIII.328–404) of the standard theological arguments, supported by appropriate scriptural authorities, to demonstrate that the Harrowing of Hell is not a robbery. It is almost as though the dreamer's lust for self-justification, suppressed in the dreamer himself, has resurfaced in Jesus. The passage is puzzling. Why should Jesus care what the devils think? Does he expect to convert them?

Thinking about questions such as these points up what many critics have noticed about Passus XVIII. It is in form a *drama* reminiscent of the mystery plays. The genre is most obtrusive in the scene of the Harrowing of Hell, but the debate of the Daughters of God is also a dramatic confrontation. The genre postulates an audience toward whom the doctrinal lessons are directed. It is not that we are watching Jesus actually defending himself before the devils. We have instead an enactment of theological argument in dramatic form, with the implicit purpose of teaching the doctrine to the audience. The drama exists not because Jesus needs to prove that God is just, but because human beings need to believe intellectually that God is just. Jesus at the end of Passus XVIII is less Jesus as person than Jesus as discourse (compare Rudd 15), Jesus as dramatis persona. The drama, a possible and perhaps necessary way to conceive Jesus' action, nevertheless itself constitutes an interpretive system—and as such, like every other human system, it interposes itself between human beings and the immediate knowledge of Jesus they desire. It is significant that Langland modulates from the debate of the Daughters of God into the actual Harrowing of Hell through the voice of a character named Book (XVIII.229ff.), in a passage that, as R. E. Kaske has demonstrated ("Patristic" 326–30), constitutes a particularly dense network of intertextuality. It is as if Langland is showing, as opposed to saying, that the mystery of this Jesus of the Harrowing cannot be directly apprehended, but must be mediated through a text.

In my reading, then, the end of Passus XVIII constitutes also a critique on Langland's part of one of the genres that he most typically exploits: the drama, or, more specifically, the debate. The drama by its na-

ture is performative. It calls for, and receives, resolution. But for a life in
progress, there is as yet no resolution. The patriarchs and prophets go to
heaven with Jesus. The Daughters of God compose their differences.
But the dreamer is left with a life still full of loose ends, a life still in the
process of creeping to the Cross.

Whatever can be said of drama can also be said a fortiori of liturgy
itself considered as performative—that is, as ritual reenactment of sacred history. When one is actually absorbed in the ritual, one is for the
moment free of the fatal itch for self-justification. But when the intellectual begins to reflect on the "meaning" of the performance, all of the
old problems come back. Why should it be so important to us to understand so exactingly the operation of God's justice, except that we are
worried about our own ability to justify ourselves? The human nature of
Jesus as dramatis persona is in a way all too human: Jesus as intellectual,
Jesus as he must be understood in dramatic terms by an intellectual who
reflects on the meaning of the Incarnation. Jesus pursues several different lines of theological argument in Passus XVIII: that he is the substitute for sinful humanity (328–29, 341ff.), that God promised sinful humanity death but not Hell forever (333), that Satan cheated human
beings by disguising himself (334ff.), that the beguiler deserves to be be-
guiled by God's disguising himself as a human being in Jesus (for example, 361), that God's kingly power is absolute and therefore able to dispense mercy to human beings (374ff.), that human sin can be expiated in
Purgatory (392ff.). But finally, everything comes down to the mystery of
the Incarnation: "Ac to be merciable to man thanne, my kynde it asketh,
/ For we beth bretheren of blood" (376–77); and

> . . . my mercy shal be shewed to manye of my bretheren;
> For blood may suffre blood bothe hungry and acale,
> Ac blood may noght se blood blede, but hym rewe.
> (394–96)

Jesus is merciful because it is of his human nature to be so. The linchpin
of all the theological arguments, and the premise of the liturgical drama,
is precisely what is not susceptible to intellectual understanding.

Langland's implicit critique of drama (and therefore of liturgy) as a
mode of intellectual understanding is perhaps behind that extremely

puzzling quotation altered from 2 Corinthians 12:4, which occurs at precisely the point where Jesus is explaining that he is of the same "blood" as human beings: *"Audivi archana verba que non licet homini loqui"* (396a). The verb *audire* has been changed from third person to first person. In the epistle, Paul explains how "a man," presumably Paul himself, was caught up into the "third heaven" and experienced "visions and revelations of the Lord" (2 Corinthians 12:1–2, RSV). Schmidt treats the quotation as an interpolation from the narrator, and reads it as Langland's "boldest claim for the value and validity of his own 'visions and revelations'" (Schmidt's note, page 483 of his edition). The pattern that Langland establishes, however, is that Jesus himself, like a lawyer in a disputation, quotes scriptural or other authoritative passages, sometimes a little cryptically, in support of his theses (for example, 340a, 350a, 361a, 379a, 391a, 401a). Either that, or the narrator is speaking in unison with Jesus, as it were, providing the proof-texts that support Jesus' argument. If we read Jesus as the speaker of line 396a, the "I" of *audivi* seems to hover somewhere between Jesus and Paul, identifying Paul's knowledge with Jesus' knowledge, and suggesting that there is some kind of human knowledge that can be revealed but not spoken. The point of Jesus' quoting the passage in this context would be to remind the audience that the mystery of his human nature, the mystery of the Incarnation, cannot be articulated fully in language or mastered through texts.

Maybe the dreamer should not want to get behind or beyond the text of the liturgy. Maybe he should be content to be absorbed in the ritual reenactment of sacred history. There even seems to be a temporary resting place in the dreamer's narrative. Deeply moved by the Easter liturgy, he awakens to thoughts of his family, and even makes gestures toward participating in the community as a more-or-less normal member of it. He dresses himself "derely, and dide me to chirche" (XIX.2), for once just like everybody else. His clothes no longer set him apart as a hermit. Even his writing seems to be taken matter-of-factly for once, as a normal sort of activity, no longer a source of shame or worry: "I awaked and wroot what I hadde ydremed" (XIX.1). As James Simpson says, "Here . . . Will's writing and church going seem to be part of a continuum" (219). But Langland shows us that he and we, as intellectuals, cannot help ourselves. We have to worry about what things mean. We postpone our pathological pursuit of self-justification, and it boils up again in our meditations on the humanity of Jesus. We want to understand how Jesus is justified. Otherwise, we cannot understand how we can be justified in him. The dreamer thinks he needs to understand the humanity of Jesus, and that is what Piers has now come to represent to him:

> I fel eftsoones aslepe—and sodeynly me mette
> That Piers the Plowman was peynted al blody,
> And com in with a cros bifore the comune peple,
> And right lik in alle lymes to Oure Lord Jesu.
>
> (XIX.5–8)

But to try to comprehend the humanity of Jesus in dramatic terms, as the dreamer tries to do at the end of Passus XVIII, leads to tedious theological argument that terminates in an encounter with the ineffable mystery of the Incarnation.

THE ALLEGORY OF THE PRESENT AGE

By Passus XIX, or so my argument goes, the dreamer has experienced two relationships with texts that are different from his habitual attempts to master them intellectually. The kind of encounter that he experiences with the gospel text is a matter of remarkable visions and strange epiphanies. The liturgical text moves and absorbs him temporarily, but as drama the liturgy only re-presents the primordial gospel event. Ideally, the resolution demanded by the genre of liturgy should reinforce the didactic purposes of the text, linking affective experience with intellectual understanding and permitting the resumption of a life edified but mundane. But after all the shouting is over and the Easter bells have rung, the dreamer as unreformed intellectual is still confronted with the mystery of the Incarnation—that which he believes he needs to understand, and that which he and we are incapable of understanding.

After the terror and triumph of Jesus' life, Passion, and Resurrection, as recounted in the gospels, there come the mundane practicalities of setting up the early Church (see Lawlor 172), as recounted in Acts. After the dreamer's visionary encounter with the gospel text and the liturgy, there comes his lapse back into the characteristic genre of the intellectual—namely, personification allegory, the genre of explanation. To explain, in this genre, means precisely to endow words themselves with agency by making explicit how they function as crucial terms in authoritative discourses. The dreamer's obsession with names at the beginning of Passus XIX is symptomatic:

> "Why calle ye hym Crist?" quod I, "sithen Jewes called hym Jesus?
> Patriarkes and prophetes prophecied bifore
> That alle kynne creatures sholden knelen and bowen
> Anoon as men nempned the name of God Jesu.
> *Ergo* is no name to the name of Jesus,
> Ne noon so nedeful to nempne by nighte ne by daye."
>
> (XIX.15–20)

The dreamer's concern, quite precisely, is the literate intellectual's concern about which name is *correct,* which term constitutes a better way to think about Jesus. Conscience explains that Jesus is called "conqueror" because he has conquered death and Hell, both for himself and for his followers:

> Mighte no deeth hym fordo, ne adoun brynge,
> That he n'aroos and regnede and ravysshed helle.
> And tho was he conquerour called of quyke and of dede,
> For he yaf Adam and Eve and othere mo blisse
> That longe hadde yleyen bifore as Luciferis cherles.
>
> (51–55)

More appositely for the dreamer, Jesus has provided a way for sinners to deal with their sin on earth:

> Ac the cause that he cometh thus with cros of his passion
> Is to wissen us therwith, that whan we ben tempted,
> Therwith to fighte and fenden us fro fallynge into synne,
> And se bi his sorwe that whoso loveth joye,
> To penaunce and to poverte he moste puten hymselven,
> And muche wo in this world wilnen and suffren.
>
> (63–68)

Conscience then modulates into his discourse on the three terms that were the object of the dreamer's search through the long middle of the poem—Dowel, Dobet, and Dobest—retelling the gospel narrative for the third time by way of "defining" these terms with reference to the life of Jesus.

Jesus "does well," is Dowel, when he changes the water into wine at the marriage feast at Cana, where "wyn is likned to lawe, and lif of holy-nesse; / And lawe lakkede tho, for men lovede noght hir enemys" (108–12). Jesus is Dobet when he feeds the hungry, heals the sick, and performs miracles: "Thus he confortede carefulle and caughte a gretter name, / The which was Dobet" (128–29). Jesus is Dobest when he establishes the Church on earth:

> . . . Dobest he [thou]ghte,
> And yaf Piers power, and pardon he grauntede:
> To alle maner men, mercy and foryifnesse . . .
>   (183–85)

The obvious implication is that only Jesus really "does well," that it is futile for sinful human beings to attempt to justify themselves by coming to understand good action in the world and then performing good action. Human beings cannot give a new law of love, or perform miracles of healing, or establish the Church. If these things are what constitute Dowel, Dobet, and Dobest, then sinful human beings cannot take even the first step: "men lovede noght hir enemys." What we ultimately come to understand is that we cannot do for ourselves what Jesus has done for us. The dreamer is not liberated from his obsession with terms and texts. An intellectual is never liberated from that. That obsession is the intellectual's way of life. But the dreamer is liberated from the illusion that intellectual understanding alone is a necessary or sufficient cause of self-justification. The thing that we would have to understand if we really were to be able to justify ourselves is the mystery of the Incarnation—how divinity can inhere in humanity—and that is what we cannot understand, but only acknowledge in the person of Jesus.

Jesus' disciples saw Jesus in his body, touched him, and knew him as persons know other persons. The fourteenth-century intellectual cannot know Jesus that way. Therefore, the dreamer's understanding of Piers changes. Immediately before Conscience explains that Jesus as Dobest "yaf Piers power, and pardon . . . grauntede" (184–85), Conscience retells the story of Thomas:

Crist carpede thanne, and curteisliche seide,
"Thomas, for thow trowest this and treweliche bilevest it,
Blessed mote thow be, and be shalt for evere.
And blessed mote thei be, in body and in soule,
That nevere shul se me in sighte as thow seest nowthe,
And lelliche bileve al this—I love hem and blesse hem:
Beati qui non viderunt et crediderunt."
And whan this dede was doon, Dobest he [thou]ghte . . .
(177–83)

That is, Jesus' granting of power to Piers in the context of Conscience's discourse appears as Jesus' way of making it possible for sinful humans to have a relationship with him (the relationship described as "belief") after the withdrawal of his bodily presence from the earth. In the simplest reading of the allegory (too simple, as it will turn out), Piers no longer symbolizes for the dreamer Jesus' human nature, the unknowable mystery of the Incarnation, but Peter and his successors the popes. What the dreamer now thinks he needs to understand is the authoritative human agency through which Jesus establishes and sustains his Church.

Two points about this development in the symbol of Piers are especially noticeable. First, Piers holds his authority precisely as custodian of texts, as I have already argued at some length in my chapter on the Prologue and on the events of Passus XIX as the healing of the Babylonian wound. Steven Justice talks about Piers's "written church," a "literary construction of which Piers becomes (in effect) an author at the moment of its building" (*Writing and Rebellion* 115). Grace says, "My prowor and my plowman Piers shal ben on erthe, / And for to tilie truthe a teeme shal he have" (XIX.262–63). Piers's "teeme" is the "foure grete oxen" (264) of the gospels—as I and others have mentioned before, Langland puns on *till/tell* and *team/theme*—and he harrows all of Holy Scripture with the help of the "foure stottes" who are the Fathers (269ff.). Piers is to sow and cultivate the seeds of the cardinal virtues (276ff.), in order to produce the fruits of love (312ff.), which will then be collected in the Church on earth (320ff.). But everything depends upon the proper cultivation of the sacred texts and the authoritative commentaries on those texts:

> Thise foure sedes Piers sew, and siththe he dide hem harewe
> With Olde Lawe and Newe Lawe, that love myghte wexe
> Among thise foure vertues, and vices destruye.
>
> (312–14)

Piers now symbolizes to the dreamer the human faculty for correct (that is, salvific) textual interpretation.

The second noticeable point is that Piers acquires this authority over texts and over the Church on earth because he has the authority necessary for dealing with human sin. Piers is able to set human beings in a proper relation with Jesus because Piers is granted the power to help men, not to justify themselves in terms of good actions, but instead to deal with their sins. The two "caples" that carry the fruits of love to the Church in the cart of Christendom are Contrition and Confession (334). And in the first place, Jesus

> . . . yaf Piers power, and pardon he grauntede:
> To alle maner men, mercy and foryifnesse;
> [To] hym, myghte men to assoille of alle manere synnes,
> In covenaunt that thei come and kneweliche to paye
> To Piers pardon the Plowman—*Redde quod debes.*
> Thus hath Piers power, be his pardon paied,
> To bynde and unbynde bothe here and ellis,
> And assoille men of alle synnes save of dette one.
>
> (184–91)

Piers as Jesus' representative on earth is empowered also through the Holy Spirit ("Grace") to provide the sacraments to sustain those who have paid their debt—to re-create Jesus' own bodily presence in the Eucharist. Conscience explains,

> Here is breed yblessed, and Goddes body therunder.
> Grace, thorugh Goddes word, gaf Piers power,
> Myght to maken it, and men to ete it after
> In helpe of hir heele ones in a monthe,
> Or as ofte as thei hadde nede, tho that hadde ypaied
> To Piers pardon the Plowman, *Redde quod debes.*
>
> (389–94)

The significance of the difference between the pardon Piers tore in Passus VII and the new pardon of Passus XIX should now, after the long middle of the poem and the visionary experiences of Passus XVI–XVIII, be strikingly obvious. It is the difference between the injunction to "do well" and the injunction to "pay your debts." The first injunction implies that it might be possible to do well, to perform good action in the world and to justify oneself in terms of that action. That is the wrong way to think about human salvation. It causes the intellectual dreamer to fall into the self-destructive game of self-justification, and it causes Piers to vanish from the poem for a long time as the dreamer works through the implications of his error. The injunction to "pay your debts," however, implies that human beings are never free of sin; that they are in themselves incapable of good action in the world; and that their task on earth is not to accumulate merit in order to justify themselves, but instead as far as possible to deal with their sinfulness. As Robert Worth Frank points out, the phrase *redde quod debes* comes from Matthew 18:21–35: "The parable is the story of the servant who, after being forgiven a large debt by his lord, turns on a fellow servant and demands payment of a lesser debt owed him—*redde quod debes*" (*Scheme* 107–8). The phrase contains a dark irony: the futile attempt to justify ourselves before others (to pay the debt for which we have already been forgiven) itself causes us to sin against others by demanding that they justify themselves before us. The only way to pay our debts is to forgive others as we have been forgiven. That understanding is the humiliating but potentially salvific conclusion of the dreamer's intellectual quest.

Line 191 says that Piers has power to "assoille men of alle synnes save of dette one." My reading of this line is close to Schmidt's: in his edition, Schmidt says that *dette* means "the binding obligation to make satisfaction [*not* the sin of debt]" (note to line 191). I would extend the meaning of *dette,* however, to cover more than just the technical requirement to perform satisfaction as a completion of the sacrament of penance. Piers, in a kind of coming full circle, has himself subsumed the proper, reformed function of the corrupt priest who challenges the pardon in Passus VII. What the priesthood cannot do for human beings, what human beings have to do for themselves, is to acknowledge sinfulness and to desire to do something about it: "In covenaunt that thei come and *kneweliche* to paye" (187; emphasis mine). The priest in Passus VII implied that a genuine pardon—a pardon that *he* would consider genuine, a pardon that would give the priesthood quasi-magical powers to do away with sin—would in itself be sufficient to justify sinners. Piers's new pardon corrects that error. Like the earlier pardon, *Redde quod debes* is conditional, but the condition it imposes does not imply that human beings can justify themselves by their own good actions.

In this new shift in the dreamer's understanding, Piers symbolizes not just Peter and the popes. Popes are sometimes corrupt, as the "lewed vicory" (413), who nevertheless evinces considerable wisdom, points out:

> Inparfit is that Pope, that al peple sholde helpe,
> And s[ou]deth hem that sleeth swiche as he sholde save.
> A[c] wel worthe Piers the Plowman, that pursueth God in doynge . . .
>
> (432–34)

Piers symbolizes, instead, the popes as they ought to be, the human agency which, though sinful itself, makes it possible for love to flourish among sinful human beings on earth. In other words, Piers remains where he has always been in the poem: just beyond the dreamer's horizon. The dreamer thinks he needs to understand this human agency, but it might be as difficult to find a good pope on earth as it is to locate Dowel. At the very moment Piers begins actually to work on earth, sin attacks the establishment of the Church: "Now is Piers to the plow, and Pride it aspide / And gadered hym a greet oost" (338–39). This is the last moment that Piers is actually present and visible in the poem. From this point to the end, Piers is only a desire. The cardinal virtues begin to be corrupted by the brewer (400ff.), the lord (463ff.), and the king (469ff.). The return of the Babylonian cacophony seems imminent.

I read the dreamer's deep depression at the beginning of Passus XX as having both an external and an internal reference: "Hevy chered I yede, and elenge in herte; / For I ne wiste wher to ete ne at what place" (XX.2–3). The external corruption of the world is bad enough, making the dreamer (and perhaps Langland himself) envision the Apocalypse and the Antichrist (XX.53). But the dreamer (and perhaps Langland himself) must also be wondering about the value of the intellectual quest and the value of literacy itself. What the dreamer's experience might suggest to him at this point is that the impulse to interpret is at its very root inseparably entangled with the impulse to dominate. Rarely—as, perhaps, with the gospel or the liturgy—there are moments when texts can become something more than instruments of one's own selfish purposes. But the intellectual always lapses back into textual interpretation in the "normal" mode, the mode that attempts to master the text. The literary genre that corresponds to this mode, in Langland's economy, is personification allegory—the genre that implies a didactic attempt to reconstruct experience completely as discourse, to offer a comprehensive explanation of the world by endowing words themselves with agency. As James Simpson puts it in another connection, "[T]he meanings of the words themselves, and the different senses of words, actually form the narrative itself: the action of the narrative is shaped out of, as it were, listings under the dictionary entries for the actants" (41). Thus "personification allegory of its nature is necessarily reiterative, since the most a word can do as actant is to play out all its senses" (Simpson 42). What personification allegory teaches the intellectual is ultimately only that discourses struggle with one another, that interpretive systems collide. The impulse to interpret produces an interior Babel corresponding with the external cacophony.

This is, as I have suggested, a humiliating lesson for the dreamer. But in the Christian economy, humility is good. The experience of the poem, for the dreamer, has been good for him precisely in the sense that his intellect has led him to a fairly clear understanding of its own impotence. Literacy, in a profound way, turns out for the intellectual to be itself instrumental like sin: an understanding of its wrongness provides the stimulus for a necessary refocusing of one's life, a *repentance* and a *redemption* in the etymological sense.

A recognition of one's own sins may ultimately be instrumental for salvation, but that makes the recognition no less depressing. In my reading, the dreamer is wondering at the beginning of Passus XX in a profound moment of self-knowledge why he has to be the way he is. He wonders why he must be an intellectual, always obsessed with texts and always lapsing back into textual hermeneutics, into the struggle of competing discourses, and into the allegorical apprehension of the world that by its attempt to freeze experience into a rational stasis falsifies reality. He wonders, as I have suggested before, whether such a life is actually worth living—not only *where* he should eat, but *whether* ("wher") he should eat at all.

At the heart of the dreamer's problem is what it has taken him most of the poem to learn: namely, the impossibility of doing well. A seem-

ingly unbridgeable gulf yawns between the human and the divine, between the sinful dreamer and Jesus. If the essential thing about the human nature of Jesus is that he does well, and if it is impossible for sinful
humans to do well, then in what sense is it possible for sinful human beings to be like Jesus? As I have argued in the preceding chapter, this
question motivates the dreamer's encounter with Need at the beginning
of Passus XX. Sinful human beings, as needy, can be like Jesus as the
self-imposed neediness of God. We imitate Jesus, paradoxically, when
we recognize our own sinfulness. In that recognition, we project an un-
attained state of completed perfection, and thus apprehend ourselves as
needy.

Furthermore, this process occurs for the intellectual in a particular
way. The intellectual, obsessed with self-justification, at first seeks to understand what it means to do well. The intellectual seeks that understanding in the place that seems natural to the intellectual: in the cacophony of contending authoritative texts. The quest issues, however,
only in the conclusion that it is impossible for sinful human beings to do
well. We sinful human beings must be justified, if at all, by identifying
ourselves with Jesus. And since we cannot identify ourselves with him in
doing well, we must identify ourselves with him in being needy. Our understanding of ourselves as needy is considerably abetted by encounters
with disease, death, and old age, such as are described at some length in
Passus XX. So the intellectual's obsession with texts, itself perhaps hope-
lessly entangled with the sinful impulse to master human experience, is
taken up into the larger providential economy. Reading is the intellectual's way of life. Our ways of reading, which make us intellectuals the sinners we are, can nevertheless become, like sin itself, instrumental to salvation. The story I have just retold, I am arguing, is the story of the
dreamer in *Piers Plowman,* and ultimately of Langland himself and of any
of his readers who as literate intellectuals share his obsessions.

But even if one's mind is straight about the crucial point, interpretation can be corrupted. The strategy that most directly deals with human
sin is the sacrament of penance. As I and others have mentioned, the
friars at the end of *Piers Plowman* corrupt the Church by corrupting the
practice of confession. Confession is, simply put, an interpretation of
the self. I think that Anne Middleton says it best:

Narration, particularly that which "speaks the self," is . . . double-edged. Its ideal use is in the service of confessional "truth-telling," the contrite return
through memory to one's past, enabling the subject to transform the present
into a new starting-point from which to make a good end. Yet first-person narration, even if nominally confessional, also carries within it a . . . hazard. In the
psychology of sin implicit in the medieval handbooks, in which the subject's capacity to see and tell the truth about himself is circumscribed by the empty recursiveness formed by his own *habitus,* such utterance is in practice equally capable of deflecting and deferring penitential contrition, enacting a fruitless and
endless auto-exegesis which keeps the narrative subject *in medias res* . . . repetition rather than revelation. . . . [O]ften for Will himself, declaration of one's
own designs quickly becomes indistinguishable from self-justification, reasons
blur into excuses, and confession repeatedly decomposes into apologia. ("Making" 248–49)

Confession lapses back into the intellectual's chronic disease of attempting to justify the self, and the friars through greed encourage the lapse.
Sir *Penetrans-domos*

> . . . gooth and gadereth, and gloseth there he shryveth—
> Til Contricion hadde clene foryeten to crye and to wepe,
> And wake for his wikked werkes as he was wont to doone.
>
> (XX.369–71)

Conscience must go on a pilgrimage in search of Piers Plowman, now
strangely absent, and the poem in one sense finishes where it began. The
dreamer believes that he needs to understand the human agency, including his own human agency as contrite sinner, that makes salvation possible, and he understands that he does not understand it—or at least, does
not understand it fully enough, since the sacrament remains subject to
corruption. The most important discovery about interpretation, after
all, is that the process of interpretation itself is grounded in a reality
outside interpretation and outside the text itself, a reality always just beyond our horizon that draws us on after it, and that is symbolized in the
poem by Piers the Plowman.

BIBLIOGRAPHICAL ESSAY 3.3

Ruth Ames's book *The Fulfillment of the Scriptures: Abraham, Moses, and
Piers* is helpful in defining the theological and literary contexts of Lang-

land's musings on the Trinity, the Incarnation, and the fulfillment of the Law. Ames sometimes compares *Piers Plowman* with the medieval drama as a didactic genre (for example, 66–68, 156–58), and much of what she says in this connection is relevant to my remarks about the liturgy as drama. Elizabeth Kirk's remarks on the way the liturgy creates social, theological, and literary community (183–87) pertain here as well. Morton W. Bloomfield's reading of *Piers Plowman* as an "apocalypse" places heavy weight on the dramatic scene in which Jesus harrows Hell as providing the nearest thing possible in the poem of an imperfect world to intellectual and aesthetic closure:

> [T]he Harrowing is the only display of Christ in His majesty before the final scene of His return; it foreshadows the Last Judgment. But Langland cannot, rooted as he is in history and especially the history of his own time, portray that Last Judgment. The Harrowing of Hell is the next best thing and a reminder to his contemporaries of the last solemn event in *Heilsgeschichte*. . . .
>   . . . In a profound sense, the powerful scene of the Harrowing of Hell is the true end of the poem, of the quest for Christian perfection which this poem exemplifies. (*Apocalypse* 124–25)

My difference with Bloomfield here is perhaps only the difference between the pessimist who sees the glass half-empty and the optimist who sees it half-full. My reading of *Piers Plowman* stresses the "not-yet," and Bloomfield's stresses the "but-soon." The inescapable image of Jesus as lawyer, given Langland's habitual attitude toward lawyers, seems to me to call out all too loudly for the hermeneutics of suspicion.

In some ways, my reading of Piers and the dreamer in general is very like Barbara Raw's. Raw sees the poem as being about the restoration of God's image in human beings. She argues:

> Whereas Piers represents the imprint of the divine image on humanity as a whole, Will stands for the particular, individual man. Piers becomes a restored image through the whole of human history, and then demonstrates the application of this new ideal to fourteenth-century society; Will, being real, not imaginary nor ideal, never becomes a fully-restored image, but follows Piers in the hope of becoming like him in the next world, and he does this in two ways, within the whole of his life and within the liturgy of one year. (168–69)

In my reading, Piers, as the sign of what the dreamer needs to understand and cannot yet comprehend, is ultimately also a sign of God—as

everything is a sign of the ultimate reality at the limit of all human interpretive systems. In my reading, Piers changes with the dreamer's
changing understanding; in Raw's reading, Piers changes with the progressive revelation of God in human history. Where I differ from Raw
is in not believing that one solves interpretive problems or achieves intellectual closure by finding the correct allegorical equation for Piers or
for the dreamer. Langland's allegory, in my reading, exists to create interpretive problems—and so the point is precisely that we do *not* fully
understand, even abstractly, what Piers is.

Stephen Barney's discussion of allegory in *Piers Plowman* ("Allegorical
Visions") is a fine short introduction to this enormous subject. Two
older discussions remain illuminating: Robert Worth Frank's "The Art
of Reading Medieval Personification-Allegory" (1953), and Elizabeth
Salter's *"Piers Plowman": An Introduction* (1963). David Aers's *"Piers Plowman"
and Christian Allegory* (1975) and Lavinia Griffiths's *Personification in "Piers
Plowman"* (1985) both demonstrate the subtleties of Langland's use of
the form. Pamela Raabe's analysis of modern critical approaches to medieval allegory is interesting and cogent (101ff.). Obviously, where I in-
dulge in simplistic characterizations of personification allegory—by
calling it, for example, the intellectual's "genre of explanation"—I am
being brutally unfair to Langland's genius, which plays on this form
with a virtuosity equivalent to his virtuosity with the long alliterative
line. In fact, the two sorts of virtuosity are not unrelated, as John
Lawlor's discussion makes clear (189–239). Langland's allegory, in my
view, yields to interpretation, if at all, only at the level of "close reading."
Langland's range within the form is so vast that critical generalizations
seem always to falsify. The tension in the poem that I am trying to pin
down by means of my brutal oversimplifications might be described as
the tension between the text considered as "open" and the text considered as "closed." The book about Langland's allegory that I cannot write
here would show how, on the microlevel and on the macrolevel of the
poem, the form that is normally expository and "closed" continually
breaks out of the conceptual and semantic boundaries it initially poses.
As Priscilla Jenkins puts it,

> [T]he allegorical habit of thought is indispensable in formulating moral con-
> cepts, but . . . since these concepts are modified by actual situations, allegoriza-
> tion itself comes under increasing suspicion. . . . Yet the desire for the idealism

and intellectual coherence of allegory cannot be abandoned. The final image of the pilgrim re-instates the allegorical, not as a statement of a scheme, but in terms of a quest for the unknown. (142)

Jenkins here seems to me to identify quite precisely the dilemma of the *litteratus*. Griffiths's work, especially, shows how Langland's personification allegory operates to keep turning world into text, things into names, story into discourse. Burt Kimmelman, as I mentioned in my Bibliographical Essay 1, reads Langland's whole poem as "an allegory about the failure of allegory" (226).

James Simpson describes the "formal changes" in *Piers Plowman* by saying that "the structure of the poem is unstable and self-consuming, undercutting itself as the inadequacy of its means of progressing is recognised" (250). Simpson sees these formal changes as having implications for "the history of reading," since "biblical texts are used in different ways as the poem proceeds" (250–51). Will changes from being a

passive receiver of biblical texts designed for moral instruction at the beginning of the poem, to being an active "reader," especially from Passus VIII forwards. Holy Church uses scriptural texts in an authoritarian and dogmatic way in Passus I, but when in Passus XI Will comes face to face with the ultimate text of the tradition to which Langland is committed, Scripture, the event is not one of passive reading, submissively accepting a "closed" text; instead, Will responds to the text of Scripture in a personal and liberating way. From this vision on in the poem, Will's "reading" of scriptural texts is more inward and poetic. (251)

Exactly like Simpson, I have been arguing that the poem is "about" reading, and that the formal structure of the poem, perhaps more than anything else, is what allows Langland to make the points about reading that he wants to make. Exactly unlike Simpson, I have been arguing that the dreamer's movement, never complete in the poem, is from "active reading" of authoritative texts—which means attempting to master those texts for one's own purposes—to salvific moments when the dreamer's pretensions to mastery are forgotten and his personality as *litteratus* is temporarily absorbed in the gospel or the liturgy. The terms *active* and *passive*, as I have mentioned before in another connection, seem misleading here. It is more helpful, in my view, to talk about the difference between regarding the soul as self-subsistent entity (which can be either "active" or "passive"), and regarding the soul as defined by its relation to God and his other creatures (where questions of "activity" and "passivity" do not come up). The dreamer as reader moves not from passivity to activity, but from understanding himself as self-subsistent, self-justifying entity to understanding himself as constituted by his relations to the texts that have formed him—from mastering texts to being mastered by them.

The idea that there is a kind of reading in which the reader is completely absorbed in and by the text is crucial for my understanding of *Piers Plowman*. This idea I find anticipated in Lawrence Clopper's assertion that Piers himself becomes "a text" (*Songes of Rechelesnesse* 296), but more directly and succinctly in Clopper's "Response" to Wendy Scase's "Writing and the Plowman: Langland and Literacy," in the *Yearbook of Langland Studies* for 1995. Clopper says that

> in *Piers Plowman* there are three exemplary "readers" of spiritual texts: 1) the "lewed" person who enacts the texts without being lettered—as Piers first does in the Visio; 2) the person who reads or interprets the letter for others—as Clergy does; and as Piers does when he repeats Clergy's teaching; and 3) the person who penetrates the script so deeply and profoundly that he becomes the text to be read—as Piers does when he tears the pardon and when in passus 19 he plows and seeds the world with Truth. ("Response" 132)

This "third kind of reading" is "an apostolic or sapiential mode" ("Response" 133). Clopper reads both the symbolism of Piers and the narrative of the poem rather differently from the way I do, but I think Clopper and I would agree that the poem on some level is about Langland's own position "[i]n the middle and on very uncertain ground indeed, for going literate rather than being a text is risky; those seduced by learning and 'lettrure' may become hypocrites at the banquet" ("Response" 134–35).

In fact, because I am reading *Piers Plowman* as "going about" textual hermeneutics, I place the major crisis in the dreamer's narrative differently than some other critics do. Because for him the main agenda of the poem is reformist, Clopper places the "turning point" of the long middle at the moment of Haukyn's confession and contrition (*Songes of Rechelesnesse* 255). John Bowers, on the other hand, says something that sounds very much like something I might say, though Bowers reaches the conclusion by a different route: "Only after the vision of the Tree of

Charity does the poem begin to rise out of the tedious tangle that di-alectic had become for most of Langland's contemporaries" (16). Other critics divide the poem as Clopper does. John Lawlor, for example, says that Passus XIV "ends a major division of the poem with Haukyn's cry for mercy," and that the dreamer "has made the greatest single stride forward in the lessons he has learnt from virtue-in-action" (136). Eliza-beth Kirk says, "Hawkin's grief marks the point at which the human spirit makes the most fundamental of all shifts, from an anthropocen-tric to a theocentric understanding of his own good and evil" (158). Simpson, as I have already mentioned, regards the fourth vision, ending with Passus XIV, as the crisis in the dreamer's narrative, a *"transitus,* a Passover from the Old Law to the New" (165). Not every critic is quite so definite about placing a major division in the poem at this point. I have discussed this problem a little more fully above, in the section of the preceding chapter that deals with the dreamer's encounter with Anima. But the issue here is whether understanding profoundly the im-plications of one's own sinfulness is enough to constitute a break-through. Certainly this understanding is presented in the poem as a necessary condition of salvation. But I am arguing that more is needed: namely, a deeper understanding of the nature of written texts, an un-derstanding of how the soul is itself like a text, and a way of relating oneself to authoritative texts that escapes the losing endgame of self-justification. Thus, in my reading, the crisis in the dreamer's narrative comes in Passus XVI, after the instruction of Anima—not just the dreamer's understanding of his own sin—prepares the dreamer for the possibility of his visionary encounter with Jesus.

WORKS CITED
INDICES

WORKS CITED

Adams, Robert. "Langland's Theology." In *A Companion to "Piers Plowman,"* ed. John A. Alford (Berkeley: University of California Press, 1988), 87–114.

———. "The Nature of Need in *Piers Plowman* XX." *Traditio* 34 (1978): 273–301.

——— . "Piers's Pardon and Langland's Semi-Pelagianism." *Traditio* 39 (1983): 367–418.

Aers, David. *"Piers Plowman" and Christian Allegory.* London: Edward Arnold, 1975.

Alford, John A., ed. *A Companion to "Piers Plowman."* Berkeley: University of California Press, 1988.

———. "The Design of the Poem." In *A Companion to "Piers Plowman,"* ed. John A. Alford (Berkeley: University of California Press, 1988), 29–65.

———. "The Grammatical Metaphor: A Survey of Its Use in the Middle Ages." *Speculum* 57 (1982): 728–60.

———. "The Idea of Reason in *Piers Plowman*." In *Medieval English Studies Presented to George Kane,* ed. Donald Kennedy, Ronald Waldron, and Joseph S. Wittig (Wolfeboro, N.H., and Woodbridge, Suffolk, U.K.: D. S. Brewer, 1988), 199–215.

———. "Langland's Learning." *Yearbook of Langland Studies* 9 (1995): 1–8.

——— . "The Role of the Quotations in *Piers Plowman*." *Speculum* 52 (1977): 80–99.

Allen, Judson Boyce. *The Ethical Poetic of the Later Middle Ages: A Decorum of Convenient Distinction.* Toronto: University of Toronto Press, 1982.

Ambrose. *Saint Ambrose: Theological and Dogmatic Works.* Translated by Roy J. Deferrari. Washington, D.C.: The Catholic University of America Press, 1963.

Ames, Ruth M. *The Fulfillment of the Scriptures: Abraham, Moses, and Piers.* Evanston, Ill.: Northwestern University Press, 1970.

Augustine. *The City of God by Saint Augustine.* 2 vols. Translated and edited by Marcus Dods. New York: Hafner, 1948.

———. *The Works of Saint Augustine: A Translation for the 21st Century. Part 3: Sermons.* Vol. 7. Translated by Edmund Hill, O.P. Edited by John E. Rotelle, O.S.A. Augustinian Heritage Institute. New Rochelle, N.Y.: New City Press, 1993.

Baker, Denise N. "From Plowing to Penitence: *Piers Plowman* and Fourteenth-Century Theology." *Speculum* 55 (1980): 715–25.

Baldwin, Anna P. "The Historical Context." In *A Companion to "Piers Plowman,"* ed. John A. Alford (Berkeley: University of California Press, 1988), 67–86.

———. *The Theme of Government in "Piers Plowman."* Piers Plowman Studies 1. Cambridge, U.K.: D. S. Brewer, 1981.

Barney, Stephen A. "Allegorical Visions." In *A Companion to "Piers Plowman,"* ed. John A. Alford (Berkeley: University of California Press, 1988), 117–33.

Barr, Helen. *Signes and Sothe: Language in the "Piers Plowman" Tradition.* Piers Plowman Studies 10. Cambridge, U.K.: D. S. Brewer, 1994.

Barthes, Roland. *S/Z.* Translated by Richard Miller. New York: Hill & Wang, 1974.

Benson, C. David. "The Function of Lady Meed in *Piers Plowman." English Studies* 61 (1980): 193–205.

Blake, William. "The Mental Traveller." In *The Portable Blake,* ed. Alfred Kazin (New York: Viking Press, 1974), 145–48.

Bloomfield, Morton W. "The Allegories of *Dobest (Piers Plowman* B xix–xx)." *Medium Aevum* 50, no. 1 (1981): 30–39.

——. *"Piers Plowman" as a Fourteenth-Century Apocalypse.* New Brunswick, N.J.: Rutgers University Press, 1962.

Bowers, John M. *The Crisis of Will in "Piers Plowman."* Washington, D.C.: The Catholic University of America Press, 1986.

Brooks, Cleanth. *The Well Wrought Urn: Studies in the Structure of Poetry.* New York: Harcourt, Brace & Company, 1947.

Carruthers, Mary. *The Search for St. Truth: A Study of Meaning in "Piers Plowman."* Evanston, Ill.: Northwestern University Press, 1973.

Clopper, Lawrence M. "Response" [to Wendy Scase, "Writing and the Plowman: Langland and Literacy"]. *Yearbook of Langland Studies* 9 (1995): 132–35.

——. *"Songes of Rechelesnesse": Langland and the Franciscans.* Ann Arbor: University of Michigan Press, 1997.

Coghill, Nevill. "The Character of Piers Plowman Considered from the B Text." In *Interpretations of "Piers Plowman,"* ed. Edward Vasta (Notre Dame, Ind.: University of Notre Dame Press, 1968), 54–86. Rpt. from *Medium Aevum* 2 (1933): 108–35.

Coleman, Janet. *"Piers Plowman" and the "Moderni."* Rome: Edizioni di Storia e Letteratura, 1981.

Cooper, Helen. "Langland's and Chaucer's Prologues." *Yearbook of Langland Studies* 1 (1987): 71–81.

Craun, Edwin D. *Lies, Slander, and Obscenity in Medieval English Literature: Pastoral Rhetoric and the Deviant Speaker.* Cambridge Studies in Medieval Literature 31. Cambridge, U.K.: Cambridge University Press, 1997.

Davlin, S. Mary Clemente, O.P. *A Game of Heuene: Word Play and the Meaning of "Piers Plowman B."* Woodbridge, Suffolk, U.K., and Wolfeboro, N.H.: D. S. Brewer, 1989.

——. *"Kynde Knowyng* as a Middle English Equivalent for 'Wisdom' in *Piers Plowman* B." *Medium Aevum* 50 (1981): 5–17.

——. "Tower and Tabernacle: The Architecture of Heaven and the Language of Dwelling with/in God in the B-Text of *Piers Plowman." Essays in Medieval Studies* 10 (1994): 99–107.

Dean, James M. *The World Grown Old in Later Medieval Literature.* Cambridge, Mass.: Medieval Academy of America, 1997.

Derrida, Jacques. *Of Grammatology.* Translated by Gayatri Chakravorty Spivak. Baltimore: Johns Hopkins University Press, 1976.

Donaldson, E. Talbot. *"Piers Plowman": The C-Text and Its Poet.* Hamden, Conn.: Archon Books, 1966.

Dunning, T. P., C.M. *"Piers Plowman": An Interpretation of the A Text.* 2nd ed. Oxford, U.K.: Clarendon Press, 1980.

———. "Structure of the B Text of *Piers Plowman.*" In *Interpretations of "Piers Plowman,"* ed. Edward Vasta (Notre Dame, Ind.: University of Notre Dame Press, 1968), 259–77. Rpt. from *Review of English Studies,* n.s., 7 (1956): 225–37.

Fish, Stanley Eugene. *Self-Consuming Artifacts: The Experience of Seventeenth-Century Literature.* Berkeley: University of California Press, 1972.

Frank, Robert Worth Jr. "The Art of Reading Medieval Personification-Allegory." In *Interpretations of "Piers Plowman,"* ed. Edward Vasta (Notre Dame, Ind.: University of Notre Dame Press, 1968), 217–31. Rpt. from *ELH* 20 (1953): 237–50.

———. *"Piers Plowman" and the Scheme of Salvation: An Interpretation of Dowel, Dobet, and Dobest.* Hamden, Conn.: Archon Books, 1969.

Galloway, Andrew. "Intellectual Pregnancy, Metaphysical Femininity, and the Social Doctrine of the Trinity in *Piers Plowman.*" *Yearbook of Langland Studies* 12 (1998): 117–52.

Gellrich, Jesse M. *Discourse and Dominion in the Fourteenth Century: Oral Contexts of Writing in Philosophy, Politics, and Poetry.* Princeton, N.J.: Princeton University Press, 1995.

———. *The Idea of the Book in the Middle Ages: Language Theory, Mythology, and Fiction.* Ithaca, N.Y.: Cornell University Press, 1985.

Godden, Malcolm. *The Making of "Piers Plowman."* London: Longman, 1990.

Goodall, Peter. "Being Alone in Chaucer." *Chaucer Review* 21 (1992): 1–15.

Griffiths, Lavinia. *Personification in "Piers Plowman."* Cambridge, U.K.: D. S. Brewer, 1985.

Hala, James. "'For She Is Tikel of Hire Tale': Word-Play in the Lady Mede Episode of *Piers Plowman* B." *Proceedings of the PMR Conference* 14 (1989): 99–126.

Hale, David G. "'The Glose Was Gloriously Writen': The Textuality of Langland's Good Samaritan." *Proceedings of the PMR Conference* 14 (1989): 127–34.

Hanna, Ralph III. *William Langland.* Authors of the Middle Ages 3. Aldershot, Hants, U.K.: Variorum, 1993.

Harwood, Britton J. *"Piers Plowman" and the Problem of Belief.* Toronto: University of Toronto Press, 1992.

Howard, Donald R. *The Idea of "The Canterbury Tales."* Berkeley: University of California Press, 1976.

Hughes, M. E. J. "'The Feffement That Fals Hath Ymaked': A Study of the Image of the Document in *Piers Plowman* and Some Literary Analogues." *Neuphilologische Mitteilungen* 93 (1992): 125–31.

Huntsman, Jeffrey F. "Grammar." In *The Seven Liberal Arts in the Middle Ages,* ed. David L. Wagner (Bloomington: Indiana University Press, 1986), 58–95.

Hussey, S. S. "Introduction." In *"Piers Plowman": Critical Approaches,* ed. S. S. Hussey (London: Methuen, 1969), 1–26.

Jakobson, Roman. "Linguistics and Poetics." In *Style in Language,* ed. Thomas A. Sebeok (Cambridge, Mass.: MIT Press, 1960), 350–77.

Jenkins, Priscilla. "Conscience: The Frustration of Allegory." In *"Piers Plowman": Critical Approaches,* ed. S. S. Hussey (London: Methuen, 1969), 125–42.

Justice, Steven. "The Genres of *Piers Plowman*." *Viator* 19 (1988): 291–306.

———. *Writing and Rebellion: England in 1381*. Berkeley: University of California Press, 1994.

Justice, Steven, and Kathryn Kerby-Fulton, eds. *Written Work: Langland, Labor, and Authorship*. Philadelphia: University of Pennsylvania Press, 1997.

Kane, George. "Reading *Piers Plowman*." *Yearbook of Langland Studies* 8 (1994): 1–20.

Kaske, R. E. "Holy Church's Speech and the Structure of *Piers Plowman*." In *Chaucer and Middle English Studies in Honor of Rossell Hope Robbins*, ed. Beryl Rowland (London: Allen & Unwin, 1974), 320–27.

———. "Patristic Exegesis in the Criticism of Medieval Literature: The Defense." In *Interpretations of "Piers Plowman*," ed. Edward Vasta (Notre Dame, Ind.: University of Notre Dame Press, 1968), 319–38. Rpt. from *Critical Approaches to Medieval Literature*, ed. Dorothy Bethurum (New York: Columbia University Press, 1960), 27–48, 60, 158–59.

Kaulbach, Ernest N. *Imaginative Prophecy in the B-Text of "Piers Plowman*." Cambridge, U.K.: D. S. Brewer, 1993.

Kean, P. M. "Langland on the Incarnation." *Review of English Studies*, n.s., 16 (1965): 349–63.

Kimmelman, Burt. *The Poetics of Authorship in the Later Middle Ages: The Emergence of the Modern Literary Persona*. New York: Peter Lang, 1996.

Kirk, Elizabeth D. *The Dream Thought of "Piers Plowman*." Yale Studies in English 178. New Haven, Conn.: Yale University Press, 1972.

Klein, Michael L. *Fragmentation and Contradiction in "Piers Plowman" and Its Implications for the Study of Modern Literature, Art, and Culture*. The Apocalyptic Discourse. Lewiston, N.Y.: Edwin Mellen, 1992.

Kuhn, Thomas. *The Structure of Scientific Revolutions*. 2nd ed., enlarged. Chicago: University of Chicago Press, 1970.

Langland, William. *"Piers Plowman": The B Version. Will's Visions of Piers Plowman, Do-Well, Do-Better and Do-Best*. Rev. ed. Edited by George Kane and E. Talbot Donaldson. London: Athlone, 1988.

———. *"Piers Plowman" by William Langland: An Edition of the C-Text*. Edited by Derek Pearsall. Berkeley: University of California Press, 1979.

———. *"The Vision of Piers Plowman": A Critical Edition of the B-Text Based on Trinity College Cambridge MS B.15.17*. Edited by A. V. C. Schmidt. London: J. M. Dent, 1995.

Lawlor, John. *"Piers Plowman": An Essay in Criticism*. New York: Barnes & Noble, 1962.

Lawton, David. "The Subject of *Piers Plowman*." *Yearbook of Langland Studies* 1 (1987): 1–30.

Mann, Jill. "Eating and Drinking in *Piers Plowman*." *Essays and Studies* 32 (1979): 26–43.

Middleton, Anne. "Introduction: The Critical Heritage." In *A Companion to "Piers Plowman*," ed. John A. Alford (Berkeley: University of California Press, 1988), 1–25.

———. "Making a Good End: John But as a Reader of *Piers Plowman*." In *Medieval English Studies Presented to George Kane*, ed. Edward Donald Kennedy, Ronald Waldron, and Joseph S. Wittig (Wolfeboro, N.H., and Woodbridge, Suffolk, U.K.: D. S. Brewer, 1988), 243–66.

———. "Narration and the Invention of Experience: Episodic Form in *Piers Plowman*." In *The Wisdom of Poetry: Essays in Early English Literature in Honor of Morton W. Bloomfield*, ed.

Larry D. Benson and Siegfried Wenzel (Kalamazoo, Mich.: Medieval Institute Publications, 1982), 91–122.

———. "Two Infinites: Grammatical Metaphor in *Piers Plowman*." *ELH* 39 (1972): 169–88.

Migne, J.-P., comp. *Patrologiae Cursus Completus. Series Latina.* 221 vols. Paris: Garnier, 1844–1903. [Abbreviated *PL*]

Mills, David. "The Rôle of the Dreamer in *Piers Plowman*." In *"Piers Plowman": Critical Approaches*, ed. S. S. Hussey (London: Methuen, 1969), 180–212.

Minnis, Alastair J. "Langland's Ymaginatif and Late-Medieval Theories of Imagination." *Comparative Criticism* 3 (1981): 71–103.

Minnis, A. J., A. B. Scott, with D. Wallace, eds. *Medieval Literary Theory and Criticism, c. 1100 c. 1375.* Rev. ed. Oxford, U.K.: Clarendon Press, 1991.

Mitchell, A. G. "Lady Meed and the Art of *Piers Plowman*." In *Style and Symbolism in "Piers Plowman": A Modern Critical Anthology*, ed. Robert J. Blanch (Knoxville: University of Tennessee Press, 1969), 174–93.

Myles, Robert. *Chaucerian Realism.* Chaucer Studies 20. Cambridge, U.K.: D. S. Brewer, 1994.

Owst, G. R. "A Literary Echo of the Social Gospel." In *Interpretations of "Piers Plowman,"* ed. Edward Vasta (Notre Dame, Ind.: University of Notre Dame Press, 1968), 22–53. Rpt. from G. R. Owst, *Literature and Pulpit in Medieval England* (New York: Barnes & Noble, 1966), 548–75.

Pearsall, Derek. *An Annotated Critical Bibliography of Langland.* Ann Arbor: University of Michigan Press, 1990.

Peirce, Charles Sanders. "Evolutionary Love." In *The Essential Peirce: Selected Philosophical Writings*, Vol. 1: 1867–1893, ed. Nathan Houser and Christian Kloesel (Bloomington: Indiana University Press, 1992), 352–71.

Pigg, Daniel F. "Imagining Feudalism in *Piers Plowman*." In *The Rusted Hauberk: Feudal Ideals of Order and Their Decline*, ed. Liam O. Purdon and Cindy L. Vitto (Gainesville: University Press of Florida, 1994), 29–46.

PL. See Migne above.

Plato. *Symposium.* Translated by Michael Joyce. In *The Collected Dialogues of Plato, Including the Letters.* Bollingen Series 71, ed. Edith Hamilton and Huntington Cairns (Princeton, N.J.: Princeton University Press, 1971), 526–74.

———. *The Symposium.* Translated by Walter Hamilton. New York: Penguin Books, 1978.

Raabe, Pamela. *Imitating God: The Allegory of Faith in "Piers Plowman B."* Athens: University of Georgia Press, 1990.

Ransom, John Crowe. *The New Criticism.* Norfolk, Conn.: New Directions, 1941.

Raw, Barbara. "Piers and the Image of God in Man." In *"Piers Plowman": Critical Approaches*, ed. S. S. Hussey (London: Methuen, 1969), 143–79.

Ricoeur, Paul. *Hermeneutics and the Human Sciences.* Translated and edited by John B. Thompson. Cambridge, U.K., and Paris: Cambridge University Press and Éditions de la Maison des Sciences de L'Homme, 1981.

Robertson, D. W. Jr., and Bernard F. Huppé. *"Piers Plowman" and Scriptural Tradition.* New York: Octagon Books, 1969.

Rogers, William Elford. *Interpreting Interpretation: Textual Hermeneutics as an Ascetic Discipline.* University Park: Pennsylvania State University Press, 1994.

Rorty, Richard. *Consequences of Pragmatism (Essays: 1972–1980).* Minneapolis: University of Minnesota Press, 1982.

Rudd, Gillian. *Managing Language in "Piers Plowman."* Cambridge, U.K.: D. S. Brewer, 1994.

Salter, Elizabeth. *"Piers Plowman": An Introduction.* Cambridge, Mass.: Harvard University Press, 1963.

Savage, Anne. *"Piers Plowman:* The Translation of Scripture and Food for the Soul." *English Studies* 74 (1993): 209–21.

Scase, Wendy. "Writing and the Plowman: Langland and Literacy." *Yearbook of Langland Studies* 9 (1995): 121–31.

Schmidt, A. V. C. *The Clerkly Maker: Langland's Poetic Art.* Cambridge, U.K.: D. S. Brewer, 1987.

———. "*Lele Wordes* and *Bele Paroles:* Some Aspects of Langland's Word-Play." *Review of English Studies,* n.s., 34 (1983): 137–50.

Simpson, James. *"Piers Plowman": An Introduction to the B-Text.* London: Longman, 1990.

Stock, Brian. *The Implications of Literacy: Written Language and Models of Interpretation in the Eleventh and Twelfth Centuries.* Princeton, N.J.: Princeton University Press, 1983.

Tavormina, M. Teresa. *Kindly Similitude: Marriage and Family in "Piers Plowman."* Cambridge, U.K.: D. S. Brewer, 1995.

Trigg, Stephanie. "The Traffic in Medieval Women: Alice Perrers, Feminist Criticism and *Piers Plowman.*" *Yearbook of Langland Studies* 12 (1998): 5–29.

Vasta, Edward. "Truth, the Best Treasure, in *Piers Plowman.*" *Philological Quarterly* 44 (1965): 17–29.

Wenzel, Siegfried. "Medieval Sermons." In *A Companion to "Piers Plowman,"* ed. John A. Alford (Berkeley: University of California Press, 1988), 155–72.

Wittig, Joseph S. *"Piers Plowman* B, Passus IX–XII: Elements in the Design of the Inward Journey." *Traditio* 28 (1972): 211–80.

———. *William Langland Revisited.* Twayne's English Authors Series 537. New York: Twayne, 1997.

Woolf, Rosemary. "The Tearing of the Pardon." In *"Piers Plowman": Critical Approaches,* ed. S. S. Hussey (London: Methuen, 1969), 50–75.

Yeats, William Butler. "Among School Children." In *The Collected Poems of W. B. Yeats,* ed. Richard J. Finneran (New York: Macmillan, 1989), 215–17.

INDEX OF AUTHORS

Adams, Robert, 143, 165–67, 184, 185, 193, 204, 206, 246
Aers, David, 277
Alford, John A., 3, 17, 74, 78, 100, 112, 114, 116, 117, 123, 126, 137, 243
Allen, Judson Boyce, 74, 76, 99
Ambrose, 157
Ames, Ruth M., 275–76
Augustine, 7–8, 21, 33, 36, 60, 63, 74, 97, 126, 132–33, 160–61, 220–21, 245
Avicenna, 245

Baker, Denise N., 204
Bakhtin, M. M., 5
Baldwin, Anna P., 77–78, 97, 112
Barney, Stephen A., 277
Barr, Helen, 70
Barthes, Roland, 11
Bede, 64
Benson, C. David, 118
Bernard of Clairvaux, 135, 257
Blake, William, 12
Bloomfield, Morton W., 18, 76–77, 276
Bowers, John M., 74, 149, 167–68, 171, 206, 279–80
Brooks, Cleanth, 5

Carroll, Lewis (Charles Dodgson), 56, 147
Carruthers, Mary, 18, 34–35, 71–74, 84, 88, 111–12, 119, 130, 137, 140–41, 160–61, 165, 167, 174, 183, 195, 201, 210, 243, 261
Chaucer, Geoffrey, 4, 13, 36, 40–41, 45, 47, 53–54, 56–57, 60, 72, 77, 86, 90, 141, 154, 172, 198
Clopper, Lawrence M., 6–7, 21–22, 139–40, 154, 165–67, 187, 204, 220, 226, 244–46, 251, 279–80

Coghill, Nevill, 242
Coleman, Janet, 204
Cooper, Helen, 40
Craun, Edwin D., 33

Dante, 33, 72, 77, 262–63
Davlin, S. Mary Clemente, O.P., 104–5, 115, 119, 181
Dean, James M., 65, 243
Derrida, Jacques, 9, 20, 70, 71
Donaldson, E. Talbot, 50, 96, 118, 133, 167
Dunning, T. P., C.M., 102, 117, 242–43

Fish, Stanley Eugene, 11
Frank, Robert Worth, 123, 139, 162, 164–65, 204, 271, 277

Galloway, Andrew, 162–63, 261
Gallus, Thomas, 98
Gellrich, Jesse M., 13, 71–72, 126
Glossa Ordinaria, 33, 35, 36, 60, 64, 157
Godden, Malcolm, 53, 120, 122, 139, 164
Goodall, Peter, 223
Gregory the Great, 33, 166
Griffiths, Lavinia, 277

Hala, James, 119–20
Hale, David G., 257
Hanna, Ralph III, 16
Harwood, Britton J., 4, 19, 75, 114, 139, 142–43, 164, 165, 167, 195, 204, 209, 241, 244, 247–48, 257
Heidegger, Martin, 56
Howard, Donald R., 141, 205
Hughes, M. E. J., 205
Huntsman, Jeffrey F., 126

Huppé, Bernard F., 33, 111, 118, 130, 134, 151, 161
Hussey, S. S., 164

Isidore of Seville, 33, 36

Jakobson, Roman, 25–26
Jenkins, Priscilla, 277–78
Justice, Steven, 7, 18, 77, 195, 269

Kane, George, 3, 50, 96, 118
Kaske, R. E., 114, 263
Kaulbach, Ernest N., 209, 228, 245–46
Kean, P. M., 106, 119
Kerby-Fulton, Kathryn, 7
Kimmelman, Burt, 6, 18, 77, 141, 278
Kirk, Elizabeth D., 121, 123, 138, 203, 226–27, 276, 280
Klein, Michael L., 24
Kuhn, Thomas, 9–10

Lawlor, John, 183, 212, 228, 259, 266, 277, 280
Lawton, David, 5, 58–59, 69, 74, 171

Mann, Jill, 130, 187, 189
Middleton, Anne, 3, 18–19, 22–23, 60, 74–75, 127, 135, 142, 177–78, 190, 191, 205, 233, 274–75
Mills, David, 176, 233
Minnis, A. J., 209, 243
Mitchell, A. G., 118
Myles, Robert, 36, 70, 74, 127, 128, 141–42

Owst, G. R., 204

Pearsall, Derek, 30, 42, 94–95, 97, 101–2, 150, 223
Peirce, Charles Sanders, 13, 15, 163, 174
Pigg, Daniel F., 78, 116

Plato, 162
Pseudo-Dionysius, 98

Raabe, Pamela, 13, 18, 53, 71–74, 119, 140–41, 165, 206, 277
Rabanus Maurus, 33, 35, 36
Ransom, John Crowe, 4
Raw, Barbara, 142, 276–77
Ricoeur, Paul, 52
Robertson, D. W. Jr., 33, 111, 118, 130, 134, 151, 161
Rogers, William Elford, 15
Rorty, Richard, 173
Rudd, Gillian, 18, 70, 73–74, 114–15, 130, 140, 173, 210, 263

Salter, Elizabeth, 277
Savage, Anne, 249
Scase, Wendy, 279
Schmidt, A. V. C., 29, 42, 50, 68, 94, 96, 101, 111, 118, 119, 123–24, 128, 133, 135, 138, 160, 221, 223, 239, 265, 271
Simpson, James, 40, 52–53, 76, 78, 84, 107, 113, 116, 119, 125, 132, 137–38, 140, 165, 192, 201, 202, 205–6, 209, 223, 231, 243, 248–49, 260, 265, 273, 278, 280
Stock, Brian, 141, 184, 220, 251

Tavormina, M. Teresa, 137, 248, 261–62
Trigg, Stephanie, 119

Vasta, Edward, 115–16

Wenzel, Siegfried, 117
Wittgenstein, Ludvig, 6
Wittig, Joseph S., 7, 40, 209, 243–47, 256
Woolf, Rosemary, 198, 200

Yeats, William Butler, 128

INDEX OF PASSAGES

B-Text

PROLOGUE: 54, 76

3: 236
4–III: 55–57
17: 33
20–III: 35–43
23–24: 96
42: 148
58–67: 122
61: 61
78–III: 122
100: 58
103: 153
109: 58
110: 153
112–17: 65–66
112–227: 44–52
144: 61
182: 58
209–10: 58, 61
221: 105–6

PASSUS I

1–2: 54, 61–62, 83
5–6: 31, 84
11: 84, 87, 108, 252
12: 35–36, 84–85
17–42: 86
43–45: 87–88
52: 24, 26–27
59–60: 88
59–64: 36
61: 85
63–64: 89
63–72: 89–90
75–78: 91

79: 109
79–80: 92
81–84: 88
83–84: 85, 92
84–85: 176
85: 100
85–86: 93, 101–2
88–89: 89
88–105: 94–97
90–91: 102
94–97: 99
95: 99
96: 106
98–99: 103
98–103: 118
104–9: 103
108: 108
111–33: 93
119: 97
119–26: 99
120: 106
123: 106
130–32: 176
130–37: 104
131: 100
134: 103
134–35: 100
134–36: 110
137: 100
138: 104–5, 181
138–39: 122, 179
140: 104
140–41: 102
142–44: 179
142–47: 218
148–49: 106
152: 107

153: 106
155: 106
156: 107
157–58: 105
159–60: 106
160: 108
188: 106
195–203: 122
202: 106
204. 106
206: 103
206–8: 100
208–9: 110

PASSUS II

1: 109
4: 109–10, 176, 179
17: 110
25–28: 110
41: 110
119: 110
119–41: 112
183: 148
185: 111

PASSUS III

3–50: 122
10: 111
120–353: 111
140: 111–12
142–52: 112
227: 112
246–54: 112
256: 112
336–50: 112–13

PASSUS IV

47–60: 113
103: 113
119–25: 122
166: 144

PASSUS V

69: 160
135–66: 122
416–22: 122
537: 176, 191
537–49: 180–81
538: 105
548–49: 196
560–629: 181–82
606: 181, 250

PASSUS VI

6: 185
9–16: 106
24–77: 103–4
78–82: 182
117: 186, 255
121: 148
133: 186
199: 186
203: 41, 187
204: 186
207: 186–87
210–11: 172
211: 187
214: 188
218–19: 187–88
225–27a: 188
228–46: 188
229: 189
256–73: 187
274: 187

PASSUS VII

1: 185
2: 67, 185
3: 183, 187
4–6: 189
5: 185
6–7: 250
18: 38–39
64–65: 41
105–6: 191

110: 184
110b: 193
111: 184, 190
115: 190, 255
116–17: 193, 231
117–20: 186
118–19: 184
119: 239
120: 200, 234
120–27: 195–96
125–26: 208, 241
126–30: 239
131–36: 191
131–39: 172
135–36: 172
137: 192
138a–39: 196
139: 199
140–52: 197
140–201: 198, 217
144–48: 198–99
144–201: 185
148: 207–8
152–54: 199
168: 197
168–70: 199–200
169: 207–8
172–78: 200–201
182: 201
188–89: 180
192: 192
195: 201
196–201: 197–98

PASSUS VIII

5–24: 202
46–57: 208–9
57: 181
70–77: 211
77: 213
109–27: 211–12
110: 181
111–13: 213

PASSUS IX

1–59: 213–14
6: 120
7: 81
16: 120
23: 120

26: 85
84: 214
99–100: 214–15
108–63: 214
184: 214–15

PASSUS X

9–11: 215
17–136: 122
37: 101
38: 148
53–57: 255
57: 135
103–25: 216
117: 229
131–34: 216
138: 216
151–52: 219
158–65: 217
170: 217
170–81: 217
182–85: 217
182–208: 107, 217–18
216–17: 217
218–19: 217–18
232: 218
243–59: 218–19
258–329: 122
331–40: 219
331–70: 224
343: 23, 225
343–453: 219
345–46: 224
371–77: 220
371–475: 122
374–77: 221
452–54: 220–21
455: 251
455–60: 220–21

PASSUS XI

1–3: 79, 224
3: 221
4–5: 251
8: 221–22
47: 222
54–57: 222
54–83: 122
60–77: 261
71–74: 222

89–104: 222
92: 148
101–2: 57
105: 223
107: 224
107–18: 203, 222–23
111–17: 223–24
116–17: 226
127–28: 225
137–40: 224
153–318: 223–27
160: 225
167–68: 225
170–71: 223
189–95: 224
204: 225
213. 225
225: 225
229a: 224–25
269: 225
272: 225
275: 225
278: 225
281–318: 122
303–8: 225
317: 225
319: 225–26
320–25: 228
323–35: 227
357–60: 229
372–74: 23
382–93: 227
411–22: 227
411–32: 228

PASSUS XII

10–11: 229
16. 57, 226–27
16–24: 231
29–32: 231
64–174: 122
71–91: 230
89a: 231
128–39: 229–30
218–39: 229
278–92: 232
288–91: 231

PASSUS XIII

7–13: 122

37–58: 235–36
61–85: 122
84: 232–33
86: 232
99: 232
103: 232
120–28: 207–8
128–30: 233
133: 208
137–40: 235
186–215: 233–35
222–25: 39, 57
235–38: 237
248: 236
249–58: 237
256: 238
285: 236
314–24: 240–41
422–60: 239

PASSUS XIV

1–2: 238, 240
16–22: 236, 238
33–34a: 238–39
36: 239
47: 239
49: 132, 238
89a. 239
97: 239
101–3: 239 40
275: 240
277: 239
322–24: 136
324–25: 252

PASSUS XV

1–3: 136, 241
1–9: 208
12: 125, 135–36
14: 81
14–15: 136
23–39: 124–25
38–39: 120–21
39a: 120
40–43: 120
44–49: 130
50–51a: 97
60–61: 135
96–102: 140, 250
99–102: 131

100: 127
111–15: 130
118: 133
146–49: 121
149: 208–9, 240
152: 121
161–62: 128, 161
165: 127
171: 127
177: 127
179: 132
186–94: 238
194: 132
209–12: 132–33, 250–51
210: 234
212: 178
220: 127
223–24: 132
228: 132
230: 127
272: 132
286–94: 132
305: 131
371: 129
385: 131
396–410: 131
414: 132
420–21: 132
458 84: 131
475–77: 131
532–33. 132
563: 132
607–10: 129

PASSUS XVI

2: 136, 242
3: 122, 240, 252
4–9: 140
4–17: 250
5–89: 253–56
10–11: 208–9
13–17: 250
16: 178
16–17: 208–9
18–20: 137, 172, 251
63–66: 254–55
86–88: 190, 255
90: 137, 256
90–166: 259
93–108: 256–57

104: 172, 178
167–70: 251–52
167–XVII.352: 257

PASSUS XVII

24–36: 258
113–18: 258

PASSUS XVIII

6–11: 260
10: 178, 262
21–26: 259
22–23: 262
36–109a: 259
110–12: 260
164: 85
328–29: 264
328–404: 263
333: 264
334–39: 264
340a: 265
341–50a: 264
350a: 265
361: 264
361a: 265
374–90: 264
376–77: 264
379a: 265
391a: 265
392–93: 264
394–96: 264
396a: 264–65
401a: 265
424–30: 261

PASSUS XIX

1–2: 265
5–8: 266
5–11: 178
12–13: 262
15–20: 267
15–33: 64
51–55: 267
63–68: 267
69–199: 259
108–12: 268
128–29: 268
170–84: 65
177–85: 268–69

183–85: 268
183–91: 179, 270
187: 271–72
191: 271
209: 85
230–34: 66
254–56: 66–67
260–74: 67–68
262–324: 269–70
263: 67
274–77: 68
277–311: 153
278–80: 1
283–90: 150
312–13: 68
331: 81
334: 270
338: 179
338–39: 272
389–94: 270
394: 24, 26–27
396–406: 69
400–406: 272
413: 272
413–62: 69
432–34: 272
463–68: 272
469–80: 69, 272

PASSUS XX

1–3: 158
2–3: 272–73
5: 148–49
6–8: 146
6–9: 150–51
14: 149
20–23: 151
21: 154
25–28: 152
29–30: 152
31–33: 152–53
33a: 159
34: 160
34–39: 160
41–48: 161–62
48–49: 146–47
53: 143, 272
53–55: 111–12, 159
74: 241
193–98: 261–62

207–13: 179
208: 262
209: 239
227–32: 155–56
232–41: 143, 153–54
232–50: 156–58
248–50: 158
341: 57
369–71: 275
381–83: 27–28
381–87: 172, 180
384–85: 155

C-Text

PROLOGUE

81–117: 42
140: 44

PASSUS I

81–82: 101–2
86–87: 95
90–100: 94
110a: 97
111–24: 97

PASSUS III

332–405a: 111

PASSUS V

1–104: 57, 60, 145, 167
99–101: 169, 174

PASSUS IX

294–95: 193–94

PASSUS XI

306–7: 159

PASSUS XII

87–XIII.128: 223–27

PASSUS XXII

6–9: 150–51
33a: 159

INDEX OF SUBJECTS

Abraham (character), 257–58, 260. *See also*
Faith (character)
abstraction, 75, 104, 127, 139, 143, 153–54, 182,
210, 213, 247, 261
acedia. See sloth
affective experience, 251–52, 262, 266
affectus, 89
agapism, 163
allegory, 72, 77, 119, 140–42, 209–10, 233,
254. *See also* genre, allegory
angel (character), 45–47, 76
angels' food (*panis angelorum*), 156–57
Anima, 90, 120, 123, 135–36, 137–40, 144–45,
148, 161, 234, 238; and dreamer, 83, 91, 97,
120–43, 178, 208–9, 240, 242, 251, 253; as
grammar, 124–29, 139, 250; gender of, 81,
90, 120–21. *See also* faculties
Antichrist, 57–58, 112–13, 143, 155, 159, 166,
180, 194, 272
apocalypse, 166, 272. *See also* genre, apocalypse
Aristotle, 106, 217, 243
asceticism, 132
Athanasian Creed, 184, 189, 193, 258–59
Augustine, 33, 60, 63–64, 74, 126, 132–33,
160–61, 218, 220. *See also* Augustinianism
Augustinianism, 176, 192–93, 198, 204, 206,
237, 243, 245, 249
Augustinisme Avicennisant, 245
authority, 18, 23, 45, 51, 54, 60, 70, 73–74,
81–82, 123, 140, 173, 191, 210, 248–49; divine, 45, 53, 65; ecclesiastical, 43, 193; secular, 43–45, 76; textual, 28, 46–47, 51, 70,
77, 88, 90–91, 199, 219, 225, 269–70
autobiographical passage (C.V.). *See* Langland,
autobiographical passage

Babel, 28, 33–40, 52, 59–70
Bakhtin, M. M., 5

baptism, 219, 222, 224, 226
beggars, 35, 41, 148, 154–156, 187–89
Bernard of Clairvaux, 132, 135, 257
Bibliographical Essays, 30; 1, 70–78; 2.1,
114–20; 2.2, 137–43, 2.3, 164–68; 3.1,
203–6; 3.2, 242–49; 3.3, 275–80
Book (character), 263
book, idea of, 13–14, 17, 22, 39–40, 71–72, 82,
128–29, 210, 224–25. *See also* Book (character); grammar; *kynde knowynge;* literacy

cardinals, 35, 38, 41, 43, 46, 58, 69
cardinal virtues, 38, 41, 68–69, 146, 150–53,
160–61, 165, 269–70, 272; fortitude, 152;
justice, 69, 94, 116, 152, 185; prudence, 1,
98, 152–53; temperance, 143, 146–47,
148–53, 156, 165
caritas. See charity, love, *caritas*
Cartesian ego-subject, 5, 16, 61, 125
catalog, 35, 37–43, 52, 56, 61, 67
Cato, 197, 199, 217–18, 219
causal explanation, 11–12, 14–15, 130
Celestial Hierarchy (Pseudo-Dionysius), 98
charity, 63, 76, 121–22, 127–28, 133, 138–40,
178, 208–9, 231–32, 234, 236, 238–41,
250–57, 262. *See also* love, *caritas;* Tree of
Charity
Charity (character), 127, 132, 257–58. *See also*
love, *caritas;* Tree of Charity
Chaucer, Geoffrey: *Canterbury Tales,* 40–41, 77,
154; double voice, 53–54, 56–57, 60, 198;
idea of the book, 13, 72, 77, 141; inorganic
structure, 4; irony, 45, 172, 198; Pardoner
as preacher, 86, 90; *Parliament of Fowls,* 47;
philosophical realism, 36, 141
class (social). *See* estates; genre, estates satire
clergy, 41–43, 45, 58, 66, 92, 95, 99–100, 105,
120–24, 127–29, 130–35, 139–40, 155,

clergy *(continued)*
  162–63, 194–96, 200, 218, 222, 225,
  229–30, 250. *See also* Clergy (character)
Clergy (character), 66, 122, 123, 155, 207–8,
  217–19, 226, 227–28, 233–35, 248, 279
cogito. See Cartesian ego-subject
Coleridgean unity, 4–6, 11–12, 14–15, 28, 56,
  72, 81–82, 228, 244
commons, 43–44, 47–49, 65–66, 69, 76,
  108, 164. *See also* estates
concordance, 76, 101–2, 117
confession. *See* penance, confession
conscience, 77, 124–25, 204. *See also* Conscience (character)
Conscience (character), 24, 42, 64–65, 69,
  81, 122, 145–46, 207, 267–70; and Clergy, 233–36; and Haukyn, 238–40; and
  Lady Meed, 111–13; and Need, 153–58;
  and Piers, 172, 180, 208, 262, 275
contrition. *See* penance, contrition
Crowned King, The, 70
C-text, 29, 42, 77, 94, 97, 111, 121, 133,
  137–38, 150–51, 159–60, 174, 193–94,
  223. *See also* Langland, autobiographical
  passage
cultus, 91, 115
cupiditas, 131, 132–33, 244

Dante, 33, 72, 262–63
Daughters of God, 85, 263–64
Deadly Sins, 155–56, 171, 176–77, 179–80,
  194
debate. *See* genre, debate
definition, 73, 76, 98–101, 105, 107, 110–14,
  127–28, 173, 210, 232–33, 243
deification, 116
Deus caritas, 1, 93, 101–7, 116–17, 122
discourse, 54, 57–61, 70, 74, 112, 135, 173,
  249, 255, 263, 273, 278
Dobest, 64, 122, 219, 232–33, 235, 236,
  268–69. *See also* Dowel
Dobet, 218, 235, 236, 268. *See also* Dowel
Doctor (character), 123, 130–31, 135, 142,
  207, 232–33, 235
document, 184, 190–95, 200, 205, 225. *See
  also* pardon
doomsday, 180, 192, 198, 200, 276
Dowel, 83, 99, 136, 198–202, 207–10,
  220–21, 232–33, 240–41, 242–43, 258;

defined by Doctor, 207, 232–33; defined
  by Clergy, 207–8, 218, 233; defined by
  Conscience, 64, 236, 267–68; defined by
  friars, 208–9; defined by Patience,
  235–36; defined by Study, 216; defined by
  Thought, 211–13; defined by Wit, 213–15;
  defined by Ymaginatif, 231–32; division
  of poem, 123, 226; as infinitive, 127, 142
drama. *See* genre, drama
dream-vision. *See* genre, dream-vision

education, 202, 207, 209–10, 211–32, 233,
  235, 241
Elde (character), 261–62
epistemology, 143, 211–12, 250, 253; and allegory, 77; and faculties, 211–19, 227–32;
  and language, 126–29, 134, 140–43, 145,
  161, 250; and texts, 181, 210. *See also* allegory; book, idea of; faculties; grammar;
  literacy; *kynde knowynge;* reading; speculative grammar
equity, 77
eremitical life. *See* hermits
estates, 28, 66–67, 95–96. *See also* genre, estates satire.
estates satire. *See* genre, estates satire
Eucharist, 156–57, 230, 238, 270

faculties, 123, 126, 138, 145–46, 209–32,
  242–49. *See also* Anima; Clergy (character); Conscience (character); *kynde
  knowynge;* Kynde Wit (character); reason;
  Reason (character); Scripture (character); Study (character); Thought (character); will (faculty); Will (character); Wit
  (character); Ymaginatif
faith, 45, 72, 89, 94–95, 108, 176, 189, 195,
  206, 219, 231, 258. *See also* Faith (character)
Faith (character), 257–60
feudalism, 38–39, 78, 93, 97, 103, 105–8, 111,
  117
fools, 136, 208, 241–42
formalist criticism, 4, 7, 11, 16, 19–28, 167,
  246–47; Russian Formalists, 260
fortitude. *See* cardinal virtues, fortitude
Fortune (character), 187–88, 221–22, 235,
  261
friars, 35, 38, 41–42, 61, 122, 140, 143, 153–58,

165, 194, 202, 208–9, 222, 274–75; anti-fraternal satire, 55, 122, 154, 222; Langland's Franciscanism. *See* Langland, William (biography), Franciscanism

gender, 90, 119
genre, 8, 53–59, 76–77, 248–49; allegory, 64, 69, 76, 127, 137, 255–57, 266–78; apocalypse, 76–77, 276; debate, 77, 202, 226, 248–49, 263–64; drama, 22–24, 44–52, 123, 185, 203, 210, 263–66, 276; dream-vision, 53–57, 145–47, 197; estates satire, 37–43, 54–57; gospel, 19, 137, 178, 255–57, 259–62, 266, 278; liturgy, 260–66, 276; narrative, 70, 74–75, 273, 275; satire, 57, 77, 130, 138–39, 142, 176–77, 196, 205–6, 222, 248–49; sermon, 53–54, 58, 62, 77, 100–101, 117
goliard (character), 45–48, 65, 76
gospel, 42, 64–65, 68, 269. *See also* genre, gospel
grace, 135, 169, 183, 192–93, 197–98, 237, 252
Grace (character), 65–68, 181, 269–70
grammar, 116, 125–29, 134–36, 147, 217; soul as, 126–28, 134–36, 139, 141–42, 148, 242, 250
Gregory the Great, 166

habitus, 75, 236–37, 275
Harrowing of Hell, 203, 263, 276
Haukyn, 39, 57, 123, 132, 136, 178, 236–42, 252, 279–80
heresy, 35–37, 108
hermeneutic circle, 7–9, 11–13, 107
hermits, 35, 38, 41, 132, 164, 236, 265
historical criticism, 4, 7, 14–15, 33–34, 119–20, 167, 242–48
Holy Church (character), 17–18, 35, 62, 81, 83–120, 122, 123, 143, 176, 179, 252
Holy Spirit, 63, 66–68, 106, 132, 137, 270
hope, 169, 231–32. *See also* Hope (character)
Hope (character), 257–58
humility, 63, 176, 273
Hunger (character), 41, 104, 172, 186–89
hypothesis, 11–15

identity, 24, 57–62, 65–69, 173
idiota. See literacy, *idiota*

imagination (faculty), 228, 243. *See also* Ymaginatif
Incarnation, 106, 116–17, 134, 156, 160–62, 203, 218, 259, 264–66, 268–69, 276
infinites, 127, 142, 207, 233, 235
intellectual. *See* literacy, of intellectual
intellectus, 89
intention, 47, 49, 51–52; authorial, 5, 50
intentionality, 36, 59, 70, 74, 124–28, 133; and literacy, 74–77, 141–43; second intention, 139
intertextuality. *See* textuality

Jesus (character), 45, 64–65, 67, 104, 106, 160–63, 172, 178–79, 230, 256–57, 262–66, 267–70, 274, 276; as Samaritan, 178, 257–60, 262
Jews, 94–95, 129, 178, 224, 230, 234, 260, 267
John of Salisbury, 126
Justice: as cardinal virtue. *See* cardinal virtues, justice; social. *See* social justice

king: Passus XIX (character), 69, 272; role of, 45–46, 51, 76–77, 94, 116. *See also* King (character)
King (character), 43–52, 65–66, 95, 99, 113
knighthood, 93–108, 117. *See also* Knighthood (character); knights
Knighthood (character), 43, 65–66, 95
knights, 38, 44, 65–66, 96–97, 98–99, 104, 116–17, 186; Christ as knight, 64, 104, 261. *See also* knighthood, Knighthood (character)
Kynde (character), 85, 157–58, 179, 213–14, 228–29, 239, 262
kynde knowynge, 19, 102, 104–5, 130, 179, 204; of charity, 208–9, 241; of Christ, 4, 88, 143; of Dowel, 136, 208, 211, 218, 241; not innate, 181; and literacy, 75, 143, 180–81; and poetry, 227
Kynde Wit (character), 43–44, 66, 180, 188
labor, 38, 41–42, 65–66, 103–4, 112, 185–86, 204, 206, 220, 234–35, 250. *See also* Piers Plowman, as good laborer; Haukyn; penance; works

Langland, William (biography), 6–7, 16, 39, 77–78, 166–67, 260; autobiographical passage (C.V.), 57, 60, 145, 167; Francis-

Langland, William (*continued*)
  canism, 6, 139–40, 165–68, 244; poetics.
  See poetics, Langland's poetics; poetry-
  writing; politics, 44, 78, 116; semi-
  Pelagianism, 192–93, 204, 206, 249
language. *See* authority, textual; Babel; book,
  idea of; discourse; epistemology; grammar; law; literacy; poetry-writing; pronoun, first person; reading; structure,
  grammatical
law: of state, 46–48, 76, 77–78, 99, 155
  (metaphorical), 165, 184; of God, 94–95,
  100–101, 117, 163, 193, 195, 205, 230–31,
  234, 248–49, 258, 268, 276, 280
lawyers, 51–52, 56, 66; Jesus as lawyer, 45,
  265, 276
Lewte, 57, 222–24
Liber de Antichristo, 166
Liberum Arbitrium. *See* will (faculty), free
  will
literacy, 40, 43, 66, 70, 74–77, 90, 141–43,
  230, 278–79; *idiota,* 204, 220; of intellectual, 7, 29, 39, 61, 72, 202, 206, 209,
  213, 220–21, 252–53, 272–73; Latin,
  35, 45, 47, 90, 113, 191; vernacular, 141–
  42
litteratus. See literacy
liturgy, 42–43, 131, 135, 225. *See also* genre,
  liturgy
logos, 115, 160, 173
love, 148, 161–64, 177, 179, 217–18, 222, 228,
  242–43, 262; *caritas,* 93, 101–9, 116–17,
  122, 132–33, 231, 236, 244. *See also* charity;
  Charity (character); fruit of cardinal
  virtues, 68, 269–70; and intentionality,
  74, 124, 141; and justice, 84; and law, 230,
  248, 258, 268; and literacy, 43, 230; love-
  dream, 137, 172, 251–52; and penance,
  195, 235–36; sexual, 261; and truth, 93,
  101–9, 114, 116–17; and unity of Church,
  63, 91, 239, 269
Lucifer, 55, 93, 96–97, 99, 106, 267
lunatic (character), 44–45

measure, 86, 112–13, 143, 152
mediation, 106–8, 111–14, 258, 263
Meed (character), 18, 27, 78, 109–14,
  118–20, 122, 143–44, 155, 176
merchants, 38, 41, 56
methodeutic, 13–16, 167

minstrels, 36, 38–39, 41, 57
Modistae, 126–27
Mohammed, 131–32
monasticism, 104–5, 243–45, 249
money, 18, 24–27, 87–88, 112, 121, 144; money economy, 38–39, 78, 87, 106–8,
  113–14, 117, 143, 149
Moralia in Job, 166
Moses, 195, 257, 260. *See also* Spes (character);
  Hope (character)
Mum and the Sothsegger, 70
mysticism, 107, 108, 109–10, 126, 132–33,
  138, 175

names, 36, 38, 46, 65, 66–68, 76, 111, 121, 125,
  130, 144, 182, 215–16, 243, 267, 278; of
  Anima, 120–21, 125, 130, 138; of cardinal
  virtues, 68, 153, 160; of God, 43, 53,
  84–85, 89, 94, 105, 115, 160–61,174,
  183–84, 213, 227; of Jesus, 64–65,
  161–63, 267–68
narrative of dreamer, 29, 77, 83, 162–63,
  171–80, 203, 206–10, 231–32, 249, 253,
  256, 262, 265, 279–80. *See also* genre, narrative
Need (character), 27, 143–45, 147–48,
  164–68, 210; and Conscience, 153–58;
  and dreamer, 83, 143–53, 158–68, 274;
  and friars, 153–58, 164–68; and Jesus,
  159–63. *See also* cardinal virtues
New Criticism, 5, 19
Nicene Creed, 260, 261–62
nihilism, 52, 66, 113, 173

originality, 8, 17, 19–22, 28, 34, 37, 54, 242
orthodoxy, 28, 37, 69, 88, 92, 108, 136, 164,
  200

panis angelorum. See angels' food
parables: feast, 224; good Samaritan, 257. *See
  also* Jesus, as Samaritan; sower, 63, 68, 132;
  unforgiving servant, 271
paraphrasibility, 19–22, 25–26
pardon, 65, 183–84, 191–92, 200–201, 205,
  222, 237–38, 250, 268, 270–72; pardon
  scene, 41, 172–73, 177, 180–209, 222, 231,
  233–34, 236, 238, 250, 255–56, 258,
  271–72, 279; pardoners, 35, 38, 41–42
Passion, 252, 257, 259–60, 266–67
patience, 139, 232, 236, 238, 241; patient

poverty, 226, 228, 240–41. *See also* Patience (character)

Patience (character), 136, 164, 232–42

patristic criticism, 21, 33, 161. *See also* historical criticism

Pelagianism, 176, 193, 198, 204, 206, 237, 249

penance, 75, 192, 200, 222, 234–36, 238–39, 271, 274–75; confession, 57–58, 75, 122, 155, 179, 222, 236, 238–39, 270, 274–75, 279; contrition, 75, 195–96, 208, 236, 238, 270, 275, 279; satisfaction, 236, 238, 271

Pentecost, 37, 63–64

Perrers, Alice, 119

persona, 6–7, 141, 168, 198, 206, 243–44, 246

Peter, 43, 56, 58, 132, 172, 191, 219, 237, 269, 272

Pharisees, 87, 90

Pierce the Ploughman's Crede, 70

Piers Plowman (character), 64, 137, 207–9, 233, 275; and Christ, 132, 178, 250–57, 259–60, 262, 266; as good laborer, 18, 38, 41, 63, 103–6, 162, 177, 180–206, 223, 237–38, 241; as hermeneutic principle, 19, 29, 175, 262, 269–70, 275, 279; and human nature, 64, 179, 266, 276; and pardon, 180–206, 222, 231, 233, 238–39; as pope, 65, 67–68, 268–72; as symbol, 29, 171–75, 180, 205, 207, 236, 242, 248, 252, 262, 276–77

Piers Plowman tradition, 70

pilgrimage, 57, 89, 185, 217, 233–34, 250, 252, 275

pilgrims, 35, 38, 41, 57, 180–81, 278

Plato, 162, 217

poetics, 25–26; Langland's poetics, 6, 18, 77, 137, 141, 143, 173, 206, 248–49

poetry-writing, 57, 75, 77, 135, 143, 206, 222, 226–27, 231, 248–49

pope, 35, 43, 134, 153, 191, 200, 237–38, 269, 272. *See also* Piers Plowman, as pope

postmodernism, 5, 11, 19–20, 46, 61, 70, 77, 173–74

poverty, 154, 162, 224–25, 236, 240. *See also* patience, patient poverty

pragmatism, 173–74

preaching, 38, 41–42, 83–86, 100, 104, 117, 126, 157, 222

predestination, 219–20, 223

pride, intellectual, 130, 176, 202, 206, 221, 223, 232, 234

Pride (character), 27–28, 97, 227, 272

private symbol, 29, 171–72, 174, 180, 189–90, 194, 201–2, 208, 236, 248, 252

pronoun, first person, 52–59, 265, 275

prudence. *See* cardinal virtues, prudence

Pseudo-Chrysostom, 133

Pseudo-Dionysius. *See Celestial Hierarchy*

psychology, 242–43, 244, 247–48; Augustinian. *See Augustinisme Avicennisant;* of conversion, 203; modern, 15, 210, 228; moral, 243–44; of sin, 75, 275. *See also* faculties

puns, 66, 67, 99, 108, 111, 119–20, 121, 185, 236–37, 238, 269

rats and mice (fable), 49–51

reading, 7–9, 42, 72, 103, 124, 125, 128, 29, 131–32, 134–35, 137, 141–42, 181–82, 249, 274, 278–79. *See also* literacy

reason, 77, 86–87, 99, 117, 145–46, 160–61. *See also* Reason (character)

Reason (character), 23, 122, 145, 227–28

Rechelesnesse (C-text), 223, 226

recursiveness, 17–19, 24–28, 29, 58–62, 73, 75, 90, 114, 175, 185, 243, 253–56, 275

Redde quod debes, 24, 26–27, 270–72

Reddite Cesari, 24, 26–27, 113–14

rich, the, 95–96, 156, 174–45, 249

Richard the Redeles, 70

Russian Formalists. *See* formalist criticism, Russian Formalists

sacrament. *See* penance

Samaritan. *See* Jesus, as Samaritan

sapientia, 73, 204, 279

Saracens, 224, 234–35

satire. *See* friars, antifraternal satire; genre, estates satire; genre, satire

satisfaction. *See* penance, satisfaction

science, 9–14; Middle English term, 130, 217–18, 228–30. *See also scientia*

scientia, 73, 210. *See also* science

Scripture, 20, 68–69, 72, 95, 101, 135, 157, 249, 269, 278. *See also* Scripture (character)

Scripture (character), 23, 203, 217, 219–26, 228, 235, 251

sermon. *See* genre, sermon

sloth, 55, 149, 176, 206, 221–23. *See also* Sloth (character)

Sloth (character), 122

social justice, 45, 87–120, 185–86, 204, 250–51

soul. *See* Anima

sower, parable of. *See* parables, sower

speculative grammar, 126–27. *See also* grammar

Spes (character), 258. *See also* Hope (character)

structure, 4–7; catalogs of occupations, 40–43, 52, 65; dramatic, 44, 52, 243; grammatical, 70, 127, 141; Holy Church's sermon, 105–9, 112; human soul, 83, 209–10, 212; narrative, 175–80; *Piers Plowman*, 3, 114, 123, 143–44, 242–43, 278; rhetorical justification, 145–53, 158, 160–61; social, 94–103; spiral, 24

Study (character), 107, 122, 215–18, 229, 247–48, 255

Symposium, 162

Te Deum, 261

temperance. *See* cardinal virtues, temperance

textuality, 17, 82; intertextuality, 22–24, 40, 117, 166, 171, 263

Theology (character), 107, 110, 112, 217–18

Thomas (apostle), 65, 268–69

Thought (character), 91, 124, 138, 211–13, 247

Tower: of Truth, 35, 84–85, 115, 173; of Babel. *See* Babel

Trajan, 223–24, 226, 231

transgressores, 95–96, 99, 106, 110

treason, 97

treasure, 112. *See also* truth

tree-image, 127–28, 131, 133, 140, 250. *See also* Tree of Charity

Tree of Charity, 122, 127–28, 137, 190, 208, 249, 250–57, 259

Trinity, 129, 160–62, 253–55, 257–59, 275–76

truth, 59, 65, 67, 72, 77, 85–108, 112, 114–18, 119, 171, 173–74, 204, 205, 257, 269–70. *See also* Truth (character)

Truth (character), 35, 53, 59, 84–85, 107, 173, 177, 180–89, 191–92, 195–96, 203, 205, 250. *See also* truth

type, 33, 35–37, 85, 90, 129, 230, 250; anti-type, 63, 132, 250

unity. *See* Coleridgean unity

Unity (Church), 44, 58, 64, 69, 81, 91, 97, 153, 155, 158, 179–80, 194, 206, 268–72

vía negatíva, 115

vis imaginativa, 245

waking episodes, 145–47, 154, 158–59, 167–68, 197, 202, 208, 261

will (faculty), 126, 132–34, 146, 160–61, 186, 234; and charity, 250–54, 256, 262; free will, 121, 137, 178, 209; and intentionality, 74, 141, 175, 180; in pardon scene, 204; and truth, 116. *See also* Will (character)

Will (character), 121, 167–68, 202, 206, 210, 261–62, 265, 275, 276, 278; and Anima, 130; and Christ, 261; and Holy Church, 115; and Ymaginatif, 245; and Need, 148–49, 158–59, 161, 165; and Reason and Conscience, 145–46; and self, 52–53, 59, 74; and Wit, 248

William of St. Amour, 166

wisdom, 73, 104–5, 160–61

Wit (character), 120, 211–12, 213–17, 243, 247, 248. *See also* Kynde Wit

Wittgenstein, Ludwig, 6

works, 89, 133, 184, 189, 209, 219, 236, 249, 258, 275; and faith, 45, 108, 176, 219, 258; and self-justification, 177–78, 198, 205–6, 216, 231–33, 251; and words, 89, 94–95, 131–32, 135, 234, 250. *See also* labor

Wyclif, John, 126

Ymaginatif, 91, 123, 227–32, 243–46, 247–48. *See also* imagination

INTERPRETATION IN

Piers Plowman

was designed and composed in Requiem Text
by Kachergis Book Design, Pittsboro, North Carolina;
and printed on 60-pound Writers Offset and
bound by Thomson-Shore, Inc.,
Dexter, Michigan.